Gender and French Cinema

Gender and French Cinema

Edited by
Alex Hughes and James S. Williams

Oxford • New York

First published in 2001 by
Berg
Editorial offices:
150 Cowley Road, Oxford, OX4 1JJ, UK
838 Broadway, Third Floor, New York, NY 10003-4812, USA

Berg is an imprint of Oxford International Publishers Ltd.

Library of Congress Cataloging-in-Publication Data
Gender and French cinema / edited by Alex Hughes and James S. Williams.
    p. cm.
Includes bibliographical references and index.
    ISBN 1-85973-570-3 (cloth) -- ISBN 1-85973-575-4 (pbk.)
    1. Motion pictures--France--History.   2. Women in motion
pictures.   3. Feminism and motion pictures--France.   I. Hughes,
Alex.   II. Williams, James S.
    PN1993.5.F7 H84 2001
    791.43'652042'0944--dc21   2001004389

British Library Cataloguing-in-Publication Data
A catalogue record for this book is available from the British Library.

ISBN 1 85973 570 3 (Cloth)
    1 85973 575 4 (Paper)

Cover illustration: Still from Jean Cocteau's *La Belle et la bête* (1946).
Courtesy of the British Film Institute.

Typeset by JS Typesetting, Wellingborough, Northants.
Printed in the United Kingdom by Antony Rowe Ltd, Chippenham, Wiltshire.

In Memory of Jill Forbes, 1947–2001
A Pioneer in French Film and Cultural Studies

Contents

Notes on Contributors ix

Acknowledgements xiii

1   Introduction 1
Alex Hughes and *James S. Williams*

2   Bodies Cut and Dissolved: Dada and Surrealist Film 19
Elza Adamowicz

3   Diva in the Spotlight: Music Hall to Cinema 35
Kelley Conway

4   'Mon cul est intersexuel?': Arletty's Performance of Gender 63
Keith Reader

5   For Our Eyes Only: Body and Sexuality in Reverse Motion in
the Films of Jean Cocteau 77
James S. Williams

6   Setting the Agenders: Simone Signoret – The Pre-Feminist Star
Body 107
Susan Hayward

7   Gender, Modernism and Mass Culture in the New Wave 125
Geneviève Sellier

8   'Autistic Masculinity' in Jean-Pierre Melville's Crime Thrillers 139
Ginette Vincendeau

9   Gender in the French Fantasy Film 1965–95 157
Guy Austin

Contents

10 Going Through the Motions: Unconscious Optics and
Corporal Resistance in Miéville and Godard's
France/tour/détour/deux/enfants   171
Michael Witt

11 The God, the King, the Fool and ØØ: Anamorphosing the
Films of Beineix   195
Phil Powrie

12 AIDS-Video: Representing the Body in Guibert's *La Pudeur
ou l'impudeur*   209
Alex Hughes

13 Gender and Sexuality in New New Wave Cinema   227
Dina Sherzer

14 Running Out of Place: Gender, Space and Crisis in Ferreira
Barbosa's *Les Gens normaux n'ont rien d'exceptionnel*
and Lvovsky's *Oublie-moi*   241
Julia Dobson

15 Identification and Female Friendship in Contemporary French
Film   255
Emma Wilson

Filmography   269

Selected Bibliography   271

Index   287

Notes on Contributors

Elza Adamowicz is a Senior Lecturer at Queen Mary, University of London. Her book publications include *André Breton: A Bibliography* (1992) and *Surrealist Collage in Text and Image: Dissecting the Exquisite Corpse* (1998). She publishes on Surrealist art and literature, Henri Michaux and Claude Cahun, and is currently researching Surrealist texts on art.

Guy Austin is a Senior Lecturer in the department of French at the University of Sheffield. He has published books on contemporary French cinema (1996) and Claude Chabrol (1999). He has a particular interest in genre and fantasy film, and is presently working on a study of modern French film stars.

Kelley Conway is Assistant Professor in the department of Communication Arts at the University of Wisconsin-Madison, and is completing a book entitled *The Chanteuse at the City Limits: Paris, Femininity and the Cinema*.

Julia Dobson has published widely on contemporary French cinema and the theatre of Hélène Cixous. She is a Research Fellow in French at the University of Wolverhampton, and teaches at the University of Nottingham and the Broadway Media Centre.

Susan Hayward is the Established Chair of French at the University of Exeter, and has published extensively on French film. Her books include *French National Cinema* (1993); *Luc Besson* (1998); and *Cinema Studies: The Key Concepts* (2000). She co-edited *French Film: Texts and Contexts* (1990 and 2000) with Ginette Vincendeau, and her current project is a major study of Simone Signoret, to be published in 2002.

Alex Hughes is Professor of Twentieth-Century French Literature at the University of Birmingham, and has published extensively on representations of gender and sexuality. She is the co-editor of the Routledge *Encyclopedia of Contemporary French Culture* (1998), and her most recent single-authored book is *Heterographies: Sexual Difference in French Autobiography* (1999).

Phil Powrie is Professor of French Cultural Studies and Director of the Centre for Research into Film and Media at the University of Newcastle on Tyne. He has published considerably on French cinema, notably *French Cinema in the 1980s: Nostalgia and the Crisis of Masculinity* (1997), and recently edited *French Cinema in the 1990s: Continuity and Difference* (1999). He has just completed a book on the films of Jean-Jacques Beineix and is currently co-authoring a student introduction to French cinema.

Keith Reader is Professor of Modern French Studies at the University of Glasgow. His publications include *Régis Debray* (1995) and *Robert Bresson* (2000). He is co-editor, with Alex Hughes, of the *Encyclopedia of Contemporary French Culture* (1998).

Geneviève Sellier teaches cinema studies at the University of Caen. She is the author of *Jean Grémillon: le cinéma est à vous* (1989) and *Les Enfants du paradis* (1992), and co-author, with Noël Burch, of *La Drôle de guerre des sexes du cinéma français: 1930–1956* (1996). She has edited special numbers of the film studies journals *1895* (on Grémillon) and *Iris* (on film, gender and cultural studies).

Dina Sherzer teaches twentieth-century literature at the University of Texas at Austin, and works on post-colonial films and novels and New New Wave film. Recent published pieces have appeared in Phil Powrie (ed.), *French Cinema in the 1990s: Continuity and Difference* (1999); the *Journal of European Studies*; *Studies in Twentieth-Century Literature*; and *South Central Review*.

Ginette Vincendeau is Professor of Film in the department of Film and Television Studies at the University of Warwick. She has published extensively in French and English on French and women's cinema. Among her books are *French Film: Texts and Contexts* (co-edited with Susan Hayward, 1990 and 2000); *The Encylopedia of European Cinema* (1995); *Pépé le Moko* (1998); and *Stars and Stardom in French Cinema* (2000). She recently edited *Film-Literature-Heritage: A Sight and Sound Reader*.

Emma Wilson is a University Lecturer in French at the University of Cambridge, and a Fellow of Corpus Christi College. Her publications include *Sexuality and the Reading Encounter: Identity and Desire in Proust, Duras, Tournier and Cixous* (1996); *French Cinema Since 1950: Personal Histories* (1999); and *Memory and Survival: The French Cinema of Krzysztof Kieślowski* (2000). She is currently working on a study of childhood trauma in contemporary cinema.

James S. Williams is Senior Lecturer of French and comparative literature at the University of Kent. He is the author of *The Erotics of Passage: Pleasure, Politics, and Form in the Later Work of Marguerite Duras* (1997) and of a critical study of

Albert Camus's *La Peste* (2000). He is editor of *Revisioning Duras: Film, Race, Sex* (2000) and co-editor, with Michael Temple, of *The Cinema Alone: Essays on the Work of Jean-Luc Godard 1985–2000* (2000). He is currently writing a monograph on the films of Jean Cocteau.

Michael Witt teaches French and film at the University of Roehampton. His doctoral research was on the film and video work of Anne-Marie Miéville and Jean-Luc Godard, and he has published articles on Godard's later work. He is currently co-editing *The French Cinema Book* for the British Film Institute.

Acknowledgements

The editors would like to thank Kathryn Earle, Sara Everett and Maike Bohn for all their help, support and patience, Susan Pritchard for her technical wizardry, and Vérène Grieshaber for helping to translate Geneviève Sellier's chapter from the original French.

–1–

Introduction
Alex Hughes and *James S. Williams*

The focus of this collection of essays, *Gender and French Cinema*, is French film in the twentieth century. Our Introduction to it is divided into several sections. In the first, we invoke particular conceptualizations and treatments of gender, before situating gender-related analysis as central to contemporary critical work on representation. In the second, we survey the space of film studies in order to profile the scope and types of gender-related reading that film, including French film, has elicited. In the third, we detail the project pursued in our volume, and outline its organization. Finally, in the fourth, we introduce the essays that compose it.

Attending to Gender

In 1949, in *The Second Sex*, Simone de Beauvoir famously affirmed the following:

> One is not born but rather becomes a woman. No biological, psychological or economic fate determines the figure that the human being presents in society: it is civilization as a whole that produces this creature indeterminate between male and eunuch which is described as feminine.[1]

In these remarks, which address the construction of feminine alterity under patriarchy, Beauvoir is doing three things. First, if she does not use the term, she is articulating a crucial, contemporary understanding of gender: one that flags up its distinctness from anatomical sex. Second, she is 'categorically refus[ing] the idea of a biological or anatomical "destiny" of any kind', firmly situating gendered subjectivity as non-natural/ontological.[2] Third, she is construing gender, or engenderment, as a productive *social* process: a process of acculturation whereby gender identity is overlaid, palimpsestically, on the sexed being, as 'an aspect of identity gradually acquired'.[3]

  Beauvoir's essay is the place where modern feminism takes off.[4] And, in its 'celebrated declaration of gender',[5] it initiates a corpus of gender-theoretical work that constitutes an essential facet of the twentieth-century epistemological canvas. *The Second Sex*'s analysis of what gender is – a social fabrication; a 'variable cultural interpretation of sex';[6] a situation in the world that is humanly created[7] – and where it is evolved (the 'man-made' realm of patriarchy), is radical. It is radical in spite of the fact that it deploys a Sartrean/Hegelian theoretical framework that is 'inextricably connected with a fundamental . . . opposition between masculine and feminine in which the feminine is associated with whatever is devalued'.[8] It is radical in its ground-breaking political, social and conceptual implications: implications that are attracting renewed critical interest today. And it is especially radical, perhaps because, by conceiving of systems of gender regulation as historically-sited and therefore transient, it encourages us to see that gender identities, as lived situations, might in future be lived differently, outside the binary masculine/feminine paradigm that is still normatively and culturally dominant.[9]

Published in the middle of the twentieth century, *The Second Sex*, if momentous, did not initially have an international impact.[10] The same cannot be said of a work of gender theory that appeared some forty years later. The work in question is Judith Butler's *Gender Trouble* (1990). Trained in philosophy, as Beauvoir had been, and manifestly in dialogue with Beauvoir, Butler works in *Gender Trouble* from a constructivist position that is indebted to Beauvoir's post-war analyses. However, the account of gender that *Gender Trouble* offers differs from that elaborated by Beauvoir in many ways, not least because it reassociates gender and sex – categories Beauvoir disassociates – and opts to anatomize not the gender constructions produced by the patriarchal order so much as those regulated within the 'obligatory frame of reproductive heterosexuality'.[11]

Gender, Butler tells us in *Gender Trouble*, is the 'repeated stylization of the body, a set of repeated acts within a highly rigid regulatory frame that congeal over time to produce the appearance of substance, of a natural sort of being'.[12] It is a '*corporeal style*': an 'act' that is '*performative*', where performative 'suggests a dramatic and contingent construction of meaning'.[13] In these statements, Butler posits gender as an enactment, imbricated in imitative and compelled bodily sig-nification. She casts gender as a bodily performance controlled by the dominant, compulsory heterosexual regime, and she moots gender performance as a mime that is inscribed on the surface of the body but appears as the effect of an interior core. Gender, in sum, constitutes for Butler a kind of (non-natural) corporeal 'doing', but not one that individuals can choose (how) to 'do'.[14] It is, moreover, a mode of 'doing' that can be done 'wrong'. That this is the case is made evident, says Butler, by the existence of 'incoherent' gender performances where gender identities, anatomical sex and sexual practices fail to mesh normatively: perform-ances where 'gender does not necessarily follow from sex, and desire, or sexuality generally, does not seem to follow from gender – indeed, where none of these dimensions of significant corporeality express or reflect one another'.[15] Such performances, Butler argues, 'run rampant within heterosexual, bisexual, and gay and lesbian contexts'.[16] They are both prohibited *and* produced by the regulatory mechanisms of gender:[17] mechanisms that require ambivalent manifestations of gender performance in order to secure as the norm gender enactments that respect the limits of a binarized either/or heteronormative paradigm, determined by the 'naturally' binarized material phenomenon of sex.[18]

In *Gender Trouble*, Butler brings sex, the body and gender together, through her articulation of gender as corporeal stylization. She problematizes the sex/gender, nature/culture distinction Beauvoir privileges, by suggesting that constrained, reiterated gender performances take place through a (sexed) body that 'has no ontological status apart from the various acts which constitute its reality', and by speculating that 'this construct called "sex" is as culturally constructed as gender; indeed . . . was always already gender'.[19] In short, she adopts a position on sex/gender that is beauvoirian in its lineage but is more radically materialist than that evident in the *Second Sex*. This evolves in *Bodies That Matter* (1993). Here, Butler turns her attention to the materiality of the sexed body. She works to understand how, as she puts it, regulatory norms of sex 'work in a performative fashion to constitute the materiality of bodies, and, more specifically, to materialize the body's sex'.[20] She shifts her focus, in other words, from gender as a corporeal style to the (materialized) matter of the body through which gender is enacted. Equally, she attends to those bodies in and through which 'abject' or non-normative gender performances are played out. In so doing, she posits the 'heterosexual imperative' as a manifestation of power that establishes 'boundaries of bodily life where abjected or delegitimated bodies fail to count as "bodies"',[21] and produces 'a domain of abject [gendered] beings, those who are not . . . "subjects", but who form the constitutive outside to the domain of the subject'.[22]

Operating in different theoretical, cultural and historical contexts, and concerned, finally, with different(ly) gendered subjects, Beauvoir and Butler are without doubt the most significant analysts of gender of the twentieth century. Their treatments of gendered subjectivity have not escaped criticism. Beauvoir's feminist exegesis of the tenor of woman's becoming has been slated for its pathologization of the biological female 'body in trouble':[23] a body Beauvoir recognizes as devalued under patriarchy, but tends herself likewise to devalue. Butler's neofoucauldian exercises in queer theoretical investigation have been deemed ultimately to elide the category of gender in favour of too exclusive a focus on bodily matters, and to neglect those elements of embodied subjectivity not circumscribed by the regulatory influence of the heterosexual Law.[24] But, taken together, the writings of these women, and the commentaries their writings have elicited, provide us with a map through which to attend productively to gender issues, understood in their broadest sense. Focused not just on what gender is but on its modes and sites of production, its imbrication in matters of anatomy, sexuality and desire, its relation to culture, history, discourse and power, and its normative and non-normative manifestations, texts such as *The Second Sex*, *Gender Trouble* and *Bodies That Matter* open up a space of gender-oriented reflection constellated with questions and concerns no less manifest in other key accounts of gender and sexual difference published during the last fifty years. These accounts include, for instance, the work on difference pursued in the psychoanalytically grounded writings of French theorists of the feminine, such as Hélène Cixous and Luce Irigaray (who, like Butler, dialogues with Simone de Beauvoir);[25] the work on the body elaborated in studies by Anglophone theorists such as Susan Bordo, Jane Gallop, Moira Gatens and Elizabeth Grosz;[26] and the dissections of the politics and discourses of sexuality/ desire produced by Diana Fuss, Teresa de Lauretis, Gayle Rubin, Eve Kosofsky Sedgwick and Monique Wittig.[27] The issues such accounts invoke were, in the last decade of the twentieth century, addressed in a growing body of texts devoted to investigations of the masculine. Masculinity, especially heteronormative masculinity, has until recently received scant attention in gender-theoretical analysis. However, as Alan Petersen signals in *Unmasking the Masculine: 'Men' and 'Identity' in a Sceptical Age* (1998),[28] questions relating to the fabrication of the male body, to the construction of masculine gender identities and to the discursification of male sexuality, straight and gay, are currently coming under increasing scrutiny, as conceptions of manhood in the modern West take their place as objects of investigation in the gender-studies environment.

In the context of twentieth-century epistemology, gender in sum became, and remains, a key category of analysis. As a number of the works cited in the preceding paragraphs confirm, a privileged focus of gender-oriented investigational work has been the realm of representation. In the contemporary literary-critical sphere, for instance, gender has been squarely established as a 'crucial determinant of the production, circulation, and consumption of literary discourse',[29] with the result that publishers' lists include today a vast array of studies that 'speak of gender' in respect of the literary endeavour. But some of the most exciting and innovative work on gender and representation has been effected with regard to visual and especially film culture, more specifically in relation to the (gendered) gaze and the situation of the cinematic spectator.[30] In the following section, this work is surveyed in some detail.

Gender Matters in the Field of Film

Work on gender and film

The most sophisticated discussions of desire and sexual politics in cinema have taken place in the field of feminist psychoanalytic film theory. This first emerged as a rethinking of the work of Freud and Lacan, Christian Metz and Stephen Heath, and sought to politicize a set of pyschological questions about gender. Theorists such as Mary Ann Doane, Teresa de Lauretis, Laura Mulvey, D.N. Rodowick and

Kaja Silverman have attempted in different ways to develop an analysis of subjectivity that would account for the pleasures of the look and the relationship of those pleasures to gender and sexual identity.[31] Barbara Creed has delineated a brief yet very useful four-stage history of film theory and psychoanalysis, and a summary of its constituent parts can be paraphrased thus:

1. apparatus theory, i.e. the work of Metz and Jean-Louis Baudry.[32] This strove to avoid the totalizing imperative of the structuralist approach by drawing on psychoanalysis as a way of widening the theoretical base of that approach;
2. the work of Mulvey, which introduced gender into apparatus theory and rebutted the naturalization of the filmic protagonist as an Oedipal hero. In her pioneering 1975 essay 'Visual Pleasure and Narrative Cinema', Mulvey exposed the position of the feminine in film as the object of the gaze. The masculine subject attempts to appropriate the cinematic gaze for his voyeuristic pleasure, and the masculine look seeks to fetishize images of women; that is, to reinvest them with the illusion of phallic plenitude, in a manner that accounts for the misogynistic violence and objectification in classic cinema;[33]
3. feminist responses to Mulvey's work, including critical studies of the female Oedipal trajectory; masculinity and masochism; fantasy theory and spectatorship (cf. Elizabeth Cowie's notion of a fluid, bisexual gaze[34]); and woman as active sadistic monster (work inspired by Kristeva's treatment of the abject maternal[35]);
4. the use of psychoanalytic theory in conjunction with other critical approaches to cinema, as in post-colonial theory, queer theory and body theory.[36]

There has, however, been sustained criticism of psychoanalytic film theory. It has been deemed to construct a monolithic spectator, and thus itself to become totalizing and repetitive; to be ahistorical, and therefore dismissive of the need to explore the micro-narratives of social change, since history is sacrificed to questions of subjectivity, its formation and its relation to ideology. Above all, psychoanalytic film theory has been critiqued for being more concerned with an ideal spectator than a real viewer, and for failing to engage with questions of class, colour, race, age or sexual preference (the kinds of issue raised, for example, in cultural studies). What underlies these various charges is a sense that, ultimately, whatever its practitioners may think, psychoanalytic theory is not a science and remains unreliable.

It is fair to say that current film theory is more selective and nuanced now in its use of psychoanalysis, for instance, in the way that it can bring together the social and the psychic in a manner derived from post-colonial theory as well as from queer theory which has introduced the concept of gender performativity to studies of filmic representation and spectatorial response. Queer theory suggests that viewers often position themselves 'queerly', that is, position themselves within gendered and sexualized spaces other than those they publicly occupy (hence the notion that the spectator does not function within any particular fixed gender and sexual category). Much attention has been paid to the body, notably in the work of Steven Shaviro, who argues for an active and affirmative reading of the masochism of cinematic experience,[37] as well as in that of Kobena Mercer, who proposes a hybridized understanding of identity that negotiates between a plurality of different positions. The result, in Mercer's case, is a recognition of 'unity-in-diversity', and the interactions between class, sexuality and ethnicity.[38]

It can never therefore simply be a question of identifying and celebrating positive images of lesbians and gay men and decrying other, more negative representations, a feature of earlier feminist and gay criticism. Indeed, queer theory sees sexual practices – whether heterosexual, homosexual, bisexual, autosexual or transsexual – as fluid, diverse and heterogeneous. As Ellis Hanson has put it in a recent collection of queer film criticism entitled *Out Takes*, queer critics 'enrich political critiques of cinematic pleasure by theorizing the psychic mechanisms of identification and desire, but they also challenge such critiques by deeming impossible any necessary conjunction, any perfect fit between ideology and desire, narrative and pleasure, the image and the subject'.[39] Just as D.N. Rodowick and others revealed Mulvey's inability to allow for the possibility of female desire outside a phallocentric context, so, Hanson argues, queer theorists have discovered that the heterocentric and exceedingly rigid structure of the look in Mulvey's analysis writes homosexuality out of existence and excites 'a political presumption – we might deem it a paranoid tendency – that views voyeurism, fetishism, sublimation, idealization, masculinity, phallic sexuality, and even identification as not merely suspect but inherently evil'.[40] Critics such as Lee Edelman, Christine Holmlund, D.A. Miller and Patricia White have redeployed the terminology of feminist film theory within queer theory, since it allows expressly for a critique of the sexual politics of representation, as well as a compelling account of desire and identity formation.[41]

Work on gender and French film

Critical works in English or French on French film directly informed by feminist or queer psychoanalytic theory are still relatively few, but include Françoise Audé's early study of French feminist filmmaking, *Ciné-modèles, cinéma d'elles: Situation des femmes dans le cinéma français 1956–1979* (1981); Susan Hayward and Ginette Vincendeau's ground-breaking collection, *French Film: Texts and Contexts* (1990); Sandy Flitterman-Lewis's *To Desire Differently: Feminism and the French Cinema* (1990); Jill Forbes's *The Cinema in France After The New Wave* (1992); and Phil Powrie's *French Cinema in the 1980s: Nostalgia and the Crisis of Masculinity* (1997). There has not yet been, however, a volume tracing the evolution of French cinema specifically in terms of gender and sexual representation, and that takes fully on board new theoretical insights in these areas. A study, for example, that would engage with the whole course of French cinema, from silent film, surrealist film, Occupation and post-war cinema, feminist avant-garde cinema of the 1970s (the cinema of Diane Kurys, Coline Serreau, Agnès Varda and especially Marguerite Duras, who experimented with the apparatus of cinema even to the point of its negation) to the 1960s–1970s work of Jean-Luc Godard and Anne-Marie Miéville (which involved extensive semiotic analysis of film and video representation, the female body and the male gaze), and more recent trends such as the *cinéma du look* of the 1980s and the New New Wave. The latter is a loose term covering an eclectic range of directors based in Paris, or the North or South, and Maghrebi-French directors, including Olivier Assayas; Jacques Audiard; Xavier Beauvois; Catherine Breillat; Mehdi Charef; Malik Chibane; Arnaud Desplechin; Bruno Dumont; Karim Dridi; Laurence Ferreira Barbosa; Robert Guédiguian; Cédric Kahn; Mathieu Kassovitz; Cédric Klapisch; Noémie Lvovksky; Tonie Marshall; Eric Rochant; Marion Vernoux; and many others.[42] The particular problems inherent in the notion of gay film-making in France have been discussed elsewhere,[43] yet one key aspect of the vitality of new French cinema is the very proliferation of out-gay directors, notably François Ozon, Philippe Barassat and François Roux. These film-makers can be seen to consolidate and develop in different ways a male gay tradition established by figures such as Jean Cocteau and Jean Genet (in films such as *Le Sang d'un poète* (1930) and the 'outlawed' *Un chant d'amour* (1950)): a tradition continued by directors as diverse as Patrice Chéreau, Jacques Demy, André Téchiné and Paul Vecchiali, and marked spectacularly by Cyril Collard's highly acclaimed and controversial *Les Nuits fauves* (1993).

The Project of *Gender and French Cinema*

Gender and French Cinema brings together critical essays by British, French and American scholars working in film or gender studies. Its task is not simply to trace and celebrate forms of gender expression in French cinema, but rather to reconceptualize and reframe the view of French cinema *tout court*. In this sense, the collection's project is very different from that of French (male) critics who recently, on the fortieth anniversary of the New Wave in France, honoured the *Nouvelle Vague* as a clear formalist break effected by male directors bent on sacralizing the status of the *auteur*. The work of such critics deliberately downplays more mundane yet equally important focuses of attention such as society, politics and gender.[44] Instead, the present volume shares goals more akin to those of the ambitious new Manchester University Press series on French Film Directors: a series that attempts to assess and re-evaluate both canonic and non-canonic French *auteurs* in the light of critical factors such as sexual difference, nation and ethnicity, and in full awareness of psychoanalysis and film theory, including feminist theories of women's film authorship. To take just one instance, Martin O'Shaughnessy's *Jean Renoir* (2000) reveals how these factors often work in contradictory ways in central films such as *La Marseillaise* (1937), and thus demand, for example, a rethinking of our common understanding of Renoir's political commitment.[45]

The studies of the MUP series may be set alongside Powrie's edited collection *French Cinema in the 1990s* (1999), which, in its second part entitled 'Inscribing Differences', illustrates how gender as a path of enquiry only makes proper critical sense when associated with questions of race, ethnicity and history. Further examples of this multi-levelled type of investigation include the work of Graeme Hayes and Carrie Tarr on sexuality and masculinity in Carax's *Les Amants du Pont-Neuf* (1991) and *Les Nuits fauves*,[46] and of Lucille Cairns on Josiane Balasko's *Gazon Maudit* (1995), which places the portrayal of lesbian desire in the larger context of French – that is to say, universalist and Republican – national identity.[47] Gender is always imbricated within history, a fact made brilliantly clear in Tarr's examination of Jean Delannoy's enormously popular 1943 film (scripted by Cocteau), *L'Eternel retour*. Tarr deftly connects the issues of masculinity and aesthetics – in particular, the 'weak' body (*douceur virile*) and ambivalent performance of Jean Marais – to the specific period of the Collaboration and the collapse of confidence in the Vichy regime in 1943.[48]

Such studies may be said to constitute a new general theoretical project in French film studies that tracks stories and histories of French cinema not covered by more traditional film history (the now classic work of André Bazin, Marc Ferro, Jean-Pierre Jeancolas, René Prédal and Georges Sadoul, for instance). As such, they can be linked to Geneviève Sellier and Noël Burch's key study of gender and cultural representation in wartime and post-war cinema, *La Drôle de guerre des sexes du cinéma français: 1930–1956* (1996), a volume all the more remarkable for being produced within the French academic context, which still remains highly suspicious of the Anglo-Saxon 'invention' of cultural studies.[49] Equally, they can be allied with the selective and subjectively rooted readings of French cinema since 1950 by Emma Wilson: readings that are possible only because they are beyond the usual norms of film history and *auteur* criticism, or the constraining categorizations of a genre-directed approach.[50]

To reiterate, the primary purpose of *Gender and French Cinema* is to explore different aspects of gender representation in French film, with gender taken in the widest, most comprehensive (Butlerian) sense: that is to say, as enmeshed with sexuality, the body and desire. In pursuing that purpose, unsurprisingly, *Gender and French Cinema* privileges questions of gender production and performance, central to the work of the gender theorists discussed earlier in this Introduction. But the collection does not restrict itself solely to investigating issues of gender (and) representation, since what is involved in any inventive rethinking of gender and French cinema is necessarily a rethinking of form and the politics of form, as inflected by other important factors and vectors of subjective location such as history, nationality, ethnicity, class, colonialism and post-colonialism. All the various well-documented aspects of the French tradition are covered in our volume: realism, stars, indigenous comedy, *auteurs*,[51] as well as movements and periods that are uniquely French. At the same time, however, new genres such as AIDS film-making and fantasy cinema, and themes often viewed as marginal such as female friendship and female gender identity in urban space, are actively promoted. For this reason *Gender and French Cinema* responds to the kind of challenge to the critic posed by a powerful new film like Claire Denis's poetic, homoerotic *Beau Travail* (1998) (an adaptation of Melville's *Billy Budd* that celebrates the male body and male camaraderie in a Foreign Legion outpost on the shores of Djibouti): a challenge that invites us to engage with French cinema and to define it in the full light of its gendered, national, historical and post-colonial contexts.

In his introduction to *French Cinema in the 1990s*, 'Heritage, History, and "New Realism"',[52] Phil Powrie talks of 'new generations': that is to say, of a new return of the political as well as realism. (Exceptions to this resurgence of political realism would be films such as Luc Besson's *The Fifth Element* (1997), a combination of French postmodern style and Hollywood action style, or what Powrie wryly calls 'a kind of hyper-postmodern transnational commodity fetish'.[53]) Powrie considers the importance and influence of the *sans-papiers* affair of 1996, and invokes the pertinence of phrases such as Guédiguian's *militantisme de proximité* (community politics) and Jeancolas's *réel de proximité*: an expression used to refer to a closeness to the sense of social change in a fragmented society, as evidenced in *beur* and *banlieue* films (French genres, although clearly influenced by contemporary black American film-makers such as Spike Lee). *Gender and French Cinema* follows in the same vein as Powrie by addressing directly the question of the national and the historical. It does so by interrogating the links between the open term 'gender' and the historical and national determinants of a cinema produced principally in France (as opposed to one that is more generally *francophone*). Moreover, it aims to convey a sense of the evolution of French film, via a historically oriented organization of chapters, and a range of critical approaches and methods. First – and in no order of priority – it contains essays concerned with key moments, movements and periods, notably dada and surrealism; the arrival of sound; cinema of the Occupation; post-1968 cinema; the New Wave; the *cinéma du look*; and the New New Wave. Second are those chapters dealing specifically with different (predominantly male) manifestations of the *auteur*, such as Cocteau, Godard, Miéville, Jean-Pierre Melville and Jean-Jacques Beineix. Third are discussions that address predominantly female stars such as Arletty and Simone Signoret and their performances within the system. Fourth, and finally, are chapters directly focused on genre, including the fantasy film, AIDS film-making and the so-called 'female film'. Here now follows a brief summary of the individual chapters.

Alex Hughes and James S. Williams

The Contents of the Volume

In Chapter 2: 'Bodies Cut and Dissolved', Elza Adamowicz probes the gender constructions elaborated in dada and surrealist silent cinema, whose practitioners were not all of French origin but which was anchored in inter-war 1920s France. Situating dada/surrealist film in its traumatic, post-Great War historical moment, Adamowicz examines how femininity, masculinity and the body are configured in films by René Clair; Marcel Duchamp; Germaine Dulac; Fernand Léger; Man Ray; Salvador Dalí and Luis Buñuel, and Hans Richter. Such films, she argues, are haunted by a 'fairground intertext': that is, a nostalgia for images of the magic theatre and the early cinema of the surrealists' childhood. Within the 'regressive' cinematic corpus they constitute, distinctions and tensions between body and non-body, Self and Other, masculine and feminine are vertiginously activated *and* exploded, in a manner that, on occasion, contests the critical credo that surrealist/dada representations were fundamentally misogynist.

Turning in Chapter 3 to the sound cinema of the 1930s and its representations of another early form of popular entertainment, the music hall, Kelley Conway investigates elaborations of gender contained in films that treat of the music hall *chanteuse* and of women's relations with the music hall environment. Her account of film-texts produced in the context of 1930s French cinema's dialogue with the culture of the music hall invokes, among other things: the star system that such films initiate and function within; their dissections of the dynamics of gender, class, social mobility and race; and their presentations of women in urban space (a phenomenon likewise explored by Julia Dobson later in the volume).

In 'Mon cul est intersexuel?', working from a star studies perspective, Keith Reader considers the gender enactments performed by Arletty in four films by Marcel Carné: *Hôtel du Nord* (1938); *Le Jour se lève* (1939); *Les Visiteurs du soir* (1942); and *Les Enfants du paradis* (1945). His analyses demonstrate how, if Arletty's star – and political – persona deters us from aligning her unproblematically with a contestatory stance, her filmic performances evince an interrogative negotiation of gender identities and boundaries that meshes richly with Butlerian notions of gender as constrained, fluid, contingent and sliding. Reader's Chapter 4 engages squarely with the interrelations of performance and performativity that Butler's gender paradigm sets up. If, however, his exegesis acknowledges the relevance of that paradigm to a reading of Arletty's screen constructions, it also goes beyond it, by revealing how *Les Enfants du paradis*, the emblem of Arletty's film career, lends itself equally to a psychoanalytically-oriented interpretation that engages Deleuzian conceptions of masochism and maternal/filial desire.

In 'For Our Eyes Only', James S. Williams pursues a reading of the cinematic corpus of Jean Cocteau that attends to the zones of uncertainty and ambiguity left unexplored in the totalizing interpretations that Cocteau's film-work has tended to elicit. Such zones include, specifically, the shared moments between men that Cocteau's films incorporate (and produce), and the current of male desire such moments bespeak. Addressing films made between 1932 and 1960, Williams's Chapter 5 concentrates on the use made in Cocteau of reverse motion photography. It anatomizes the complex, unsettling dynamic of viewing that Cocteau's investment in this technique engenders, and it positions that dynamic, finally, as evidence of an 'anal erotics' of viewing inherent in – and essential to – the lure of Cocteau's cinema.

In Chapter 6: 'Setting the Agenders', Susan Hayward, like Keith Reader, takes as her focus the performance(s) of a female star persona: Simone Signoret. Establishing Signoret's commitment to feminist politics as equivocal, she proposes that, this notwithstanding, the 'star body' that Signoret incarnated was, not unlike that of Arletty, intrinsically contestatory, proffering a challenge to the ideology – notably, the sexual/gender ideology – of mid-century France. Hayward concerns herself especially with two of Signoret's films: *Les Diaboliques* (1955) and *Les Mauvais Coups* (1960/61). Her analysis suggests that, in these star vehicles, as in other films of the 1945–1960 era, Signoret's performances attest to a play with gender fixity and a degree of sexual ambiguity that not only fascinated audiences of the time, but also, more significantly, refused to leave intact normative, post-World War Two images of submissive or fetishized femininity.

The feminine incarnations of the female star persona are also anatomized, albeit less centrally, in Geneviève Sellier's Chapter 7: 'Gender, Modernism and Mass Culture in the New Wave'. Here, Sellier addresses the key place in French cinematic and cultural history occupied by New Wave auteurist film. She begins by locating the cinema of the New Wave as inflected both by a modernist aesthetic defined against mass cultural forms allied to the feminine, and by a conception of the creative artist and the male subject grounded in a misogyny associated with the Romantic literary tradition. She proceeds to a reading of New Wave films made in the early 1960s by François Truffaut; Claude Chabrol; Jacques Rozier; Louis Malle, and Jean-Luc Godard. Taking as her focus the accounts of sexual difference and sociocultural identity that these narratives provide, she argues that their configurations of masculinity and femininity (a femininity equated with alienation, objectification and popular culture) evince the New Wave's imbrication in a profoundly masculinist vision of gender relations.

Misogyny is likewise taken to task in Chapter 8, '"Autistic Masculinity" in Jean-Pierre Melville's Crime Thrillers'. Here, Ginette Vincendeau concentrates on late films in Melville's mid-century corpus: *Le Samouraï* (1967); *Le Cercle rouge* (1970); and *Un flic* (1971). Her discussion of Melville's manipulations of the crime thriller/gangster genre dissects the intertextuality and extreme androcentrism of his cinematic work, and considers the appeal that that work exerts: an appeal that derives, Vincendeau affirms, from the combination of Melville's stylistic virtuosity and his compelling depiction of a masculinity that is introspective, self-absorbed, death-driven and tragic. In this chapter, Vincendeau signals that gender, notably in the masculine mode, is in no way peripheral to Melville's films. Rather, gender is enmeshed with all aspects of his cinema: its *mise en scène*; decor; narrative preoccupations, and its dialogue with the sociocultural context in which it came into being.

Concerned, no less, with male-authored cinema, and with an eye to more recent film production as well as that of the mid-century moment, Guy Austin in Chapter 9 explores articulations of gender and genre in French fantasy film, specifically: François Truffaut's *Fahrenheit 451* (1966); Roger Vadim's *Barbarella* (1967); and Luc Besson's *The Fifth Element* (1997). Austin examines how, in French fantasy film-texts, stock gender models are mobilized or undermined. Austin's commentary attends especially to the depiction, within the fantasy format, of the archaic mother; the Pygmalion/Galatea paradigm; the performative masculine; and the androgyne. It establishes French fantasy film as less locked into a monolithic lexicon of gender representation than we might expect, and as the site of challenging treatments of masculinity.

From the 1970s to the present, Anne-Marie Miéville and Jean-Luc Godard have employed modes of altered motion in their collaborative ventures and individual projects. In Chapter 10, a close reading of the second of their collaboratively-made television series, *France/tour/détour/deux/enfants* (1978), Michael Witt pulls this phenomenon apart, allying it to the renderings of the 'disciplined' body – and the body that refuses the normalizing process – that the series incorporates. Engaging both with Foucauldian theory and with the pre-cinematic science of Etienne-Jules Marey, he foregrounds the representation and decomposition of the corporal in *France/tour/détour/deux/enfants*. His account of Godard-Miéville's political anatomy of the body contextualizes it in terms of the growth of feminism in 1970s France and of the recent history of French pornographic cinema, analyzing in detail the formal tool – video – that it employs. Witt constructs a rich exegesis of Godard-Miéville's videographic treatments of the body, and their revitalization of cinema as a vibrant creative form.

In a further discussion of the masculine, Phil Powrie's Chapter 11 deals with films made by Jean-Jacques Beineix in the 1980s and early 1990s: films that, like those of Luc Besson, belong to the self-consciously aesthetic *cinéma du look*. In contrast to that adopted in a number of chapters in this volume, Powrie's approach engages directly with Lacanian psychoanalytic theory. His reading centres at once on the reception of Beineix's films and on the presentation, within them, of his young male protagonists, or YMPs. It situates these wilting, 'anamorphic' male/filial subjects in their relation both to the (increasingly degraded) Father and to the spectator, vis-à-vis whom, Powrie argues, they function as lures for the gaze, or *trompe-l'oeil* figures. Powrie contextualizes the visual 'trap' the YMPs constitute in terms of Beineix's attraction to images as loci of disruption: an attraction that issues from his determined rejection of the New Wave *cinéma de papa* and the critical establishment associated with it.

In Chapter 12, 'Aids-Video', Alex Hughes opts also to examine a filmic treatment of the 'fading' male subject. Her concern, however, is the visual work of Hervé Guibert, specifically the video-diary *La Pudeur ou l'impudeur* that Guibert made between June 1990 and March 1991 shortly before succumbing to the ravages of AIDS. Drawing on the writings of Foucault, Lee Edelman and Simon Watney, Hughes begins her discussion by mapping a homophobic matrix of images and narratives that reconstruct the gay male body – more particularly, the gay body-with-AIDS – as unnaturally legible. Then, by examining the bodily self-representations offered in *La Pudeur* (and in Guibert's photographic self-portraits), she works to show how Guibert's AIDS-video counters both normative, prejudicial configurations of the gay/AIDS body and the voyeuristic reading gaze that unfailingly interprets the symptoms of AIDS as ciphers of a scorned homosexual degeneracy.

In her Chapter 13 on the New New Wave, a cinema she situates as firmly tied to social issues and concerns current in contemporary France (and as far less mired in a misogynist mind-set than its New Wave precursor), Dina Sherzer investigates images of sexuality and gender roles contained in a selection of films made by French male directors of the 1990s. These films, she argues, convey messages about social mutation, notably in the spheres of gender, sexuality and ethnicity, that are likewise to be found in the writings of French sociologists. The New New Wave directors, she suggests, because they register societal evolution in their film-narratives, depict modes of subjectivity congruent with an evolving, late twentieth-century social environment in which existential choices and ways of being are more free, although more unstable, than ever before.

In her Chapter 14 dissection of two 1990s films made by contemporary French women directors, Laurence Ferreira Barbosa's *Les Gens normaux n'ont rien d'exceptionnel* (1994) and Noémie Lvovsky's *Oublie-moi* (1994), Julia Dobson considers the complex relations that obtain between urban space, the conventions of gendered mapping allied to representations of the cityscape, and the fabrications of gender that our occupation of the urban realm produces. Deploring the absence in recent French films of truly innovative conceptualizations of the woman/city dynamic, she scrutinizes the treatments of urban, gendered subjectivity provided in *Les Gens normaux* and *Oublie-moi*: narratives that foreground the situation of the woman subject-in-crisis in the public, city environment. Both films, she argues, seek to offer radical visions of women and/in the city in a manner that, among other things, effects a disruption of cinematographic space. But they also embrace, albeit ambiguously, modes of narrative closure that threaten to re-enclose the female subject-in-crisis in related, limiting environments: those of domestic space and the romance subplot with which tales of women in the city are all too often entwined.

Emma Wilson in Chapter 15, the last in our volume, explores the contemporary French female friendship film, and the issues of identification and desire it raises. Wilson's presentation is informed by the work of theorists such as Teresa de Lauretis and Jackie Stacey, situating French female friendship film in relation to its more established US counterpart, and delineating its history. Wilson's reading investigates three recent instances of the genre: Martine Dugowson's *Mina Tannenbaum* (1993) and *Portraits Chinois* (1995), and Erick Zonca's *La Vie rêvée des anges* (1998) (a film also dissected by Sherzer). In pursuing her readings of these film-texts, Wilson's object of attention is the relational dynamics that female friendship film – female and male-authored – articulates, and the intersections of affective and sexual attraction that it addresses. She optimistically concludes that contemporary French female friendship film, if it deals as much with antagonism and betrayal as with intimacy (obliging the viewer to reflect on the complexity of women's investments in each other) at least eludes the masculine/feminine, oppositional logic of heterosexuality by attending precisely to differences between women.

Notes

1. S. de Beauvoir (1972), *The Second Sex*, trans. H. Parshley, Harmondsworth, p. 295. 'On ne naît pas femme: on le devient. Aucun destin biologique, psychique, économique ne définit la figure que revêt au sein de la société la femelle humaine; c'est l'ensemble de la civilisation qui élabore ce produit intermédiaire entre le mâle et le castrat qu'on qualifie de féminin'. S. de Beauvoir (1949), *Le Deuxième Sexe II*, Paris, p. 13.
2. T. Moi (1994), *Simone de Beauvoir: The Making of an Intellectual Woman*, Oxford and Cambridge, Mass., p. 162.
3. J. Butler (1998), 'Sex and Gender in Simone de Beauvoir's *Second Sex*', in E. Fallaize (ed.), *Simone de Beauvoir: A Critical Reader*, London and New York, pp. 29–42, p. 30.
4. See D. Kaufmann (1986), 'Simone de Beauvoir: Questions of Difference and Generation', *Yale French Studies*, 72, pp. 121–31, p. 128.
5. M. Dietz (1992), 'Introduction: Debating Simone de Beauvoir', *Signs*, 18, pp. 74–88, p. 74.
6. Butler, 'Sex and Gender', p. 31.
7. S. Kruks (1998), 'Beauvoir: The Weight of Situation', in Fallaize, *Simone de Beauvoir*, pp. 43–71, p. 59.

8. C. Mackenzie (1998), 'A Certain Lack of Symmetry', in R. Evans (ed.), *Simone de Beauvoir's The Second Sex*, Manchester, pp. 122–58, p. 123.

9. Butler's essay 'Sex and Gender' (cf. p. 40) detects in *The Second Sex* a promise that gender identity, elaborated under different cultural norms, might 'proliferate into a multiple phenomenon for which new terms must be found'. Butler recognizes however that Beauvoir herself is not consciously entertaining the possibility of genders other than those of 'man' and 'woman'.

10. On the reception of Beauvoir's text, see R. Evans (1998), 'Introduction: *The Second Sex* and The Postmodern', in Evans, *Simone de Beauvoir's The Second Sex*, pp. 1–30, p. 1.

11. J. Butler (1990), *Gender Trouble: Feminism and The Subversion of Identity*, London and New York, p. 136. The following survey of Butler's treatment of gender draws on A. Hughes and A. Witz (1997), 'Feminism and the Matter of Bodies: From de Beauvoir to Butler', *Body and Society*, 3, pp. 47–60.

12. Butler, *Gender Trouble*, p. 33.

13. Ibid., p. 139.

14. Butler clarifies this point in her later study *Bodies That Matter*. See J. Butler (1993), *Bodies That Matter: On the Discursive Limits of 'Sex'*, New York and London, p. x.

15. Butler, *Gender Trouble*, pp. 135–6.

16. Ibid., p. 135.

17. Ibid., p. 17.

18. See Butler, *Bodies That Matter*, pp. 124–5.

19. Butler, *Gender Trouble*, p. 136, p. 7.

20. Butler, *Bodies That Matter*, p. 2.

21. Ibid., p. 15.

22. Ibid., p. 3. By 'abject' here, she refers to all those beings whose sexed identifications fail to adhere to heteronormativity.

23. See Hughes and Witz, 'Feminism and the Matter of Bodies', pp. 47–52.

24. See ibid., pp. 55–7.

25. Relevant here are L. Irigaray (1974), *Speculum, de l'autre femme*, Paris; L. Irigaray (1977), *Ce Sexe qui n'en est pas un*, Paris; and H. Cixous/C. Clément (1975), *La Jeune Née*, Paris. These are translated as *Speculum of the Other Woman* (1985, Ithaca); *This Sex Which Is Not One* (1985, Ithaca); *The Newly Born Woman* (1986, Minneapolis).

26. See for example S. Bordo (1993), *Unbearable Weight: Feminism, Western Culture, and the Body*, Berkeley and London; J. Gallop (1988), *Thinking Through The Body*, New York; M. Gatens (1996), *Imaginary Bodies: Ethics, Power and Corporeality*, London and New York; E. Grosz (1995), *Space, Time, and Perversion*, New York and London; E. Grosz (1994), *Volatile Bodies: Toward a Corporeal Feminism*, Bloomington and Indianapolis.

27. See, for example, D. Fuss (ed.) (1991), *Inside/Out: Lesbian Theories, Gay Theories*, New York and London; T. de Lauretis (1994), *The Practice of Love: Lesbian Sexuality and Perverse Desire*, Bloomington and Indianapolis; E.K. Sedgwick (1990), *Epistemology of the Closet*, Berkeley and Los Angeles. See also T. de Lauretis (1993), 'Sexual Indifference and Lesbian Representation', in H. Abelove, M. Barale and D. Halperin (eds), *The Lesbian and Gay Studies Reader*, New York and London, pp. 141–58; G. Rubin (1993), ' Thinking Sex: Notes for a Radical Theory of the Politics of Sexuality', in ibid., pp. 3–44; M. Wittig (1993), 'One Is Not Born A Woman', in ibid., pp. 103–9; M. Wittig (1996), 'The Straight Mind', in S. Jackson and S. Scott (eds), *Feminism and Sexuality: A Reader*, Edinburgh, pp. 144–9.
28. A. Petersen (1998), *Unmasking the Masculine: 'Men' and 'Identity' in a Sceptical Age*, London, Thousand Oaks and New Delhi.
29. K.K. Ruthven (1984), *Feminist Literary Studies: An Introduction*, Cambridge, p. 9, cited in E. Showalter (ed.) (1989), *Speaking of Gender*, New York and London, p. 1.
30. For a discussion of this phenomenon, see N. Mirzoeff (ed.) (1998), *The Visual Culture Reader*, New York and London, pp. 391–7.
31. See, for example, M.A. Doane (1987), *The Desire to Desire: The Woman's Film of the 1940s*, Bloomington and Indianapolis (a study of gender dynamics in classic melodrama); M.A. Doane (1991), *Femmes Fatales: Feminism, Film Theory, Psychoanalysis*, London and New York; T. de Lauretis (1984), *Alice Doesn't: Feminism, Semiotics, Cinema*, Bloomington and Indianapolis; L. Mulvey (1989), *Visual and Other Pleasures*, Bloomington and Indianapolis; D.N. Rodowick (1991), *The Difficulty of Difference: Psychoanalysis, Sexual Difference, and Film Theory*, London and New York; K. Silverman (1992), *Male Subjectivity at the Margins*, London and New York; K. Silverman (1988) *The Acoustic Mirror*, Bloomington and Indianapolis. See also S. Heath (1979), *Questions of Cinema*, London; E.A. Kaplan (1983), *Women and Film: Both Sides of the Camera*, London and New York; E.A. Kaplan (ed.) (1990), *Psychoanalysis and the Cinema*, London and New York; T. Modleski (1988), *The Women Who Knew Too Much: Hitchcock and Feminist Theory*, New York and London; C. Penley (1989), *The Future of an Illusion: Film, Feminism, and Psychoanalysis*, Minneapolis; G. Studlar (1988), *In The Realm of Pleasure: Von Sternberg, Dietrich, and the Masochistic Aesthetic*, Urbana.
32. See C. Metz, (1974), *Language and Cinema*, trans. D. Jean, The Hague; C. Metz (1982), *The Imaginary Signifier: Psychoanalysis and Cinema*, trans. B. Brewster, C. Britton, A. Guzzetti and A. Williams, Bloomington and Indianapolis; J.-L. Baudry (1976), 'The Ideological Effects of the Basic Cinematographic Apparatus', *Film Quarterly*, 27, pp. 39–47.
33. See L. Mulvey (1975), 'Visual Pleasure and Narrative Cinema', *Screen*, 16, pp. 6–18.

34. E. Cowie (1984), 'Fantasia', *m/f*, 9, pp. 76–105.

35. See, for example, B. Creed (1993), *The Monstrous-Feminine: Film, Feminism and Psychoanalysis*, London and New York.

36. See B. Creed (1998), 'Film and Psychoanalysis', in J. Hill and P. C. Gibson (eds), *Oxford Guide to Film Studies*, Oxford, pp. 77–90, p. 79.

37. See S. Shaviro (1993), *The Cinematic Body*, Minneapolis.

38. See K. Mercer (1993), 'Dark and Lovely Too: Black Gay Men in Independent Film', in M. Gever, J. Greyson and P. Parmar (eds), *Queer Looks: Perspectives on Gay and Lesbian Film and Video,* London and New York, pp. 238–56.

39. See E. Hanson (ed.) (1999), *Out Takes: Essays on Queer Theory and Film*, Durham and London, in particular pp. 1–19, p. 12.

40. Ibid., p. 13.

41. See, for example, L. Edelman (1994), *Homographesis: Essays in Gay Literary and Cultural Theory*, New York and London; C. Holmlund (1993), 'Masculinity as Multiple Masquerade: The 'Mature' Stallone and the Stallone Clone', in S. Cohan and I. Hark (eds), *Screening the Male: Exploring Masculinities in Hollywood Cinema*, London and New York, pp. 213–29; Fuss, *Inside/Out: Lesbian Theories, Gay Theories.* Fuss's collection contains essays by Miller, White and Richard Dyer, among others.

42. See F. Audé (1981), *Ciné-modèles, cinéma d'elles: Situation des femmes dans le cinéma français 1956–1979*, Lausanne; S. Flitterman-Lewis (1990), *To Desire Differently: Feminism and the French Cinema*, Urbana and Chicago; J. Forbes (1992), *The Cinema in France After The New Wave*, London; S. Hayward and G. Vincendeau (eds) (1990), *French Film: Texts and Contexts*, London and New York; P. Powrie (1997), *French Cinema in the 1980s: Nostalgia and the Crisis of Masculinity*, Oxford. See C.-M. Trémois (1997), *Les Enfants de la liberté*, Paris, for an extensive summary of contemporary *jeune cinéma*.

43. See O. Heathcote, A. Hughes, and J.S. Williams (eds) (1998), *Gay Signatures: Gay and Lesbian Theory, Fiction and Film in France, 1945–1995*, Oxford and New York, in particular the Introduction (pp. 9–17). The volume includes B. Rollet and J.S. Williams, 'Visions of Excess: Filming/Writing the Gay Self in Collard's *Savage Nights*' (pp. 193–208).

44. See, for example, A. de Baecque (1998), *La Nouvelle Vague, portrait d'une jeunesse*, Paris; J. Douchet (1998), *Nouvelle Vague*, Paris; M. Marie (1997), *La Nouvelle Vague: Une école artistique*, Paris.

45. See M. O'Shaughnessy (2000), *Jean Renoir*, Manchester, in particular Chapter 4, 'The Popular Front Years'. Other titles in the series edited by Diana Holmes and Robert Ingram include their own *François Truffaut*; *Agnès Varda* (Alison Smith); *Diane Kurys* (Carrie Tarr); *Luc Besson* (Susan Hayward); *Coline Serreau* (Brigitte Rollet); *Georges Méliès* (Elizabeth Ezra); *Claude Chabrol*

(Guy Austin); and *Bertrand Blier* (Sue Harris). On feminist film authorship, see C. Grant (2001) 'Secret Agents: Feminist Theories of Film Authorship', *Feminist Theory*, 2, pp. 113–30.

46. See C. Tarr (1999), 'Gender and Sexuality in *Les Nuits fauves*', in P. Powrie (ed.) (1999), *French Cinema in the 1990s: Continuity and Difference*, Oxford, pp. 117–26; G. Hayes (1999), 'Representation, Masculinity, Nation: The Crises of *Les Amants du Pont-Neuf*', in ibid., pp. 199–210.

47. See L. Cairns (1998), '*Gazon Maudit*: French National and Sexual identities', *French Cultural Studies*, 9, pp. 225–37. Cairns concludes rather pessimistically that what may appear an iconoclastic French film turns out, in fact, to be a sop to millennial anxieties about crises of national identity, since it offers 'traditional, Latin France as a model of French national identity generally: tolerant, relaxed enough to have fun, but ultimately committed to preserving the two foundation-stones of its identity – the family, and the Law of the Father, which is what, in the end, it is all about' (p. 236).

48. See C. Tarr (1998), '*L'Eternel retour*: Reflection of the Occupation's Crisis in French Masculinity?', *Sub-stance*, 87, pp. 55–72. As this book went into production, we became aware of the existence of Lucy Mazdon's edited collection *France on Film*. See L. Mazdon (2001), *France on Film: Reflections on Popular French Cinema*, London. This includes essays on gender-related topics by Darren Waldron, Lucille Cairns and Emma Wilson.

49. See N. Burch and G. Sellier (1996), *La Drôle de guerre des sexes du cinéma français: 1930–1956*, Paris.

50. See E. Wilson (1999), *French Cinema Since 1950: Personal Histories*, London.

51. See Ginette Vincendeau's valuable historical overview of French cinema in G. Vincendeau (ed.) (1996), *The Companion to French Cinema*, London, pp. 1–11. Vincendeau uses Louis Delluc's notion of a 'really French cinema' to examine popular traditions of French cinema, specifically realism, performance (i.e. stars), indigenous comedy, and *auteurs*.

52. See Powrie, *French Cinema in the 1990s: Continuity and Difference*, pp. 1–21, p. 15.

53. For Powrie, heritage cinema is the hegemonic cinema in France today, precisely because its anchoring in French history makes it the most easily identifiable 'national' cinema, even if it can also be very melodramatic and in thrall to its Hollywood cousins (cf. ibid., p. 20).

2

Bodies Cut and Dissolved: Dada and Surrealist Film

Elza Adamowicz

Un pied un oeil le tout mélangé aux objets.

Fernand Léger

The Lady Vanishes (twice)

In 1921 Marcel Duchamp and Man Ray are said to have shot a short film in which Duchamp shaves the pubic hair of Baroness Elsa von Freytag-Loringhoven, an eccentric German-born New York dadaist.[1] The film was lost during processing (Duchamp having tried to develop it in a dustbin lid), but at least one photograph marking the event has survived.[2] This dada performance (and its variants)[3] raise a number of questions about gender, ideology and spectatorship in dada – and, by extension, surrealist – film practice. These pertain to gender relations in the paradigm of male film-maker and female subject; to sexual (in)differentiation in the erasing or (literal) dissolving of body parts of a persona who appears as an extension of Elsa's androgynous self-performances in the streets of New York; to shifting (self-)identities in the projection of Duchamp's alter ego on to the body of the Other; to the appropriation of popular entertainment codes in the perverse transformation of the woman's body; and to the unsettling position of the spectator, confronted with a (virtual) film that is both deliberately artisanal gag and unsettling *mise en scène* of castration. Some of these issues will be discussed in this chapter, which will explore the aesthetic, intertextual and ideological contexts that inform the contradictions and tensions of gender construction in dada/surrealist films.

While dadaists and surrealists produced a large number of virtual films in the 1920s, the corpus of actual film production is relatively insubstantial. The surrealists' own listings fluctuated over the years, determined primarily by disputes and conjunctural strategies. Films listed as 'surrealist' in the *Dictionnaire abrégé du surréalisme* (1938), for instance, correspond to a historical moment when Artaud was a reviled actor, and dadaist extras had to be co-opted to produce a substantial list. My own corpus focuses on the silent films of the 1920s and includes René Clair's *Entr'acte* (1924) (scenario by Francis Picabia); Man Ray's *Retour à la raison* (1923) and *Emak Bakia* (1926); Marcel Duchamp's *Anémic cinéma* (1926); Fernand Léger's *Ballet mécanique* (1924), Man Ray's *Etoile de mer* (1928) (scenario by Robert Desnos); Germaine Dulac's *La Coquille et le clergyman* (1928) (scenario by Antonin Artaud);[4] Hans Richter's *Vormittagsspuk* (1928); and Luis Buñuel and Salvador Dalí's *Un Chien andalou* (1929). Critics have distinguished dada films, with their focus on the illusory cinematic apparatus (the eye of the camera), from surrealist films as a simulacrum of the psychic apparatus (Dali's 'other side of the eye').[5] But my discussion, which focuses on aspects related to both the so-called dada mechanistic and the surrealist *merveilleux*, shows that the two movements are historically and aesthetically interwoven. My aim is to study the ambivalence of these films as both apparently nostalgic (in their engagement with the fairground intertext) and radically modernist (in their montage techniques). Moreover, adopting a film-viewing mode learned from dadaists André Breton and Jacques Vaché, who would enter several cinemas in succession to view random sequences of films, creating their own incongruous montage, my analysis will involve a zapping process that focuses on features shared by the films under discussion without denying their specificity as *auteur* films.

The Post-War Context

The disruptive experience of the 1914–1918 war, its mutilated and disfigured bodies, wounded psyches and hysterical disorders, brought about fundamental shifts in the way the body was conceptualized and identity was constructed.[6] In response to this disruption, post-war reconstruction programmes saw a return to rationalism, marked in the aesthetic field by a revival of the classical paradigm of the body represented as an organic whole (as in Picasso's Ingresque nudes or in Léger's machine-bodies of technological utopias). This was a new start, aimed at suppressing the traumatic images of the dismembered limbs and dislocated minds of the soldiers in the trenches blasted by mechanized warfare, or the alienated condition of the munitions factory workers. The dadaists and surrealists reacted against this process by privileging art forms based on spontaneity, chance and the irrational. They produced images of the body as dysfunctional machine, as fragment, fetish or fantasy: images that expose rather than suppress the disfigured limbs and violence to the integral body. The instability of the male self-image, the shifting identities of female images and the images of gender indifferentiation found in their films can also be linked to the collapse of the nineteenth-century myth of the heroic individual; to French women's demands for social emancipation in the 1920s; and to the feminization of society engendered by growing consumerism, accompanied by the appearance of the androgynous figure of the New Woman and resulting shifts in gender-specific identities. These social disruptions partly explain the dadaists' and surrealists' regression to pre-war intertexts – to the nostalgic images of the magic theatre or the early cinema of their childhood – as a magical re-enactment of childhood, a form of resistance against modernity. In the bodies depicted are inscribed both trauma and potential liberation, whether in the tragic-ludic replay of Oedipal scenarios or in the fragmented or exploded body as source of anxious separation from, or joyful transgression of, the constraints of the classical body.[7] In such exploratory shifting reconfigurations of the body and the self, distinctions – body/non-body; animate/inanimate; self/Other, masculine/ feminine – collapse in the dissolves and clashes between disparate elements.

The Fairground as Intertext

While exalting the 'savage eye' of automatism,[8] the surrealists actually adopted a number of conscious strategies in their film-making, parodying contemporary film genres: the avant-garde abstract cinema;[9] slapstick comedy; the expressionist and melodramatic film.[10] They also turned to pre-war cinema, the films of Georges Méliès and the Lumière brothers, themselves informed by popular entertainment models of the end of the nineteenth century, and in particular the fairground and the magic theatre. Even as they parody such outdated modes of spectacle, the surrealists play nostalgically with the magical fantasmagoric images of *fin de siècle* entertainment grounded on excess (the carnivalesque, the burlesque or the ecstatic), and play with illusion and displays of primal or infantile emotions. In *Anémic cinéma*, for instance, we find memories of fairground optical devices such as the chromatrope (a lantern slide made up of two patterned glass discs revolving in opposite directions to produce circular revolving images); in *Emak Bakia*, the deforming mirrors of fairground booths. Like Méliès's films, dada and surrealist films generally favour the isolated gag over a sustained narrative:[11] in *Entr'acte* there are revolving fairground dolls with balloon heads alternately inflating and deflating; bearded ballerinas; a female dancer dissolving to water; a hunter hunted and shot; a funeral procession led by a camel.[12] The male protagonist often appears in the guise of a magician who controls and transforms reality, as in the corpse turned magician conjuring away the funeral procession in *Entr'acte*, or the clergy-man-(al)chemist in *Coquille*, conjuring up the woman's head trapped in a vase. As a replay of a fairground performance, the film-as-spectacle sometimes screens the magician-*cinéaste* himself, as in the opening shot of *Emak Bakia* of Man Ray as cameraman, or the shot of Léger filming his own reflection in a deforming mirror in *Ballet mécanique*. More tellingly, the magic theatre or trick film intertext provides the cliché of the male conjuror performing magical acts on a female subject, as in the prologue of *Un Chien andalou*. This sequence – with its elaborate *mise en scène*; its build-up of suspense (knife-sharpening, moon-slicing, eye-slitting); the frontality of shots that produce a deliberately theatricalizing effect, showing Buñuel himself as conjurer-*cinéaste* and objectifying the female protagonist as passive spectacle – belongs to the magic theatre's or early cinema's 'catalogue of magical misogyny', that included such displays of sadistic penetration as 'sawing a woman in half' and 'shooting through a woman'.[13] The opening sequence of *Chien* can also be seen as an appropriation of the fairground waxwork displays designed to educate (and shock) the public, with their presentation of physical ailments or operations, such as the waxwork of a cataract operation where the disembodied hand of an assistant holds open the eye of an apparently compliant woman that the doctor's scalpel prepares to pierce.[14] Elsewhere, the close-up shots of female legs, breasts or eyes evoke memories of the fairground female assistant sawn into pieces, while the transformation of body parts – breasts dissolved to buttocks or seashells; underarm hair to sea-urchin; a ballerina's legs to an opening and closing flower – allude to the substitution tricks played out by the male magician on his female subject. The paradigm of bodies fragmented, transformed or dissolved in the fun-fair or early cinema – the bearded lady; exploding heads; levitating bodies; amputated limbs – is characteristic of the carnivalesque space of popular entertainment. These limit-bodies seem only slightly subversive: the sawn-up woman is reassembled; the vanished lady is conjured back, as in Méliès's *L'Escamotage d'une dame* (1896). Popular entertainment formulas operate at the outer limits of social codes, articulating the pre-conscious rather than fully sustaining the social order. According to John Cawelti, 'formulas enable the audience to explore in fantasy the boundary between the permitted and the forbidden and to explore in a carefully controlled way the possibility of stepping across this boundary'.[15] The spectators thus relive their fundamental fears and impulses in a framed context within which they can manage their anxieties or sadistic impulses.[16] For Linda Williams, Méliès's films present a symbolical reenactment, obsessively repeated, of mastery over the threat of gender difference, played out in the scenarios of dismemberment/reintegration or disappearance/reappearance of the woman's body.[17]

What is the effect of dada/surrealist appropriations of fairground tricks and magical transgressions, particularly in their representations of gender relations? Does the parodic reworking of early cinematic codes in the corpus under discussion reinforce or subvert patriarchal order? In declaring above that surrealist films are both nostalgic and radical, I am suggesting that the answer lies in apparently antithetical readings.[18] In an initial reading, dada/surrealist film can be seen to reinforce the misogynistic ideology encoded in *fin de siècle* entertainment of male domination and female submission. Such a reading is supported by Xavière Gauthier in her polemical work *Surréalisme et sexualité* (1971),[19] which was the first feminist critique of surrealism as a deeply misogynistic movement dominated by men. Gauthier, who focuses on surrealist painting, argues that both the celebration and the violation of the female body are played out as defences against male castration fears. Read through Gauthier's optic, the films under discussion here appear to reinforce traditional patriarchal positions on the level of both narrative and spectatorial position. The stock melodramatic tropes of male domination and female subjugation (cf. the eye-slitting scene in *Chien*; the confessional scene in *Coquille*); the replays of the Oedipal scenario; the image of woman as passive spectacle (frontal shots), icon (close-ups) or fetishized object (starfish or head bottled in a jar) for the active male gaze can be seen to invite the narcissistic identification and scopophilic (fetishistic) pleasure of the spectator.[20]

In dada/surrealist film practice, familiar tropes of femininity (subjugation, instability, dissimulation) appear to be reactivated through the topos of magic and dream. So the cliché of woman subjugated is euphemized – that is, poeticized – as magical transformation, informed by desire.[21] This explains not only the fetishistic focus on body parts, manifest in the superimposed images of Rose Wheeler's legs getting out of a car in *Emak Bakia*, but also the transformation of the female body: a body shot in a mirror that shatters into a star-shaped pattern, reifying as starfish (*Etoile*), or whose head is distorted and dissolved (cf. Kiki de Montparnasse, in *Emak Bakia*). Similarly, figures of dissimulation (goggles, lipstick or veil) renew the cliché of feminine instability through the paradigm of dream and magic. In *Coquille*, for instance, the female protagonist is constantly changing, appearing sometimes with a huge swollen cheek, sometimes with her tongue fantastically extended, sometimes with a horribly bloated chest.

This first reading may lead one to conclude that the surrealists were too close to the topos of magic as a poetic means of transforming reality to challenge, radically, the moral and social conventions encoded in early fantasmagoria or trick film. Yet Walter Benjamin explains surrealism's turning to the outmoded objects and modes of entertainment of the nineteenth century as a form of fascination that, far from being melancholic, is revolutionary. He suggests that 'surrealism is the death of the nineteenth century through comedy': a rewriting of the nineteenth century's texts that offers a critique of its dominant ideology.[22] The radical nature of dada/surrealist film practice is evident in the parodic strategies of the film-maker as 'inventor-*bricoleur*' with regard to early cinematographic techniques.[23] The deliberately artisanal shooting (hand-held camera; blurred image; jerky 'automatic' shots) and editing techniques (rapid cuts; awkward dissolves; irrational juxtapositions or superimpositions) foreground the film-text as a product of *bricolage*, a collage of fragments that refuse to stick together, defamiliarizing conventional perception.[24] Furthermore, disruption on the diegetic level foregrounds the work of the signifier, preventing passive consumption of the film. In the last part of *Entr'acte*, for instance, when the (resuscitated) hunter leaps through the words *la fin* on the screen, closure is playfully denied,[25] while in *Chien* the absence of diegetic coherence disorients the viewer, leaving 'desire engaged and unfulfilled'.[26] The centrality of this objective is clear in André Breton's 1951 account of early surrealist cinema, 'Comme dans un bois', where he discusses the formal strategies of defamiliarization (*pouvoir de dépaysement*) exploited in the silent film, its ellipses and interpolated shots, irrational associations and rhythmic structures.[27] Such disruptions destabilize the spectator, who is assaulted not only indirectly, through the formal and narrative techniques enumerated above, but also quite directly, in the cannon or boxing gloves aimed at the camera in *Entr'acte*; the violence of the eye-slitting scene in *Chien*; the confrontation with the female character as the active subject of the gaze (cf. Kiki de Montparnasse, in *Entr'acte*); or the sequence of four women opening their eyes and staring at the camera in *Emak Bakia*. Far from passively succumbing to the male gaze, these female characters repeatedly counter that gaze with their own intense look. Thus the visibility of the cinematic apparatus exposes (or perversely celebrates?) its fetish function, preventing spectatorial identification with the screened fiction.

Rosalind Krauss has commented on the process of fetishization made visible in surrealist photography. Gauthier attacked surrealist representations of women as fundamentally misogynist, declaring that surrealist woman was essentially a 'male forgery'. Krauss's analysis of surrealist photography, however, explores *how* surrealist images of women are forged, focusing on techniques of defamiliarization – techniques relevant also to film, such as multiple exposure; doubling; rayographs; and negative printing – that expose the distortions of the (female) body as fictional. Krauss thus adumbrates for surrealism a metadiscourse on 'male' and 'female' positions: a comment on the patriarchal fetishization of woman.[28] In her analysis of Georges Bataille's pornographic texts, Susan Sontag takes the radical argument a step further, arguing that such texts are transgressive, 'breaking through the limits of consciousness', and hence emancipatory.[29] If one adopts a similar line with regard, for instance, to Buñuel's film, it can be argued that, through his exploitation of visually and psychically shocking scenes of violation (cf. the image of the knife-penis and eye-vagina as an explicit enactment of the sexual act), he allows unconscious desires to express themselves, disrupting the stable symbolic order in a liberating movement that transgresses the constraints of bourgeois repression. In similar vein, elaborating on Krauss's discussion of photography, Susan Rubin Suleiman reads surrealist perversions of the normative body, in their images of the hybrid/fragmented body as well as in their parodic intertextual practices, as the rebellious actions of the son against paternal law, hence as liberating.[30]

In sum, we can choose to construe the distorted image of the woman produced in dada/surrealist film as the sign of a dehumanizing misogynistic attitude or to understand the perverse transformations of the woman as an act of liberation of the psyche from repressive constraints. That such antithetical readings recommend themselves reflects the often contradictory explorations of gender relations in surrealism. An investigation of the surrealists' debates on sexuality ('Recherches sur la sexualité' 1928–32) reveals their complex attitudes towards sexual issues. While they loudly posit gender difference, they also express the desire to collapse difference, as Breton's remarks reveal:

If I place love above everything, it is because it is for me the most desperate, the most despairing state of affairs imaginable. My own depersonalisation in this realm is precisely all that I wish for. As to my submission, it is so bound up with domination that I am entirely taken over by it.[31]

An ambivalent approach to gender relations is evident in Man Ray's *Retour à la raison*, a three-minute film produced in twenty-four hours as part of the programme for a dada *Soirée du Coeur à barbe*, organized by Tristan Tzara in 1923.[32] An example of improvised *bricolage*, the film was collaged from ready-made material, kineticized rayographs (objects such as nails and pins placed on photosensitive paper and briefly exposed to light) and short filmed sequences: a brightly lit merry-go-round; a field of daisies; rotating objects; a distorted 'phonetic poem'. Among these, shots of a nude female torso, headless and armless,[33] are montaged in a sequence of rapid shots of rotating objects, including a paper spiral and suspended eggboxes. (A still from the film is reproduced in the first issue of *La Révolution surréaliste* of 1924.) The light and shadow patterns of a curtain are projected on to the female body in a slowly rotating movement in a shot then inverted, and in a play on positive and negative images as on a screen, suggesting magic-lantern images as well as the process of the rayographs. Depersonalized and abstracted, the body can be seen as reified mannequin, as optical illusion, or as reduced to skin-deep light patterns. Yet the patterns moving across the body, evoking tattoos or scars, animal stripes or the bars of a cage, transform the body into a fluid shape whose contours are dissolved in the light and shadow patterns projected on to and around it, denying the body contained through the process of defamiliarization analyzed by Krauss, and celebrating the body as light, space and movement.[34] Moreover, the female body, in *Retour à la raison*, is a screen for the projection of Man Ray's desires and anxieties about the stability of his own self-image. It works as a form of displaced self-portrait, and confirms that the surrealist quest for the Other, in the guise of female torso, starfish or seashell, often mediates a search for self-identity.[35] 'The search for the other', writes Gérard Durozoi of Breton's relation to Nadja, 'is always a search for the self. The Other who haunts me will reveal to me who I am.'[36]

But surrealist film-images of the male body are not always displaced through the representation of the female Other, nor do they always adhere to the fixed codes of the male magician discussed earlier. They betray an ambivalence similar to that evinced in images of the female body: an ambivalence that signals both nostalgic regression and a radical exploration of an exploded identity.

Dada films offer a playground for adolescent boys to indulge in playful antics and portray a world out of control. We see this in *Entr'acte*, where Duchamp and Man Ray play chess on Paris rooftops, and in the practices of the all-male cast of Hans Richter's *Vormittagsspuk*, where beardless faces sprout beards, bodies are dismembered or decapitated, a disembodied head becomes a target or a rotting mask, severed hands wave and men engage in frantic and fruitless activities, walking vertically, crawling, climbing up and down ladders, unable to control hats, their collars flying, ties untying, revolvers revolving without human agency. Richter's film (a non-French production, but an excellent vehicle for the fairground intertext characteristic of French surrealist/dada cinema) was read as a political satire portraying the destabilization of German society with the rise of National Socialism.[37] *Coquille* presents the shifting identities of a 'man in black' as alchemist; child; clergyman, or criminal; as doubled (as a general); feminized (his habit lengthens into a wedding-train); self-absorbed and literally self-absorbing. In *Chien*, likewise, the main protagonist is both duplicated and feminized: he lacks stable contours (hole in hand), is conjoined with the animal (ants emerging from flesh) or reified in objects washed up as flotsam.[38] Male characters are engaged in fruitless chases (after hats or women); Oedipal conflicts left unresolved; frustrated romances; failed alchemical quests;[39] or ever repeated gestures in incomplete narratives where desire is constantly thwarted. Through such figures of destabilization – bodies lacking stable contours or identity, actions lacking in finality – the male self is foregrounded as the decentred subject, split, fragmented, displaced or dissolved in the Other.[40]

Like the magician-figure at the end of the nineteenth century, who asserts his independence from industrialization[41] (and who was often a very competent designer), the dada/surrealist film-maker turns to outdated forms of entertainment and pastiches the material effects of early film, in a challenge to post-war modes of modernity. Against the realities of adulthood, he regresses to infantile sexual fantasies (masturbatory sequences, gratuitous sadistic violence) or Oedipal struggles against reified father-figures (the floating general, the B-movie cop-dad who removes the son's feminine frills). Against the Taylorized body of the worker on the assembly-line, he celebrates, in a playful critique, the fragmented or dysfunctional body in the surrealist exquisite corpse.[42] Against the narrative of the disjunctive body as a tale of loss, where body parts refer to an absent whole, to the (almost forgotten) narrative of a collective or individual traumatic past (wounds of the battlefield; alienation of the factory floor; exile from the nursery), the dadaist plays out the consciousness of the illusion of wholeness or differentiation by regression to a state of play that, according to D.W. Winnicott, can be considered as a 'sort of ticking over of the unintegrated personality':[43] an exploration of the self as multiple and joyfully unstable.

The awareness of the disintegration of self – euphemized as playful fragmentation – is conjoined, in sum, with a fascination for an exploded identity. Commenting on the ambivalence of such a position, Sidra Stich notes that the 'self, then, moves outside of itself, taking on the likeness of the other while experiencing both the exaltation and the discord of such a possibility'.[44] The principle of a stable unified ego was challenged by the surrealists, who rejected notions of identity as essentialist concept or ontological given, in favour of understanding identity as a mobile construct, constantly remodelled by objective chance. The body is not a closed entity but a privileged site of the encounter between desire and reality, with the result that the comforting/constraining limits of the body and the subject are constantly transgressed or exploded.[45] This awareness is clearly articulated by Jacques Lacan, for whom the notion of the unified self is grounded on an illusion and constantly threatened by regression:

> Here we see the ego, in its essential resistance to the elusive process of Becoming, to the variations of Desire. This illusion of entity, in which a human being is always looking forward to self-mastery, entails a constant danger of sliding back again into the chaos from which he started; it hangs over the abyss of a dizzy Ascent in which one can perhaps see the very essence of Anxiety.[46]

In their texts and images, the surrealists explore processes of becoming and desire that disrupt the supposed unity of the ego.[47] The self as a distinct(ive) identity is constantly decentred, displaced or dissolved in the Other: the double as symbolic representation of the irrational self or as the woman (the unconscious coded feminine). The self is mediated via the mythical persona of conjuror, criminal or clergyman; the shattered body parts; the synecdoches of box and frills reified as flotsam. The limits of the self are explored concretely in the absence of fixed bodily contours, in dissolves to the non-body (animal; object; light; rhythmic shapes), transgressing the limits between self and Other, masculine and feminine.

Migrating Body Parts

The shifting spaces of gender difference are evident in the playfully fetishistic substitutions and displacements of dada/surrealist films, as in the sequence in *Emak Bakia* where female dancers in tutus are shot from below through glass, cutting to upper bodies that have been transformed into bearded men, in a playful reworking of the fairground paradigm of the bearded lady or hermaphrodite. Such isolated gags, however, unintegrated into a sustained narrative, fail to have a lasting resonance for the spectator. But the 'dance between genders'[48] sequence in *Chien*, where body parts disappear (Batcheff loses his mouth) or migrate between the male and female protagonists (female hair to male face), while it appropriates the optical tricks of the fun-fair, is profoundly disturbing in its ambiguity. The male is de-faced, castrated, feminized, while the threatening female protagonist asserts her femininity by vigorously applying lipstick, defying her companion with her phallic tongue. The death-head moth sequence that immediately precedes this prepares us for the disturbing migration of attributes: through a series of dissolves and iris-shots the moth turns to monster, while shots and counter-shots link it to both the male and female characters, so that the monster can be read as the double of the male expressing animal sexuality, or of the female as avatar of the vampire.[49]

A similar ambiguity, both playful and disturbing, is effected through the conflation of gender codes in *Anémic cinéma*. Duchamp's experiments in optical machines or 'roto-reliefs' are pursued in this film, in which a motionless camera films ten rotating disks inscribed with circular eccentric patterns alternating with nine disks printed with spiral texts. The film has been classified with the abstract avant-garde films of the 1920s (those of Richter and Eggeling) that explore the visual rhythms of moving abstract shapes. Yet Duchamp's film (like the paintings and collages of Picabia or Ernst) undermines the abstract film genre and the machine aesthetic by infiltrating them with the irrational and the erotic. Man Ray retitled it *Obscenema*,[50] and indeed the rhythmic movement of projecting and receding spirals suggests body parts and bodily sensations (lung; breast; eye; sexual organs; pulsating heart; sexual activity),[51] while the alliterations and anagrams of the spiralling texts have sexual connotations.

If Thomas Elsaesser interprets the closed circuits, the mirror effects and punning mechanisms of *Anémic cinéma*'s texts as essentially auto-erotic ('The cinema-machine has become a bachelor-machine'),[52] Dalia Judovitz sees in the visual ambiguity, conjoined with the wordplay of the spiralling texts, the creation of a transitional object, a 'pun whose undecidable character informs its erotic character'.[53] The shifting meanings produced by verbal play parallel the shifting gender identities suggested by the revolving disks, where concave alternates with convex and male flows into female. Yet such phenomena produce less the surrealist resolution of opposites in the figure of the androgyn, or a collapse into the *informe* of gender indifferentiation, than an oscillation between male and female positions (as in *Chien*).[54] This is a form of play where fixed gender codes are relaxed rather than renounced, not only (on the level of representation) in favour of fluctuating signs marking the shifting spaces of male and female signifiers, but also (on the level of the filmic text) as a more generalized eroticism, created through the rhythmic movement of the images. Furthermore, these figures present an oscillatory movement undecidably located between the body and the non-body, the human and the mechanical. A similar oscillation is exploited in Léger's film *Ballet mécanique*, where a moving piston cuts to the bulging stomach of a pregnant woman, and shots of Kiki's head are interpolated with revolving machine parts and saucepan covers, so that machines and bodies are on the point of fusing. Moreover, rapid montage generates a rhythmic movement that eroticizes, hence defamiliarizes, mechanical objects.

Convulsive Identities: The Lady Vanishes (*bis*)

'L'identité sera convulsive ou ne sera pas', writes Max Ernst.[55] Whether oscillating between male and female gender positions or engaged in a generalized eroticism, the dada/surrealist body is the site of conflicting impulses articulated and maintained as tension, multiplicity, play: impulses that both deny and exacerbate difference. In dada/surrealist practice, the filmic medium is a privileged medium for staging such ambivalent identities, in its shifting signifiers, dissolves, diegetic disruptions or optical tricks that make bodies merge or explode, multiply or disintegrate, reify or resuscitate, denying the stability of the body as a distinct(ive) unity. 'The principle of montage was supposed to shock people into realizing just how dubious any organic unity was', writes Adorno.[56] The disjunctive self is inscribed formally in the film body in montage techniques that make visible their wounds, grafts and cuts.

This discussion has explored the fluid remappings of identity and the body in the shifting, often perverse images of the body incorporated in dada/surrealist film. Such unstable images problematize our reading of the surrealist filmic text. On the one hand, the couple composed of the male magician-*cinéaste* and the female victim appears to invite complicitous projections of the masculine gaze and combative protests of the female spectator. On the other, the disruptive strategies encoded in surrealist film disorient perception, and elicit a reading grounded in a disruption of the symbolic order produced through the exploration of the trans-gressive body. Moreover, surrealist film-makers explore the body, whether male or female, as a limit-form of anthropomorphic representation. For example, for his film *Retour*, Man Ray laid the photographic negative of a nude woman shot partly through glass over several individual frames, and printed it directly on to the film strip, so that the body, reduced to abstract shapes, becomes invisible to the eye on screening.[57] And in the ladder sequence of *Vormittagsspuk*, the male body becomes a rhythmical abstract form. Such bodies exceed their anatomical limits and become other, part of a generalized eroticism suggested by the rhythmic qualities of the images. Limit-forms of corporeal representation constitute a radical revision of the (classical) body as contained or framed, and by extension a revision of identity as fixed and immutable. While the exploration of limit-bodies in dada and surrealism radically questions oppositional categories such as masculine and feminine, abstract and concrete, animate and inanimate, human and animal, the convulsive identities constructed from the shifting signifiers, incomplete narratives and interpolated shots are not resolved in the magic flourish of the conjuror Breton's dialectical wand.

Notes

1. See J.-M. Bouhours and P. de Haas (eds) (1997), *Man Ray directeur du mauvais movies*, Paris. p. 10. Performance artist, poet, sculptor, shop-lifter, the Baroness's eccentric appearance in the streets of New York, head shaved and painted, coal

scuttle as hat, birdcage as necklace, was a dada event. She was considered as the 'first American dada'; the 'only one living anywhere who dresses dada, loves dada, lives dada'. See J. Heap (1922), 'Dada', *Little Review*, p. 46.

2. This is reproduced in F.N. Naumann (1994), *New York Dada 1915–23*, New York, p. 208.

3. These include Duchamp's 'rectified ready-made' of the Mona Lisa with added moustache, goatee beard and title 'LHOOQ' (she has a hot ass), published in the dada review *391* (March 1920), and the invitation card sent by Duchamp for his 1965 exhibition, representing a playing card with the effigy of the Mona Lisa with the inscription 'rasé LHOOQ' (shaved LHOOQ).

4. For a discussion of the Artaud-Dulac controversy regarding *Coquille*, see S. Flitterman-Lewis (1990), *To Desire Differently: Feminism and the French Cinema*, Urbana and Chicago, pp. 98–140.

5. See T. Elsaesser (1996), 'Dada/cinema?', in R.E. Kuenzli (ed.), *Dada and Surrealist Film*, Cambridge, Mass. and London, pp. 13–27, pp. 19–20; and R. Fotiade (1995), 'The Untamed Eye: Surrealism and Film Theory', *Screen*, 36, pp. 394–407, pp. 400–1.

6. See M.L. Roberts (1994), *Civilization Without Sexes: Reconstructing Gender in Postwar France 1917–1927*, Chicago and London.

7. For Sidra Stich, 'the anxiety of dislocation and the rapture of possibility meet' in the surrealist body. S. Stich (1991), *Anxious Visions: Surrealist Art*, Berkeley and New York, p. 24.

8. 'All the films I made were improvisations. I did not write scenarios. It was automatic cinema.' Man Ray, quoted in Kuenzli, *Dada and Surrealist Film*, p. 3.

9. For a discussion of the Surrealists' ambivalent relationship to contemporary avant-garde practices, see Fotiade, 'The Untamed Eye'.

10. The surrealists were fascinated by serials such as *Fantômas*, with Musidora as Irma Vep (anagram of vampire), and *Les Mystères de New York*, with Pearl White (*perle vite*), for their power to sustain suspense and provoke mystery.

11. Narrative is not however absent from Méliès's films. See the excellent analysis, based on Christian Metz's categories, offered in E. Ezra (2000), *Georges Méliès: The Birth of the Auteur*, Manchester.

12. *Entr'acte*, based on a scenario outline by Francis Picabia, was originally shown during the intermission of Picabia's 'instantanist' ballet *Relâche*.

13. L. Fischer (1979), 'The Lady Vanishes: Women, Magic, and the Movies', *Film Quarterly*, 33, pp. 30–40.

14. This is illustrated in *Le Corps en morceaux* (exhibition catalogue, Musée d'Orsay), Paris, p. 56.

15. J.G. Cawelti (1976), *Adventure, Mystery, and Romance: Formula Stories as Art and Popular Culture*, Chicago and London, p. 35.

16. 'Carnival, after all, is a *licensed* affair in every sense, a permissible rupture of hegemony, a contained popular blow-off as disturbing and relatively ineffectual as a revolutionary work of art'. T. Eagleton (1981), *Walter Benjamin: Towards a Revolutionary Criticism*, London, p. 148.

17. L. Williams (1981), 'Film Body: an Implantation of Perversions', *Ciné-Tracts*, 12, pp. 19–35. Williams elaborates on Lucy Fischer's 1979 analysis of the rhetoric of magic, while rejecting the latter's argument that Méliès appropriates the woman's procreative powers.

18. My reading is informed by Susan Gubar's discussion of Magritte's painting *Le Viol* and the antithetical debates on art and pornography it has engendered. See S. Gubar (1987), 'Representing Pornography: Feminism, Criticism, and Depictions of Female Violation', *Critical Inquiry*, 13, pp. 712–41.

19. X. Gauthier (1971), *Surréalisme et sexualité*, Paris.

20. L. Mulvey (1975), 'Visual Pleasure and Narrative Cinema', *Screen*, 16, pp. 6–18.

21. See H. Bellmer (1957), *Petite Anatomie de l'inconscient physique ou l'anatomie de l'image*, Paris.

22. W. Benjamin (1983), *Das Passagen-Werk*, Frankfurt, p. 584; W. Benjamin (1979) 'Surrealism: The Last Snapshot of the Bourgeoisie', in *One Way Street and Other Writings*, London, pp. 225–39.

23. Elsaesser, 'Dada/cinema?', p. 18.

24. Man Ray refers to *Emak Bakia* as a 'series of fragments, a cinepoem with a certain optical sequence [which] make up a whole that still remains a fragment'. See Man Ray (1927), 'Emak Bakia', *Close-Up*, 1, p. 40.

25. '[I]n the end, the narrative corpus, like the corpse in the story, refuses to be put away and must suffer one last repetition and reversal'. R. Abel (1984), *French Cinema: The First Wave 1915–1929*, Princeton, p. 382.

26. Ibid., p. 485. For a discussion of the production of desire in Buñuel's films, see L. Williams (1981), *Figures of Desire: A Theory and Analysis of Surrealist Film*, Urbana.

27. A. Breton (1951), 'Comme dans un bois', *L'Age du cinéma*, 4–5, pp. 26–30.

28. R. Krauss (1991), 'Photography in the Service of Surrealism', in R. Krauss and J. Livingston (eds), *L'Amour Fou: Photography and Surrealism*, London, pp. 15-54. Kuenzli criticizes Krauss for remaining silent about the violation to the female body. See R.E. Kuenzli (1991), 'Surrealism and Misogyny', in M.A. Caws, R.E. Kuenzli and G. Raaberg (eds), *Surrealism and Women*, Cambridge, Mass. and London, pp. 21–5.

29. S. Sontag (1981), *Styles of Radical Will*, New York, p. 58.

30. S.R. Suleiman (1990), *Subversive Intent: Gender, Politics, and the Avant-Garde*, Cambridge, Mass. and London, pp. 146–50.

31. These remarks are cited in J.P. Imrie (ed.) (1992), *Investigating Sex: Surrealist Research 1928–1932*, London and New York, p. 88.

32. See Man Ray (1963), *Self-Portrait*, Boston, pp. 260–4.

33. See Mary Ann Caws's spirited attack of surrealist representations of the female body: 'Headless. And also footless. Often armless too; and almost always unarmed, except with poetry and passion. There they are, the surrealist women so shot and painted, so stressed and dismembered, punctured and severed: Is it any wonder they have (we have) gone to pieces? It is not just the dolls of Hans Bellmer, lying about, it is more. Worse, because more lustily appealing, as in Man Ray's images'. M.A. Caws (1991), 'Seeing the Surrealist Woman: We are a Problem', in Caws, Kuenzli and Raaberg, *Surrealism and Women*, pp. 11–16, p. 11.

34. Caws comments on this image that 'in no way is the body deformed, it is rather augmented by its natural possibilities'. M.A. Caws (1986), 'Ladies Shot and Painted: Female Embodiment in Surrealist Art', in S.R. Suleiman (ed.), *The Female Body in Western Culture: Contemporary Perspectives*, Cambridge, Mass. and London, pp. 262–87, p. 275.

35. See Flitterman-Lewis, *To Desire Differently*, p. 127, for a discussion of the clergyman's pursuit of the female protagonist as a quest for the self.

36. 'La recherche de l'autre est toujours recherche de soi. A travers l'autre qui me hante se révélera à moi qui je suis.' G. Durozoi (1974), *André Breton: L'Ecriture surréaliste*, Paris, p. 189.

37. M. von Hofacker (1998), 'Richter's Films and the Role of the Radical Artist, 1927-1941', in S.C. Foster (ed.), *Hans Richter: Activism, Modernism, and the Avant-garde*, Cambridge, Mass. and London, pp. 122–44, p. 132.

38. For a discussion of the instability of the male protagonist in *Chien*, see P. Drummond (1977), 'Textual Space in *Un chien andalou*', *Screen*, 18, pp. 65–7.

39. I. Hedges (1996), 'Constelled Visions: Robert Desnos's and Man Ray's *Etoile de mer*', in Kuenzli, *Dada and Surrealist Film*, pp. 99–109.

40. For an excellent analysis of masculinity in Buñuel's films, see P.W. Evans (1995), *The Films of Luis Buñuel*, Oxford.

41. See P. Hammond (1974), *Marvelous Méliès*, London, p. 103.

42. See H. Foster (1993), *Compulsive Beauty*, Cambridge, Mass., p. 152.

43. D.W. Winnicott (1971), *Playing and Reality*, New York, p. 55.

44. Stich, *Anxious Visions*, p. 35.

45. The question of the shifting images of (self-)identity in surrealism is explored in E. Adamowicz (1998), *Surrealist Collage in Text and Image: Dissecting the Exquisite Corpse*, Cambridge, pp. 129–58.

46. J. Lacan (1953), 'Some Reflections on the Ego', *International Journal of Psychoanalysis*, 24, pp. 11–17, p. 15.

47. Linda Williams bases her reading of Buñuel's films on Lacan's theory of the subject.

48. 'This hilarious sequence compresses an extraordinary range of sexual signifiers into a dance between genders.' D. Ades (1995), 'Surrealism: Fetishism's Job', in A. Shelton (ed.), *Fetishism: Visualising Power and Desire*, London, pp. 67–87, p. 78.

49. For a discussion of the ambivalence of the monster in film, see L. Williams (1984), 'When the Woman Looks', in M.A. Doane, P. Mellencamp and L. Williams (eds), *Re-Vision: Essays in Feminist Film Criticism*, Los Angeles, pp. 83–99, p. 87.

50. Man Ray, *Self-Portrait*, p. 12.

51. Jean-Jacques Lebel reads the spiral shapes as a kind of gigantic Cyclops whose eye acts as a screen for suggestive metamorphoses. See J.-J. Lebel (1959), *Sur Marcel Duchamp*, Paris, p. 52. See also T. Mussman (1966), 'Anemic Cinema', *Art and Artists*, 1, pp. 48–51; and R. Krauss and Y.-A. Bois (1997), *Formless: A User's Guide*, New York, p. 135.

52. Elsaesser, 'Dada/cinema?', p. 24.

53. D. Judovitz (1996), 'Anemic Vision in Duchamp: Cinema as readymade', in Kuenzli, *Dada and Surrealist Film*, pp. 46–57, p. 53.

54. For a discussion of the androgyne in *Anémic cinéma*, see K. Martin (1975), 'Marcel Duchamp's *Anémic cinéma*', *Studio International*, 189, pp. 53-60. For a discussion of the *informe*, see R. Krauss (1991), 'Where's Poppa?' in T. de Duve (ed.), *The Definitively Unfinished Marcel Duchamp*, Cambridge, Mass. and London, pp. 433–62, p. 457.

55. M. Ernst (1970), *Ecritures*, Paris, p. 269.

56. T. Adorno (1984), *Aesthetic Theory*, New York and London, p. 223.

57. See photogrammes reproduced in Bouhours and de Haas, *Man Ray*, pp. 38–9.

3

Diva in the Spotlight: Music Hall to Cinema
Kelley Conway

Introduction

When we think of 1930s French cinema, images of the dilemmas of masculinity are likely to dominate our memories. In *Le Jour se lève* (Marcel Carné, 1939), Jean Gabin ruminates over the past in a sparsely furnished bedsit; in *La Belle Equipe* (Julien Duvivier, 1936) and *Gueule d'amour* (Jean Grémillon, 1937), a virile male community is threatened or destroyed by a beautiful woman; in *La Grande Illusion* (Jean Renoir, 1937), an aristocrat officer creates a diversion so two men can escape a prison camp. Our sense that this cinema tells primarily of men seems confirmed by a statistical analysis of the credits of feature films made in the 1930s.[1] This reveals that, by far, male actors held the majority of the lead film roles in 1930s French film. Appearing in the top tier of the compilation are those actors who each performed in more than thirty films and played the starring role in at least eighty per cent of them: Armand Bernard; Jules Berry; Albert Préjean; Charles Vanel; Henri Garat; Raimu; and Harry Baur.[2] There are no corresponding actresses with the same degree of visibility in 1930s French film.[3]

Striking though it is, this disparity tells us little about the decade's decidedly ambivalent cinematic construction of femininity. French films of the 1930s tend to ask spectators to either desire or despise their female characters. This is reflected in the dichotomous female 'types' of such films: the *ingénue* and the *garce* (tart or bitch). The *ingénue* appears in both a passive guise – Annabella in *Hôtel du Nord* (Carné, 1938) or Jacqueline Laurent in *Le Jour se lève* – and a vivacious, 'modern' mode – Danielle Darrieux in *Un mauvais garçon* (Jean Boyer, 1936) and *Club de femmes* (Jacques Deval, 1936). At the other end of the spectrum, we find the seductresses incarnated by Viviane Romance in *La Belle Equipe* (Duvivier, 1936), Mireille Balin in *Gueule d'amour* (Grémillon, 1937) and Ginette Leclerc in *La Femme du boulanger* (Marcel Pagnol, 1938). The *ingénue* typically serves as the object of desire of the film's much older, male lead.[4] The *garce*, on the other hand, possesses the power to disrupt the narrative, driving men to murder or suicide, but has a flat, undeveloped quality that we see in the *ingénue* as well. Both female types are defined in relation to the male protagonist.

There are a few exceptions to this dichotomous representation of women. Arletty, a venerable symbol of working-class Paris in 1930s and 1940s cinema, is famous for her nasal *argot* and her *bons mots* in *Hôtel du Nord* and *Le Jour se lève*. As Madame Raymonde or Clara, she projects an appealing independence and complexity. The ethereal, enigmatic sexuality she manifests in Carné's *Les Visiteurs du soir* (1942) and *Les Enfants du paradis* (1945) makes her a cipher, a particularly effective 'screen' on to which spectators could project fantasies about gender indeterminacy and national identity during the Occupation. The other major exception to the *ingénue/garce* dichotomy is Edwige Feuillère, the *aventurière* of 1930s cinema. She plays high-class thieves, for instance, in a comic register akin to that of Hollywood screwball comedy heroines, Carole Lombard and Katherine Hepburn. Throughout the 1940s, Feuillère was called the *grande dame* of French cinema, due to her theatre background and her portrayals of strong, aristocratic women in *De Mayerling à Sarajevo* (Max Ophüls, 1940); *La Duchesse de Langeais* (Jacques de Baroncelli, 1941); and *L'Aigle à deux têtes* (Jean Cocteau, 1947).

Yet there is a tradition of representation in 1930s French film that presents a version of femininity quite different from the *gamine* and the *garce*. This tradition is that of the *femme-spectacle*. Female performers from the world of music hall brought their performance styles to the sound cinema. Dressed in fabulous feathered, sequined costumes and descending the ubiquitous staircase surrounded by troops of devoted male chorus singers, music hall revue stars Mistinguett, Josephine Baker, Florelle and Jane Marnac brought their star images of glamour and social transcendence to 1930s cinema. A second type of *femme-spectacle* also appears in 1930s cinema: the *chanteuse réaliste*.[5] While the music hall queen is associated with spectacle, power and class mobility, the realist singer evokes powerlessness, the proletariat and/or the underworld, performing songs about prostitution, urban poverty and female desire. A mainstay of late nineteenth-century *café-concert* and the music hall of the inter-war period, the realist singer also performed in the sound cinema. The two best-known realist singers of the 1920s and 1930s, Fréhel and Damia, appear in many films, including *Pépé le Moko* (Duvivier, 1936) and *La Tête d'un homme* (Duvivier, 1932), respectively.

The cinematic roles of the revue star and the realist singer compel us to think about how a cinema deemed irretrievably 'masculine' imagines icons of female power, and about how the sound cinema addresses a form of live entertainment it had eclipsed, the music hall. How does 1930s French cinema, celebrated for its moody poetic realist films about proletarian male outsiders, address the glitzy, imperious *meneuse de revue*? How do films about the music hall tap the realist vein of 1930s cinema and song? The deeply contradictory images of femininity in *Faubourg Montmartre* (Raymond Bernard, 1931), *Zouzou* (Marc Allégret, 1934), *Paris-Béguin* (Augusto Genina, 1931) and *Le Bonheur* (Marcel L'Herbier, 1935)

– films that take place in the world of the music hall and feature real music hall performers – will be the focus of this chapter.

First, a glance at the relationship between music hall and the cinema in the 1930s is in order.[6] Despite the post-World War One success of spectacular revues offering star performances by singers such as Mistinguett, the fortunes of the French music hall began to decline in the late 1920s and early 1930s. The Olympia and the Moulin Rouge closed within a week of one another in 1929, reopening soon after as cinemas.[7] In 1932, the Bataclan and the Gaîté-Rochechouart became cinemas, while the Eldorado was demolished.[8] One strategy adopted by the ailing music hall was to 'look back' toward the nineteenth-century *café-concert* era.

The *café-concert* emerged in the late eighteenth century, offering inexpensive food and drink and musical entertainment to a mixture of working-class and bourgeois customers. Typically, the entertainment consisted of a singing perform- ance in the back room of a modest bar. By the 1860s, the *café-concert* entered its 'golden era', taking in both dives in the Latin Quarter and the working-class suburbs and song palaces in the centre of Paris. Large *salles* seating one thousand or more spectators, such as the Alcazar and the Eldorado, clustered along the Champs- Elysées and the *grands boulevards* in the ninth and tenth arrondissements. The atmosphere of the *café-concert*, raucous yet nominally respectable, offered a new social space in which boundaries typically separating people by class and gender were challenged. The environment of the *café-concert* produced the first popular, populist female singing star: Thérésa (1837–1913), singer of bawdy parodies of the ballad. *Café-concert* performers created and circulated star images, endorsing consumer products and publishing autobiographies. Despite the increased size of its halls and nascent star system, however, the *café-concert* remained economically accessible to most spectators, retaining its boisterous atmosphere and its interaction between performer and spectator. The centrepiece of an evening's entertainment at the *café-concert* continued to be the *tour de chant*, the performance of four or five songs in a row by one singer.

In the 1880s, the music hall offered variety acts and even more monumental performance spaces. While the music hall did not exactly displace the *café-concert* – they co-existed from the 1880s to the pre-1920s – the *tour de chant* slowly ceded its place to the revue, a series of independent numbers featuring kicklines, sumptuous costumes and large, complex sets. The technology-dependent revue constituted a new scale of spectacle, offered less direct interaction between performer and spectator, and engendered a new kind of female star, the *meneuse de revue*. Female stars, already prominent in the *café-concert*, continued to serve as the icons of this new entertainment. Mistinguett, Josephine Baker, Florelle, Jane Marnac and others projected appealing images of glamour and social mobility with their elaborate costumes, dancing, and both comic and realist singing.

When, in the early 1930s, the music hall was in trouble and the *café-concert* only a *Belle Epoque* memory, many music halls tried to revive themselves by recreating the *café-concert* atmosphere. In an attempt to recapture the conviviality of that entertainment space, as well as to capitalize on the stars of *tour de chant* still in circulation, music halls featured Fréhel, Damia and many others. Another strategy adopted by the music hall was a joining of forces with its primary competitor, the sound cinema.

The cinema's fortunes were linked with those of the music hall long before the 1930s. Indeed, until around 1910, the music halls (as well as the *cafés-concerts* and *fêtes foraines*) were the primary exhibition locations for French film.[9] The Eldorado, the Olympia and the Casino de Paris introduced the short film as one of the many 'numbers' in their shows, starting in 1896 or 1897.[10] Conversely, cinema programmes were supplemented by live acts well into the post-World War Two era. Damia, Lys Gauty and other realist singers performed regularly in cinemas such as the Gaumont-Palace, the Rex, the Olympia and the Alhambra.[11]

Another kind of interaction operated between the music hall and the cinema when films told stories set in the music hall. For example, in 1935, Ophüls directed *Divine*, an adaptation of Colette's *Music Hall Sidelights*. A backstage musical about a country girl's initiation into the seamy world of a third-rate music hall in Montmartre, *Divine* revels in the music hall's backstage chaos, its female nudes, the orientalist décor of its revue and its clandestine ring of narcotic-sellers. The most interesting interaction between the music hall and the cinema for our purposes, however, occurred when music hall divas took their stage acts to the screen. At a time when the music hall was declining, Allégret's *Zouzou*, Genina's *Paris-Béguin* and L'Herbier's *Le Bonheur* celebrate it, building narratives around the revue star and elaborate revue sequences. Bernard's *Faubourg Montmartre* contrasts the revue star and the realist singer, registering ambivalence about the music hall. Featuring performances from Florelle, a prominent revue star (and quite a well-known film actress, too) and from realist singer Odette Barencey, *Faubourg Montmartre* conveys a host of meanings relating to femininity, the pleasures and dangers of urban space, and shifts in French popular entertainment.[12]

Faubourg Montmartre

Faubourg Montmartre, an adaptation of a novel written by Henri Duvernois in 1912, is a melodrama about the struggle of the Gentilhomme sisters to support themselves in the seductive, treacherous world of Montmartre.[13] Ginette (Gaby Morlay) is a naïve yet plucky seamstress working in a couturier's workshop, while her older sister Céline (Line Noro) works as a prostitute. Charles Vanel plays Dédé, Céline's pimp and a drug dealer. Pressured by Dédé, Céline has been urging Ginette to start working the streets too. The sisters are virtually alone in the world: their ageing father is a travelling salesman, apparently oblivious of the fate that awaits his vulnerable young daughters in Paris. Ginette and Céline are perched precariously on the verge of poverty and take in a provincial lodger, Frédéric, an awkward young man who reads poetry and loves the theatre. Frédéric will eventually rescue the younger sister, Ginette, from the fate that befalls Céline: prostitution, drug addiction, the asylum.

Like many 1930s French films, *Faubourg Montmartre* contains stock characters from the Parisian criminal underworld – the pimp and the prostitute – and attempts to capture the visual texture of an exoticized Parisian space, in this case Montmartre. The film's fascination with a flashy, bustling nocturnal Paris is revealed immediately. Sounds of traffic accompany an image of a street sign reading Rue du Faubourg Montmartre. There is a high-angle, long shot of the neighbourhood at night, revealing busy streets and neon signs, including one that advertises Le Palace, a music hall. An ageing prostitute walks along the pavement, wearing a fur coat and an animal-print scarf. Another middle-aged prostitute passes, a weary expression on her face. From inside a café, a pimp surveys the women. Contemporary critics noticed the film's representation of the cityscape and praised its views of the street, the movements of the crowd and its little bistros.[14]

Despite this, it appears that the film was not well attended. One critic complained that its characters were of the pre-World War One moment. Bernard, this commentator says, failed to update sufficiently the 1912 source-text: 'One encounters only very rarely fathers as blind as M. Gentilhomme, hussies as sloppy as his older daughter, Céline, and virgins as fierce as his younger daughter, Ginette . . .'.[15] Another admires the movie, but speculates that Bernard's 'bold' and 'moving' film is too *noir* for elegant audiences on the Champs-Elysées, despite its 'deceptively optimistic' ending.[16] He sees a disjunction between its setting and narrative, claiming that the film's representation of the *faubourg*, with its lights, flashing signs, dance halls and sumptuous music halls, has little in common with Duvernois's 1912 portrait of the *quartier*: 'No neighbourhood in Paris has changed its face more in twenty years and in such a sparkling décor this drama of poverty and prostitution is conspicuously out of its element'.[17] *Faubourg Montmartre* is, in fact, concerned precisely with the tension between 'old' and 'new' Paris. On the one hand, the film treats of a pre-war Paris where prostitutes walk the streets and popular entertainment is comprised of a woman singing a realist song in an intimate setting. On the other, there is the post-war, glittering surface of 'modern' Paris, defined by its music halls, brisk pace and 'modern' woman – a poor but independent *midinette*, thoroughly at home in the city. This tension, uneasily resolved by the film, is played out in its juxtaposition of two different musical numbers.

The first occurs when the sisters and Frédéric go to the music hall. There, the sisters' cousin Irène (Florelle) is performing in a revue. The sequence begins with a high-angle shot behind the balcony seats where Ginette, Céline and Frédéric sit.

The spectators are seated according to their class: our characters are up in the cheapest seats, with the most active, boisterous part of the audience. Down below, on stage, Florelle sings against the backdrop of a kickline of feather-clad women holding parasols. Ginette is delighted with the spectacle and chatters throughout the scene. She knows all the dancers' names. Irène sings a cheerful tune similar to those sung by Mistinguett and Florelle herself in the music halls of Paris in the late 1920s and early 1930s. In the middle of her song, Irène looks directly at the sisters in the balcony seats and calls out 'Bonjour, Céline et Ginette!'. Ginette yells 'bonjour' back, proud to know a star. But other audience members stare disapprovingly. In this instant, *Faubourg Montmartre* stages/reflects a transitional moment in popular entertainment, where (some) spectators want to believe that the intimacy of the *café-concert* is still present in the music hall experience. But, as the other spectators' disapproval indicates, that intimacy between performer and audience is now inappropriate or illusory.[18]

Starting around the turn of the century and intensifying after World War One, the 'pact' between performer and spectator was modified by/in the shift from the neighbourhood *café-concert* to the rationalized, commercial entertainment of the music hall. The *café-concert* spectator, accustomed to smoking, drinking and interacting with performers, evolved into the more sedate, prosperous music hall spectator. *Faubourg Montmartre* simultaneously mourns the real Palace music hall and the sense of community and congenial mixing of classes lost in the phasing out of the *café-concert*. The film's characterization of the successful music hall star compounds its expressions of ambivalence with regard to the music hall. The star of the revue, Irène, appears to provide a pleasurable viewing experience to her audience. But her performance of warmth and gaiety are later shown to be just that: a performance. The social-climbing Irène is unsympathetic to the financial problems of Ginette and Céline, despite her own difficult past. She even seduces Frédéric, whom Ginette has started to love. It is, in fact, Irène's thoughtless seduction of the lodger that precipitates Ginette's near-fall into prostitution. After the evening at the music hall and Irène's apartment, Ginette cries to Céline that, the following day, she will put on the finery her sister has provided and accompany her out.

The film's second musical performance occurs the next evening at a gathering of prostitutes that includes the pimp, Dédé. A middle-aged woman we have never seen (Odette Barencey) begins to sing a realist song written for the film. Barencey was a second-tier performer in the *café-concert* and music hall, a respected *chanteuse* at the best *concerts de quartier*. In the 1930s, like Damia and Fréhel, she was invited to perform in music halls that sought to revive the *tour de chant*. Barencey looks rather like Fréhel: she is a large woman with a weathered face. She delivers a riveting performance in a song about prostitutes working the Rue du Faubourg Montmartre. The scene opens just as she is finishing its first verse:[19]

They don't show their true face
Hidden under the everyday smile
Those who, from morning to evening,
And often from evening to morning,
On the Faubourg pass by in order to be seen.
They stroll alongside shop windows
And seem to think of nothing
Except showing their humble faces
But they are not bodies without souls
The little women.

Ell's n'montrent pas leur vrai visage
Caché sous le sourir' d'usage,
Celles qui, du matin au soir,
Et souvent du soir au matin,
Au Faubourg pass'nt pour se fair' voir.
Ell's s'ballad'nt le long des vitrines
Et semblent ne penser à rien
Qu'à montrer leur humble bobine,
Mais ce n'sont pas des corps sans âmes
Les p'tit's femm's.

A close-up lingers on Barencey's face as she sings:

And there are kids
Like ghosts
Who pace up and down the pavement
At twilight,
Looking each evening for
An idiot of a man
Offering a sum to hear some
Words of love.
They'll have to, to amuse them,
Whether they're faint,
Broken-hearted,
Without believing that it
Lasts forever
Because everything happens on the faubourg, one day.

Et y a des mômes
Comm' des fantômes
Qui déambulent sur le trottoir,
Au crépuscule,
Cherchant chaqu' soir

Un idiot d'homme
Offrant un' somme pour s'entendr' dir' des mots d'amour.
Il faudra, pour les amuser,
Qu'elles soient pamées
L' coeur brisé
Sans croir' qu' ça doit
Durer toujours
Car tout arriv' dans le Faubourg, un jour.

Only the prostitutes who are not hungry, the song tells us, have the luxury of rebelling against their plight. But despite these material conditions, the women hold out hope for love:

On the Faubourg, they aren't all beautiful
There are some pallid ones who are rebels
Perhaps it's because they have less appetite
It's useful to have a small appetite
If one seeks to be virtuous
But the street is inexorable
And destiny is stubborn.

Au Faubourg, elles sont pas tout's belles
Y en a des pâl's qui sont rebelles
C'est p't'êtr' qu'ell's ont moins d'appétit
Car c'est util' pour la vertu,
D'avoir un estomac petit.
Mais la rue est inexorable,
Et le destin est très têtu.

The sequence is structured by a series of close-ups that constitute a departure from the visual style of much of the film. The camera lingers on each woman's tired, longing face, as she stares at the singer, mesmerized. The room is dim and smoky, unlike the brightly lit music hall where Irène performs. Shots of eerie-looking dolls are interspersed with close-ups of the women's faces. The setting appears to be a cheap, furnished room where prostitutes and pimp have gathered before work. Typical of realist songs, 'Faubourg Montmartre' evokes the daily lives of prostitutes, humanizing them and capturing the monotony and heartbreak of their lives. The sequence communicates a sense of female community and a moment of comfort in an otherwise bleak existence.

The performance also initiates a powerful opposition to the revue sequence, in terms of the representation of the internal audience. While the realist singer and the community of prostitutes cannot offer Ginette the giddy spectatorial pleasure she experiences at the music hall or the financial safety net of the bourgeois family, they furnish the solace of female solidarity in a difficult existence. In the music hall sequence, Ginette transgresses by attempting to breach the gap between performer and audience when she shouts 'bonjour'. Eschewing the kind of reaction her outburst at the music hall elicits, the prostitutes respond out loud to the song they listen to. Between two verses of Barencey's performance, one woman exclaims 'Ah! You know men'. Likewise, in contrast to the hierarchical seating at the Palace, the prostitutes sit loosely in a circle, each in intimate proximity to the performer. In further contrast to the relatively static 'tableau' perspective used on Irène/Florelle and the chorus line at the music hall, the camera here moves in and out of the group of women, providing close-ups and medium shots of the singer and her audience from a variety of angles. While Irène's performance offers artificial, mass-produced gaiety, Barencey's reflects the texture of the difficult yet compelling lives of the prostitutes and their tenuous sense of community. The film's critique of modernity, then, operates through the construction of two different urban spaces and different types of entertainment: the modern music hall, with its kicklines and glamorous star, and the furnished room, with its 'authentic' prostitutes and realist song.[20]

Faubourg Montmartre also elaborates distinctly different scenarios relating to the trajectory of women living on the margins of society. Just as Florelle represents the 'upper class' of the world of entertainment, Barencey is the 'working class' of that universe. The larger narrative trajectory of Ginette and Céline further mimics this polarization of women's material condition, again using 'place' to comment on class structure and the female condition. Neither remains on the rue du Faubourg Montmartre for long. The film's resolution of the 'problem' of two poor, unmarried sisters living in Paris is to 'save' Ginette by marrying her off and moving her to the country, while disposing of Céline who becomes a cocaine addict, in an asylum. Ginette, then, after hovering precariously between the positions of *midinette* and prostitute, gets pulled miraculously into the upper class. The political conservativism of this solution is tempered, however, by the film's representation of Ginette's relationship to Paris.

While on one level the film folds Ginette into the bourgeois, provincial family, it also acknowledges that she cannot forget the city. Despite its apparent valorization of provincial life, care is taken to represent the pleasures available to women in the city. Early on, Ginette giggles and eats chocolate with her friend on a busy boulevard. She clowns around at work with girlfriends and behaves irreverently toward a wealthy customer. When she leaves the couturier's at the end of her working day, she is jostled by the crowd, eyed by an older man, and followed. But she is no victim of the hustle and bustle; she contributes to it. She buys a snack from a street vendor and argues about the price, participating in the ebb and flow of city life. She is a spunky young woman vulnerable to prostitution, but fully at home in the urban environment.

While Ginette moves away from rue du Faubourg Montmartre, this Parisian space remains with her. The signifying power of the words 'Faubourg Montmartre' is made clear near the end of the film, when Ginette has moved to the provinces, initially seeking refuge with Frédéric and his mother. Dédé tracks her down and tries to take her back to the city. When she refuses to return to Paris with him, he gossips to the villagers. All he needs to say in order to discredit Ginette is that she is from Faubourg Montmartre. Scandalized, the villagers burn effigies of Ginette and Frédéric. The provincial setting will eventually serve as a haven for Ginette, but at this moment it is a place of intolerance and ignorance.

The film ends with a representation of Paris that emphasizes its seductiveness more than its infamy. The final sequence takes place in the sweetshop belonging to Ginette's aunt in Paris. Ginette calls her aunt from the country, finally accepted in her provincial life, but missing Paris nonetheless. She telephones because she wants to hear the noises of Paris. The aunt obliges and holds the telephone out to the rue du Faubourg Montmartre. It is here that the film ends, with the valorization of the city: a demonstration of its aural texture and seductiveness. Despite the film's moralistic solution to the sisters' dilemma, it communicates the magnetism of the urban space and the ideal of female community not found in bourgeois marriage.

The urban landscape and its connection with femininity persists even in films that do not feature a realist singer, as the analyses of the remaining films in my corpus will reveal. The films under consideration all include the music hall queen as protagonist. In contrast to *Faubourg Montmartre*, they aim to celebrate the music hall queen by placing her at the centre of the narrative. *Zouzou*, *Paris-Béguin* and *Le Bonheur* bring together the powerful female star with the virile 'man of the people'. They juxtapose the worlds of the working class (or, in the case of *Paris-Béguin*, the underworld) with that of the glittering music hall, aligning thereby gender difference and class difference.

In *Zouzou*, *Paris-Béguin* and *Le Bonheur*, the realist tradition is absorbed and contorted by the character of the music hall queen. The values allied with Barencey in *Faubourg Montmartre* are associated in these films with a male protagonist. Jean Gabin (in *Zouzou* and *Paris-Béguin*) and Charles Boyer (in *Le Bonheur*) play characters imbued with the authenticity previously attributed to female singers in many other 1930s French films. Here, the men are emissaries of the working class or the underworld, while the women move up the socio-economic hierarchy. As we shall see, this elevation in the status of the *chanteuse* is carried out with considerable ambivalence.

Zouzou

Zouzou stars Josephine Baker, the American dancer who made her *début* in 1925 at the Théâtre des Champs-Elysées in the *Revue Nègre*. At first glance, it may seem curious to include Baker in a study of the place of the French revue star and the realist singer in 1930s French film. After all, Baker's appeal in 1920s and 1930s France responded to a very different fantasy circulating in French culture, that conflated 'blackness', 'femininity', 'animalistic sexuality' and 'primitivism'. The qualities she evoked according to the mythology of this fantasy seem very different from those of both the revue star (class mobility, glamour) and the realist singer (the tragic life lived in the marginal landscapes of Paris). However, much like the French stars of the *café-concert* and musical hall, Eugénie Buffet, Yvette Guilbert, Fréhel and Mistinguett, Baker utilized the intertext of her own life to construct an appealing star image that dovetailed with French fantasies of social transcendence and exotic 'otherness'. First, she incarnated the poor girl from the slums of St Louis who astounded Paris at the *Revue Nègre*. Next, in the late 1920s, she metamorphosed from the girl in the banana skirt to the *grande dame du music-hall*. Elegant, French-speaking, in possession of a trained singing voice, she became the glamorous *Parisienne* heading up revues at the Folies-Bergère and the Casino de Paris.[21]

Both of Baker's sound films, *Zouzou* and *Princesse Tam-Tam* (Edmond Gréville, 1935), were written for her, and recycle the 'rags to riches' and 'primitive to *parisienne*' narratives at the centre of her star image. The realist singer renders the marginal spaces of Paris exotic: the fortifications, the faubourgs, the rough dance hall and the old *café-concert*. Baker utilizes the same mechanism, but trades instead on the exoticism of America, jazz, the jungles of Africa and the South Seas, and supplements this image with the patina of Parisian music hall glamour.

Zouzou opens in Toulon during the childhood of Zouzou (Baker) and her adoptive brother Jean (Gabin). Zouzou and Jean perform as circus freaks with their kindly adoptive father, Papa Mélé (Pierre Larquey). Mélé displays the children as twins, claiming that they are a 'miracle of nature' from an island in the Polynesian archipelago. Their parents, he explains to the fascinated fairground audience – a Chinese mother and a 'redskin' father – turned the children away because their colours did not match those of their parents. Racial difference is the stuff of spectacle, as is sexual difference. Indeed, our first glimpse of Zouzou is through the eyes of a group of young boys who peep at her in her dressing room tent as she applies white powder to her face.

The children grow up: Jean becomes a sailor while Zouzou and Mélé move to Montmartre and Zouzou finds work as a laundress. *Zouzou*, like *Faubourg Montmartre*, contrasts two different kinds of singing performance that we may broadly differentiate as realist and spectacular. The realist performances draw on the intimacy and working-class character of the *café-concert* and the *bal musette*, while the spectacular performances take place in the modern music hall. Both Baker and Gabin, in fact, perform in the realist style early in the film in settings other than the music hall. Zouzou sings in the laundry; Jean on the dance floor of the *bal musette*. Another performer represents the 'false' values of the modern music hall: Miss Barbara (Ila Merry), the capricious blond star whose heart is with her Brazilian lover, not the overweight patron underwriting her show. The 'tragedy' of the film is that, in the end, Zouzou is relegated to the artificial, joyless universe of the music hall, leaving Gabin in the arms of another laundress and in the warm, 'authentic' realist world.

Zouzou's first singing performance occurs at the laundry where she works and is an improvised parody of the singing style of Miss Barbara. She sings 'C'est lui' to her fellow laundresses:[22]

> Twenty times a day, by the dozens
> Very smitten gentlemen
> Offer me a queen's life
> So that I'll give myself to them.
> There's only one who knows how to please me
> He's ugly and doesn't have a penny
> His stories aren't always clear,
> I know this very well but I don't give a damn
>
> For me there's only one man in Paris, it's he!
> I can't do anything about it; he has my heart!
> I think I've lost my mind
> He's so thick
> That he doesn't get it
> For me there's only one man in Paris, it's he!
> I'd go through a mouse hole for him!
> Each day, I adore him even more.
> For me there's only one man in Paris
> And it's he!
>
> Vingt fois par jour, par douzaines
> Des Messieurs très amoureux
> Me props'nt un' vie de reine
> Pour que je m'donne à eux.
> Y en a qu'un qu'a su me plaire
> Il est moche et n'a pas l'sou
> Ses histoir's ne sont pas claires,
> Je l'sais bien mais j'm'en fous
>
> Pour moi y a qu'un homm' dans Paris, c'est lui!
> J'peux rien y fair', mon coeur est pris par lui!
> Je crois qu'j'en perds la tête,
> Il est si bête
> Qu'il ne l'a pas compris

Pour moi y a qu'un homm' dans Paris, C'est lui!
Je pass'rais dans un trou d'souris, Pour lui!
Chaque jour, je l'adore
Bien plus encore.
Pour moi y a qu'un homm' dans Paris
Et c'est lui!

Like Barencey's song in *Faubourg Montmartre*, 'C'est lui' is presented as Zouzou's own fabrication, performed for the members of her community. Zouzou sings at the urging of her fellow laundresses, who gather around her in a circle. Centred in the frame, Zouzou sings directly to them. One laundress even pretends to be Zouzou's orchestra, accompanying her with a harmonica. Zouzou sings joyously, screams, tosses laundry into the air, rolls her eyes, contorts her face and hams it up with great verve.

This performance sequence features a rather unusual relay of the gaze between the characters, as well as between the performers and the implied film audience. Although she is centred in the frame, Zouzou never once looks into the camera, as if to imply that this spectacle is for the laundresses only and not the film's spectators. Just as unusual for the classical cinema is the 'reciprocal gaze' between Zouzou and her fellow laundresses: a gaze between the female performer and her female spectators, as it were. The sequence lacks point-of-view shots that might grant us a closer, voyeuristic look at Zouzou. In a cinema that usually accords the power of the gaze to male characters and (implied) male spectators, *Zouzou* seems to privilege, if only briefly, a non-controlling gaze at the female performer.

The scene cuts directly, mid-song, to the performance of the 'real' music hall star, Miss Barbara, rehearsing the same song at the music hall. In contrast to Zouzou's audience of laughing laundresses who participate in the performance, Miss Barbara's auditors are the music hall director and her fawning protector. She sings in a flat voice utterly lacking in conviction. She is depressed because her true love, a Brazilian man who 'takes her like a jaguar', is leaving Paris.

The film's next performance occurs in a *bal musette*, where Zouzou, her laundress friend Claire (Yvette Lebon) and Jean go to dance. While dancing with Claire, Gabin sings, accompanied by the accordion band in a jaunty waltz called 'Viens Fifine':[23]

Ah! Come along Fifine;
From the Rue des Halles to the Rue d' la Huchette
We knew Fifine, the queen of the dance hall.
At night when she passes by rolling her eyes,
More than one guy from the neighbourhood
Says to her willingly

Come along Fifine
Come along Fifine
To the little dance hall Sébasto[pol]
Oh! Oh! Oh! Oh! Oh! Oh!

Ah! Viens Fifine:
De la rue des Halles à la rue d' la Huchette
On connait Fifine, la rein' des bals musette
Le soir quand elle passe en roulant des mirettes,
Plus d'un gars du quartier
Lui dit sans s' fair' prier:

Viens Fifine
Viens Fifine
Au p 'tit bal du Sébasto
Oh! Oh! Oh! Oh! Oh! Oh!

Other dancers join Gabin on the chorus, and, like Zouzou's performance in the laundry, his number is integrated into the narrative. He sings, casually and spontaneously, to Claire and Zouzou in the *bal musette*, a mythical space of working-class community. Gabin's performance does not isolate him from his community spatially or reduce him to a 'spectacle': he moves about the floor among other dancing couples, singing 'naturally'. Here, as in his other singing performances in 1930s films, Gabin's conduct consolidates his membership in the community of the proletariat.[24]

Zouzou's second performance begins with the aura of friendly female complicity we saw in the laundry scene, but becomes something different. While delivering laundry to the music hall, Zouzou cavorts with chorus girls in a dressing room. They dress Zouzou in a sparkly, scanty costume. She runs to show it to Jean, now an electrician working at the hall. Jean directs Zouzou to the stage while the curtain is closed and shines a flood light on her, ostensibly to test the lighting. He instructs her where to stand, directing her to 'stay put'. She begins to dance, casting shadows in the shapes of animals on the wall. Unbeknownst to Zouzou, Jean raises the curtain, exposing her to the music hall directors sitting in the empty theatre. In contrast to Zouzou's improvised performance in the laundry, it is Jean who 'directs' the spectacle of Zouzou. This spectacle is made up, in part, by a huge black shadow – an extreme, dehumanizing abstraction of a black woman. Her dance, in which she imitates the head-bobbing movements of a chicken, walks on all fours and does the Charleston, reproduces the combination of sensuality, animality, jazz and primitivism that Baker had symbolized for French audiences since her *début* in the *Revue Nègre*.

Zouzou offers a literal enactment of the mechanism explored fruitfully by feminist film theory: the production of female spectacle orchestrated by a man for the desiring gaze of male spectators. In *Zouzou*, this construction, in a perfect rehearsal of the theoretical model, both participates in the fetishization of the female body and reveals the aggression inherent in it. We watch, along with Jean and the producers, while Zouzou dances. But when she realizes her antics are observed, she flees in horror and, suddenly, we too are complicit. Crucially, the sequence represents the music hall stage as an alienating space outside the woman's control, in which she is subject to manipulation and scrutiny. In contrast to her song in the laundry, Zouzou's music hall performance is, quite literally, authored by, and presented to, men.

Zouzou's next performance occurs once again on the music hall stage, but this time it is as a fully-fledged star that she performs. When Jean is falsely accused of murder and needs money for his defence, Zouzou agrees to perform at the music hall in order to raise funds. Ironically, Zouzou replaces Miss Barbara, the woman she had previously mocked and who has now abandoned the stage to follow her Latin lover. Perched in a huge bird-cage wearing a feathered costume, Zouzou sings 'Haïti':[25]

> In a beautiful blue countryside
> Very far, very far under other skies
> I lived happily
> But it's all over
> Alone in my exile today
> I sing with a stricken heart
>
> Ah, who will give me back my country, Haiti
> Yes, you are my sole paradise, Haiti
> When I recall
> Your forests so beautiful
> Your grand horizons
> Far from your shores
> The most beautiful cage
> Is only a prison
> Yes, my desire, my love call, Haiti
> Is to see you again, Haiti.
>
> Au beau pays bleu
> Bien loin, bien loin sous d'autres cieux
> Je vivais des jours heureux
> Mais tout est fini
> Seul dans mon exil aujourd'hui
> Je chante le coeur meurtri

Ah . . . qui me rendra mon pays, Haïti,
Oui, c'est toi mon seul paradis, Haïti
Quand je me rappelle
Tes forêts si belles
Tes grands horizons
Loin de tes rivages
La plus belle cage
N'est qu'une prison
Oui, mon désir, mon cri d'amour,
Haïti
C'est de te revenir un jour, Haïti.

Once again, we have a representation of racial difference as a mark of the 'primitive' and the exotic. The feathered costume, gilded cage and reference to a love call point to both Zouzou's construction as an untamed creature and a confining metaphor for a certain image of spectacular women. As in this sequence, Baker came to represent any number of 'exotic' cultures, playing, for example, an Arab Tunisian woman in *Princesse Tam-Tam*.

Zouzou's exchange of the camaraderie of the laundry and the *bal musette* for imprisonment in the music hall is completed in the final sequences. Between numbers during the opening night of her revue, Zouzou manages to identify the real murderer and secure Jean's release. Back at the music hall, she sings 'C'est lui' again, this time dressed in a satin evening gown. The performance lacks both the element of parody and the appreciative female audience from the laundry. There are no reaction shots of the music hall spectators and this isolates further her performance from any sort of context or community, underscoring the difference between the performance space of the music hall and that of the *bal* and the laundry.

The shift in performance context of a song from a more 'private' to a public domain carries with it unfortunate consequences for the female protagonist. Zouzou's success in the music hall coincides with the loss of the man she loves. Jean does not recognize Zouzou's sacrifice and chooses her friend Claire instead. Zouzou may have experienced a class rise – she has exchanged her simple cotton dresses for a fur-trimmed suit – but has lost the only thing she wants: Jean. The film closes with an image of Zouzou singing 'Haïti' for the hundredth time in her gilded prison.[26] The music hall itself functions here as a cage: an oppressive milieu for both Miss Barbara and Zouzou. Notwithstanding the rather extraordinary revue sequences in *Zouzou*, the film mounts a critique of this artificial world, valorizing, on the narrative level at least, the working-class camaraderie and modest urban spaces of the dance hall and laundry.

Baker's performances in *Zouzou* evince not only the intertext of the realist representation of the proletariat essential to realist singer texts, but also that of the different stages of Baker's life as it was disseminated in her autobiographies and publicity. At the beginning of *Zouzou*, she is the poor little black girl defined by the spectacle of her race. Her acrobatic shadow dance at the music hall, directed by Jean, corresponds to her *Revue Nègre* phase with its emphasis on exoticism and racial Otherness but also on real talent. Finally, her star appearance in the music hall revue evokes the 'real' 1930s Baker: the elegant *meneuse de revue* who has conquered Paris. Zouzou may have lost her man, but has gained something that was a crucial aspect of every music hall revue star's persona: citizenship in Paris.

The film's treatment of Parisian urban space is similar, in some ways, to that of other 1930s French films. The gritty fortifications and enchanting Les Halles in *Coeur de Lilas* (Anatole Litvak, 1931); the courtyard in *Le Crime de Monsieur Lange* (Renoir, 1935); and the prostitutes and honking cars on rue du Faubourg Montmartre in *Faubourg Montmartre* have their counterparts in *Zouzou*. Scenes of everyday life in Montmartre are represented with detailed texture and considerable affection. Zouzou shops in friendly daytime Montmartre, while Jean's inadvertent involvement in murder takes place in a noirish, nocturnal Montmartre familiar from poetic realist films. However, once Zouzou becomes a music hall star, she leaves working-class Montmartre and enters a paste-diamond Paris. In the opening night revue sequence, an elegant Zouzou sings against the backdrop of an outrageously stylized Paris, represented by the huge obelisk of the Place de la Concorde and the distorted bridges of the Seine. Clearly, the Paris Zouzou has won is not *Paris populaire*. This 'Paris' offers the *chanteuse* only the admiring glances of male chorus singers, denying her an authentic love affair with a 'real' man. This trade-off characterizes all the films featuring the music hall queen and is explored more fully below.

Paris-Béguin

Paris-Béguin anticipates poetic realism in its low-key lighting and recreation of the shadowy, nocturnal universe of prostitutes and criminals. But the film is just as indebted to the backstage musical, chronicling the rehearsals and opening night of a music hall revue in which real-life music hall star Jane Marnac performs both a realist song and a revue number. One of the paradoxes of *Zouzou* is that its female protagonist experiences a vertiginous class rise and achieves social ascendancy in the glittering Paris of the music hall world, at the expense of personal happiness and the presence of a 'real' man in her life. *Paris-Béguin* likewise features a rich, powerful star denied the man she loves. The plot concerns a star named Jane Diamond (Jane Marnac) who cannot perform her songs with sincerity until she experiences the virility of the *réaliste* universe through her attraction to a dangerous gangster, Bob, played by Gabin. On opening night of the show, however,

Jane loses Bob. In the first of Gabin's many photogenic deaths in 1930s cinema, he is gunned down in front of the music hall by a rival gangster.[27] Like *Zouzou*, *Paris-Béguin* plays out a fantasy around the encounter between the rich female star and the virile 'man of the people'.[28]

The film opens in Jane's sumptuous apartment before she has met Bob. The opening scene, remarkable for its camera movement and construction of a fragmented space, establishes Jane as an imperious star leading a decadent life. The camera travels slowly through her luxurious, cluttered bedroom to the strains of a jazzy tune on the radio. High-heeled shoes, a fur coat, cigarettes, a slumbering lap dog and an empty champagne bottle are strewn about. A close-up reveals a woman's legs as she puts on stockings. A tight close-up fragments Jane's face as she applies mascara. She speaks rudely to her protector on the telephone, then leaves for the music hall where she must rehearse.

At the Folies de Paris, a fictitious music hall, the rehearsal of the revue 'Paris-Béguin' is underway. Jane observes a rehearsal of a dance, judging it idiotic. The rehearsal of her own number, the 'Moroccan Tableau' is fraught with problems. The narrative concerns the rape of a woman by a North African gang leader, and her eventual love affair with him. Jane speaks the first lines of the scene in an old-fashioned declamatory style with one arm raised, gesturing toward the sky. She then interrupts the rehearsal, claiming that the story feels false because a woman would never fall in love and allow an intruder to spend the night with her. She demands of the author that he change the scenario. She is at the top of the power hierarchy, ruling over servants, a lover, the revue director, the revue author and fellow actors. Crucially, all the men shown thus far are emasculated: her wealthy but ridiculous protector, the over-wrought director and his incompetent assistants, the elderly, foppish author of the revue, and especially Jane's co-star, clearly coded as homosexual. When he learns that his role in the revue may be diminished, he stomps furiously off, his male lover in tow. In response, Jane stamps her foot and demands 'a man, a man, a man!' ('un homme, un homme, un homme').

Paris-Béguin mourns the emasculation of the modern music hall, critiquing its imperious female star, its artificiality and its homosexual male star, who undergoes here a specifically 'oriental' feminization in that his role within the Moroccan revue is that of the Arab male character. As if in answer to Jane's demand for a 'real' *homme* (straight, white and French), the following sequence introduces Bob, a hardened yet seductive gangster. A modern apache, he wears eyeliner, a fedora, a pinstriped suit and two-toned patent leather shoes. Bob's milieu is carefully established: the scene begins with a shot of the elevated *métro* line, an icon of *Paris populaire*, as a train pulls into the Barbès-Rochechouart station. According to the film's promotional material, this sequence was meant to evoke specifically the intersection of the Boulevard de la Chapelle and the Rue de la Charbonnière, known for prostitution.[29] The publicity proudly notes that 'real regulars from the boulevard' were used as extras in the location shooting, indicating a 'professional consciousness and care for the truth pushed to the extreme limit which does honour to French production'.[30]

Bob enters a bistro to plan a jewel heist with fellow gangster, Dédé (Jean Max). He encounters Gaby (Rachel Berendt), a prostitute and his former lover.[31] 'Je suis chipée pour toi', she says, using underworld *argot* to express her desire for him. But Bob spurns her and brags of other conquests. Later, as a reinforcement of this popular atmosphere, one of Mistinguett's realist songs plays on the bistro phonograph, nursing Gaby through her depression. In *Paris-Béguin*, the working-class bistro represents the 'modern', 'authentic' world in contrast to the artificial, feminized, orientalist universe of the music hall.

Paris-Béguin continues its alternation between Bob's *noir* universe and the star's opulent surroundings. After drinking champagne and flirting at an elegant rest-aurant, Jane returns home. While in her bath, she hears a sound and finds Bob in her room. They size one another up in a series of shot/reverse shots. Bob reveals his revolver. A smile spreads across his face; he stares at her exposed leg. The phallic gaze and fetishistic camera work prefigured in the opening sequence could not be more explicit here. Jane stares back mutely, fascinated and horrified. When she breaks away and calls for help, Bob kisses her brutally and leads her to bed off-screen, ignoring her cries of protest. The following morning, Bob slips away, leaving the jewels. Jane awakens and smiles contentedly, caressing the bed Bob has just left.

The effect of this sexual encounter, coded initially as a rape, is a radical shift in Jane's personality and performance style. In a repetition of the opening sequence, the transition from boudoir to theatre could not possibly be in greater contrast. At the dress rehearsal for the revue, she is affectionate toward the music hall personnel. The ballet she found idiotic is now 'charming'; she deems unnecessary the reduction in her stage lover's role. Her objectification/subjugation by Bob results in a complete loss of her mastery, figured here as amiability if not utter compla-cency. Furthermore, she restages the rape in the music hall narrative, orchestrating her powerlessness in a highly ambivalent if suggestive gesture that does nothing to restore her primacy in this space. She requests that the Arab threaten her with a revolver instead of a sabre, and that he kiss her brutally when she tries to call for help. In short, she transforms the exotic context of her North African showpiece to that of the Montmartre underworld. Once her stage lover has been killed by the guard, she sings a realist song called 'C'est pour toi que j'ai le béguin' over his dead body.[32]

The audience of music hall performers and stagehands, particularly the female spectators, is hypnotized by Jane's performance. Four separate reaction shots reveal women mesmerized by Jane's antics: one strokes her feather boa absent-mindedly, while another eats a chocolate bar. Jane's song recounts a *béguin* (crush) that begins promisingly but ends violently, with the woman shooting her lover dead as he tries to leave her. It illustrates not exactly what we have just seen on the stage, but rather, predicts the outcome of the relationship between Bob and Gaby. The link between Jane's emotions and her 'authentic' expression of them made possible by her encounter with underworld masculinity is underscored in the sequence that takes place the following night during the opening performance of the revue.

Just before Jane's performance, Bob is shot dead in front of the music hall. The visually striking scene is filmed in low-key lighting, with an emphasis on the formal beauty of an iron fence nearby that casts shadows in the shapes of bars along the wall. The scene climaxes with Bob dying gracefully in the arms of Jane beneath a huge, abstract poster of the music hall star, much like the art deco posters created for Mistinguett by Gesmar in the 1920s. A fade connects a shot of Jane cradling Bob in her arms to that of Jane cradling her stage lover during the performance she gives later in the music hall. She sings 'C'est pour toi que j'ai le béguin' for the second time, crying genuine tears. This time it is the well-to-do spectators who are transfixed by this expression of authentic emotion. We saw earlier how Jane's performance, infused through Bob with the virility and authenticity of the underworld, affected her fellow female performers. Now this experience also filters to the bourgeois spectators of the modern music hall. Jane has taken the realist song from the seedy hotel room and the laundry to the music hall stage, recapturing, for a moment, the intimacy, emotion and authenticity missing from the music hall experience.

Like *Faubourg Montmartre*, *Paris-Béguin* wants to give us both the *frisson* of the underworld and the sophistication of the music hall. Despite Jane's devastation, the show must go on. Here, *Paris-Béguin* finally fulfils its other function: the celebration of the *music-hall à grande revue*. Jane pulls herself together and performs the final number which features a troupe of male chorus singers in top hats and tails, as well as women in evening gowns and feathers. Forming a glittering, colourful kaleidoscope, the dancers ascend and descend the huge staircase dominating the stage. Reversing the film's earlier ridicule of the music hall's artificiality and incompetence, this sequence celebrates its visual beauty and spectacular effects. Jane appears at the top of the staircase, wearing an enormous feather headdress and sparkly black tights. She descends regally and sings the other song written for the film, 'Paris-Béguin', in her quavering operetta soprano. In contrast to her performance of the realist song that elicited intense involvement on the part of the internal spectators, this sequence eschews 'reaction' shots of the audience, privileging instead a view of the performance consisting of frontally-shot long takes.

In the logic of the film, then, it takes a sexual encounter with a 'real' man – an emissary of the underworld defined in opposition to the aristocratic cuckold and the effeminate men of the glittering music hall world – to tap Jane's sexual potential.

This process can be read as both a valorization of the exoticism and authenticity of the marginal people/spaces of Paris, and a textual mechanism for containing the 'woman on top'. Jane's encounter with Bob can be taken not only as a utopian sexual awakening, but also as a foreclosure of her position of control. If their 'lovemaking' was a quasi-rape, the conquest is short-lived according to the terms set by the man, for the morning after their encounter, Bob flirts with Jane's assistant, hinting that Jane will shortly usurp a different male subjectivity: that of the cuckold, a figure once possessed of authority, but subsequently undermined.

Le Bonheur

Another 1930s French film, *Le Bonheur*, critiques the overarching ego and power of a female music hall star. The film is an adaptation of boulevard playwright Henry Bernstein's melodrama *Le Bonheur*, created at the Théâtre du Gymnase in 1932 with Yvonne Printemps. In both play and film, Charles Boyer played a man of modest means who, disgusted by the cult of celebrity, shoots a star. He is convicted of the crime and spends time in prison. On his release, the former anarchist and the star (played by Gaby Morlay in the film) fall in love. In Bernstein's play, the star is a theatre actress. L'Herbier's film, which enjoyed critical and popular success, transforms Bernstein's theatre star into a film star, thereby not only mounting a critique of the star system but characterizing the cinema as a hypnotizing, emasculating medium.

Philippe Lutcher (Boyer) is a caricaturist for *L'Anti-Sociale*, an anarchistrevolutionary newspaper. He is assigned to sketch the arrival at the train station of the star Clara Stuart, just back from Hollywood. That night, Philippe attends Clara's singing performance, given before the screening of her latest film. Wearing a feathered costume connoting excessive luxury, the prima donna sings a waltz about the fragility and happiness of love to enthralled, mute spectators.[33] Clara's mesmerizing power is emphasized in close-ups of Philippe and Clara that create the illusion that she is singing directly to him. Philippe is shown to experience, despite himself, the hypnotizing power of the star's performance.

The active spectator is thus transformed into the compliant spectator when the female singer appears. In depicting this, L'Herbier's film taps a tradition of ambivalence toward the female singing star we can trace back to the mid-nineteenth century.[34] However, the opposition to the power held by the *chanteuse* has shifted somewhat. In the mid-nineteenth century, critics were afraid that *café-concert* star Thérésa would incite unrest: that her working-class 'aggression' would spill out into the streets or contaminate bourgeois strata – bourgeois women in particular. Here, we have a critique of the female star's ability to paralyze, to render apolitical the (male) spectator. *Le Bonheur* updates this lament, critiquing both the power of the diva in live performance and the cinematic apparatus: its star system; publicity operation; its hypnotic power over spectators; and its highly rationalized spectacle of technology and dehumanized performers.

In the sequence following Clara's performance, Philippe attempts to murder her. His motive, he explains at his trial, was the desire to commit an anti-social act by killing a powerful person. He reasons that, in today's world, the contemporary figure whose murder would garner maximum publicity was not the traditional holder of power, the politician for example, but the new idol: the film star. However, once in the theatre, he finds himself transfixed by Clara, transformed from anarchist to compliant spectator. This potentially subversive theme in *Le Bonheur* – the protest against the paralyzing neutralization of the anarchist – is neutralized itself, as we shall see, by the end of the film.

Just as Philippe has been unexpectedly touched by Clara, Clara is now strangely attracted to Philippe. She testifies at his trial, begging the judge to show mercy. Philippe spends a few years in prison, then is united with Clara on release. Their passion flourishes until Clara decides to make a film chronicling Philippe's attempt on her life and their subsequent love. Philippe protests that the story is his. Responding that is is hers, too, she proceeds to make the film in secret. He leaves her, but not explicitly for her appropriation of their private love story for a narrative destined for a mass audience. Oddly, he explains that he is abandoning Clara because he realizes that her ex-husband, a minor character played by Jaque-Catelain, still loves and needs her. He leaves Clara not with bitterness, but with tenderness and self-sacrifice, asking only that she direct her special 'look' at him while singing in her films – a look he will recognize, he tells her. The final image is a close-up of Philippe gazing longingly at Clara on the screen, dreaming that she is singing directly to him. The representation of Clara singing in a movie at the end of *Le Bonheur* replicates her earlier mesmerizing effect, depicted in the live performance shown at the beginning of the film. Whether in the music hall or the cinema, *Le Bonheur* implies, female performance possesses an overwhelming and destabilizing power, rendering spectators mute, incapable, apolitical.

Like *Paris-Béguin*, *Le Bonheur* celebrates the male protagonist with ties to *le peuple* at the expense of other, feminized male characters and especially at the expense of the female protagonist possessed of wealth and power. Although Philippe is not, properly speaking, a proletarian figure – he is a lawyer and painter turned anarchist – he is nevertheless aligned with the working class through his humble surroundings and opposition to the power structure of his society, incarnated in the dominant cinema idol. Clara's manager (Michel Simon) and husband (Jaque-Catelain) are 'inadequate' men: Simon's character is ridiculed for his homosexuality and Catelain plays an idle, impoverished aristocrat. Just as in *Paris-Béguin*, in *Le Bonheur* a female star is flanked by a homosexual and a compliant aristocrat in order to highlight the virility of the proletarian-identified male. Likewise, Philippe is posited as an 'authentic' man, sensitive to his surroundings, whereas Clara is cast as egotistical and artificial.

Le Bonheur's construction of gender is unusual not only on the thematic level, but also in terms of its visual style. During the sequence where Clara performs live, the film's representation of her as object of desire is fairly conventional: her body is highly fragmented, and lighting and costumes abet a process of fetishization. But Philippe is framed in a fashion usually reserved for female characters in the classical film. In this and many other sequences, his face is filmed in lengthy, filtered close-ups as he watches Clara, enthralled. Moreover, the close-ups that align their gazes are highly ambiguous. Philippe's gaze is not the masculine look that freezes the body of a woman, reducing her to an erotic image. It is that of a helpless animal, caught in the headlights of an oncoming car. Clara's gaze, directed at Philippe through the editing, reduces him, as well as the other spectators, to paralysis. He is revealed to be 'too close' to the image, reflecting the more traditional construct of the woman's 'excessive' proximity to the image taken up by Mary Ann Doane in her defining 1987 study of the woman's film.[35]

Although it would be unwise to infer that its 'feminization' of a masculine character functions to overturn the gender hierarchy that traditionally accords men primacy, we can, nonetheless, identify in *Le Bonheur* an important disruption in gender coding. A norm is disturbed on the level of the visual organization of the gaze and in terms of cinematography, and this coincides with the film's unusual portrayal of a socially powerful female protagonist. The scenario of alienation represented in *Le Bonheur* operates, further, in opposition to what Dudley Andrew identifies as the more prevalent tendency in French cinema at this time. Through its direct address of stars, that cinema evoked the memory of simpler forms of pleasure: of a lost community surrounding street singers; of revellers at spontaneous outdoor stage shows; of good times in the army, and so forth. As France's economic and international situation grew more complex, as its increasingly urban citizens became more alienated, the cinema served to stabilize them with the security of a former identity, the persistence of an endless *Belle Epoque*.[36] The effect of Gaby Morlay's Clara could hardly be more different from the impact of realist singer Odette Barencey's presence in *Faubourg Montmartre*. Rather than transport her spectators back in time to an imaginary space of community and melancholy, Clara isolates them in a cold, mechanized relationship with her image. *Le Bonheur*'s internal spectators, far from interacting with the singer, as the laundresses did in *Zouzou*, are hypnotized and mute.

In sum, the character of the music hall queen constitutes in 1930s French film a rich focus – and site – of anxieties and desires centred around gender and class issues. As we have seen in the four films discussed above, the queen is used as a vehicle whereby the music hall as institution is simultaneously celebrated and critiqued. These films reveal her impossible will to 'have it all'. In *Zouzou*, *Paris-Béguin* and *Le Bonheur*, the star wants both glamour and social power (denied to the lowly realist singer figure in 1930s films) and the intimacy, authenticity and underworld allure of the realist singer's universe.

Ultimately, the trajectory of realist values (working-class camaraderie, authenticity, and so on) I have mapped in my dissections of these four films is not haphazard. In the first, *Faubourg Montmartre*, this impulse resides in a historical realist singer (Barencey). Next, in *Zouzou*, the realist tradition is embodied by a male-female duo (Baker and Gabin). In the third film, *Paris-Béguin*, it is invoked by the figure of a woman-liberated-through-the-intervention-of-a-man (Marnac), when a virile, underclass gangster transmits his 'realist' values to a frigid, unaffecting artist, thawing her innate expressive self which she then takes to the music hall stage. Finally, *Le Bonheur* locates its realist values squarely with(in) the character of a man who cannot, in the end, successfully transfer them to the woman. This trajectory leads not only further and further away from the thrilling, communal dynamism of the underworld towards the dehumanized, spellbinding attractions of the music hall and the cinema, but also it displaces the woman. The idealized images of laundresses and prostitutes generating female performance for a female community in *Faubourg Montmartre* and *Zouzou* give way to the construction of male spectatorship evident in the classic fetishization and objectification of the spectacular image of women (*Zouzou* and *Paris-Béguin*), and, finally, to the disenfranchisement of both the internal male spectator and the female star (*Le Bonheur*).

Notes

1. M. Lagny, M.-C. Ropars and P. Sorlin (1986), *Générique des années 30*, Paris, pp. 179–83.
2. Lagny, Ropars and Sorlin note that there were two actresses, Colette Darfeuil and Marguerite Moréno, who appeared in over thirty 1930s films, but they drop out of the top tier of the chart when we take into account the relatively high number of small roles they played. Women were certainly visible in 1930s French cinema, but were far less likely to play the lead role in a film.
3. Ginette Vincendeau also signals the relative paucity of prominent actresses in 1930s French film, in G. Vincendeau. 'French Cinema in the 1930s: Social Text and Context of a Popular Entertainment Medium', unpublished PhD thesis, University of East Anglia, 1985, p. 179. Taking as an example the top movies in the 1936 and 1937 survey, and comparing the number of leading actors and actresses of equal stature, we find on the male side: Raimu; Pierre Fresnay; Victor Francen; Charles Boyer; Jean Gabin; Louis Jouvet; Fernandel; Guitry; Charles Vanel; Michel Simon; and Harry Baur. Actresses are represented only by Gaby Morlay; Danielle Darrieux; Annabella; Arletty; Edwige Feuillère; and Marie Bell.

4. G. Vincendeau (1988), '"Daddy's Girls" (Oedipal Narratives in 1930s French Films)', *Iris*, 8, pp. 70–81.

5. This chapter focuses primarily on the revue star in 1930s films, but the realist singer provides an important contrast to this figure, and I sketch out her function as well. For a more extensive treatment of the realist singer, see K. Conway (forthcoming), 'Flower of the Asphalt: Popular Song, Gender, and Urban Space in 1930s French Cinema', in P. Robertson and A. Knight (eds), *Soundtrack Available: Essays on Film and Popular Music*, Durham and London.

6. For a more complete exploration of the relationship between the music hall and the cinema, see K. Conway (forthcoming), *The Chanteuse at the City Limits: Femininity, Paris and the Cinema*, Berkeley and London.

7. J.-C. Klein (1991), *La Chanson à l'affiche: Histoire de la chanson française du café-concert à nos jours*, Paris, p. 75.

8. Ibid., p. 75.

9. R. Abel (1994), *The Cine Goes to Town: French Cinema 1896–1914*, Berkeley and London, p. 16.

10. Ibid., 16.

11. P. Chauveau and A. Sallée (1985), *Music-hall et café-concert*, Paris, p. 34.

12. Two different film versions of *Faubourg Montmartre* were made. The first, apparently no longer extant, was released in 1924 and directed by Charles Burguet. In both versions, Gaby Morlay plays the young, innocent Ginette. Morlay (1893–1964) was a veteran theatre actress who played comic, melodramatic and boulevard roles. Closely associated with the theatre, Morlay was one of the most visible actresses in 1930s French cinema, but is best remembered today for the martyr-mother she portrayed in the most popular film of the Occupation, *Le Voile bleu* (1942).

13. For a useful discussion of the melodrama and femininity in relation to poetic realism, see G. Vincendeau (1989), 'Melodramatic Realism: On some French Women's Films in the 1930s', *Screen*, 30, pp. 51–65.

14. G. Champeaux (1933), 'Faubourg-Montmartre', *Gringoire*, 2.

15. Ibid. 'On ne rencontre plus qu'exceptionnellement des pères aussi aveugles que M. Gentilhomme, des drôlesses aussi avachies que son aînée Céline, des vierges aussi farouches que sa cadette Ginette . . .'.

16. G. Charensol, 'Faubourg Montmartre' [Publication Unknown], *Faubourg Montmartre* Dossier, Collection Rondel, Bibliothèque de l'Arsenal, Paris.

17. Ibid. 'Nul quartier de Paris n'a plus complètement changé de visage en vingt années, et dans un aussi brillant décor ce drame de la misère et de la prostitution se trouve singulièrement dépaysé'.

18. Sallée and Chauveau, *Music-hall*, p. 174. The music hall Irène sings in is the Palace, then a real music hall located at 8, rue du Faubourg-Montmartre, in

the ninth arrondissement. A thousand-seat hall was opened at this location in 1921. Initially called the Eden, it did not succeed and was sublet in the following two years to a number of people who tried producing operettas, literary theatre and revues. In 1923, legendary music hall directors Oscar Dufrenne and Henri Varna purchased the Eden and renovated it, transforming it into one of the top Parisian music halls. They changed the name of the Eden to the Palace, to associate it with the Palace of London, a music hall with which Varna and Dufrenne exchanged talent. Varna, considered an innovator, created some thirty successful revues for the Palace.

19. 'Faubourg Montmartre': Lyrics, Raymond Bernard; music, André Roubaud.

20. Fittingly, in light of *Faubourg Montmartre*'s valorization of the intimate realist song over the glitzy revue number, the Palace changed its formula the year after *Faubourg Montmartre* was made. Varna, alone after the 1933 murder of his business partner, attempted to recreate the turn-of-the-century *café-concert*. He changed the hall's name to the Alcazar, in honour of the former monument to Parisian song where Thérésa sang in the 1860s. In 1933 and 1934, Varna presented a series of variety programmes, and hired stars such as Mayol, Georgius, Charles Trenet, Lys Gauty, Marianne Oswald, Yvette Guilbert, Damia and Fréhel: comic and realist singers, as opposed to *meneuses de revue*. But the retreat to an old formula did not take; the Alcazar closed its doors in 1939. It reopened at the end of year under the name of Le Palace, only to fail once more. The Palace's last revue was performed in 1940: in 1946, it became a cinema.

21. For more information on Baker's career trajectory see J. Kear (1996), 'Vénus noire: Josephine Baker and the Parisian Music-hall', in M. Sheringham (ed.), *Parisian Fields*, London, pp. 46–70; P. Rose (1989), *Jazz Cleopatra: Josephine Baker in Her Time*, New York; and J.-C. Baker and C. Chase (1993), *Josephine: The Hungry Heart*, New York.

22. 'C'est lui': Lyrics, Roger Bernstein; Music, Georges Van Parys. This was one of Baker's signature songs. Although Baker sings a realist song here, her voice was not that of the traditional realist singer: her fluty soprano is closer to that of Florelle or Yvonne Printemps, the operetta singer.

23. 'Fifine' or 'La Java des Marsiallo': Lyrics, Géo Koger, Henri Varna et E. Audiffred; Music, Vincent Scotto, 1934.

24. A sustained analysis of male singing performances in 1930s French cinema is beyond the scope of this study, but the star images and singing performances of Préjean, Jean Sablon, Tino Rossi, Charles Trenet and Maurice Chevalier clearly merit closer analysis. For an analysis of working-class spaces of entertainment in 1930s French films, see G. Vincendeau (1992), 'From the Bal Populaire to the Casino: Class and Leisure in French Films of the 1930s', *Nottingham French Studies*, 31, pp. 52–70.

25. Lyrics, Géo Koger and E. Audiffred; Music: Vincent Scotto, 1934.

26. The bird-cage motif also recalls the cage-like mask worn by the only other black actress to star in a 1930s French film: Laurence Clavius. For a fascinating contrast to Baker's roles, see Clavius in *Daïnah la Métisse*, Grémillon's 1931 film about an elegant black woman's encounter with a working-class white man on a cruise ship. This film, written by Charles Spaak and starring Charles Vanel and Clavius, was brutally cut to a sixty-minute version by its producers, Gaumont-Franco-Film-Aubert, prompting Grémillon to disavow the work.

27. Duvivier was undoubtedly influenced by this scene, for Gabin's death in *Pépé le Moko* is quite similar. Betrayed by a woman of the underworld (the Casbah), he dies beautifully behind a fence that resembles prison bars.

28. Francis Carco, the novelist, playwright and screenwriter, wrote the scenario for *Paris-Béguin*, as well as the lyrics to its two songs.

29. A. Corbin (1990), *Women for Hire: Prostitution and Sexuality in France after 1850*, trans. A. Sheridan, Cambridge, Mass. and London, p. 136.

30. 'Conscience professionnelle et souci de la vérité poussés à la limite extrême . . . qui font honneur à la production française'. *Paris-Béguin* Dossier, Collection Rondel, Bibliothèque de l'Arsenal.

31. It appears that Gabin's character is to be understood not as Gaby's pimp but as her lover. Although the *amant de coeur* of a prostitute was quite often, in fact, her pimp, Gabin's main occupation seems to be that of a thief. As in *Pépé le Moko*, Gabin's gangster avoids the unsavory characterization of pimp. See Corbin, *Women for Hire*, pp. 155–61, for a discussion of the different modes of procurement and the representation of the *souteneur*.

32. 'C'est pour toi que j'ai le béguin': Lyrics, Francis Carco; Music, Maurice Yvain, 1931.

33. 'Le Bonheur n'est plus un rêve': Lyrics, Louis Poterat; Music, Billy Colson, 1935.

34. See Conway, *The Chanteuse at the City Limits*.

35. M.A. Doane (1987), *The Desire to Desire: The Woman's Film of the 1940s*, Bloomington and Indianapolis.

36. D. Andrew (1995), *Mists of Regret: Culture and Sensibility in Classic French Film*, Princeton, p. 121.

−4−

'Mon cul est intersexuel?': Arletty's Performance of Gender
Keith Reader

Stars, Performance and Performativity

A major development in film studies over the last twenty years or so of the twentieth century has been the emergence of the star as a figure of at least equivalent importance to that of the director, aureoled in auteurist splendour since the heyday of the *Cahiers du cinéma*, if not before. There are a number of reasons for this phenomenon, prominent among them an increased emphasis on film-making as a collaborative process, and a greater interest in cinema as a popular cultural form and as industry – an industry whose major 'products' are, naturally, its stars. Probably as important as either of these reasons, however, is the greater scope that star-studies affords to investigations of gender, now all but omnipresent in the cultural studies context. One of the first major works in the star-studies field – Edgar Morin's *Les Stars*, of 1972 – hints at this *avant la lettre*, in its assertion that 'the preponderance of women gives the star system a feminine character' ('la prépondérance féminine donne au *star system* un caractère féminin').[1] This statement is illustrated, of course, by the feminine gender accorded, in French, to the words *vedette* and *star*. It was, however, Richard Dyer's *Stars* (1979) that did most to establish gendered star studies as a dominant paradigm in the English-speaking world. Dyer's invocation of sexual ambiguity in his discussion of figures as disparate as Montgomery Clift and Katharine Hepburn developed analysis offered in his edited volume *Gender and Film* (1977).[2] And scholars such as Susan Hayward and Ginette Vincendeau, with their work on Simone Signoret and Jean Gabin respectively, have more recently placed a star studies approach firmly at the centre of work on French film in the United Kingdom.

Many more women have, unsurprisingly, become celebrated as stars than as directors (though in France, at least, the balance has shifted in recent years), providing thereby a focus for female as well as male spectators. The star as crossroads of gendered identification and desire has become a major phenomenon in film studies: a phenomenon closely linked with the notion of performance. Performance is obviously at the centre of the Arletty persona, for her two best-known roles are as performing artists (Clara in *Le Jour se lève* (1939) and Garance in *Les Enfants du paradis* (1945), both by Marcel Carné), and her streetwalker in Carné's *Hôtel du Nord* (1938) is a variation on that figure. 'Performance' is, however, a more complex and often less precisely used term than we might suppose, particularly in its relevance to questions of gender. So some refinement and clarification of it will be useful, before I move to analyze Arletty's performances.

The cover of Victoria Best and Peter Collier's 1999 edited volume *Powerful Bodies: Performance in French Cultural Studies*[3] describes performance as 'the latest and most challenging development in French cultural studies'. It might be tempting to say that performance dominates cultural studies *tout court*, so ubiquitous (and defining) a term has it latterly become. The upsurge of interest in film, currently occupying no less significant a place than literature on many an academic syllabus, has obviously been propitious to this evolution. Even more crucial has been the influence of queer theory, which has moved beyond an earlier, feminist preoccupation with fixed-but/because-antagonistic genders to a more inclusive and labile approach, epitomized by the work of Judith Butler. It was Butler who, in *Gender Trouble*, declared that 'gender ought not to be conceived as a noun or a substantial thing or a static cultural marker, but rather as an incessant and repeated action of some sort'.[4] Performance, variously marked also as 'parody' or 'masquerade', has become the privileged signifier for this notion of gender-as-action, but one whose use is not without problems. In the gender-theoretical context, 'performance', taken in the bodily or theatrical sense, stands in a complex relation to 'performativity', used in the sense in which J.L. Austin deploys the term in *How To Do Things With Words* (1975):[5] that is, in respect of speech-acts that bring about a situation rather than merely describing one. ('I now declare this swimming-pool open' serves as a suitably uncontentious example of the latter.) Performativity, in its linguistic sense, clearly depends on an outside system of constraints and conventions, whereas the notion of gender as performance has often, and erroneously, been taken to mean an unbridled bodily voluntarism of a distinctly utopian kind. Butler's later *Bodies That Matter* recognizes this, arguing against 'the reading of [gender] "performativity" as wilful and arbitrary choice' and seeking instead to 'recast [it] as a specific modality of power as discourse'.[6]

What has all this to do with Arletty's performance(s)? Play with gender, most marked in Carné's *Les Visiteurs du soir* (1942), is, we shall see, a fairly constant feature of them, and suffuses her off-screen persona as well. Guillaume Hannoteau's remark, reported in Denis Demonpion's *Arletty*, that 'there are two real men in France: de Gaulle and Arletty' ('il y a deux mecs en France: de Gaulle et Arletty')[7] is an ironic allusion at once to Arletty's collaborationist activities under the Occupation and to her 'masculine' assertiveness. Michel Perrin's *Arletty*, published in Calmann-Lévy's evocatively titled *Masques et Visages* series, speaks of her as 'a double creature, a woman in her heart and a man in her head' ('un être double, femme par le coeur, homme par le cerveau').[8] These are two among a number of references to the gender ambiguity that is so fundamental to Arletty-as-star. Arletty's performances – on- and off-screen, one might say, given that the interplay between the two is constitutive of the star persona – make up the 'incessant and repeated action' that, for Butler, characterizes gender. But it would be a step too far to conclude from that that they break free from the imprisoning male/female dichotomy into a world of 'willful and arbitrary choice'. Perrin's conventional assignation of Arletty's femininity to the heart and her masculinity to the head should be enough to warn against that. Arletty partakes of some of the most tenacious archetypes of modern femininity – the whore-with-a-heart-of-gold in *Hôtel du Nord*; the *femme fatale* in *Les Enfants du paradis*; the incestuous mother-figure in Roger Richebé's *Gibier de potence* (1951) – androgynously inflecting and subverting, rather than overcoming or escaping, them. Her two explicitly lesbian roles would appear to conform still more to type – a hesitant formulation, since I have been unable to see her in the first of these, Jean de Limur's *La Garçonne* (1935). Here she plays Niquette (literally, 'little fuck'), a 'depraved young lesbian' (*jeune lesbienne dépravée*)[9] who is part of the debauched life from which the film's heroine is rescued by the loving devotion of a (male) childhood friend. In Jacqueline Audry's adaptation of Sartre's *Huis clos* (1954), her Inès is a fairly conventionally 'mannish', if not quite butch, lesbian. I shall be concentrating here on some of her major, and more widely accessible, heterosexual roles. But, before moving on to these, let us first look at the off-screen Arletty, and the ways in which she might be taken to inflect and subvert stereotypes of gender.

Arletty: Life and Myth

Arletty was born Léonie Bathiat in the then working-class Paris suburb of Courbevoie in 1898, and died in Paris in 1992. She started her performing career as a fashion model. Her film career began in 1931, but it was not until 1938, and *Hôtel du Nord*, that she attained real star status. Her performance in this film was marked by two characteristics that became the foundation of her star persona: the (oxymoronic?) feminine raucousness of her voice and her street-wise repartee. These make of her 'an *enfant de Paris* in her own right'.[10] It was, as we have already seen, for Carné that her most celebrated performances were given, and Jacques Siclier's description of her as 'the most beautiful woman in Carné's films, the only one who is really a woman' ('la plus belle femme des films de Carné, la seule vraiment femme')[11] is all the more fascinating, and perhaps ambiguous, in the light of Carné's homosexuality. She conspicuously lacked the voluptuousness of younger contemporaries such as Ginette Leclerc or Viviane Romance, as Siclier implies when he says that 'what would be pornographic in a film with Viviane Romance becomes a source of comedy with Arletty' ('ce qui serait pornographique dams un film joué par Viviane Romance devient ressort comique avec Arletty').[12] Although this is changing, the comic in cinema has been a domain largely associated with men, for all the presence of female figures such as Mae West, with her camp performances and what David Thompson has described as 'her sailor's roll'.[13] Michel Simon's alleged exclamation concerning Arletty – 'Those aren't breasts, they're walnuts!'('C'est pas des seins, c'est des noix!') – further stresses her androgyny, unmatched in my view by almost any major actress of her period except Katharine Hepburn (cf. in particular Hepburn's cross-dressing role in George Cukor's *Sylvia Scarlett* (1935)). Marlene Dietrich provides an interesting contrast with Arletty: superficially similar in her sassiness, her habit of playing 'non-respectable' characters, and the power she exerts over men, she is nevertheless far more unambiguously marked as feminine.[14] Arletty, like Dietrich, is a gay icon,[15] but of a more equivocal kind. This point is suggested a contrario by Gaylyn Studlar, when she points out that in most Dietrich films, there is no strong male protagonist. This, Studlar affirms, leads to a direct 'projection of male fantasy onto the woman'[16] that would surely be much more difficult to achieve in the universe of Arletty's films, where strongly male figures – François (Jean Gabin) in *Le Jour se lève*; Frédéric Lemaître (Pierre Brasseur) in *Les Enfants du paradis* – abound.

Arletty's career, like that of so many others in French cinema, tailed off after the War, as a result, many would argue, of her collaborationist activities during the Occupation. These she ascribed largely to her love-affair with the German officer, and later diplomat, Hans Soehring. Her (in)famous self-justificatory remark 'My heart is French, my arse is international!' ('Mon coeur est français, mon cul est international!') has acquired mythical status. While this observation may appear only tangentially relevant to our concerns here, its combination of sexual *franc-parler* and a species of political indifference, or at least promotion of the individual above any sense of collective solidarity, is revelatory. Arletty fits into a tradition particularly important in France by virtue of the strength of the post-revolutionary state: a tradition of *anarchisme de droite* (right-wing anarchism), populist, cynical, irreligious and mistrustful of the idea of progress.[17] That tendency was a priori unfavourable to the fervour of the Resistance, and her place within it is suggested by Arletty's perhaps paradoxical combination of libertarian sexual attitudes and profound social cynicism. She had numerous lovers, mostly but not all male, refused ever to marry, and rejected the idea of having children. For Arletty, '"A child is always somebody who one day will be dead". And I would never be a soldier's mother!' ('"Un enfant, c'est toujours un futur mort". Et moi, mère de soldat, jamais!')[18] – sentiments that might seem to evoke Simone de Beauvoir rather than somebody who was briefly imprisoned at the Liberation. Yet, in the context of the *anarchiste de droite* tradition, they are entirely of a piece with her effective collaboration and subsequent unwillingness to show repentance. Her lifelong refusal to vote – a sturdily *anarchiste de droite* stance if ever there was one – has been trenchantly commented upon by Françoise Audé in the following terms:

If, as I do, one believes that Arletty was lucid and perceptive, one can also believe that one new development of the twentieth century, that of women as citizens, passed her by. She was not quite a modern woman.[19]

Arletty's gender ambivalence is particularly troubling, for me at least, in this light. The unreconstructed individualism that subtends *anarchisme de droite* makes it very difficult to align her with even the most free-wheeling, or, to reprise Butler's terminology, 'wilful and arbitrary', gender or queer theory. It is as if the persona rose up in cynical refutation of the possible implications of the performance. There is, however, no reason to allow a collaborator to have the last word on her own work, so I shall now examine four of the major films – all by Carné – across which Arletty's performances of gender are most fruitfully articulated.

Hôtel du Nord

This is the only one of Carné's acknowledged major films not to have been scripted by Jacques Prévert, whose mordant and iconoclastic wit contributed much to the director's success. Jean Aurenche and Henri Jeanson's screenplay does, however, provide Arletty with ample fuel for her *gouaille*, or sharp-tongued repartee. (Appropriately, in view of her throaty delivery, the colloquialism derives from the same root as *gorge* (throat).) As in the other films to be discussed, Arletty's character, the prostitute Raymonde, is contrasted with a more innocent younger woman – here Renée (Annabella), who comes to the hotel with Pierre (Jean-Pierre Aumont), intending to fulfil a suicide pact. Renée is poor but honest – after the pact fails she returns to the hotel to work as a waitress – and, despite her dalliance with Renée's pimp Edmond (Louis Jouvet) while Pierre is in prison, remains ultimately loyal to her true love. Annabella's image – that of the 'the young girl with her tender smile, nervous gestures and shy voice' ('jeune fille au sourire tendre, aux gestes effarouchées, à la voix timide')[20] – is at the antipodes of Arletty's, and the more seasoned actress benefits, here, as later in *Le Jour se lève*, from the blandness of her foil.

Raymonde qua prostitute is constructed as an at least potential object of male desire, though that potential is not always realized: she returns from working beneath the elevated *métro* tracks one day to bemoan the fact that fifty-seven trains went past while she was waiting for her next customer. But what of the female spectator's possible view of her? Recent work on spectatorship – I am thinking in particular of Jackie Stacey's *Stargazing* (1994) – has foregrounded same-sex identification, irrespective of the sexual orientation(s) of the individual spectator. (Stacey speaks of 'the possibility of homoeroticism in the forms of fascination between women available to *all* women in the cinema audience'.)[21] There seem to me to be two ways in which Arletty's Raymonde provides such a focus. While as a prostitute she is clearly exploited, and while her relationship with Edmond is anything but idyllic, her adroitly cynical way with words often enables her to hit back. Carted off in a police van because her papers are not in order (in keeping with the *anarchiste de droite* persona), she wryly observes: 'If you want a good catch, you've got one' ('Pour une belle prise, c'est une belle prise'). More famously, when Edmond declares that he needs a change of atmosphere (for which, read female companion), Raymonde raucously retorts: 'Atmosphere! Atmosphere! Do I look anything like an atmosphere?' ('At-mos-*phè*-re! At-mos-*phè*-re! est-ce que j'ai une gueule d'atmosphère?'). In no other of her best-known films does Arletty deploy verbal agility – generally, of course, seen as a male prerogative – so pungently, as a weapon of defence and attack alike.[22]

Secondly, Raymonde's story – like that of Renée but less predictably – seems to have a happy ending. Not content with denouncing him in their shouting matches which degenerate into physical violence, she gives Edmond away to the underworld rival who shoots him, in a classic gesture of *femme fatale* 'betrayal', and finds solace with the lock-keeper (Bernard Blier), who calls her 'my little queen' ('ma petite reine') and tucks her up in bed. Some sort of quasi-conjugal respectability and escape from the life of the streets – in the light of her age and periodic difficulty in attracting punters, 'retirement' might be a more gracious formulation – is evidently beckoning to her. Arletty's/Raymonde's *gouaille* has served not only to protect her against the degradation of her life with Edmond, but to bring that life to an end and conceivably to open a new one. In none of the other films we shall consider does Arletty's character's story suggest so positive a *dénouement*.

Le Jour se lève

Le Jour se lève covers a far smaller canvas than *Hôtel du Nord*, focusing as it essentially does on the love quadrangle between François (Jean Gabin), Valentin (Jules Berry), Françoise (Jacqueline Laurent), and Clara (Arletty). François shoots his rival Valentin dead and, at the end of the film, shoots himself, in order to avoid capture by the police. Gabin's role as icon of French working-class masculinity was never more marked than here, drawing strength from the camply mincing mannerisms of Berry who provides him with an ideal foil. The film gave Jacqueline Laurent her first and only major role, perhaps unsurprisingly: the heavily diluted femininity of her performance throws into relief even more strongly than Anna-bella's in *Hôtel du Nord* the knowingly sensual-yet-caring qualities of Arletty. It is noteworthy that, of the four couples whose makings and unmakings are the main narrative thread of the film, only Valentin and Françoise are not seen together on screen, as though his 'effeminacy' and her pallid innocence would not have generated the requisite charge to convince an audience.

This is pertinent because the impact of Arletty's performance seems to be dependent on the three others to which it relates. As in *Hôtel du Nord*, she is first seen forming a couple with a man she despises (she intentionally drops Valentin's top hat, emblem of his social aspirations, during the introduction to his performing-dog stage act), and from which she is to escape, more rapidly than in *Hôtel du Nord*, because of the instant rapport she achieves with François. Yet she is not quite so androdependent as this might suggest, for on leaving Valentin she does not go straight to François, but moves into a hotel room opposite the block of flats in which he lives.

This encoding of the Arletty persona as sexually and emotionally independent is reinforced when François visits her in the hotel one Sunday and finds her showering. He alludes to her as 'Truth rising out of the well' ('la Vérité qui sort du puits') – with 'Truth', obviously, being understood in its 'naked' sense. That sense would have been all the more obvious had the original version of the sequence, in which Arletty was seen entirely unclothed, survived the Occupation censors. A clandestine still photograph[23] shows her holding a sponge, nipples clearly visible, and smiling enticingly – an extremely daring pose by the standards of the time. Arletty's comment on the scene, more than forty years later, is of a piece with the *franc-parler* element of her character: 'At the time it was considered bold. But it was really quite natural. A man is in love with an eighteen-year-old girl. He sees me, a much older woman, in the shower, and thinks: "Hey, this lady's not too bad"'.[24]

Clara/Arletty is thus counterposed to the insipid Françoise, and the seeming unconcern with which she moves from one lover to another, along with the *déshabillé* in which she is frequently seen, evoke a seductress, or even a *garce* (tart), in the mould of Viviane Romance's Gina in Duvivier's *La Belle Equipe* (1936). But, as in *Hôtel du Nord*, this brazenness is only part of a more complex, perhaps more softly 'feminine', persona. In her final scene with François, Clara speaks of their relationship with rueful resignation – 'Luckily we don't love each other' ('Heureusement qu'on s'aime pas') – and settles for a return to the world of catchpenny entertainment she has but recently forsaken, indignantly rejecting any idea of happy memories in tones straight from *Hôtel du Nord*: 'Do I look like somebody who makes love with memories?' ('Est-ce que j'ai une gueule à faire l'amour avec des souvenirs?'). The melancholy that imbues this scene is more marked still in her final appearance in the film, at the bedside of Françoise, who has collapsed on learning of François's plight and is (somewhat unconvincingly) delirious. Françoise, clearly unaware that Clara is in the room, says: 'He doesn't love Clara, it's not his fault' ('Il n'aime pas Clara, c'est pas d'sa faute'). Clara tries to calm her, before turning away with a sob that rings truer than anything else in this scene. Why, or rather for whom, is she sobbing? For the shattered innocence of her rival in love, an emotional and very probably also a sexual victim of Valentin? For François, whom she may have loved more intensely than she has been willing to admit? For herself, her ageing femininity, and the loss she is in the process of facing? The undecidability of her grief reflects that of her character: maternal rather than vengeful on the first hypothesis; passionate rather than cynical on the second; brought face to face with a wasted life and the ageing process on the third. The overwhelming emotion likely to be generated by François's suicide may act to mask the less clear-cut, but nevertheless profound, tragedy of gender and age implicit in Arletty's final sob: a tragedy that, as we shall now see, is echoed and amplified in her later work for Carné.

Les Visiteurs du soir

The plot of *Les Visiteurs du soir* – a fairly preposterous medieval farrago sometimes, interpreted a trifle underconvincingly, as an allegory of the Resistance – is almost the least important thing about the film. Carné and Prévert construct in it a thoroughly camp visual and verbal universe: a *féerie* complete with implausibly dazzling white castle and, for its time, notable special effects, especially in the use of stopped motion. Within that universe, complex love intrigues unfold between the castle's various denizens and the Devil's emissaries, Gilles (Alain Cuny) and Dominique (Arletty). The ambiguous gender of Dominique's name inflects, as it is determined by, that of the character, who arrives at the castle disguised as a young man. The gender confusion that this provokes is all the more unsettling for a present-day audience, probably unused to conventional representations of the Middle Ages, since Arletty's 'male' disguise puts her strikingly elegant, and clearly female, legs on display. It is she who immobilizes the celebration of the betrothal of Renaud (Marcel Herrand) and Anne (Marie Déa), so that she and Gilles can entice the couple away from each other. The crucial difference between them is that Gilles genuinely falls in love with Anne, for which crime the lovers are turned to stone at the end by the Devil (Jules Berry), though their hearts continue to beat as one. Dominique, on the other hand, describes herself as an emotional blank, incapable of true feeling, and thus as a much more authentic representative of the Devil than the over-sensitive Gilles.

For Turk, Dominique's character is unequivocally feminine, in its embodiment of 'values which, for millennia, have been ascribed specifically to women: treachery, carnality, and the responsibility for humankind's fall from grace'.[25] Her treachery is certainly not in doubt: as well as enticing Renaud away from Anne, she inflames Anne's widowed father Baron Hugues (Fernand Ledoux), leading to a joust in which Hugues kills his son-in-law-to-be, and to Hugues's frantic pursuit of Dominique when she finally leaves the castle. Yet her carnality is somewhat more ambiguous. She tells the Devil that she is incapable not only of love or suffering, but of joy or pleasure – hardly the assertion of a carnal woman (or man), belied in part though it is by the Arletty persona and the sensual throatiness of her voice. We are closer here to the fatalistic catatonia of Greta Garbo at the end of

Mamoulian's *Queen Christina* (1934) than to the carnality of a Dietrich, or indeed of Arletty herself in the two roles previously discussed.

The film's period stylization and the often funereal pace of the acting work not only against any sense of carnality, but more generally against clear-cut gender bipolarity. Marie Déa picks up where Annabella and Jacqueline Laurent left off as an innocent foil to Arletty, albeit a somewhat more persuasive one than either of her predecessors. It is, however, the varyingly 'demasculinized' males that do most to destabilize the polarities of gender. Baron Hugues has led a lonely, brooding existence since his wife's death; Renaud shows little sign of attraction towards Anne, a perception doubtless abetted by knowledge of Marcel Herrand's homo-sexuality; and Alain Cuny's performance as Gilles is so wan and languid as to drain him of any suspicion of masculinity. Even the Devil, thanks to Berry's mannered performance, is lacking in the machismo we might feel entitled to expect. In this effete world, and thanks as much to the performances that surround Arletty's as to her own, 'Dominique jostles normal codes of erotic attraction'.[26] There is certainly rich gender ambiguity in the scene where Renaud surprises Baron Hugues and Dominique together, the latter still in male disguise. If, as Turk argues, Arletty's performance is nevertheless not androgynous, this is true only on a somewhat over-holistic reading of the term: a reading that deems it to denote 'the capacity of a single person of either sex to embody the full range of human character traits'.[27] Such an embodiment would be a tall order at the best of times: in a world as bleached of carnality, as bled of testosterone, as that of *Les Visiteurs du soir*, it smacks of the impossible. Carné may have been, as Turk avers, 'attempting to turn Arletty into an emotionless icon'.[28] And, by contrast with her more robust perform-ances in *Hôtel du Nord* and *Le Jour se lève*, she is certainly subdued, erotically and in a more general sense. Yet enough of her former *élan* and 'male' manipulative skills, as evidenced by her determining role in the film's narrative *dénouements*, remain to ensure that her performance, along with Berry's, is the film's most memorable. Washed-out and exhausted her androgyny may be, but androgyny it surely remains.

Les Enfants du paradis

Arletty's role as Garance in *Les Enfants du paradis* has come to stand metonymic-ally as the quintessence of her entire career, right through to her unhappy isolation at the end which seems to prefigure that to which she was to be condemned at the Liberation. To speak of Garance as in any sense androgynous may in this context seem problematic, if not downright absurd. Loved passionately by two very dif-ferent men, the mime Baptiste (Jean-Louis Barrault) and the actor Frédéric Lemaître (Pierre Brasseur); loved platonically by a third, Lacenaire (Marcel Herrand, more clearly designated here than in *Les Visiteurs du soir* as homosexual); and loved with absurd possessiveness by the Comte de Montray (Louis Salou), she is the crossroads and focal point of so many different kinds of male desire that, more than any other role in pre-war French cinema, hers has come to stand for femininity in all its enigmatic inconstancy.

This apparently unequivocal femininity is further emphasized by Garance's narcissism – she is often seen in, or gazing into, a mirror – and the passivity that makes of her 'a distant and self-absorbed "moon goddess"'.[29] In these respects, she appears as a classic female object of male desire. Yet that is a role her relationship with Baptiste in particular works to undercut or subvert, in two different and at least partially contradictory ways. Baptiste's feminine qualities are plain from the outset, notably through the association of his dreamy melancholy with the moon, most marked when he appears as Pierrot in the masquerade in which Frédéric plays Harlequin and Garance Columbine. He is counterposed to the more blusteringly virile Frédéric in several ways that go to reinforce this sense of femininity. Frédéric generally plays speaking parts while Baptiste, as though victim of a para-Lacanian lack, always mimes. Frédéric has a variety of female lovers whereas, until his marriage with Nathalie (Maria Casarès), Baptiste, so far as we are aware, has none. Indeed, he turns away from Garance in their first encounter, in a 'virtual coitus interruptus' that 'is a necessary consequence of . . . his deliberate withdrawal from the sight of Garance's cleavage'.[30] Moving as rapidly as possible beyond the simplistically Freudian conclusion that what Baptiste is really frightened of is the spectacle of (his own possible) castration, we may legitimately infer, with Jill Forbes, that Baptiste is 'struggling with the nature of his desire'[31] – that desire thereby being marked, like Carné's own, as homosexual. Forbes's reading is grounded in a view of 'gender as performance'[32] that owes much to Butler and to those gender theorists, such as Joan Rivière and Eve Kosovsky Sedgwick, whose work preceded hers.

We shall return to (Arletty's) 'gender (as) performance' and to the ways in which it intersects with the cognate notion of performativity in due course. For the moment it is enough to note how Arletty as emblem of femininity – an emblem that, according to Forbes, 'hardly comes alive'[33] in this film – is contested if not supplanted by the gay icon status whose existence we have already noted. That, however, does not exhaust the range of gendered possibilities she embodies, extremely important among which is that of the mother. This may at first appear bizarre, given Arletty's own strident rejection of motherhood and the fact that in none of her major screen roles does she play a mother. But the 'mother' referred to here is to be understood less in a biological than in a figurative sense, deriving from Gilles Deleuze's construction of a certain kind of mother-figure in *Masochism* (1967).

The 'Deleuzian mother' is above all a pre-Oedipal figure. Rather like her opposite number, Kristeva's 'father of individual prehistory' ('père de la préhistoire individuelle'), invoked in *Tales of Love* (1983), she harks back to a period before, or outside, the classic Freudian castration scenario. Deleuze's masochist is not, like Freud's various *dramatis personae*, a 'real' human being, but a literary figure: the protagonist of Sacher-Masoch's novella *Venus in Furs*, reproduced as *La Vénus à la fourrure* along with Deleuze's commentary – a fact that may alleviate any anxieties about the congruence of his analysis with empirical reality. (That reality, for some of us at least, may of course be significantly improved and enriched by the availability of an erotic, non-castratory mother figure.) For Deleuze, the masochist desires to expiate his (gendered) similarity with the Father and to act out a narrative in which he will be (re)born of the pre-genital *mère orale*. This accounts for 'the theatrical impression which is conveyed at the point where the masochist's feelings are at their deepest, and his pain and sensation most intensely experienced'.[34] Sexual consummation, for the Deleuzian masochist, is not denied so much as delayed, in a narrative that recounts 'the triumph of the oral mother, the abolition of the father's likeness and the consequent birth of the new man'.[35]

The evident theatricality of *Les Enfants du paradis* makes these remarks particularly pertinent to the film, and to Arletty's and Barrault's performance of gender within it. The consummation of Baptiste's union with Garance is not denied when he rushes away in the first part of the film: it is delayed, by several filmed years and two filmic hours, until very near the end. The Deleuzian masochist actively desires and seeks this delay, very much in the same way as Baptiste flees the all too willing Garance on their first encounter. Turk, following Gaylyn Studlar, has it that masochistic regression 'allows not only for primary identification with the mother but for "the pleasurable possibilities of gender mobility through identification" as well',[36] as if Baptiste had so thoroughly interiorized Garance's femininity that he has no need for direct erotic experience of it. Why that need makes itself felt only much later, by which time Baptiste has equipped himself with a sexual *curriculum vitae* in the shape of a wife and son, is a question to be addressed very shortly.

Baptiste's masochistic persona, viewed in a more lay sense as well as via Deleuze's more refined use of the term, is scarcely in doubt, from his first appearance when his father is loudly and publicly denouncing his uselessness through to his final, and increasingly unavailing, pursuit of Garance at the end. To affirm this is emphatically not to describe Garance as in any sense 'sadistic'. One great value of Deleuze's analysis is that it uncouples the sadistic from the masochistic universe, treating each as 'a separate world, with different techniques and different effects'.[37] Baptiste and Garance, for all that they come from the same theatrical milieu, in one way at least inhabit 'separate worlds', which, a common-sense view of the film's ending (and there are worse ways to read it) suggests, may make their final parting inevitable. Yet their union – one of the great filmic archetypes, and probably the greatest, of impossible love in European cinema – does achieve consummation, only to be destroyed again immediately afterwards, leaving Garance alone and frozen-faced in the uneasily narcissistic image on which, memorably, the film concludes. This image is doubtless the apogee of her, and Arletty's, performance. But to understand what has led up to it, we need to look again at the notion of performativity, in the sense in which Butler speaks of it as 'a specific modality of power as discourse'.

Baptiste is a sexual innocent at the time of his first encounter with Arletty, whose self-attributed innocence – 'I am as I am. I like those I like to like me, that's all' ('Je suis comme je suis. J'aime plaire à qui me plaît, c'est tout') – is of a very different order. The words she utters to reassure him ('Love is so simple' ('C'est si simple, l'amour')) may thus have a negative effect, performatively provoking the very anxiety they are supposed to alleviate. Yet, in the medium term, they turn out to be justified, for it is after they have been spoken – and unforgettably spoken, to judge by the ease with which they are recalled in the later meeting – that Baptiste enters into what at least appears to be a happy marital and family life. Love has, it would seem, indeed turned out to be simple for him – considerably more so than for Garance, whose performance of her own straighforwardness has proved to be profoundly ironic, but who, as benevolent *mère orale*, has been able, for a while at least, to confer love upon Baptiste.

The medium term, of course, does not last for ever, and Garance's reappearance makes it plain that 'c'est si simple, l'amour' can now become true for Baptiste outside the world of his marriage. Baptiste-the-father is occluded by Garance-the-mother, who finally unites erotically with Baptiste-the-son – until the 'real' Baptiste-the-son, all too appropriately named after his father, appears with *his* mother to put an end to this gloriously father- and thus guilt-free variant on the family romance. 'Power as discourse' finally turns out to lie on the side of the nuclear family, however incongruous that denomination may appear in so non-realistic a world as that of *Les Enfants du paradis*. If this performativity determines the film's 'unhappy ending', it is not, however, the whole story. The fantasy world in which gender does not matter – in which, be one 'straight' or gay, 'c'est si simple, l'amour' – lives on, in the dreamlike (Lacanians would say imaginary) form that was always its only possible habitat. That is what this commentator at least likes to think lies behind Arletty's eyes, and within Garance's imagination, in the film's final shot.

Notes

1. E. Morin (1972), *Les Stars*, Paris, p. 93.
2. R. Dyer (1979), *Stars*, London; R. Dyer (ed.) (1977), *Gender and Film*, London.

3. V. Best and P. Collier (eds) (1999), *Powerful Bodies: Performance in French Cultural Studies*, Berne.

4. J. Butler (1990), *Gender Trouble*, New York and London, p. 112.

5. J.L. Austin (1975), *How to Do Things with Words*, Oxford and New York, 1975.

6. J. Butler (1993), *Bodies That Matter*, New York and London, p. 187.

7. D. Demonpion (1996), *Arletty*, Paris, p. 59.

8. M. Perrin (1952), *Arletty*, Paris, p. 14.

9. Arletty, in collaboration with M. Souvais (1987), *'Je suis comme je suis . . .'*, Paris, p. 114.

10. J. Forbes (1997) *Les Enfants du paradis*, London, p. 56.

11. J. Siclier (1957) *La Femme dans le cinéma français*, Paris, p. 50.

12. Ibid., p. 59.

13. D. Thompson (1975), *A Biographical Dictionary of the Cinema*, London, p. 610.

14. I am indebted to Jill Forbes for this insight.

15. See Arletty/Souvais, *'Je suis comme je suis . . .'*, p. 91.

16. G. Studlar (1990), 'Masochism, Masquerade, and the Erotic Metamorphoses of Marlene Dietrich', in J. Gaines and C. Herzog (eds), *Fabrications – Costume and the Female Body*, London and New York, pp. 229–49, p. 248.

17. This concept is trenchantly developed in P. Ory (1985), *L'Anarchisme de droite*, Paris.

18. M. Souvais (1999), *Arletty, de Frédéric Lemaître aux Enfants du paradis*, Paris, p. 98.

19. 'Si l'on croit – c'est mon cas – à la lucidité et à la perspicacité d'Arletty, on peut estimer qu'elle est passée à côté d'une nouveauté du vingtième siècle, la citoyenneté féminine. Elle n'était pas tout à fait moderne'. F. Audé (1992) 'Arletty', *Positif*, 382, pp. 66–71, p. 67.

20. See J.-L. Passek (ed.) (1987), *Dictionnaire du cinéma français*, Paris, p. 9.

21. J. Stacey (1994), *Stargazing: Hollywood Cinema and Female Spectatorship*, London and New York, p. 29.

22. Her *demimondaine* 'Marie qu'a d'ça' in Jean Boyer's *Circonstances atténuantes* is an even more splendid example in a less celebrated, but hilarious, film.

23. Reproduced in E.B. Turk (1989), *Child of Paradise*, Cambridge, Mass. and London, p. 167.

24. See ibid., p. 166.

25. Ibid., p. 208.

26. Ibid., p. 206.

27. Ibid., p. 207.

28. Ibid., p. 206.

29. Forbes, *Les Enfants du paradis*, p. 60.

30. Turk, *Child of Paradise*, p. 316.
31. Forbes, *Les Enfants du paradis*, p. 63.
32. Ibid., p. 62.
33. Ibid., p. 63.
34. G. Deleuze (1991), *Masochism*, trans. J. McNeill, New York, pp. 101–2. 'L'impression d'un théâtre, au moment même où les sentiments sont le plus profondément vécus, les sensations et les douleurs le plus vivement éprouvées'. G. Deleuze (1967), *Présentation de Sacher-Masoch*, Paris, p. 88.
35. Deleuze, *Masochism*, p. 101. 'comment la mère orale triompha, comment la ressemblance du père fut abolie, comment en sortit l'Homme nouveau'. Deleuze, *Présentation*, p. 88.
36. Turk, *Child of Paradise*, p. 293.
37. 'un monde à part, avec d'autres techniques et d'autres effets'. Deleuze, *Présentation*, back-cover note.

For Our Eyes Only: Body and Sexuality in Reverse Motion in the Films of Jean Cocteau

James S. Williams

Indeed, in a film, the text is a little thing. It is essential to make it invisible. The primacy of the eye over the ear obliges the poet to tell his story in silence, to connect images, to provide for their slightest backward motion and the slightest relief.

Jean Cocteau

Merde! Merde! Merde! Merde! Merde!
(The Poet in *Le Testament d'Orphée*)

Is it possible to discuss Cocteau's films without reducing them to a fixed paradigm or phantasmatic? This question arises upon reading two relatively recent and important studies that discuss Cocteau's cinema in terms of masochism and castration: Naomi Greene's account of pain and pleasure within the Deleuzian context of a masochistic aesthetic,[1] and Daniel Gercke's more Freudian analysis of bodily and filmic ruins, scars, woundings, fissures and ruptures, including Cocteau's own 'prosthetic' figure at the start of his first film, *Le Sang d'un poète* (1932).[2] Both studies confirm Danielle Chaperon's increasingly influential claim that all Cocteau's work is the performance of an ascetic and victim perpetually condemned to abortive encounters with the Unknown, and thus to produce work founded on masochistic obstinacy.[3] It is not difficult, of course, to see the appeal of Deleuze's theory of masochism in the case of Cocteau.[4] Like the work of Sacher-Masoch, on which Deleuze's theory is based, Cocteau's autobiographical film trilogy – *Le Sang d'un poète*; *Orphée* (1950); and *Le Testament d'Orphée* (1960) – invariably involves the poet's subservient and ambivalent relation to an icy and powerful woman who turns him into a victim and obedient slave. Such figures include the androgynous figure and statue in *Le Sang d'un poète*; the cruel and impassive Princess in *Orphée*; the archer Diana in *La Belle et la bête* (1946); and Minerva, Goddess of Reason, in *Le Testament d'Orphée*, who carries in one hand a shield with the device of Medusa's severed head, and in the other a javelin which she hurls straight into the back of the Poet from a raised dais. As Greene demonstrates, Cocteau's universe is one of persecution and tribunals where law is all-powerful but unknowable: a world without real fathers, or rather cluttered with impotent fathers (cf. the various characters played by Marcel André in *Les Parents terribles* (1948) and *La Belle et la bête*). Faced against these odds, the masochist transforms living sensuality into phantasy and art, and the stylistic signs of this disavowal or neutralization of reality in Cocteau's films include dramatic suspense and suspension (literally of characters against walls); waiting and paralysis; the framing of mirrors and keyholes; statues and severed heads; and the creation of *tableaux vivants*, notably in the Hôtel des Folies dramatiques of *Le Sang d'un poète*.[5] Gercke gives these ideas an interesting Freudian twist when he considers images in *Le Sang d'un poète* such as the opening shot of the falling chimney tower, whose path to self-destruction is suspended until the end of the film. His central argument, however, is that the flower in *Le Testament d'Orphée* substitutes finally for the disembodied mouth/wound of Cocteau's first film, and that this logic is fetishistic since marked by the conspicuous disavowal of an absence.[6] Yet to posit such a clear development in fantasy across the Cocteau corpus runs the risk of overdetermining it, a risk succumbed to by the critic Milorad in his exhaustive and strictly Freudian dissection of *Le Sang d'un poète*. For Milorad, Cocteau's work as a poet replaces a real complex – the Oedipal murder of the father – and thus represents an attempt to redeem the Oedipal crime.[7] In such a totalizing reading, aesthetic sublimation becomes simply recuperation, purification and self-absolution.

Zones of uncertainty and ambiguity exist within Cocteau's cinema, however, that are simply left out of such all-encompassing accounts. Nor do they correspond to the usual norms of gay aestheticism: for example, the exaltation of the false as beautiful as proposed by Marcel Eck in *Sodome* (1966).[8] What, after all, are we to make of those moments of apparent narrative breakdown that are so visible in Cocteau's films but which have never been properly addressed? I am referring to the extensive use of reverse motion photography that, by the time of *Le Testament d'Orphée*, becomes so endemic to Cocteau's method that there is no indication at all in the published screenplay that many of the events described are created through this process. Whole sequences are passed off by Cocteau almost as if natural: a photograph of Cégeste materializes in the flames of a fire and, rolled up, leaps into a gypsy woman's hands; broken pieces of the same photograph are thrown into the sea out of which Cégeste (Edouard Dermit) immediately issues, landing on to a cliff to present the Poet (Cocteau) with an Hibiscus flower; the flower is later reconstituted by the Poet after he has torn it apart, and so on. In some cases, the events of reverse action are not even mentioned in the screenplay, for instance, Cégeste's jerky placing of a death mask on to the Poet's face with the word 'Obey!' after the mask suddenly rises from the ground into his hands. More fundamentally for the viewer, there are moments of real confusion in *Le Testament d'Orphée* when it is no longer clear whether filmic time is going forwards (the time of projection) or in reverse (the time of shooting). Such seemingly indiscriminate use of the device has provoked more than one critic to declare that it has become like an empty shell, an embarrassing personal tic, or worse, pure trickery à la Méliès: an inevitable effect of Cocteau's final switching of interest from space (his comprehensive play with mirrors and reflections in *Orphée*) to time, made an explicit theme of *Le Testament d'Orphée*.[9] Gercke, too, characterizes Cocteau's use of *trucages* as naive when he argues that the filmic apparatus, by suspending or reversing moments of prior collapse (Cégeste's magicial arrival from the sea; the sudden rising upright of the Poet following his 'death' in *Le Testament d'Orphée*), shows disavowal as the temporal inversion of castration. The 'uncanniness of the special effect', Gercke explains, 'obliges the viewer to perceive the (res)erection as illusory. The erection is put under erasure, and the male body is reborn as its own fetishistic double, manifestly unable to coincide with itself'.[10]

It may be true, as Gercke asserts, that the stiffly erect male bodies in *Le Testament d'Orphée* end up merely 'miming' the fetishized female phallus of the Hibiscus flower. Certainly, Cégeste rising from the sea 'like a stamen' to land 'under the flashing beam of the lighthouse' (Cocteau's words in the screenplay) is whoppingly phallic, and it vies in mocking extravagance with the ascension by Belle and Prince Charmant at the end of *La Belle et la bête* (shot in reverse motion although confected in the laboratory as a special effect). Yet Gercke's appealing idea is directly complicated by the obvious fact – not usually acknowledged – that just as there are different types of *trucage* in Cocteau's films (whether produced through *mise en scène*, the camera or the laboratory),[11] so, too, there are distinctive forms of reverse motion photography. The first kind are clearly those moments of resurrection and metamorphosis that were already complex manoeuvres during their filming, and that require the actor to fall backwards without bending his knees. They can be linked to those dramatic feats of *mise en scène* that Cocteau inherited from the theatre, such as Marais falling backwards down a flight of stairs in *L'Aigle à deux têtes* (1947), and that he brings together under the term *le merveilleux direct*. Yet there are also other, far more subtle moments that privilege less the dynamic flow of movement produced (the surging jump forwards into the frame, etc.) than the object of the movement. I am referring to such instances in *Le Testament d'Orphée* as a self-portrait by Cocteau slowly coming into being by means of a rag; a flower forming in human hands petal by petal; or Cégeste's accusation against Cocteau his creator, played in reverse and thus totally scrambled (the original words: 'Have you ever wondered what would happen to me after Heurtebise and the Princess were arrested? Did you stop to think that you were leaving me alone in such a place?').[12] Nothing particularly remarkable was experienced for these moments to be produced. They belong to 'reel' time in the sense that they are a pure phenomenon of the camera, at once impersonal and objective, and not otherwise visible. As with the first set of cases, however, they entail some form of initial *chute* or pre-collapse, as if the act of erasing, dismantling or destroying (and that includes destructive words against one's creator) were intrinsic to creation. To use an expression recently formulated by Jean-Luc Godard in *Histoire(s) du cinéma* (1988–98), a work of intensive videographic montage that refers explicitly to Cocteau and takes to new technical levels his work in de- and re-creation, 'only the hand that effaces can write' ('seule la main qui efface peut écrire').

In view of the complexities involved, can we then approach the use of reverse motion photography in Cocteau's films without resorting simply to the phallus, even in its castrated form? Jean-Paul Fargier's answer is to consider the question in Orphic terms, a strategy frequent among Cocteau critics. He suggests that reverse motion represents a wish on Cocteau's part to do what only television can do: that is, perform an instant replay. (Many of the interior scenes in *Le Testament d'Orphée* are, in fact, staged in a studio.)[13] To film a fall in reverse seems to accelerate the movement's speed (*re-bondir*), since inverted time does not pass at the same speed as forward time, a fact that *Orphée* itself hints at with the mysterious phrase relayed from the Zone: 'Silence goes faster backwards' ('Le silence va plus vite à reculons'.) Yet Cocteau himself, who approached film as a form of research and a response to specific questions raised by the medium, never explained in any great detail his reasons and motivations for using reverse motion photography. Here is one brief moment, however, when he discusses its use in *Le Testament d'Orphée*, concentrating on the second type we have established. He appears to deny the possibility of ascribing any particular meaning or interpretation to the process other than as performance:

> There is never a symbol. There aren't any with the flower. I chose the Hibiscus because there are Hibiscus flowers growing at Mme Weisweiller's, and because it's convenient to tear apart. In addition, it's Cagliostro's flower. When I reconstitute it, my hands are like animals. They're detached from me and live like creatures. But it's not enough simply to film in reverse motion; I must all the time play with my hands in such a way that it doesn't seem as if it has been shot in reverse. There is as much creativity here as in a scene played by Madame Réjane or Madame Sarah Bernhardt. I'm not boasting. I'm trying to show you how much work it all constitutes.[14]

The Cagliostro reference is to the eighteenth-century Count Alessandro Cagliostro, the Italian adventurer notorious throughout Europe as a necromancer and alchemist who narrowly missed death by the Inquisition in 1791. While fleeting, it is enough to place Cocteau's use of reverse motion photography firmly within a general metaphysical context of death and transfiguration. For indeed, not only the events of phallic rising obtained through reverse motion, but all moments of film record a process of resurrection and metamorphosis. In *Le Testament d'Orphée*, when asked by the Princess during his mini-trial to define 'film', Cocteau in his role as Poet talks in the oxymoronic and quasi-erotic terms of a static ejaculation: 'A film is a petrifying source [and fountain: *source*] of thought', adding: 'A film revives dead acts. A film allows one to give a semblance of reality to unreality.'[15] Cocteau is referring here both to cinema's documentary aspect (in which he absolutely believed) and to the fact that reality and action have first to be sacrificed and 'shot' ('cinema is death at work', to cite his famous phrase) in order to be resurrected by the projector on the screen. Hence, all events of resurrection in the film may be said to figure the filmic process itself.

Yet the real force of Cocteau's words in the quoted extract is both his admission of stagecraft required to make the manual process of restoration appear as if natural, and his very incomprehension and fascination at the strange, animal and beast-like forms produced by film stock moving in reverse. These images are like vesicles of raw data waiting, if not to be interpreted, then at least processed in some way as concrete evidence. But evidence of what, precisely? How literally should we take Cocteau's wish to go into, and as it were 'behind', people and objects? I want to explore these questions in the particular context of Cocteau's presentation of the male body which, I will argue, is intimately linked to the events of reverse motion photography even when the human body is not actually visible. I will attempt to show that the many risings, rebirths and resurrections of the poet, along with his fateful encounters with super-phallic women – events by which most critics recognize a Cocteau film – represent merely a lavish decoy, one that is ultimately 'immaterial' to the viewing experience and akin to the false 'happy ends' between man and woman which seal *La Belle et la bête* and *Orphée*. Indeed, by emphasizing the 'monstrous' nature of reverse motion, I will suggest that there is another sexual economy operating in Cocteau: one that has very little to do either with the spectacle of the phallic regime or of masochism conventionally defined.

Let us establish some of the immediate effects of reverse motion photography created by Cocteau. Reverse motion pushes body and object to the verge of abstraction and, through providing a new angle on reality, reveals what is normally hidden from view – the material, open core of the Real, or what Cocteau calls the 'invisible' or 'inevitable *invisibility*'.[16] It is, in effect, a use of *trucage* to uncover the *truc*, or the materiality of the Thing, for Cocteau provides glimpses not only of accidental beauty and charm but also of the ugly and formless, even the grotesque and abject. The unforeseen frothing-up of the water during Cégeste's jump in reverse motion is described variously by Cocteau as a 'monstrous' and 'atomic flower'.[17] More troublingly insistent and invasive, however, because more protracted, are those shots of the weird, bulbous shapes of the (already obscene) Hibiscus petals some-how crystallizing in Cocteau's hands, or the smudged black lines of the drawing taking painful, humanoid shape. These images appear even gross and disgusting, like a ghastly sub-stage or perhaps remainder of creation. They echo in form the hollowed out and rock-strewn cavernous spaces of the quarries in Le Val d'Enfer (the Baux-de-Provence), where so much of the exterior action in *Le Testament d'Orphée* takes place. In this last film, the collection of shifting, amorphous images seem, in fact, like the many dissolves, to have been generated out of the smoke that curls and lingers after the opening image (also shot in reverse) of a soap-bubble hitting a pointed knife, a motif that culminates in the smoke wafting gently out of the Poet's open mouth after his 'death', and which is eventually replayed in forward motion at the end of film. Such moments might be said to correspond to those other forms of the grotesque and base matter in Cocteau's other films played out at the level of character and emotion, most obviously la Bête in *La Belle et la bête* but also the evil dwarf Achille in *L'Eternel retour* (scripted by Cocteau although directed by Jean Delannoy, 1942); the malevolent, vengeful Présidente in *L'Aigle à deux têtes*; and the stifling and wretchedly jealous Yvonne in *Les Parents terribles* (the latter two roles played by Yvonne de Bray, herself a *monstre sacré* of French theatre and one of Cocteau's *grands fauves*).

This degree of abandonment to the monstrous surprises of the machine is a sign of Cocteau's absolute commitment to *monstration*, or the act of showing forth (Latin: *monstrare*, to show): that is, to presenting events mimetically in individual shots as opposed to narratively (Cocteau talked of 'disconnected images' (*images décousues*)). Film offers an endless 'petrifying' source of thought because it can engineer moments of non-control when matter takes over, and moreover it can *show* the results. It delivers proof of the impossible. So potentially momentous is this process that, for his encounter in reverse motion with an Hibiscus flower, Cocteau will even don a professor's gown. As he says in his preface to *Le Testament d'Orphée*, 'if the film wanted it that way to begin with, it must have had its reasons, or . . . reason had nothing to do with it. And I was content to obey'.[18] This process is further intensified by Cocteau's common practice of 'accidental synchronism', a form of montage whereby the music on the sound-track, even a specially composed score, is deliberately divorced from the image, resulting in moments of counterpoint but also unheralded and fortuitous connections. The whole mysterious effect is poetry itself, as Cocteau explains in *Du cinématographe* where he underlines the peculiar balance of control and chance that is involved: 'instead of losing all control as happens in dreams, I celebrate the marriage of the conscious and unconsciousness which gives birth to this terrible and delicious monster called *poetry*'.[19]

What excites Cocteau above all is that indeterminate zone between creation and decreation, forming and deforming. If he never discussed in detail this process in his own work, he recognized and celebrated something equivalent in the art of El Greco where, in paintings such as *The Martyrdom of St Maurice and his Legions*, the male body is presented like a frozen, deathly eternity but can also burst forth in a kind of vibrant sexuality or 'explosion of the line'.[20] Claude Foucart has already shown with regard to Cocteau's poetry that, just as an El Greco painting comes into being when the body is 'unmade' and transformed into an *élan* as if by a thunderbolt, so the Coctelian male body mutates and vibrates in 'exquisite decom-position' as the poem develops, becoming even 'a single monster of joy' ('un seul monstre de joie'). That is to say, the *endroit* (the right side out) becomes the *envers* (the wrong side out).[21] Yet how ought we to view Cocteau's materialist method of film that takes us directly into the ecstatic flux of both human and non-human objects? We could perhaps view the process of reverse motion photography in religious terms, not only due to its remarkable resurrectional qualities (the written preface to *Le Testament d'Orphée* even features a poem entitled 'Phoenixology') but also on account of the Christian associations and iconicity evident in Cocteau's filmwork (associations that, it must be said, Cocteau never sought actively to advertise). One thinks of the many trials and sufferings of the Poet in *Le Sang d'un poète* and *Le Testament d'Orphée* where he is killed like a martyr to the artistic cause for which he was born (and perpetually reborn). At the end of this last film, the Poet, expecting to be arrested by the angels of Death from *Orphée*, lifts up his arms in front of the two police motorcycles as if to plead for mercy, before being 'crucified' (Cocteau's own term in the screenplay) by Cégeste on the rocks of the road. It could perhaps also be argued that la Zone in *Orphée* constitutes a depiction of Hell, since it presents '[a] no man's land between life and death. One is neither completely dead there, nor completely alive'.[22] In fact, if we retain the strong pictorial aspect of Cocteau's film-making, it may be possible to view the present-ation of the monstrous as further evidence of that 'enigmatic', paradoxical body that Jean Louis Schefer opposes to doxical figuration in Western painting, a tradition rooted in perspectival and volumatic space. Schefer champions works of art such as Uccello's *Deluge* and films such as Tod Browning's *Freaks* (1932) that provide figurations of unformed, deformed or freakish bodies, all attached in different ways to the elements of time and memory.[23] Such a comparison is encouraged by the fact that *Le Sang d'un poète* is dedicated as a 'collection of allegories' to the memory of Uccello, as well as of Pisanello, Piero della Francesca and Andrea del Castagno, all of whom Cocteau characterizes as 'painters of coats of arms and enigmas'. There is even an explicit reference in *Le Sang d'un Poète* to Uccello. Its fourth episode is called 'The Profanation of the Host', the title of one of the six episodes of a predella by Uccello entitled *Miracle of the Host*.[24] The particular episode chosen by Cocteau (one that had already intrigued André Breton suf-ficiently for him to include it in his 1928 novel *Nadja*) is notable for its self-consciously stray sense of perspective in the foreground of the usurer's home. This is a moment when Uccello, a master of the art of perspective, chose to play against his own rules.

While this type of religious, aesthetic reading would have the virtue of insisting on Cocteau's controlled play with non-control, it would still not do full justice to the physical and sensory experience of watching reverse action moments that demand our rapt attention to objects in process. In their sheer materiality and strangeness, such moments could be said, after all, to have more in common with Arcimboldo's human heads formed of animals, flowers, fruits and stones: the expression of a pantheistic vision of the world. Nor would such a reading take into proper account Cocteau's own precise statement regarding *Le Sang d'un poète* that, while 'every poem is a coat of arms' and 'must be deciphered' (the first words of the film),[25] his cinema deliberately rejects symbols, substituting 'acts, or allegories of these acts, that the spectator can make symbols of if he wishes'.[26] In fact, Cocteau's moments of reverse motion bring the viewer face to face with an Otherness which he or she can neither incorporate nor expel. For these events, along with the constant transfer in Cocteau's work of sounds and sensations between and across surfaces (the many close-ups of eyes and mouths in action; the sound of rubber gloves being stretched; gloved hands entering a vat of mercury; a half-naked body jumping into a tank of water; the magnified sound of human breathing), throw objects into dramatic 'relief' – a major critical and evaluative term for Cocteau – and transform the filmic medium into a living organism. Not just the mirror in *Orphée* but the entire screen of a Cocteau film undulates like water to become a giant lung of movements and drives, inflations and deflations, penetrations and ejections (cf. the reverse-action moments of expulsion from the mirror – a tank of water – in *Le Sang d'un poète*, or from the sea in *Le Testament d'Orphée*). The real interest of mirrors for Cocteau is surely less in their play of reflection and specularity than in the direct human contact they can provoke. One thinks, for example, of the camera's attention to Marais's breath secreted on the surface of the mirror during his first reflection in *Orphée*, an image that has too quickly been classified as a case of male narcissism, yet merges through super-imposition into an outside puddle of water. (In his written presentation of *Orphée*, Cocteau states simply that mirrors are a means of seeing oneself grow old and thus of approaching death.)[27] So overwhelming, indeed, is the power of objects in Cocteau that, in the case of *Le Testament d'Orphée*, the shot of the Poet's blood causes the black and white screen to break out in colour. The image of blood runs through the very veins of Cocteau's films, beginning with the blood oozing pain-fully and yet erotically from the mouth of the schoolboy struck down in *Le Sang d'un poète*. ('Blood is flowing out of his mouth, forming bubbles. He moans, and half opens his eyes. This picture should be painful to see'.)[28]

If the rhythm of flowing blood 'makes us turn our head away' (Cocteau), it also contributes directly, like the breath of wind in *Orphée* and *Le Testament d'Orphée*, to the peculiar mood and atmosphere of Cocteau films, both thematically and at the most visceral level. Cégeste tells the Poet in *Le Testament d'Orphée*: 'That flower is made from your blood, and has adopted the same rhythms as your destiny.'[29] For blood is linked to the *syncope*, a recurring word in Cocteau and used most often in its meaning of a loss of consciousness due to a sudden transient failure of blood supply to the brain. Here is how Cocteau describes the phenomenon of the *syncope* as it relates to film:

The sort of rapture which carries us away on contact with certain works rarely results from an appeal to tears or an effect of surprise. To repeat, it is rather provoked in an explicable way by a gap opening on to the unexpected.

This opening will occur in a film just as in a tragedy, a novel or a line of verse. The rapture will not arise out of the film being amenable to stratagems. It will arise out of some error, some syncope, some lucky encounter between the attention and lack of attention of its author.[30]

The unforeseen gaps and errors Cocteau is talking about here are precisely those spasms and vibrations of energy produced by the *glissandi* of reverse motion, in conjunction with the always unanticipated slowing down of characters' movements through slow motion; the occasional quick-fire zoomings in and out of the camera; the slow emergence and melting away of people and objects through dissolves; and the often vertiginous camera angles and framings of his films (in particular high and low angles) that serve to give every frame such a knowing and ironic edge. The extreme, physical 'rapture' of form this creates is perhaps best described by Steven Shaviro in *The Cinematic Body* (1993), a study of embodied cinematic vision that proposes a dynamics of film-viewing at once mimetic, tactile and corporeal.[31] Shaviro does not discuss Cocteau, yet long before Cronenberg, Fassbinder and Warhol, Cocteau was creating a 'proliferation of affect' by facilitating multiple interactions, affects and transformations of bodies on screen. His films institute for extended moments a similarly ambivalent, viscerally real and at times terrifying, non-signifying body, defined now not as an object of representation but as a *zone* of affective intensity. Such moments of excitation, according to Shaviro, can even offer the intoxicated viewing body a 'shattering' masochistic pleasure of obsessive passivity and abjection, due to the spectator's abandonment to free-floating sensation and visual fascination. Shaviro's concept of masochism in film has little to do with the elaborate contracts of Sacher-Masoch. Underpinning his idea of masochistic excitement – via the work of Leo Bersani – is Jean Laplanche's theory that fantasy, or the imaginary expression and fulfilment of a desire, is itself a sexual 'perturbation' (*ébranlement*) related in origin to the emergence of the masochistic sexual drive. This psychic disturbance is essentially an experience of pleasure as pain, and thus already a form of masochistic sexual excitement.[32]

Shaviro's 'cinematic body' brings out the truly radical nature of Cocteau's investment in reverse motion photography, an 'image-*en-procès*' where film literally regresses (becomes *in-fans*) and provides disturbing glimpses of primary erotic matter. Is it possible, in addition, to accord some type of sexuality to such regression? Cocteau never ventured into this area, although in one account of *Le Testament d'Orphée*, as if aware of the film's internal, diffuse eroticism, he had recourse to the then new word *gamberger* which he attempted to define typically in terms of (non-)control and which clearly carries echoes of *gerber*, slang in French for 'to vomit' and also (of women) 'to masturbate':

> This time, in my film, I took great care to ensure that the tricks were in the service of the internal line of the track and not the external line. They have to help me make this line as supple as that of a man who 'thinks hard' [*gamberge*], to use this admirable term which is not in the dictionary. To think hard means to let the mind follow its course without any control and without corresponding either to dreaming, or rêverie, or daydreaming; to allow our most intimate ideas – those most imprisoned within us – to take flight and pass without being seen by the guards. Everything else is merely 'thesis' or 'brio', and both these repel me.[33]

If we remind ourselves of the close images and forms liberated in reverse motion, many possess a strong oral component, notably the close-up of reversed words in Dermit's mouth and, one might argue, his 'vomiting up' by the sea on to land. These complement the many oral images conceived in forward motion, including the disembodied mouth drowning in the poet's hand in *Le Sang d'un poète* (an effect of superimposition) and the Tiresias-type statue of the Idol in *Le Testament d'Orphée*, out of whose three mouths spew ribbons of writing. Yet there is another more urgent dimension and valency to the viewer's experience of reverse motion in Cocteau's films. This will become clear if we consider the reactions Cocteau himself claimed to have witnessed during a screening of *Le Testament d'Orphée* when, to confuse matters even further, one reel was played backwards, producing effectively a double reversal:

> Filmed backwards . . . a track reveals a universe, a form of behaviour and such a plausible language that this bizarre language could even be learned. Seeing me depart from the edge of the abyss without any fear, the projectionists couldn't prevent themselves from shouting out warnings each time the movement backwards made me approach the same abyss by my back.[34]

This anecdote is instructive for illustrating again how keen Cocteau is to extend and universalize the wondrous world of reverse-motion photography. Yet it also – and this is a typical Cocteau manoeuvre – insists simultaneously on uniqueness and difference, since it indicates the particular danger that lurks at the rear in his films. All the various formal gaps and openings in Cocteau's cinema are linked in some way to this virtual, yet utterly physical, concrete gulf that can suddenly open up from behind. What is even more mysterious is that this gaping void impinges almost exclusively upon Cocteau's male characters. Indeed, we need to draw a clear and necessary distinction between reverse motion as a principally male phenomenon in Cocteau and those more routine dissolves or superimpositions that affect male and female figures alike. Let us, in fact, pause for a moment to consider more general aspects of *mise en scène* and framing in Cocteau's films, since the very act of looking and turning back in Cocteau is defined as a male activity and enticement.

In the first exterior scene of *Le Testament d'Orphée*, the Poet slowly turns around as if to begin cruising the 'man-horse' he has just passed. This is a young man dressed in a black leotard with a long black horse's tail and head who also stops to turn around and lift off his mask. The Poet then follows him into the gypsy camp where he is pictured provocatively combing his mane, the mask resting on his knees. Following the Poet's eventual retreat from the camp under the man-horse's intense gaze, the voice-over commentary states: 'I did not like that man-horse. I guessed that he was drawing me into a trap, and that I would have been wiser not to follow him.'[35] The drama of the male gaze is later repeated in the scene in the quarry where the Poet meets his double (that is, the image which the public has fabricated of him), who looks at him only when he turns his back. It is in *Orphée*, however, that the dangerous attraction and fascination of looking and turning back is most developed. Just as Eurydice enjoins Orphée not to look back according to the legend and the law (which Orphée will thereby subvert), so the Princess of Death warns Cégeste of the terrible risk involved by referring to the Biblical myth of Lot, where Lot's wife was turned into a statue of salt for having dared to look back at the city of Sodom ('Will you ever learn not to look back? There are some who play this little game and are changed into statues of salt').[36] The male gaze thus carries a dangerous, sodomitical charge, one that is continually played out in Cocteau. Orphée himself is obsessed with the ramifications of looking back long before the legendary injunction is even declared, as evidenced in his early rebuke to Heurtebise who counsels rest: 'Thanks! For sentences to begin again as soon as I've turned my back'.[37] When he does finally entrap himself by seeing Eurydice, it is naturally in the rear-view mirror of Heurtebise's talking Rolls that relays the strange pronouncements by Cégeste. At that moment, the image of Eurydice disappears immediately, yet what is left on the viewer's retina is the oval shape of the mirror itself that stands metonymically for the car with its gliding curves and folds. This is the car that first brought Orphée and Heurtebise together and in the specific context of reverse motion. When he was first driven to the Princess's residence, Orphée was sitting directly with his back to Heurtebise, the driver. At the same time, the landscape into which the car was moving was shot in negative as a rear projection. At one stage, as the car crosses a railway line and pulls away into the distance, we see Orphée and Heurtebise positioned in line through the back window of the car, leaving us again with a circular oval image that decreases in size as the car progresses forward. The gaze of Heurtebise visible in the rear-view mirror is formally extended by the back window, thus creating an all-male space of shapes and forms in which the Princess, sitting on the back seat, barely figures. The viewer participates directly in this circulation of male gazes because positioned behind the car and directed to look through the window towards Orphée and on to Heurtebise. We might compare this dense image with the shot of the male servants' behinds in *La Belle et la bête*, lined up in series through the windows of the carriages in which they are carrying Belle's sisters, as well as with the sequence in *Le Testament d'Orphée* where two young semi-naked swimmers simulate a dog, the first donning a mask of Anubis (an Egyptian god of the dead), the other wearing a dog's tail and holding the first by the hips as they frisk past and behind the Lady.

The implication of such stylized scenes of male vision and formation is clearly that looking from an angle, on the move, and most importantly from behind, is the privileged viewing position in Cocteau's cinema. This is never resolved or straightened out by means, say, of a standard shot/counter-shot arrangement, which is rare to non-existent in Cocteau, who studiously avoids the subjective presumption of point-of-view shots and ensures that his characters retain their status as his 'creatures'. It is highly significant that, during the first penetration of the mirror by the Princess and Cégeste in *Orphée*, the viewer is positioned already from within (that is, we are placed inside the Zone and watch from a low angle as the figures glide through at a tangent). This goes hand in hand with a type of 'reverse' contact with objects enjoyed uniquely by the male characters. Eurydice and even the Princess remain oblivious to the complex movements and configurations available in the Zone, where, for example, almost as a joke, during Orphée's first descent, a boy glazier passes first in front of Heurtebise as a real presence, and then behind him in the form of a prefilmed rear projection. Moreover, only men can experience together the magnetic forces of attraction and repulsion between themselves and objects. In *Orphée*, gloves serve not merely to penetrate the mirror – they also become an object of mutual exchange between Orphée and Heurtebise. Before they enter the Zone together Heurtebise appears to throw Orphée the gloves for him to wear, yet the action has, in fact, been shot in reverse, magnifying their rubbery effect. The same action is replayed in forward motion at the end of the film, as though the two characters are 'in' on a trick together. In the case of the 'unreasonable' Hibiscus flower in *Le Testament d'Orphée*, this is first presented by Cégeste to the Poet as an emblem of the Poet's destiny, but when Heurtebise attempts to return it as a gift to the Poet after his trial, the latter immediately refuses it; the camera promptly zooms back away from the object as if in curious empathy. Once in the Poet's hand it can often disappear, as when later it wafts away from under the sign *Pièges* ('Traps') (the accompanying bars of music reprise those that greeted our very first sighting of the flower in Cégeste's hand). It has become the object of some mysterious male force, as though (to quote the screenplay) 'Heurtebise, invisible, were lifting it away from him'.[38] It will eventually reappear at the end of the film when the Poet's ID card, falling to the ground between a policeman's boots, is suddenly transformed into an Hisbiscus flower, to be blown away by the car carrying the new wave of youth.

Such shared, composite moments between men in Cocteau's films have never really been acknowledged, yet they constitute an indefinable current of male desire with its own secret code and knowledge. This is formalized explicitly in *Orphée*, just after Eurydice has been spirited away by the Princess, and Orphée and Heurtebise finally meet together in close proximity in the conjugal bedroom. As Heurtebise comes up to Orphée from behind and slides his hand slowly into frame to rest on Orphée's shoulder, Orphée asks: 'How do you know such formidable things?', to which Heurtebise replies: 'Don't be naive. One isn't a driver like I am without knowing certain . . . formidable things.'[39] As with the multiple penetrations of the mirror into the Zone in *Orphée*, where we linger behind the character long enough to share the experience of a hand making contact with mercury, the viewer participates directly in this process. (The passage through the mirror by the Princess is almost perfunctory by comparison, as is the rapid restoration by reverse motion of the mirror that she smashes into pieces at one point prior to her return to the Zone.) This demonstrates once again that the real focus of interest in Cocteau is not the direction of the movement (here, the rather obvious phallic gestures of penetration) but rather, as in reverse motion, the presence of the object in all its new-found richness and posterior depth.

What I am arguing, in fact, is that the secret knowingness of male characters by means of objects is tied up directly with a Cocteau film's own playful, erotic knowledge of itself when it goes into reverse motion and makes objects out of human forms. This process culminates in the climactic scene of *Orphée* when, at the Princess's command (typically, she herself is not physically involved in the action), Orphée is 'killed' in the Zone in order that he might 'climb back up time' and return with Heurtebise to the real world by walking backwards. Shot from behind with his back to the wall, Orphée is suffocated by the hand of Heurtebise who appears as if to take him from behind while Cégeste holds down his feet. Here is how Cocteau savours this mock, gay Pietà in his screenplay:

> Heurtebise slips abruptly behind Orphée, closes his eyes and puts his hand over his mouth. Cégeste runs up from the left and holds down Orphée's legs with his outstretched arms. They immobilise him . . . Heurtebise lets go of Orphée's mouth and eyes and Orphée lets his head hang backwards, as if asleep . . . Orphée is seen asleep standing up, his head resting backwards on Heurtebise's shoulder, and Cégeste is up against Orphée's legs where he remains, curled up and still . . . The camera frames the two profiles – one upright, the other turned upside down – of Heurtebise and Orphée.[40]

The ravishing of Orphée has obvious counterparts, of course, in Cocteau's other films: the body of the black angel shot in negative over the schoolboy lying prone on the ground in *Le Sang d'un poète*, and the final shot of Cégeste 'crucifying' the Poet on the rocks before they both dissolve in *Le Testament d'Orphée*. In the case of the latter, what is stressed visually is the pushing of Cocteau's rear onto the stone surface, as though the only way out is via the rear. This is a kind of anal dissolve back into the bowels of the earth (cf. Cégeste's ironic comment: 'After all, the earth is not your country' ('La terre, après tout, n'est pas votre patrie')). At the same time, the gestures of the two men seem almost in preparation for a scene of oral sex, with Cégeste's legs bent down ready and the Poet's hands outstretched as though on a rack and waiting, perhaps like Ganymede, for Zeus to lift him away. (Cocteau refers in discussion of the film to the Poet's rapture (*enlèvement*) by Cégeste.)[41]

Such remarkable erotic focus on the male behind, part of a strong desire, if not compulsion, in Cocteau to look and take *a tergo*, is connected directly to the only image in Cocteau's cinema that he himself identified as erotic: the moment in *Le Sang d'un poète* when the poet (Enrique Rivero), having 'crawled, rolled and rubbed' his way along the corridor of the Hôtel des Folies dramatiques, is shot from behind on his knees as he peers through the keyhole of Room twenty-three, the room of the Hermaphrodite. Rivero is half-naked, his arms outstretched, and his buttocks protruding potently in his tight, pulled-up trousers. Cocteau's description in the screenplay is precise and to the point: 'Close-up of the poet putting his hands against the door and leaning against it. His back arches. The image should be sensual.'[42] If this arresting image of sensualness and Cocteau's comment on it have been recognized, they have not been followed up. Milorad is content to note 'an audacious allusion, exceptional in the author, to passive homosexuality' (Milorad qualifies this as 'frightening').[43] I propose that we rest a little longer on the image of Rivero's arching back, however, in order to appreciate its particular anal force within the context of the Hôtel des Folies dramatiques (the name of which, it is worth recalling, was derived from a popular cinema in Paris). For here Cocteau offers a *mise en scène* – as well as a concrete *mise en abyme* – of the normally phallicly defined scopic drive: we are invited to fix our eyes close-up on the poet as he steals his gaze through the various keyholes. The process is made fully self-reflexive at the keyhole of 'Room nineteen, Celestial Ceiling' where, as he tries to gain a better view of the Chinese opium den, the poet's gaze is met, in the terms of the screenplay, by the '[k]ey-holed shaped close-up of a *slit* eye approaching from the opposite direction'[44] (my emphasis). It is not clear for the viewer whether this is a reverse shot of the poet's eyes or another pair of eyes. All we know is that, at this particular moment, the subject of the gaze appears to become the object; active becomes passive; and the (slit) eye takes on the shape of the poet's (slit and curved) behind. The act of vision imposes itself, therefore, as both reversible and anal, a point that is underscored shortly afterwards when the poet is expelled backwards out of the mirror into his room (accompanied for those brief seconds by 'a religious choir of childish voices'). As such, it is intimately related to the sexual ambivalence of the Hermaphrodite who, with an incomplete, disembodied torso featuring a 'real male leg and real male arm', lifts

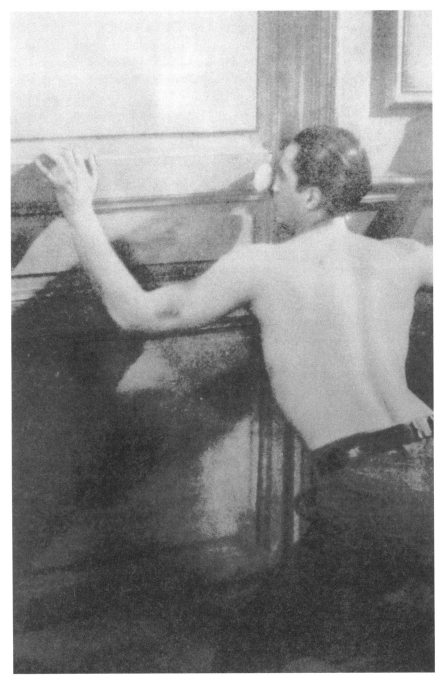

Figure 5.1 Enrique Rivero as the Poet in the Hôtel des Folies dramatiques, in Jean Cocteau's *Le Sang d'un Poète* (1932). Courtesy of the BFI

up a loin cloth covering the crotch and discloses a sign announcing the threat s/he represents: *Danger de mort* ('Danger of death'). Undifferentiation – at its most threatening in anality – is the real attraction and temptation, at once 'abysmal' and irresistible, that Cocteau's cinema sustains and is sustained by.[45]

That we should view this complex sensual moment in *Le Sang d'un poète* as emblematic of a general anal erotics of viewing in Cocteau's cinema – as opposed, say, to simply being a further expression of Cocteau's theory of art as herma-phroditic self-fertilization – is confirmed if we go briefly 'behind' the main corpus of films to consider the case of the little-known and rarely seen 16mm short, *La Villa Santo-Sospir* (colour, 1951), some of whose key moments (notably the petal restoration scene) will be transplanted later into *Le Testament d'Orphée*. This avowedly amateur work, where the elements of male body, natural object, physical space, rear viewing and the material effects of the camera are all simultaneously in play, indicates the path where Cocteau's cinema is always heading: a fact that perhaps explains why, in a diary he kept at the time, Cocteau considered the film an 'indiscretion' that should remain in safe obscurity for as long as possible. The tone of the film appears wonderfully light, its bright, summer documentary style enhanced by the fresh, compliant faces of Dermit and Mme Alec Weisweiller (the future Lady of *Le Testament d'Orphée*). Again, Cocteau ensures from the outset, almost effortlessly, an eclipse of the phallus: the new lighthouse on the Cap Santo-Sospir is shown hidden in scaffolding, an image that will be constantly repeated. There are recurring shots, too, of a water sprinkler revolving deliriously in a virtual send-up of virile male sexuality, while waves break orgiastically on to the rocks below in periodic inserts. In addition, and pushing the limits of public taste, Cocteau pictures himself campily mounted on life-size sculptures of animals. He is in equally playful and teasing mood on the sound-track, staggering certain details and promising to show some images later as he takes us on a tour of the villa that he has 'tatooed' with drawings and representations of Narcissus; Holofernes; Ulysses; sailors; the fishermen of Villefranche; Dionysus; Orpheus; Christ; Satan, and so forth. Clearly, since this is not his home (the villa belongs to Mme Weisweiller), Cocteau is never going to reveal the personal secrets of his own 'closet'! Instead, like a magic, prehistoric grotto of marvels, the drawings and silhouettes of naked men that he has assembled and superimposed over the surface of the villa's walls draw us deeper into the villa's own recesses, its tatooed skin constituting the very surface of the film. This creation of a continuous, sensuous and entirely self-reflexive environment, into which we are invited to sink with voluptuous pleasure, expands the endlessly enticing vat of mercury in *Orphée* and the 'night' through which the poet appears to swim back and forth in slow motion filling the frame in *Le Sang d'un poète*. It might even be said to correspond to Aaron Betsky's generalized concept of mirror space in his recent study of the relationship between architecture and same-sex desire. Queer mirror space is free and open, Betsky writes, and its goal is orgasm. It is a 'space in which your body dissolves into the world and your senses smooth all reality into continuous waves of pleasure. It only lasts for a moment, but during that movement you give yourself over to pure pleasure made flesh'.[46]

Yet *La Villa Santo-Sospir* is offered fundamentally as formal instruction in the techniques and sensations of reverse filming and viewing. It is an experiment in the newly accessible Kodachrome process of *contretype* (the name for an inter-mediate negative print derived from the original negative) that, according to Cocteau, 'disturbs [*perturbe*] colours at will'. He presents himself to the inter-pellated viewer (*vous*) as a willing hostage to cinematic fortune ('it is what the chemical baths wish, not me!'), and recommends that we step back from certain images in order to discern the empty spaces around the 'significant lines' – 'the insignificant lines must become significant' ('les lignes insignifiantes doivent devenir signifiantes'). Yet if potential new sites of signification are created, Cocteau also leaves it entirely to the viewer to formulate their erotic meaning. Taking as an example his own astonishing painting, *The Slaying of Holofernes*, that emphasizes less the Judith and Holofernes drama than the swarthy bodies of the sleeping guardsmen rolled up over themselves (a fact underlined when he revisits the painting in *Le Testament d'Orphée*), Cocteau states simply that to throw light in front of a painted image using Kodachrome film produces the abnormal effect of painted glass lit from behind. Furthermore, if Cocteau talks at length, even verbosely, about technical forms and processes, he never acknowledges the pervasive use of reverse motion photography in *La Villa Santo-Sospir*, which thus constitutes its great 'unsaid'. In fact, the intense and restless skirting with power-lessness that we have been witnessing in Cocteau's major films takes on a more far-reaching form here, since it is primarily his own body that he submits to the gaping voids and reversals possible in reverse motion photography. He films himself engaged in a range of bizarre activities: playing *boules* with and almost 'on to' and 'over' himself; 'peeling back together' petals of flowers; waiting to receive fragments of pottery that fly up into his hand; sketching forms by means of a rag; and so on. As in Cocteau's other films, there are moments when it is not clear whether we are experiencing forward or reverse motion: his own arm is pictured dropping down slowly in consecutive shots (but is it actually rising?); waves crash irregularly into themselves (or is it really back on to themselves?). The difference here, however, is that Cocteau deliberately sows doubt in the viewer's mind at the beginning of the film. After the opening series of views of the water-sprinkler in manic motion, we gradually realize in retrospect that it was rotating unnaturally in an anticlockwise direction. This realization undermines any confidence we might have in the direction of future shots: a dilemma Cocteau renders explicit when he films himself at one point in a high-angle silhouette giving an account of the geography of the area that cannot be followed, still less verified. This process of slow realization recalls in pictorial terms anamorphosis: a process of enormous interest to Cocteau and one where a picture (or part of a picture) gives a distorted image of the object represented until it is seen from a particular angle or by means of a special lens or mirror, whereupon it appears in lifelike aspect.[47] Unlike the classic example of anamorphosis, however, Holbein's painting *The Ambassadors*, that leads the viewer to a distorted skull, symbol of the brevity and nullity of all terrestrial goods, there is no obvious meaning to be read into Cocteau's perversion of cinematic form in *La Villa Santo-Sospir*, where object and aim are made continually reversible. Instead, we are forced to contemplate and accept permanent confusion and uncertainty. Yet paradoxically, this reality also ensures that we react with heightened sensitivity to all the visual forms displayed, which we must now take on their own terms and enjoy, simply and erotically, for what they are.

It is precisely the reversible, material effects of the cinematic machine in Cocteau's films, where we are brought face to face with the black hole of the Real, that encourage us to read the rear and reverse forms of movement and vision involving the male body through *mise en scène*, angle and framing as part of a mobile, anal erotic zone. The anal zone constitutes, of course, like the oral and phallic, one of the three main stages in the subject's libidinal economy determined by Freud, and it functions in Cocteau's films as the loose, indeterminate ground of all activity, long before the phallus can even attempt to rise (and fall). Which is to say, the more intrinsically filmic that film becomes in Cocteau – to repeat: the strange forms produced in the camera are not available or even conceivable during shooting – the more focused it is on what lies at the rear. The true, literal force of the Zone in *Orphée* as both a '*no man's* land' and site of *ruination* of men's habits (Heurtebise: 'It [the Zone] is made up of the memories of men and the ruins of their habits' ('Elle est faite des souvenirs des hommes et des ruines de leurs habitudes')) is now fully revealed. If *Le Testament d'Orphée* marks the culmination of Cocteau's experimentation in film, it is only because it takes to a new level a process of anal erotics set in motion by *Le Sang d'un poète* with its view of the framed, tight ass – the curve and slit – of the young poet. Ironically, the female figures in Cocteau's cinema end up incarnating the phallic instance because they are denied the additional anal pleasures of desymbolization and undifferentiation. (Chaste Minerva announces herself in *Le Testament d'Orphée* as 'The sad column. The virgin with an iron mask'.) In an interesting twist to the often-levelled charge of misogyny, Cocteau never allows his female characters the possibility of voluntary self-reification: when not turned into items of exchange (Heurtebise to Orphée: 'Je vous l'offre' [i.e. Eurydice]), they are instructed to get down on all fours like an animal simply to remain hidden from view. If women are active at all in Cocteau's films, it is only in a penetrative way through deadly acts of Reason (piercing, wounding). Hence, Mme Weisweiller may appreciate the queerness of the two-man dog in *Le Testament d'Orphée* ('I must say, everything is topsy-turvy [*de travers*] today', she exclaims), yet she remains at a safe distance from it while clutching her erect parasol.

La Belle et la bête, with its multiple manual protrusions from behind, sideways and below (the live arms holding candelabra and serving food from underneath the table, the smoking mouths and eyes of the caryatids) does no more than thematize and render explicit, therefore, what is always throbbing beneath and behind the surface of the screen in Cocteau's cinema: the erotic lure of the anal Other. Bearing in mind the homoerotic gender performance of *La Belle et la bête* as analysed by Susan Hayward (whereby Marais is the male suitor Avenant, Prince Charming and the linguistically confounding *la* Bête in feminine garb all rolled into one),[48] the recurring visions of terrible and abject matter in Cocteau may be viewed as an irresistible drawing out of the rectum in *rectus*. Queerness so defined is able, in return, to proliferate and establish itself as the 'normal'. At the end of *Orphee*, after Heurtebise and Orphée have returned from the Zone, the room is itself described now as the Zone.[49] The term 'Zone' could surely be said to apply not simply to the other world beyond the mirror, but to the entire enchanted, and ultimately unknowable, space – that literal, erotic *mise en abyme* – of a Cocteau film. As Cocteau puts it later in *Le Testament d'Orphée*: 'This body which contains us does not know ours./ What lives in us is lived in./ And these bodies, one inside the other/ Form the body of eternity.'[50] The viewer is obliged to enter this end-ZONE and experience the reversal and dispersal of the ONE: that is to say, a pre-specular, post-narcissistic, regard for the Other derived via – among other privileged objects – the framed male body.[51] For if Cocteau allows us to enjoy these at once regressive and generative moments, he also demands that we treat them seriously for what they are. They are not available for interpretation precisely because they are beyond interpretation or symbolization, as vague and stubbornly obscure as the very terms *truc*, *bête* and *zone*. 'We' are made privy to this process and wholly complicit with it, far more intensively even than Belle, who takes a while to grasp the complex nature of the pleasures handed to her in the warm, generous habitat of *la Bête*.

The theoretical implications of such non-phallic pleasure will become even clearer if we turn briefly to Lee Edelman's remarkable study of the visual rhetoric of anality in Alfred Hitchcock's *Rear Window* (1954), a film directly concerned, like so much of Cocteau's film-work, with vision and the scopic drive.[52] Edelman shows how an anal eroticism structures the rhythm of the whole film, disrupting narrative momentum to offer the glimpse of a purely rhythmic repetition that includes flashes of light and the shots of a blinding hole. The logic of the unconscious manifests itself in each of the protracted fade-outs that rhythmically punctuate *Rear Window*: fade-outs that articulate cinema's primal cut, or the enabling fissure that holds us tight with the strength of a sphincteral grip before its redemption through marriage to the order of visual productivity in the form of continuity editing and the hetero-genetic castration fetish.[53] The anal rhythm of *Rear Window* thus contradicts the clear-cut definition of sexed human characters invested with sexual identities through the logic – redemptive because also repro-ductive – of the castratory cut. According to Edelman, Hitchcock's film possesses an awareness of the anal hole as the lining of vision itself. Moreover, '[t]his return of the hole to consume the visual images it invariably frames testifies anew to the doubleness of vision, to the contradictions of desire, by which an anal libido compulsively burns its way through the Symbolic screen'.[54] In short, what *Rear Window* reveals is the 'originary' cut that threatens to rupture the Symbolic's signifying structure from within: the cut that marks the place of drives resistant to signification. In other words, '[a]ll vision takes place *through* the rear window it proposes to take the place *of*'.[55]

Edelman's account of *Rear Window* bears out what we have observed in Cocteau's films: namely, the anal foundation of vision and its central status as a compulsion. Yet Cocteau does not disavow or deny this anal dimension – there is no blind spot here as such. All his films invite us at different levels to look in the rear-view mirror and contemplate the originary castration, of which the herma-phrodite in *Le Sang d'un poète* is but a spectacular denial yet also a clear acknowledgement. Indeed, like the slowly gliding Sphinx at the end of *Le Testament d'Orphée* (and Edelman reminds us that Sphinx is etymologically cognate with 'sphincter', derived from the Greek *sphingein*, 'to hold tight'),[56] Cocteau positively revels in those moments of ambivalence and anal play when it is not clear that what we are watching is in the process of being formed or deformed – moments that totally undermine narrative continuity yet also, perversely, miraculously, ensure it. Edelman's study enables us, furthermore, to appreciate the particular importance of such odd scenes as the Poet's waiting inside the empty caves in *Le Testament d'Orphée*: a scene that is structured as a series of long and extra-long shots and where the dramatic detail is delayed. This turns out eventually to be the back-side of the court-usher (Yul Brynner) that occupies the frame while he bows down in front of the table, gradually to reveal the Poet's face in the upper portion of the frame. In a mockery of the shot/counter-shot formation, we are then positioned behind the Poet's *derrière* as he also bends down at the table, at which point he is instructed by the usher *not* to sign his name. ('There is no point in that. Go in without knocking.') What this brief scene exposes are the repudiated pulsions of the anus and the syncopated rhythms of withholding and producing: rhythms that make the anus the common denominator of such libidinal cuts or divisions as those between auto- and allo-eroticism, or between preserving and destroying the object. Cocteau's dazzling array of phallic shapes and forms – part of the poet's interminable, tragic ceremonial of life, death and resurrection, the bread and butter of his personal symbolic – constitutes, in the final analysis, nothing more than a customized, ornamental 'frame' for these other deeper, more intrinsically filmic pleasures generated internally within the camera. Indeed, the apparently extraneous, minor moments of rear and reverse motion in Cocteau's work actively challenge the castratory clarity of the more spectacular, frontal risings and resurrections produced through the very same process. It is not merely that Cocteau ensures a ruination of phallic masculinity, but that he actually proposes the site of this ruination – the insecurity and uncertainty of the abject and anal – as the very 'seat' of filmic thought. In view of the many close-up moments of intricate hand play in reverse motion photography – Cocteau's restoration of the Hibiscus flower next to the open rim of a flower pot, his drawing of the portrait by means of a rag – might we not also view these primary pleasures as a filmic version of 'fisting-as-*écriture*', Eve Kosofsky Sedgwick's term for Henry James's more private literary moments?[57] What else is one to make, after all, of those shots in *Orphée* of gloved hands slowly penetrating *into* resistant mercury and also penetrating *out of* it (the same shot in reverse): actions that seem even further provocative when reproduced in stills as set poses? Filmed in close-up, it is as if the projection screen had become an enormous membrane, an extension of the back passage of Saint-Cyr in the Zone through which Heurtebise and Orphée are painfully blown along, holding hands and in 'bizarre poses', as if by an immense force of suction.

Sublimation in Cocteau can therefore never be as simple as saying that filmic inversions and reversals provide formal evidence of his own 'inversion', or that they create a tension of styles between the straight and vertical (penetration; phallic piercings; risings) and the curved and circular (the rotating spiral of the herma-phrodite; the rolling Rolls; the dislocated mouth cupped in the poet's hand; a revolving pipe-cleaner figure; swirling water-sprinklers).[58] Certainly that tension exists, and it is there already in the opening credits where Cocteau usually writes the title – and sometimes more – in a cursive, childish writing before sealing it with his signature of the star. Yet from the very beginning of his film practice, in his prefatory remarks to *Le Sang d'un poète*, Cocteau had a profound and prescient sense of what really lies behind phallic 'axes', 'muzzles' and 'towers' of artistic sublimation – the raw material of blood and tears. He conveys this in the form of a rhetorical question: 'How much blood, how many tears in exchange for those axes, those muzzles, those unicorns, those torches, those towers, those martlets, those seedbeds of stars and those fields of blue!'[59] In a much later general account of artistic sublimation entitled 'Inedit féodal', he insists unequivocally on the 'depraved' sexual basis of supreme artistic endeavour:

> this sublime spirituality [Shakespeare etc.] is again, I repeat, a *debauchery and monstrous depravation* of the mind. Moreover, all lyricism is debauchery of the mind and results from depravation. If this depravation is hidden, it gives the work it inhabits a secret which impregnates it, flees from it, and envelops it with a *mysterious phosphorescence*.

It's in this way that certain peaceful works propose an enigma and become a vehicle between an artist's stormy soul and other souls like it. It must be a mechanism of this kind which accords the *Mona Lisa* the exceptional status it occupies. In short, a kind of rottenness where flies come to gather.[60] (my emphasis)

In Cocteau's own case, as we have seen, poetic gloss and phallic lift provide merely the distraction for a work shimmering in ambiguous textures and anfractuosities. This may help to explain his continued, almost pedantic insistence on the richly mysterious term 'cinématographe' as opposed to the now devalorized 'cinéma'. Furthermore, while he may refer almost instinctively to the process of creation and reception in phallic terms, reiterating phrases such as 'erections of the soul' and the 'hardening' of the work's moral progress, it is always with a giddy and excited leaning towards the potentially uncontrollable 'insignificant lines' ('my line is one of shocks and risks', as he once memorably put it).[61] In his astonishingly frank acceptance speech upon receiving in 1956 an honorary degree from the University of Oxford, Cocteau reminded his academic audience that we are both stirred by art as if by an 'internal erection *beyond our control*' and provoked by a 'kind of psychic sexuality'. In fact, the success of a Cocteau film is to be measured directly by the very 'insurmountable disturbance' it produces,[62] since, as we have seen, it can never be isolated from the immediate viewing experience where so much is reserved for the special pleasure of our eyes only. Forty years on from his death, Cocteau's extraordinary capacity to shatter one's preconceptions and illusions – not only about his work but also about the cinematic apparatus itself – is a marvellous thing.

Notes

In the notes that follow, all translations are my own unless otherwise indicated.

1. N. Greene (1988), 'Deadly Statues: Eros in the Films of Jean Cocteau', *The French Review*, 61, pp. 890–8. Greene, who emphasizes Cocteau's presentation of *Le Testament d'Orphée* as a 'striptease of the soul' both hallucinatory and oneiric, argues that Cocteau's masochistic film aesthetic is part of his general *désobéissance* regarding the rules of cinema. She links this idea of transgression to the creative artist's wish to scandalize the public which, as in the case of Pier Paolo Pasolini, may be regarded as one of sadomasochistic self-punishment and self-wounding.

2. See D. Gercke (1993), 'Ruin, Style and Fetish: The Corpus of Jean Cocteau', *Nottingham French Studies*, 32, pp. 10–18. Gercke's analysis of the 'jaunted, castrated, hysteric, dazzling' male bodies in Cocteau's films is premissed on a comparison of Cocteau's notion of the 'great night of the human body' with Freud's theory of the unconscious (cf. p. 10).

3. See D. Chaperon (1990), *Jean Cocteau: La Chute des angles*, Lille, and (1994) 'Jean Cocteau, un enfer tapissé de plumes', *Revue des Sciences Humaines*, 233, pp. 7–10.

4. G. Deleuze (1991), *Masochism*, trans. J. McNeill, New York; G. Deleuze (1967), *Présentation de Sacher-Masoch*, Paris. Deleuze's theory hinges on the suffering child/masochist undergoing a process not only of desexualization but even of death in order that a new self freed of the superego and sexuality can be born uniquely of the mother who, through disavowal, magically possesses a phallus.

5. See Greene, 'Deadly Statues', p. 894.

6. See Gercke, 'Ruin, Style and Fetish', p. 11.

7. Milorad (1981), '*Le Sang d'un poète*: Film à la première personne du singulier', *Cahiers Jean Cocteau*, 9, pp. 269–334. Milorad (who also edited the *Cahiers Jean Cocteau*) makes extensive use of his own intimate knowledge of Cocteau's life and work, as well as of Cocteau's father (who killed himself and was most probably a closet gay) and lovers such as Raymond Radiguet, whom Milorad links to the paternal figure of the angel of death in *Le Sang d'un poète*. Nothing is left to chance by Milorad. In Cocteau's unconscious, he writes, the homo-sexual love object always links back fatally to the figure of Cocteau's father whom it thus reincarnates. For this reason, death becomes one of the key attributes of the gay love object (e.g. the boy Dargelos in *Le Sang d'un poète*). According to Milorad, homosexual love in Cocteau is accompanied uncons-ciously by a desire for murder and emasculation, followed immediately by punishment through the eternal law of 'an eye for an eye'. Milorad ultimately reduces the entire corpus to this one compex, making all female subjets and objects of death and deathliness in Cocteau representations of the paternal figure of suicide.

8. See also R. Dyer (1990), *Now You See It: Studies on Lesbian and Gay Film*, London, pp. 63-74, which places Cocteau within a high literary tradition of gay aestheticism, one of cult as cultivation. Dyer makes the valid point that the heterosexuality of the Orpheus/Eurydice legend is simply displaced in *Orphée* into a relationship between Eurydice and Heurtebise, while Orphée's passion is reserved for Death (the Princess) and Cégeste whom he has seen die in an accident.

9. See C. Rolot and F. Ramirez (1992), 'Le Rôle des trucages dans la "Poésie de Cinéma" de Jean Cocteau ou "les tours d'Orphée"', *Quaderni del Novecento Francese*, 15, pp. 163–75, pp. 173–4. Rolot and Ramirez list a two-fold increase

in cinematic tricks between *Orphée* and *Le Testament d'Orphée*. For the record, they list 23 *zones* in *Orphée* (17 are due to *mise en scène*, the seven crossings through the mirror being of a different nature), 47 *plages* in *Le Testament d'Orphée* (60 per cent are mechanical, and even when *plages mixtes,* mechanically derived tricks are the greater: 20 cases of appearance/disappearance by superimposition, 10 instances of reverse motion photography, and 6 sequences of slow motion). Rolot and Ramirez emphasize the importance of the title of *Le Testament d'Orphée* to argue that in his last film Cocteau is focusing exclusively on the 'unreal of time', and that what is really 'tricked' is narration (i.e. the play with different time zones). It could be argued, however, that there is even more work on time in the narration precisely because there is more exploration, or 'distortion', of space and the system of visual representation. My contention, in fact, will be that Cocteau's intricate play with the mirror in *Orphée* – where the extensive use of stand-ins produces some reflections which are clearly false but which we are prepared to believe in anyway, so powerful is the overall effect – is effectively taken to a new level in *Le Testament d'Orphée* through reverse motion photography, whereby impossible actions and events can occur and still be read as real precisely because they have been filmed (part of Cocteau's general concept of cinematic truth or *vérisme*). In both cases, what is showcased is the physicality and sensation of objects.

10. Gercke, 'Ruin, Style and Fetish', p. 17.
11. See D. Dittrich (1997), 'Les Chiffres du poète – Les "Trucs" du cinématographe', *Oeuvres et Critiques*, 22, pp. 170–84. Dittrich shows the degree of confusion and overlap in Cocteau's use of the terms *trucages*, *truc* and *(la) truca* (special lab effects), that cover both discoveries and 'faults' and can also, of course, refer to sound-effects. Cocteau claimed not to indulge in *truca* although this is patently not always the case.
12. J. Cocteau (1985), *Two Screen Plays: The Blood of a Poet/The Testament of Orpheus*, trans. C. Martin-Sperry, London and New York, p. 102. 'Vous êtes-vous demandé ce qui m'arriverait après l'arrestation de Heurtebise et de la Princesse? Avez-vous pensé une minute que vous me laissiez seul et où?'
13. See J.-P. Fargier (1992), 'La Marche arrière', *Vertigo*, 9, pp. 101–3.
14. 'Il n'y a jamais de symbole. Il n'y en a pas dans la fleur. J'ai choisi l'hibiscus, parce qu'il y a des hibiscus chez Mme Weisweiller, parce que c'est commode à déchirer. De plus c'est la fleur de Cagliostro. Quand je la reconstitue, mes mains sont des animaux. Elles sont détachées de moi, elles vivent comme des bêtes. Mais il ne suffit pas de tourner à l'envers, il faut, tout le temps, que je joue avec mes mains de telle sorte que ça n'ait pas l'air d'être tourné à l'envers. Il y a là autant de création que dans une scène jouée par Madame Réjane ou par Madame Sarah Bernhardt. Je ne me vante pas: j'essaie de vous montrer

combien tout cela représente de travail.' J. Cocteau, with J. Domarchi and J.-L. Laugier, (1960), 'Entretien avec Jean Cocteau', *Cahiers du cinéma*, 19, pp. 1–20, p. 10.

15. *Two Screen Plays*, p. 104. 'Un film est une source pétrifiante de la pensée. Un film ressuscite les actes morts. Un film permet de donner l'apparence de la réalité à l'irréel.'

16. J. Cocteau (1972), *Cocteau on the Film: Conversations with Jean Cocteau recorded by André Fraigneau*, trans. L. Traill, introduced by G. Amberg, New York, p. 17.

17. Domarchi and Laugier, 'Entretien avec Jean Cocteau', p. 10.

18. *Two Screen Plays*, p. 74. 'Si le film l'avait voulu à l'origine, c'est qu'il avait ses raisons où la raison n'avait que faire. Et je me contentais de lui obéir.'

19. '[. . .] au lieu de perdre tout contrôle comme il arrive dans le rêve, je célèbre les noces du conscient et de l'inconscience qui mettent au monde ce monstre terrible et délicieux qu'on appelle *poésie*'. J. Cocteau (1988), *Du cinématographe* (rev. edn), Paris, p. 150.

20. See J. Cocteau (1943), *Le Mythe du Gréco*, Paris.

21. See C. Foucart (1997), 'Cocteau et l'écriture du corps', *Oeuvres et Critiques*, 22, pp. 185–96. Foucart refers also to the long unpublished poems 'Le Rythme grec' and 'Un ami dort', the latter of which includes the line 'Love turns lovers into a single monster of joy'.

22. 'Un no man's land entre la vie et la mort. On n'y est ni tout à fait mort, ni tout à fait vivant.' E. Freeman (ed.) (1992), *Jean Cocteau, Orphée: The Play and the Film*, London, p. 64.

23. See J.L. Schefer (1995), *The Enigmatic Body: Essays on the Arts*, trans. P. Smith, Cambridge, in particular 'The Plague' (pp. 37–53) (on Uccello's *Deluge*), and 'Cinema' (pp. 108–38).

24. See Milorad, '*Le Sang d'un poète*: Film à la première personne du singulier', pp. 310–12. Uccello's predella depicts in anti-semitic terms the profanation of a consecrated host. A Jewish usurer throws on to the fire a consecrated Host he had obliged a Christian woman to give him and it quickly begins to bleed. The woman is eventually hanged, and, in the particular episode chosen by Cocteau, soldiers assail the usurer and his family in their home. The usurer will eventually be burned alive just as he had burned the host. The 'host', of course, while a specific reference to Christ whose sacrifice upon the Cross and in the breaking of bread at the Last Supper is commemorated liturgically in the Eucharist, is derived more generally from the Latin *hostia*, meaning a victim sacrificed to the gods to propitiate their anger. In *Le Sang d'un poète*, the 'host' is the schoolboy struck down and 'profaned' by his school-friend Dargelos's snowball. This Christian/pagan tension is explored as one among many in F.-J. Albersmeier (1997), 'Tensions intermédiales et symbolique

multimédiale dans *Le Sang d'un poète* de Jean Cocteau', *Oeuvres et Critiques*, 22, pp. 162–9.

25. *Two Screen Plays*, p. 8. 'Tout poème est un blason. Il faut le déchiffrer.'
26. Ibid., p. 8. 'et leur substitue des actes ou allégories de ces actes, sur lesquels puisse symboliser le spectateur, si bon lui semble'.
27. *Jean Cocteau, Orphée*, p. 65.
28. *Two Screen Plays*, p. 46. 'Le sang lui coule de la bouche et y forme des bulles. Il gémit. Il entr'ouvre les yeux. Cette image doit être pénible.'
29. Ibid., p. 107. 'cette fleur est faite de votre sang, elle épouse les syncopes de votre destin'.
30. 'L'espèce de ravissement qui nous transporte au contact de certaines oeuvres provient rarement d'un appel aux larmes, d'un effet de surprise. Il est plutôt, je le répète, provoqué de manière inexplicable par une brèche qui s'ouvre à l'improviste.

    Cette brèche se produira dans un film au même titre que dans une tragédie, un roman ou un vers. Le ravissement ne viendra pas des facilités qu'il offre aux stratagèmes. Il viendra de quelque faute, de quelque syncope, de quelque rencontre fortuite entre l'attention et l'inattention de son auteur.', J. Cocteau (1995), 'Du merveilleux au cinématographe', in *Jean Cocteau: Romans, Poésies, Oeuvres diverses*, Paris, pp. 890–4, p. 892.
31. See S. Shaviro (1993), 'Film Theory and Film Fascination', *The Cinematic Body*, Minneapolis, pp. 1–65, pp. 50–65.
32. See J. Laplanche (1976), 'Aggressiveness and Sadomasochism', in *Life and Death in Psychoanalysis*, trans. J. Mehlman, Baltimore. Laplanche analyzes a passage from Freud's 'Instincts and their Vicissitudes' (1915) to demonstrate that not only is the masochistic fantasy fundamental, but also it is within the suffering position that all pleasure resides.
33. 'Cette fois, dans mon film, j'ai pris bien garde à ce que les truquages soient au service de la ligne interne et non pas de la ligne externe de la bande. Ils doivent m'aider à rendre cette ligne aussi souple que celle d'un homme qui "gamberge", pour employer ce terme admirable mais qu'on ne trouve pas dans notre dictionnaire. Gamberge signifie laisser l'esprit suivre son cours sans contrôle et sans correspondre ni au rêve, ni à la rêverie, ni à la rêvasserie, permettre à nos idees les plus intimes (les plus emprisonées en nous) de prendre la fuite et de passer sans être vues devant les gardes. Tout le reste n'est que "thèse" et "brio". L'un et l'autre me rebutent.', Cocteau, *Du cinématographe*, p. 143.
34. 'Tournée à reculons . . . une bande révèle un univers, une manière d'agir et une langue si plausible que cette langue bizarre se pourrait apprendre et que, me voyant partir du bord du vide sans crainte, les projectionnistes ne pouvaient s'empêcher de pousser un cri d'avertissement chaque fois que le recul me

faisait m'approcher de dos du même vide.', R. Pillaudin (1960), *Jean Cocteau tourne son dernier film*, Paris, p. 11.

35. *Two Screen Plays*, p. 94. 'Cet homme-cheval m'avait déplu. Je devinais qu'il m'attirait dans un piège et que j'aurais mieux fait de ne pas le suivre.'

36. 'Apprendrez-vous jamais à ne pas regarder en arrière. A ce petit jeu, il y en a qui se changent en statues de sel.', *Jean Cocteau, Orphée*, p. 100.

37. 'Merci, pour que les phrases recommencent dès que j'aurai tourné le dos.', *Jean Cocteau, Orphée*, p. 88.

38. *Two Screen Plays*, p. 120. 'comme si Heurtebise, invisible, la lui enlevait'.

39. 'Orphée: Comment savez-vous toutes ces choses redoutables? Heurtebise: Ne soyez pas naïf. On n'est pas le chauffeur que je suis sans apprendre certaines choses . . . redoutables.', *Jean Cocteau, Orphée*, p. 101.

40. 'Heurtebise, brusquement, se glisse derrière Orphée, lui ferme les yeux et la bouche avec les mains. Cégeste arrive en courant par la gauche et empoigne les jambes d'Orphée à pleins bras. Ils l'immobilisent . . . Heutebise lâche la bouche et les yeux d'Orphée qui laisse sa tête pendre en arrière, comme endormie . . . On voit Orphée endormi debout, la tête en arrière sur l'épaule de Heurtebise, Cégeste contre les jambes d'Orphée où il demeure, recroquevillé, immobile . . . L'appareil cadre les deux profils. L'un droit, l'autre à la reverse, de Heurtebise et d'Orphée.', Ibid., p. 122.

41. Cocteau, *Du cinématographe*, p. 142.

42. *Two Screen Plays*, p. 32. 'Gros plan du poète qui met ses mains contre la porte et s'y applique. Son dos se creuse. L'image doit être sensuelle.'

43. Milorad, '*Le Sang d'un poète*: Film à la première personne du singulier', p. 304. Cocteau's promotion of the passive position elsewhere in his work is worth emphasizing. See, for example, his poem 'L'Ange Heurtebise' from the collection *Opéra* (1925–7), directly cited by Cocteau in *Le Testament d'Orphée*. This includes the following lines: 'L'ange Heurtebise, d'une brutalité/ Incroyable saute sur moi. De grâce/ Ne saute pas si fort./ Garçon bestial, fleur de haute/ Stature.', Cocteau, *Jean Cocteau: Romans, Poésies, Oeuvres diverses*, p. 331 ('The angel Heurtebise, with an unbelievable/ brutality jumps on to me. For goodness sake!/ Do not jump so hard/ Bestial boy, flower of high Stature'). In Milorad (1979) 'Esquisse d'une théorie de la sexualité', *Cahiers Jean Cocteau*, 8, pp. 132–41, which brings together a variety of published and unpublished texts by Cocteau, Milorad shows that this literary representation of gay sex, where the passive partner is not at all feminized or effeminate, contrasts with Cocteau's other recorded view that homosexuality is primarily an 'exchange of forces' and a matter of virility (cf. p. 135). Milorad suggests, probably correctly, that when Cocteau celebrates sexual force and the active penetrative role, he is really indulging in wishful thinking and secondary rationalizations. The biographical specifics of Cocteau's sexuality, however, are beyond the scope and focus of this chapter.

44. *Two Screen Plays*, p. 31. 'On voit, en gros plan, dans un cache en forme de trou de serrure, un oeil bridé qui s'approche en sens inverse.'

45. It is perhaps worth noting here Cocteau's generalized notion of sexual activity. Already in *Opium* (1930) he was proposing that a 'normal man' ought to be capable of making love with anyone and anything, since all that really counts is the sexual act itself, not the particular person or individual involved. As Milorad rightly remarks in 'Esquisse d'une théorie de la sexualité' (cf. pp. 136–7), this bears comparison with Freud's polymorphous pervert and may help, in part, to explain Cocteau's interest in Walt Whitman.

46. A. Betsky (1997), *Queer Space: Architecture and Same-Sex Desire*, New York, p. 21.

47. See, for example, J. Cocteau (1981), 'Notes autour d'une anamorphose: un phénomène de réflexion', *Cahiers Jean Cocteau*, 9, pp. 245–57, where Cocteau extends the notion of anamorphosis to include also the perception of time, or what he calls 'ce capharnaüm du temps'.

48. See S. Hayward (1990), 'Gender Politics – Cocteau's Belle is not that Bête: Jean Cocteau's *La Belle et la bête* (1946)', in S. Hayward and G. Vincendeau (eds), *French Film: Texts and Contexts*, London and New York, pp. 127–35. Emphasizing those moments in the film of la Bête's narcissism, autoeroticism and erotico-voyeurism, Hayward reveals how the linguistic conditions that govern recognition and identity have been removed. *La* Bête is referred to simultaneously as *il* and *elle*, a fact complemented by his/her appearance (the curves of the robe and curved lace collar, matched by lace around the boots). Hayward argues that 'misrecognition occurs through the shifting of the representations of la Bête's 'otherness' (cf. p. 130). Hence, although all three main roles are melded at the point of transformation into one – Marais – this cannot be considered pure narcissism because reflection can no longer occur. It is the moment of participation in desire of which Cocteau speaks in *Le Livre blanc* (1928); that is, the moment when a young man unknowingly presses his fully naked body against a two-way mirror, on the other side of which stands the narrator. Hayward concludes very persuasively that the final transformation of la Bête into Prince Charming provoked by the shooting of Avenant in the back by Diana's arrow represents homoerotically the release into beauty and love of one man by another.

49. 'La chambre. On les voit traverser le miroir et entrer dans la chambre. La zone.' *Jean Cocteau, Orphée*, p. 123. 'The bedroom. We see them crossing through the mirror and entering the bedroom. The zone.'

50. *Two Screen Plays*, p. 107. 'Ce corps qui nous contient ne connaît pas les nôtres./ Qui nous habite est habité./ Et ces corps les uns dans les autres/ Sont le corps de l'éternité.'

51. One might compare this type of post-narcissistic engagement with otherness with Leo Bersani and Ulysse Dutoit's concept of difference as a 'non-threatening supplement to sameness', as expressed in their study of a more recent gay filmmaker, Derek Jarman. See L. Bersani and U. Dutoit (1999), *Caravaggio*, London. Here, they privilege those moments in Jarman where tenderness is revealed as dependent on a certain degree of self-recognition in the object we reach toward. Unlike specular narcissism, the narcissism represented during such moments facilitates contacts with the world rather than imprisoning the subject in solipsistic relations to others. A non-antagonistic relation to difference, they argue, 'depends on this inaccurate replication of the self *in* difference, on our recognizing that *we are already out there*. Self-love initiates the love of others; the love of the same does not erase difference when it takes place as a dismissal of the prejudicial opposition between sameness and difference. Difference can then be loved as a non-threatening supplement to sameness' (cf. pp. 71–2). The conclusion Bersani and Dutoit reach in their study of Jarman's *Caravaggio* (1986) enables us to grasp the full power of the final, anally directed image of *Le Testament d'Orphée* where Cocteau is 'crucified' by Dermit and they both then slowly dissolve: 'The replicability of being gives rise to an expansive rather than a self-enclosing narcissism . . . *Caravaggio* emphasizes the ontological dignity of an uncertain or fleeting visibility, of pushing beyond our form in order to circulate within universal similitudes . . . In identifying himself with Caravaggio's identification with Christ, Jarman submitted to the beneficent martyrdom of art. . . . a suffering (a loss of self) exactly identical to a potentially ecstatic Passion, that of self-dispersion. *Caravaggio* entombs that nakedly anxious self, resurrecting it, transformed, as ontological disclosure, as uncircumscribable reappearances within the plentitude of Being.' (cf. pp. 80–1).

52. See L. Edelman (1999), '*Rear Window*'s Glasshole', in E. Hanson (ed.), *Out Takes: Essays on Queer Theory and Film*, Durham and London, pp. 72–96, p. 83. Edelman invokes D.A. Miller (1991), 'Anal *Rope*', in D. Fuss (ed.), *Inside/Out: Lesbian Theories, Gay Theories*, New York and London, pp. 119–41. This latter piece first proposed the anus as a site and rhythm of cutting.

53. Edelman, '*Rear Window*', p. 83.

54. Ibid., p. 90.

55. Ibid., p. 92.

56. Ibid., p. 79.

57. See E.K. Sedgwick (1993), 'Is the Rectum Straight?: Identification and Identity in *Wings of the Dove*', in *Tendencies*, Durham and London, pp. 73–106. Referring in particular to James's 'Notebooks', Sedgwick shows that James's highly charged associations concerning the anus did not cluster around images of the phallus, but rather the hand (cf. p. 99). Crucially for our discussion,

Sedgwick argues that the fisting image offers a switchpoint between those polarities which a phallic economy defines as active and passive (cf. p. 101). It could be argued that such moments in Cocteau's work as his 'crucifixion' by Dermit constitute a deliberate attempt on his part to reverse in art the power dynamic that clearly exists with his lovers-cum-collaborators, where he effectively always holds the phallus. This dynamic is made spectacularly clear in a photograph by Robert Doisneau taken in 1949 during the shooting of *Orphée* called simply 'Jean Marais, Jean Cocteau', where Cocteau, looking towards the camera amusedly, directs the index figure of his outstretched hand towards the back of Marais who stands in front of him, apparently unaware. The sexual and aesthetic implications of the Cocteau-Marais partnership are discussed at length in J.S. Williams (forthcoming), *Jean Cocteau*, Manchester.

58. See in this regard M. Mourier (1997), 'Quelques aspects de la poétique cinématographique de Cocteau', *Oeuvres et Critiques*, 22, pp. 152–61, on style in *La Belle et la bête*. Mourier proposes *La Belle et la bête*, with its Doré-like flowing curbs (the 'serpentine extravagances' of the famous sheet scene) and Vermeer-like concision and clarity (the film's 'disturbing strangeness'), as a form of resolution of two major opposing strands in Cocteau's work. At no time, however, is this double movement linked to questions of gender or sexuality.

59. *Two Screen Plays*, p. 8. 'Que de sang, que de larmes, en échange de ces haches, de ces gueules, de ces licornes, de ces torches, de ces tours, de ces merlettes, de ces semis d'étoiles et de ces champs d'azur!'

60. 'cette spiritualité sublime [Shakespeare, etc.] est encore, je le répète, *une débauche, une dépravation monstrueuse* de l'esprit. Au reste, tout lyrisme est une débauche de l'esprit et résulte d'une dépravation. Si cette dépravation se cache, elle donne à l'oeuvre qu'elle habite un secret qui l'imprègne, s'en échappe, l'enveloppe d'une *phosphorescence mystérieuse*. C'est de la sorte que certaines oeuvres calmes proposent une énigme et deviennent un véhicule entre l'âme tumultueuse d'un artiste et d'autres âmes qui lui ressemblent. Ce doit être un mécanisme de ce genre qui vaut à la Joconde la place exceptionnelle qu'elle occupe. Bref, une manière de pourriture où viennent se mettre les mouches'. J. Cocteau (1979), 'Inédit féodal', *Cahiers Jean Cocteau*, 8, pp. 142–4, p. 143.

61. See 'De la ligne' (from *La Difficulté d'être*) in Cocteau, *Jean Cocteau: Romans, Poésies, Oeuvres diverses*, pp. 962–6, p. 965. 'ma ligne est de chocs et de risques'.

62. See J. Cocteau (1956), *Discours d'Oxford*, Paris.

–6–

Setting the Agenders: Simone Signoret – The Pre-Feminist Star Body
Susan Hayward

Introduction

In 1971, Simone Signoret (1921–85) signed up to the *Manifeste des 343 'Salopes'*, a petition signed by French women in the public eye who had had illegal abortions or who advocated women's right to abort. In two interviews given in 1973, to *La Tribune de Genève* and *Elle*, she is on record as saying the following in relation to abortion and the *MLF* (the French feminist *Mouvement de Libération des Femmes*):

> I have sided with the women of the *MLF* as long as they have acted in challenging and even provoking ways, as for example with free abortion on demand.[1]

> Without them [the *MLF* activists], this terrible problem of abortion would still be where it has languished for so long.[2]

> Let her who has never miscarried shut up. I have, and the MLF activists deserve everybody's thanks.[3]

But equally, disassociating herself from the *MLF*, she states:

> I didn't wait for these ladies of the *MLF* in order to become emancipated . . . I don't like the *MLF* racism against men . . . I leave them entirely when they practise racism, sexism as the intellectuals say; that is, when they reject man.[4]

In her *Tribune de Genève* interview, moreover, Signoret readily admits that she is not a 'woman's woman', being far more moved by a man's sorrow than by a woman's tears. A few years later, in discussion with Jacques Chancel (*Radioscopie*, 11 November 1976), she again acknowledges that she is not a feminist, but adds that she has nothing against the *MLF* and supports their struggle for equal pay and free abortion. She has never been a victim of men, she claims, and ascribes her lack of feminist tendencies to the fact that 'I am deeply Mediterranean and, by instinct, submissive to the man I love' ('Je suis profondément méditerranéenne et d'instinct soumise à l'homme que j'aime').

This chapter is not therefore going to contend that Signoret was a feminist before her time. Rather, it will read her through what I shall term her performativity. I take performativity here to refer to the star persona's body as site of (gender and sexual) performance, to the body-as-performance. What my discussion will propose is that by virtue of her particular mode of performativity – a performativity through which (particularly in post-war films up until 1960) she plays with gender fixity and which gave pleasure to men and women equally – Signoret, as star and body text,[5] disturbed audiences more profoundly than contemporaries such as Jeanne Moreau and Martine Carol. The first part of the chapter delineates the earlier phase of Signoret's career (1945–1960), and provides a broad study of her star body. The second part scrutinizes two films (*Les Diaboliques* (1955) and *Les Mauvais Coups* (1960/1961)), and takes as its central focus Signoret's play with sexuality. In the conclusion, I shall suggest that her performativity incorporates a politicization of the (gendered) body: a politicization that Signoret carries forward into her post-1960 films and that caused her to be considered as much a *monstre sacré* in the domain of politics as in cinema. And I shall argue that it is in this light that we can today view Simone Signoret as a 'pre-feminist' star body.

Before beginning, however, it is worth pausing for just a moment to situate Signoret vis-à-vis a number of other French female star bodies. Jeanne Moreau (b. 1928), who became a fetish-star of the French New Wave, was perceived (argu-ably with Anna Karina, b. 1940) as the first modern woman and first star body since Arletty to project a troubling eroticism. Unlike Moreau, Signoret never became a New Wave icon.[6] Indeed, as Signoret herself says, in the minds of the New Wave film-makers, she was part of the *cinéma de papa* they rejected.[7] She was, however, only seven years Moreau's senior. Furthermore, what is sometimes forgotten with regard to Moreau is that, until she met Louis Malle and starred in his first film, *Ascenseur pour l'échafaud* (1957), and more especially his *Les Amants* (1958), in which she enacts an orgasm on screen, she played a variety of roles that were not too dissimilar to Signoret's (tart, call girl, and so forth). The major difference is that Moreau often took on secondary or lesser roles, as opposed to the central roles Signoret assumed. Moreau's work with Malle would change all that. But, until her collaboration with Malle, Moreau, in a sense, played against the stage/star persona for which she was more renowned. Her film career, then, commenced around the same time as Signoret's. She appears in fanzines in the early 1950s, as did Signoret and Martine Carol. Currently, we tend to forget that Moreau was in the public eye in the 1950s, because her true years of stardom were the 1960s. And her sexually challenging self-enactments as androgyn or as double-gendered really only began with François Truffaut's *Jules et Jim* (1961).

Within sound cinema history, it is almost certainly Arletty who first presented a challenge – as a woman – to gender fixity. Although Arletty always publicly denied her lesbianism, within the inner studio circle her proclivities were well known.[8] But, given that she was placed under house arrest after the Occupation for sleeping with the (male) enemy, it would seem safer to credit her with being bisexual. Undoubtedly, her own gender and sexual mutability contributed to her striking star performances: performances that were strong and rude, attracting men and women alike. I have argued elsewhere that Signoret assumed Arletty's mantle of gender disruption through her own performativity.[9] Signoret was not only a beauty in the 1940s and 1950s, but gave every evidence of intelligence, lucidity and, especially, insolence. Her beauty was not that of Martine Carol (a female matinée idol if ever there was one), nor that of Brigitte Bardot. If Bardot embodied 'total' beauty, then Signoret transcended beauty, or was more than beauty alone. As Signoret said, beauty enervates ('la beauté agace'),[10] and can provoke stereo-typing, as Bardot certainly discovered. Stereotyping was a danger for Signoret, too, especially given that, in the heyday of her beauty, she was typically offered roles as a prostitute or a scheming woman. Signoret was aware that the body-text, once on display, was potentially an unliberating text to inhabit. The challenge was to make it function as a system of signs that communicated not myths of woman but something else. Meeting this challenge has been Signoret's trajectory since her earliest triumphs through to her very last film. Signoret's work gives us to believe that she is always already more than her sex. In illustration of this, later on in this chapter, I shall examine two of her star vehicles (*Les Diaboliques* and *Les Mauvais Coups*) as exemplars of her resistance to the ideological construction of the gendered subject.

Signoret – The 'Beauty' Years: Fifteen Years in the Frame (1945–1960)

Simone Signoret first achieved notoriety in her second major film role – that of a prostitute – in Marcel Blistène's 1946 film *Macadam*. But she had already come to attention as the beautiful Lili, a barmaid working in Northern Africa, in Yves Allégret's 1945 war/Resistance film, *Les Démons de l'aube*, a film whose kiss scene, for the critic Georges Baume, was the revelation of Signoret: 'she made of this kiss one of the most healthily erotic moments of cinema of that period'.[11] These early central roles won her the prestigious Suzanne Bianchetti award for most promising actor/actress in 1947. By 1948 she was on the front cover of *Cinémonde*, one of France's top film magazines. And by 1949, *L'Ecran français* – the leftwing film weekly – published a six-part series on her entitled 'Simone Signoret: L'Enfant du Siècle'. Critical reviews of her performance were already signalling her difference from other young and somewhat more established stars. She was 'devilishly seductive', 'disturbing'.[12] She was distinctive, in short, and stood out as such.

So much has been made of Signoret's post-1960 loss of looks that it is worth reminding ourselves that it was some fifteen years after her first major role that her beauty began to decline (albeit rapidly), by which time she was forty years old. I do not propose to dwell on this deterioration in this chapter, since I have discussed it elsewhere.[13] What I wish to do first, rather, is to map out Signoret's filmography from 1945 to 1960 (see Table 6.1) and thereby to give an overview of the film genres and types of role she embodied. Excluding two films where she had very small cameo roles, Signoret made eighteen films during this period, averaging just over one film per year, although some years were fallow and others quite rich. And she engaged in four categories of film genre. First, she made Resistance or political films, in which she is part of the resisting ensemble. Second, there are the tart (*garce*) films in which she plays either a golden-hearted prostitute

Table 6.1 Films with Simone Signoret, 1945–1960

Resistance/political	Tart/garce	Melodrama	Thriller
Les Démons de l'aube (1945/6)	Macadam (1946)		
Against the Wind (1947)	Dédée d'Anvers (1947/8)	Fantômas (1947)*	
	L'Impasse des deux anges (1948)	Le Traqué (1950)*	
	Manèges (1949/50)	Ombre et lumière (1950/1)	
	La Ronde (1950)	Thérèse Raquin (1953)*	
	Casque d'or (1951/2)	Room at the Top (1959)	Les Diaboliques (1954/5)
Les Sorcières de Salem (1956/7)	La Mort en ce jardin (1956)	Les Mauvais Coups (1960/1)	
	Adua et ses compagnes (1960/1)		
3 films	8 films	6 films	1 film

N.B. Where two dates are given, the first is the production date, the second the release date.

or a scheming woman, always a product of the working class. (Sometimes, she is a schemer or a gangster's mistress who makes it into the middle class.) Third, she starred in melodramas. In these latter films, in which she is located as middle-class, she is either the victim of someone else's scheme, or a central player, or a winner/loser in a love story. Finally, we must not forget her thriller films. Signoret only acted in one true thriller, *Les Diaboliques*, where once again she is middle-class: however, certain of her melodramas border on the thriller format (asterisked in Table 6.1 to show that they cross genres).

Table 6.1 reveals that Signoret is more readily identifiable with so-called women's genres (cf. the two central columns), but does make inroads, as a central player, into two film categories conventionally taken as men's genres (Resistance and thriller films). In two of the films in which she does so – *Against the Wind* and *Les Diaboliques* – Signoret embodies a woman of force. In the first, she is a Belgian resister who must eventually gun down the traitor in the group. Furthermore, she is one of the senior organizers in the Resistance cell and has, in consequence, considerable authority. She occupies then, on two counts at least, positions within this type of film that are traditionally identified as more masculine than feminine. Similarly, in *Les Diaboliques*, she is no straightforward *femme fatale*. She stands in a place of power, in which she directs the action of murder and sees it through to the bitter end. She is without remorse once she is caught for her crime, and goes to her death head held proudly high. She is, in sum, as completely bad as any male cinematic counterpart would be.

There are further things that we can say in relation to the eighteen films under discussion here. Signoret was a stunning beauty during the period in which they were made, so we need to reflect on the sort of body-spaces/texts she occupies within them. In order to do so, I want to focus on the first category of film invoked above, Signoret's Resistance or political films. In these films, her star body is both sexualized and politicized. She holds true to her principles, engaging in verbal show-downs with people who show either treachery, cowardice or lack of solidarity. She also kisses in two of them, and is the agent of the kiss, not the receiver. She kisses the timid (and virginal) young soldier in *Les Démons de l'aube*, with the intense erotic impact referred to above. Her kiss in *Against the Wind* is filmed with an extraordinary sensuality, moving into full close-up on her closed eyes whose stunning long eyelashes caress her radiant cheeks. The same shot holds the fullness of her lips as she desiringly seeks out her lover's mouth. It is a truly dangerous kiss, and it is Signoret who kisses; she goes toward her man and embraces him fully. In *Sorcières*, the third film in this category (loosely about the MacCarthy era in the United States, if transplanted to the seventeenth century), Signoret embodies the cold and principled Elizabeth Proctor, and does not kiss. However, even here, Signoret's sensuality seeps through, if only the once, in the scene where Elizabeth's husband goes to her bed. Other actresses would have played this with the same coldness that is attributed to Elizabeth throughout: a coldness that endures until the closing scene when Elizabeth finally gets in touch with her feelings, so that by the end of the film she is able to express love for her husband.

In this category of films, then, we witness a star body that expresses its full potential, or comes to a realization of its full potential, as woman and political activist. We need to consider the political and social context of post-war France in order to understand just how powerful the roles Signoret embodied were, and to intuit the subversive tenor of the alternative images these roles offered to spectators of France's modern womanhood. This was a time when France as a nation was heavily embroiled on the international front in its colonial struggles, and on the domestic front was attempting to encourage women back into the private sphere of the home to produce babies. Two types of control or censorship were in force during the period 1945–1960. First, there was censorship of a political order, in relation particularly to the Algerian war. The political climate in France over the question of Algerian independence gave rise, on the government's part, to a fear of civil war. So, for example, information on the Algerian conflict was to all intents and purposes blacked out. Protests and civil unrest were met with severe reprisals. As Signoret herself says, demonstrating against the Algerian war in the 1950s was a far more dangerous activity than participating in the anti-Vietnam protest marches of the late 1960s.[14] Second, control of a sexual order was imposed on women in an effort to resolve France's demographic difficulties. Women were paid to stay at home and reproduce, through the provision of all sorts of family benefits: benefits that increased the more babies they conceived.[15] Set against this constraining censorship of the female body, Signoret's performativity or star persona/body sits uneasily with the dominant ideology of the 1945–1960 era, in that it suggests that woman has a powerful role to play and enjoys a forceful autonomy. This autonomy is no less political than sexual. Signoret's bodily performances, in her films of the post-war period, speak out first for the female presence within the Resistance (French films about the Resistance were almost exclusively male-oriented); and second, for the female voice of dissent raised against the repressive climate produced by the cold war in particular and, more generally, by political hypocrisy of all kinds.

Let us now return to our chart and to further readings of Signoret's body-as-text. Unsurprisingly, female sexuality is very much at the heart of the other three categories of film the chart delineates. And, while all of the films cited are black and white, they posit issues of colour and the body as a first consideration. Take Signoret's hair – a significant matter when it comes to lighting. At first her hair was red, to match her grey-green eyes. This coloration excellently reflected her radiant and insolent young womanhood (cf. *Dédée d'Anvers* (1948)). But, if shot differently, it could signal a sharp contrast between her hair (as dark, albeit red) and eyes (limpid and sparkling), bringing out a troubling ambiguity. This occurs in *Macadam*, for example, with the result that the question of how to read Signoret becomes primordial for the audience. By the time of *Casque d'Or* (1952), the hair was blond, allowing Signoret's face in close-up to admit a far greater degree of luminosity, a luminosity essential to the depiction of a woman (Marie) passionately in love. Her alive sexuality is palpable on screen. The audience, no less than Manda (Marie's lover), cannot fail to feel it. By 1955 – the time of *Les Diaboliques* – the glorious mound of hair (red, once again, for *Thérèse Raquin* (1953)) is gone. Now it is blond once more, but cropped into a short, gamine hairstyle, the better to emphasize ambiguous, disturbing sexuality.

It has often been said of Signoret that she was her eyes and her lips; that a flicker of her glance, a narrowing of her eyelids, a pout of her mouth spoke volumes.[16] Normally, a make-up artist would seek, for example, to diminish the fullness of a star's lips through a careful application of liners and fillers. But, with Signoret, such rules went out of the window. In film after film of the period 1945–1960, her lips glisten in their fullness, sensuality and expression of desire. Make-up drew attention to her lips, as did lighting to her eyes. Signoret could express the gamut of feelings from hatred to love through her facial features. In fanzines of the time (and, equally, in the more serious film journals), her gaze is often described as ironic, volcanic, cruel and disturbing;[17] her mouth as redolent with an erotic sensuality.[18] And it is as if her body only had to follow the aura her eyes and lips conveyed. In short, Signoret's eyes and lips functioned metonymically in her performances (and in reviews of her roles) as ciphers for the whole body. That they did so produced a number of effects, one of which I wish to scrutinize particularly.

What I would like to suggest here is that because of the metonymic, erotic power of her eyes and lips, Signoret's *body* was not fetishized, or visibilized, as an erotic object in the same way, say, as Martine Carol's and Brigitte Bardot's bodies were. Signoret is never shot in the nude (Carol and Bardot were). However, in her intimist moments/shots – where she is simply dressed in a négligée or a silken slip – she is nonetheless highly erotically charged by virtue of all the visual information proffered *before* the shot. Established as profoundly erotic by her eyes and lips, she does not need to be 'seen'. We already know more than enough, and what we know is 'more' (that is, transcends standard figurations of the sexualized feminine). If, moreover, Signoret has agency over her erotic being in the films addressed here, she likewise, I would propose, normally controls her outcome within the narrative (the rare exception is Buñuel's *La Mort en ce jardin* (1956), where she is shot dead by a madman). Her endings may mostly be tragic, culminating in death or the loss of a lover. But, whatever their tenor, it is she who has the power over closure.

Signoret represented force, never nubile, fetishized sexuality. Certainly, her beauty allowed her immediately to be a presence on screen. But what enabled her to take control, I would argue, was first her lack of narcissism, and second her lack of fixity. These phenomena, coupled with a gestural intelligence and a verbal economy, made her more than simply pleasing to the eye. She was pleasing to the mind as well, provoking the kind of pleasure in viewing associated with Arletty. She was a strong woman star persona, at a moment when films were by and large vehicles for 'fixed' images of woman-as-sex-kitten or submissive female.[19] The next section of this discussion focuses further on Signoret's play with gender and sexual fixity, and particularly on Henri-Georges Clouzot's *Les Diaboliques* and François Leterrier's *Les Mauvais Coups*. I will treat these films in reverse chrono-logical order, primarily because *Les Diaboliques* is well known to readers (it is available on video) while *Les Mauvais Coups* is not, so a more detailed presentation of it is necessary. For reasons of economy, I will use this latter film to framework my main argument around sexuality and desire, before I tie that argument into a shorter discussion of *Les Diaboliques*.

Ambiguous Desire

Although many filmographies of Signoret's work and histories of French cinema give 1960 as the release date for *Les Mauvais Coups*, it was premiered in Paris in May 1961. However, I have counted it among Signoret's 1945–1960 films because it was due for release in 1960 and because its numerous intertexts make it pertinent to the analysis offered in this section.[20] The reason for the delay was political, and related to Signoret's status in the eyes of the state. In September 1960 she signed the 'Manifeste des 121' that denounced the sending of troops to Algeria. In response to the manifesto, the state banned any persons who were signatories to it from appearing in or on state fora (radio, theatres, tv), and withdrew funding from films that had connections with those signatories. Leterrier's film, in consequence, suffered delays. Its governmental subsidies were withheld during the last stages of shooting. These financial difficulties caused significant problems at the post-production stage and the film had to wait a further seven months until its release – a release that coincided with the lifting of the ban.[21]

Les Mauvais Coups was François Leterrier's first film. He had worked as an assistant with Yves Allégret (Signoret's former husband) and played the escaped man in Robert Bresson's *Un condamné à mort s'est échappé* (1956). Much is made in critical reviews of Leterrier's film of the Bressonian influence. Certainly, the slow pacing and the way the characters' psychology (or inner torment) gradually unfolds have something of a Bressonian feel, as does the choice of a non-actor for the central male role of Milan (Signoret's husband in the film). The starkness of the exterior shots (filmed in October in Saint-Fargeau and along the Loing river, near Auxerre in the Yonne) makes us think briefly of Bresson.[22] However, Leterrier's shots are lush in their starkness, and at times there is a strong contrast of light and dark. At others a terrible dampness emanates from the misty morning shots and the general wetness of the landscape. Shot in dyaloscope, these rural images, because they are spread so wide, achieve a heaviness and darkness that make them painful and violent in their beauty. In short, Leterrier's shots lack the flattened, bleached-out effect that Bresson strove for, and are richer and more redolent with explicit meaning than those produced by Bresson's austere style. Leterrier thus transcends Bresson's style to achieve his own.

In *Les Mauvais Coups*, based on a 1959 Roger Vailland novel of the same name, Signoret plays Roberte, the disabused and disaffected wife of a former racing driver, Milan. Roberte and Milan have rented a property on a Château estate for a year, during which time Milan intends to write his autobiography. Roberte, a former Paris socialite, renowned for her brilliance, beauty and excesses (notably in gambling), gave up her exciting (to her) life to be with Milan on the racing circuit, after which their passion died. Theirs is a love-hate relationship. Roberte drinks heavily to compensate for their lost passion and eventually commits suicide when Milan takes off on his own to start up a racing career once more. But it is what occurs within this petrified relationship, what Roberte does and the games she plays, that are of interest here. Milan and Roberte have a marriage without sex. In its place they exchange cruelties, banalities and occasional words of love. Milan goes to prostitutes from time to time. He once had an affair with a bosom friend of Roberte's, a younger woman called Juliette. For a brief while, a triangular relationship was sustained, until Roberte banished Juliette. When a new school-teacher, Hélène (Alexandra Stewart), arrives in the village, Roberte decides to take charge of a situation that, she is convinced, will lead to Milan's seduction of the young woman. There are three key moments within this process. First, Roberte befriends Hélène. She then fills her in on the emptiness of her marriage. Finally, she attempts to make Hélène over into her own former self, ostensibly in the hope that this will rekindle Milan's passion for her. Milan in the meantime perceives the traps Roberte is setting and decides to leave before succumbing to Hélène's charms.

What concerns me here is Roberte's play with Hélène. Far more is at stake in that play than the above synopsis indicates. Indeed, a contemporary reviewer recognized that the two women's preoccupation was not really with Milan but rather with each other. For that critic, tellingly, the Roberte/Hélène dynamic was the only element of Leterrier's film that gave it any drama and made it come alive.[23] There is an extraordinary tension between Roberte and Hélène, that reaches a number of peaks within the narrative. There are three pivotal scenes or moments that are as much about sexual connection as they are about identity and power. It is worth recalling that *Les Mauvais Coups* was made six years before Ingmar

Bergman's *Persona* to which it bears some resemblance, particularly with regard to the relationship between its women protagonists. Indeed, there is one shot of Roberte and Hélène, framed as a reflection in a mirror in which Roberte is making Hélène over as herself, that announces Bergman's more famous shot of Liv Ullmann and Bibi Andersson in a similar pose. Both shots turn on a fusion of identity and, of course, on the narcissistic mirror-moment – and in this latter respect invoke not only the issue of self/Other misrecognition but also the death of the subject.

The three pivotal scenes referred to above accrue in intensity. In the first, Roberte, Hélène and Milan are returning by car from an evening's play at the Casino. Roberte falls asleep on Hélène's shoulder. Once back indoors, in the *salon*, Roberte asks Hélène to fix her a drink. Previously, it was always Milan who carefully measured out the tots of alcohol: now it is Hélène who executes precisely the same gesture. Roberte, lying on a sofa, seizes Hélène's wrist and pulls her down to sit next to her. Hélène wipes away Roberte's tears. Roberte falls asleep and, as Hélène moves to leave, she kisses Roberte on the forehead. Milan, impassive, watches the women. Hélène tells him 'je l'aime'. The second scene takes place in Roberte's bedroom. Hélène, who has just come in from the rain, with Milan, stands by the window gazing out. Her pose reminds Roberte of the day, ten years earlier, when Milan declared his love for her and of the happiness his avowal provoked. As she narrates the story, she draws Hélène closer to her and then pulls her onto the bed. Roberte re-enacts the scene of Milan's declaration of love with Hélène as her former self, and herself as Milan. At this point Milan (again a silent witness) storms out angrily, declaring 'that was ten years ago' ('c'est il y a dix ans'). Undaunted, Roberte goes on evoking the past. Holding Hélène's face tenderly between her hands, she tells of Milan's first great betrayal: a betrayal involving Octave, a friend of his and a man passionately in love with Roberte. Milan deliberately omitted to deliver Octave's plea that Roberte should see him before she took off with Milan. Because she never came, Octave committed suicide.

The final scene between the two women centres on a complex play of mirror-images and ultimately on a seduction whereby Roberte transmutes Hélène into her own former self. It takes place both in the *salon* and in Roberte's bedroom. There are seven sets of mirror-images. In the first six, Roberte and Hélène are framed as follows:

1. Both are reflected in a mirror: Hélène is in the foreground and Roberte in background.
2. Roberte is reflected in the mirror: Hélène is in the foreground and not in the mirror.
3. and 4. Both women are reflected in the mirror in medium close-up: Hélène is slightly in front of Roberte; Roberte is doing Hélène's hair.
5. Both are reflected in the mirror: Hélène in background; Roberte in foreground, in the far right bottom corner, as she serves herself a drink.

6. Both are reflected in the mirror in close-up: Hélène is now completely made-up as 'Roberte'; Roberte is slightly in front of Hélène.

During this sequence of images, Roberte dresses Hélène, applies make-up and does her hair. At each stage, she makes comments about Hélène's body ('you have beautiful breasts, you must show them off' ('tu as de beaux seins, il faut les montrer'), 'your hair is so silky' ('tes cheveux sont soyeux')), caresses her hair and shoulders and, when she has completed the transformation, kisses Hélène on the forehead. When Roberte asks her how she feels, Hélène replies 'I frighten myself a bit' ('je me fais un peu peur'), echoing Milan's earlier words to Roberte: 'you frighten me' ('tu me fais peur'). The masquerade/transmutation is complete. At the same time as it is evolving, Roberte tells Hélène about Juliette. The paradox is, of course, that Roberte is drawing Hélène in (and into) her own image, all the better to throw her at Milan. Hélène will become Roberte's previous self in this game of travesty. Milan has already made it clear, however, that he will not seduce Hélène, so the game, in Roberte's mind, becomes one in which lost ten-year-old scenarios might be replayed. It is in order to replay them that she takes over Hélène's body completely. The erotic interest, for Roberte, is to 'become again' the desired body she once was, through the medium of Hélène's body. And, because she has been so sucked into Roberte and Milan's story, Hélène's desire – despite her fears – is to become Roberte and thus to appeal acceptably, as a rejuvenated Roberte, to Milan. Both women, in sum, desire a body (Roberte's) that essentially no longer exists but that hangs between them in the mirror as a tremendous attraction. They are, in other words, attracted to each other for what they are – each is – *not*: a phenomenon reflected in the current of misrecognition and narcissism that runs through their relationship. But their attraction ensures that a lesbian narrative is quite palpably present in the sequence of shots, giving the mirror-scene its tension and erotic suspense.

As if to underscore the 'danger' of this homoerotic attraction, the whole sequence is intercut with shots of Milan outside in the bleak and wintry landscape, shooting at ravens. He eventually kills one and brings it home, bursts in on the women, throws the carrion bird down at Roberte's feet and storms out. The set of shots includes the seventh mirroring-shot, which is as follows:

7. Milan enters the frame briefly: Hélène is in the background, Roberte in middle-ground and Milan in the foreground. Milan explodes with anger (once more) and leaves.

Milan, then, fails to remain as a third presence within the mirror. He asserts no patriarchal veto over the (misrecognitional) desire between the two women. He throws down an emblem of treachery and denunciation – the raven (*corbeau*, in

French) – and leaves. The strength of and between the two women disempowers Milan, who can only respond to it by an angry gesture that suggests their perfidy.

In *Les Diaboliques*, the lesbian intertext is far stronger, doubtless because in the novel on which it is based (*Celle qui n'était plus*, by the *série noire* duo Boileau and Narcejeac), it is the women protagonists who are lovers. Clouzot changed the plot-line and heterosexualized the narrative. His decision was presumably motivated less by concern about censorship (other lesbian films were made in the 1950s in France) than by the fact that he wanted his wife, Vera, to play the role of the woman married to a ruthless, sadistic headmaster with whom she runs a boarding school just outside Paris. It meant that Signoret (who plays a schoolteacher) was cast as the headmaster's mistress, rather than as the lover of his wife. For all that, the lesbian text seeps through. In the original story, the two women plot to kill off the husband who suffers from a weak heart. Clouzot reverses the tale, so that it is the husband (played by Paul Meurisse) and Signoret who plot against the wife (now the character with a heart disorder). In order for the plan to succeed, the mistress (Nicole) has to befriend the wife (Christina). This she does by ganging up with her against the husband (Michel), who behaves quite brutally towards the two of them, to the point of giving Nicole a black eye. (His sadism also includes publicly humiliating his wife and forcing her to eat disgusting food.) The two women enter into complicity against Michel: a complicity that, to the viewer, is utterly convincing, since we do not know until the last thirty seconds of *Les Diaboliques* that Michel and Nicole were plotting to provoke Christina's eventual heart attack. In other words, we are led to believe that what we are seeing is the truth, the duplicity being revealed only at the last minute.

During the period (the major part of the film) in which we observe what we receive as the truth, we witness the close friendship between the two women. Although, as one schoolteacher remarks, they should be rivals, in fact they are close allies. Indeed, within the film, we see more two-shots of Nicole and Christina than, say, of Michel and Nicole (who are almost never in a two-shot). Michel mostly appears in three-shots with his wife and mistress. Thus, the actual framing of the characters lulls us into a conviction that the relationship between Nicole and Christina is a close, even intimate one. At one point the two women are framed in a bedroom window in their nightclothes, Nicole (Signoret) wearing dark pyjamas and Christina (Vera Clouzot) in a white nightie. This light/dark motif runs throughout. Signoret/Nicole wears dark, severe dresses with straight skirts firmly belted at the waist, while Vera/Christina wears light-coloured patterns with full skirts that hint at her Latin-American origins. The only reversal in colouring is with the hair: Nicole's hair is blond and cropped short, whereas Christina's is long and dark. However, this reversal does nothing to undo the image of Christina's exotic foreignness and femininity, offset against Nicole's more masculinized appearance. Thus, Christina comes over as the exotic fragile female and Nicole as a strong-willed modern woman. She is purposeful and no-nonsense, even hard-nosed and tough. She is certainly masculinized in relation to Christina, teaching maths and science, 'hard', male-identified subjects, to Christina's 'soft', languages (English). Nicole smokes cigarettes in a 'masculine' manner, pulling the butt from her mouth with her thumb and forefingers and stamping it out on the ground with considerable force.

Not all is masculine in Nicole, however. Her black high-heels and deep red nails are coded markers, within thriller conventions, of her *femme fatale* status. They ensure that, iconically speaking, she incarnates a female persona well-established in *film noir*, whose clothing positions her as the (safely contained) phallic woman.[24] But, and this is a key point about Clouzot's film, the apparent investment in *noir* iconography manifest in *Les Diaboliques* is undermined by other aspects of Nicole's clothing. Other things intrude to pull that investment up short. The dark sunglasses Nicole favours and her casually worn cardigan suggest a sporty persona (ready for tennis), at odds with the languorous *femme fatale*. And even that persona (the sportswoman) is destabilized by the fact that Nicole knits (presumably for herself – a new white cardigan perhaps). When she walks, with her grand strides, she comes over as sexually powerful, predatory even. But here again, something is incomplete. It is as if she is lacking a target. There is no hint of passion between herself and Michel (as, indeed, there cannot be, if the twist in the tail of the narrative is to remain a secret). Hence, the sexual power she embodies must find another outlet. This comes in the form of Nicole's relationship with Christina.

As in the previous film discussed above, Signoret takes charge of the other woman. In his *Sight and Sound* review,[25] Derek Prowse speaks of Signoret as 'big and dominating' and of Vera Clouzot as 'small and harassed'. Within these sets of contrasts, Nicole looms as the dark shadow to Christina's virginal translucence. Their relationship is not quite 'butch-femme' but borders on it: Nicole orders Christina about magisterially but also comforts her when she is abused by Michel. But of course, as with all the other embodiments mentioned above, the tension stops short. In a sense, the heterosexualizing of the narrative prevents it from having conviction, denaturalizes it, forces it to grinding halts. Several critics of the time make the point that the plot of *Les Diaboliques* is empty, absurd.[26] This judgement is too harsh, although, as I have suggested here, something does not quite gel. The film is full of suspense and minute observations that make it compelling to watch. And what makes it particularly fascinating are the moments when the complicity of its central women protagonists is forefronted. The murder scene where the two women drug and eventually drown Michel in the bath is a masterful piece of horror. And yet we are not without sympathy for these women, who have suffered greatly at the sadistic hand of the man they are now (apparently) ridding themselves of.

Conclusion

Earlier in this chapter, I argued that Signoret's performativity gave the lie to the dominant ideology of post-war France, and I suggested some of the processes whereby it did so. In both of the films discussed above as 'Ambiguous Desire', we can see such processes at work. In the case of *Les Mauvais Coups*, Signoret's star text – the texts and contexts her star persona refers to, or connects with – can be read as political. So, too, with regard to *Les Diaboliques*, can her star body, her bodily performance. This is not least because in both instances, as star text and body, Signoret invokes the Algerian war. I have already sketched out the background to *Les Mauvais Coups*, and indicated how the controversy attached to Signoret's star text – to Signoret as star persona – made Leterrier's film fall victim to censorship, delaying its release. In *Les Diaboliques*, the murder scene described above points up other aspects of the censorship of the post-war era, namely the censorship that masked the use of torture in Algeria by the French army. (This was known as clean torture because it entailed torture by water, as in the bath scene of *Les Diaboliques*, or by electricity.) Effectively, in both films Signoret's (female) body is not silenced: it is/becomes a politicized, contestatory body with agency within, and effects upon, the political arena.

As discussed under 'Ambiguous Desire', the politicization of Signoret's body goes still further once that body enters the domain of sexuality. I have showed how Signoret's bodily performativity can be read as sexually ambiguous, as permitting or inviting a queer reading. In order to grasp the full significance and impact of her ambiguous play with sexuality, her performances in *Les Mauvais Coups* and *Les Diaboliques* must be considered with an eye to the historical moment at which they came into being. These performances stand out as different from those of other top-billing female stars of the time (stars who included Michèle Morgan, Micheline Presle and Danielle Delorme) because, within them, Signoret does not play a singular, straight part. That they offer 'more' is always evidenced by Signoret's gesture, clothing, allure and speech. Repeatedly in interviews, Signoret speaks of disliking the bother of dressing and making-up, of not being interested, in sum, in female masquerading. Readily admitting that she does not 'dress well', she talks of wanting to be comfortable in her clothes and of preferring slacks to dresses. For a woman – particularly a woman in the film industry, where looks are everything – to perceive and speak of the (gendered) self in such ways in the 1950s was extremely modern and liberal. Signoret offered a different kind of freedom from that incarnated by Bardot, with her naked feet, bouffant hair and gingham dresses. She embodied the freedom of a sexually potent woman, as opposed to the infantile-nubile sexuality Bardot conveyed. She performed as a woman who was certain about her multiple subjectivities and who did not seek to confine them on film. This was the power that made her appearance on screen so magnetic: that made spectator after spectator speak of how their eyes were immediately drawn to, and made aware of, her screen 'presence'. (We should note that, with regard to Signoret, the word is unquestionably 'presence', not 'body'.) In *Les Mauvais Coups* and *Les Diaboliques*, the exemplary films considered here, Signoret's freeplay with sexuality is certainly contained. The narratives that represent it suggest that perfidy and treachery are never very far removed from its embodiment. This attempt at containment is unsurprising. It is, however, an attempt that does not work. The seductive play with alterities that we can detect in Signoret holds us in full sway throughout the performance, throughout her performances.

The play in Signoret's performativity was to endure for another twenty-five years and some twenty-five more films. Her body was her politics and her politics her body – she remained true to both throughout her life. She fought lastingly for causes she believed in, particularly for those without a voice. She would lend her voice to help, as one might lend a hand. Small wonder, then, that she stands as an icon of womanhood for many still today and that, despite her affirmations to the contrary, she is both a star and a pre-feminist star body.

Acknowledgement

I wish to thank the British Academy for the Small Grants Award that made possible the research for this chapter. This grant and a research grant from the University of Exeter have funded research for a larger project on Simone Signoret (a book commissioned by Continuum).

Notes

1. 'J'ai suivi les femmes du *MLF* tant qu'elles ont été contestataires, provocatrices même, par exemple pour l'avortement libre.' *La Tribune de Genève*, 28 February 1973. This and further citations from Signoret, as well as citations from reviews of her work, are taken from press cuttings held at the Bibliothèque de l'Arsenal, not all of which provide page references.
2. 'Sans elles, cet atroce problème de l'avortement serait encore où on l'a si longtemps laissé.' *Elle*, 11 June 1973.
3. 'Que celle qui n'a jamais fait de fausse couche ferme sa gueule, moi j'en ai fait, et les manifestantes du *MLF* méritent les remerciements de tout le monde.' Ibid.
4. 'Je n'ai pas attendu ces dames du *MLF* pour être émancipée . . . Je n'aime pas le racisme *MLF* contre l'homme . . . Je les quitte complètement à partir du

moment où elles font du racisme, du sexisme comme disent les intellectuels, c'est-à-dire qu'elles renient l'homme.' *La Tribune de Genève*, 28 February 1973.

5. When I use the term 'star text' in relation to Signoret, I refer to the narratives and contexts with which Signoret, as star persona, intersects and which she evokes.

6. Signoret did however appear in the work of some of the *Cahiers du cinéma*'s fetish film-makers (Costa-Gavras; Buñuel; Allio), and lent her name and acting time to get aspiring film-makers' first projects produced (Baratier; Bozzuffi).

7. See *Télérama*, 30 July 1975.

8. Signoret, who played a small part in *Boléro* (Jean Boyer, 1941), which starred Arletty, recalls how Arletty made a pass at her. In response to questions about the episode and her reaction to Arletty, Signoret has said: 'je la fuyais. Parce qu'elle voulait me sauter dessus' ('I fled from her. Because she wanted to make a pass at me'). See J.-P. Josselin (1995), *Simone: Deux ou trois choses que je sais d'elle*, Paris, p. 65.

9. See S. Hayward (1995), 'Simone Signoret 1921–1985: The Star as Sign – the Sign as Scar', in D. Knight and J. Still (eds), *Women and Representation*, Nottingham University of Nottingham Press (WIF occasional papers): pp. 57–74, p. 73.

10. Signoret, quoted in P. Durant (1988), *Simone Signoret: Une vie*, Lausanne, p. 166. I am aware that 'beauty' is a not unproblematic term, but constraints of space prevent me from addressing its complexities here.

11. 'Elle faisait de ce baiser l'un des moments les plus sainement érotiques du cinéma de ces années-là'. *Cinémonde*, 2 April 1954.

12. 'Séduisante en diable' (*Cinémonde*, 9 April 1946); 'troublante' (*Cinémonde*, 28 October 1947).

13. See Hayward, 'Simone Signoret 1921–1985', pp. 60–6.

14. See Signoret's interview with Guy de Belleval in *La Tribune de Genève*, 1 April 1967.

15. See C. Duchen (1994), *Women's Rights and Women's Lives in France, 1944–1968*, London and New York.

16. See, for example, D. de Vorges (1986), *Le Maquillage: cinéma, télévision, théâtre*, Paris, p. 60.

17. See, for example, *Cinémonde*, 30 October 1951; 23 April 1952.

18. See, for example, *Cinémonde*, 23 October 1953.

19. In numerous films, Bardot embodies such fixed images (cf. *Et Dieu créa la femme* (1956)), prevalent in all sorts of representational media. For example, the popular historical romances of the 1950s, while they gave women some initial power, were only too quick to absorb it back into a male-dominated plot.

20. By 'intertext', I mean that the film-text meshes with, or invokes, numerous other, often hidden, narratives: narratives relating to lesbianism; the Algerian crisis; Signoret's ban from state-funded venues; the backgrounds of the director Leterrier and Roger Vailland, the novelist on whose book the film was based, and so on.

21. See Signoret's account of this in S. Signoret (1975), *La Nostalgie n'est plus ce qu'elle était*, Paris, p. 293.

22. It is worth remembering that Bresson's *Mouchette*, to which some of the exterior shots of Leterrier's film could be compared, was not made until 1966.

23. See the review in *Motion Picture Herald*, 27 November 1963, p. 938.

24. The appearance (dress, high-heeled shoes, painted nails, etc.) of the *femme fatale* in *film noir* is conventionally referred to/understood as phallic. But the phallicity of the *femme fatale* must be recognized as 'safely' contained by her encasing clothing. This apparel is the target of, and appeals to, the fetishizing male gaze that seeks to deny female difference (Lack) and thus avert castration anxiety. Equally, though, it contains/restrains a female phallicity that might otherwise pose a threat.

25. See *Sight and Sound*, Winter 1955–6, p. 149.

26. See, for example, *Cahiers du cinéma*, 3, March 1955, p. 20.

Gender, Modernism and Mass Culture in the New Wave

Geneviève Sellier

Introduction

Breaking with the aesthetic/stylistic approach that has dominated to date the study of French New Wave cinema (in the Anglo-Saxon world included), my project in this chapter is to analyse New Wave films made around 1960 from a critical perspective grounded in the history of cinematic representation. My purpose is to understand the nature of, and to highlight what was at stake in, the cinematic renewal constituted by the emergence of the New Wave: a renewal initiated by a young generation of film-makers who made their mark on the French cinematic scene between 1957 and 1962. My decision to privilege a particular moment in the history of French cinema and to locate it as distinctive relates both to questions of French cultural policy and film production (in 1956, the quality subsidy came into force; in 1959, the *avance sur recettes* system was established; the late 1950s and early 1960s witnessed a marked increase in the number of *début* films) and to questions of reception (audience figures began to fall at this time; American rather than French movies began to top the charts; and the first critical assessments of the New Wave were published at the end of 1962, in the journals *Cahiers du cinéma* and *Positif*).[1] Between 1957 and 1962, around 150 film-makers had their first film commercially distributed, so that *début* films averaged some thirty per year (previously, fifteen per year had been the norm). Tellingly, however, none of these *cinéastes* was a woman (Agnès Varda had made her first full-length film, *La Pointe courte*, in 1954), a phenomenon that signals a major discordance between the creative renascence represented by the New Wave and the evolution of women as creative and social subjects in their own right.

Viewed against the canvas of French cultural history, the emergence of the New Wave marked a moment at which a new mode of artistic expression was born and legitimated. Its methods of production and consumption notwithstanding – methods that allied it to the industrial – French cinema in its New Wave guise entered the realm of Art: a fact evidenced by the institution of the various forms of financial subsidy cited above. The dialogue with issues of individual freedom that young

New Wave directors embarked on in their cinematic productions secured New Wave film's status as an art form, not least because an engagement with freedom and singularity, from Romanticism onwards, has been a hallmark of the work of art. The New Wave manifested itself as a rebellion of 'young Turks'. It targeted France's cinematic *tradition de qualité* – a mode of film production that sought to render France's cultural heritage accessible to all – and did so in the name of creative innovation: an innovation unconcerned with 'academic' conventions and rules. And New Wave cinema privileged the individual against the collective/ patriarchal; against, that is, cinema as mass culture. The majority of New Wave films distanced themselves from the 'popular' cinema of the mid-century era, effectively by according a central place to a male protagonist whose point of view is the dominant perspective of the film in which he features. In these films, as in the Romantic tradition of the *Bildungsroman*, it is usually a young man, a kind of alter ego of the New Wave *auteur*, with whom the spectator empathizes and identifies.

Michelle Coquillat has shown how, influenced by its most famous precursor, the Jean-Jacques Rousseau of *La Nouvelle Héloïse* (1761), Romanticism is subtended by a claim to self-generation on the part of the male artist: an artist who 'ontologically' associates creation and masculinity, and defines woman in terms of contingency, nature, reproduction.[2] In the Romantic optic, the artisan, humbly subject to the rules of Beauty, is displaced by the inspired thinker, the solitary prophet, for whom artistic fraternity is the only valid social bond. This valorization of individual singularity over social hierarchy and the collective environment is articulated in most of the great Romantic texts, through a treatment of the tragic destiny of the male hero. The hero's destiny turns on an entrapment that takes the form of his love for a woman who causes him to lose his creative capacities or, more generally, his ability to be himself. The fundamentally misogynist dimension of Romanticism (expressed, paradoxically, through the highly moving female characters who people Romantic narratives) establishes as mutually exclusive the construction/consolidation of male subjectivity and man's love for woman. It is a dimension that is no less in evidence in most New Wave films, which, with the same tragic overtones, present as fateful the mismatch between male subjective evolution and love.

To elucidate further the cultural tradition with which the New Wave allies itself, we must refer to the manner in which the domain of artistic creation has been mapped out in France since the mid-nineteenth century. In *After the Great Divide: Modernism, Mass Culture and Postmodernism* (1986), Andreas Huyssen observes with regard to Flaubert's invention of modernism that the modernist stance tends to oppose the 'bad object' that is mass culture consumed by women to the 'good object' that is the 'authentic' culture generated by male artists.[3] If we reflect on Flaubert's ironic treatment of Emma Bovary's taste for what, today, we would term 'trashy novels', novels full of swooning heroines and their dashing, brave-but-emotional male consorts, we are unfailingly reminded of modes of pre-New Wave French popular cinema (especially those genres targeted at women, melodramas and sentimental comedies) against which the New Wave defined itself.

Modernist works, according to Huyssen, are characterized by their self-referentiality. They seek to articulate a purely individual mind-set rather than the collective consciousness; they aim to be as experimental as scientific research; they elaborate a singular language with which to express themselves; and they reject classic systems of representation, challenging the primacy such systems accord to verisimilitude, realism, and the signification (to cite Roland Barthes) of 'what has been'. They are hostile both to the bourgeois culture of the quotidian and to the mass culture of entertainment. Analyzing mass-market American films, the *Cahiers du cinéma* critics – by emphasizing the most abstract aspects of their *mise en scène* and by disregarding the sociocultural context of their production and consumption – gave impetus to the modernist, distanced gaze on cinema that the most innovative films of the New Wave worked to mobilize. The same narrative hallmark likewise became peculiar to a certain type of French 'new novel', notably in the work of the most visible author of the heterogeneous *nouveau roman* movement, Alain Robbe-Grillet.

However, for all that Robbe-Grillet collaborated with Alain Resnais in *L'Année dernière à Marienbad* (1960), cinematic modernism in early 1960s France was different from that which was emerging in literature, not least because, as Alexandre Astruc proposed in his famous article on the *caméra-stylo*, filmic creation, unlike literary creation, was only just becoming a 'moyen d'expression', a 'langage'. Astruc's article, which can be viewed as a manifesto of cinematic modernism, is underpinned by an opposition between mass culture and individual creation. Cinema as art, it signals, is in its infancy. Its first step must be the affirmation of the cinematic creator's subjectivity, against the conventions of collective cultural production, and in a *véritable écriture*, produced by a cinematic *auteur* whose camera writes as an author writes with his pen.[4] The *cinéastes* of the New Wave foregrounded both their subjectivity and their film-writing, in order to affirm themselves as creators. The contradiction between the two stances, romantic and modernist, that they adopted was only superficial. That this is so is apparent in films such as François Truffaut's *Tirez sur le pianiste* (1960) or Jean-Luc Godard's *Le Petit Soldat* (1960–1963), and it is without doubt the case that it is the admixture engendered by its dual cultural inheritance that renders New Wave cinema so original.

To take the case of *Tirez sur le pianiste*, the film chooses a modernist mode of *cinécriture* to construct and represent wounded masculine subjectivity. The breaks in tone and the mixing of genres that Truffaut brings to his adaptation of a *roman noir* by David Goodis appeal slyly to a cultured audience without, however, challenging our capacity to empathize with Truffaut's unhappy hero, Charlie Kohler. Charles Aznavour, with his attractive ugliness, his diminutive stature and his hangdog expression, in tandem with the crippling shyness his character evinces, his muteness, and his truncated career as a virtuoso musician, offers an emblem of vulnerable masculinity. The cyclical structure of the narrative, which revolves around two catastrophes, the first set in the story's prehistory, confirms the inescapability of Truffaut's male character's tragic fate. The film links great concert music (that of the cultured elite), which Charlie has had to give up, to an ancient form of popular music, the music of the world of the *café-concert*, where Charlie is associated with Bobby Lapointe, a singer of quasi-nonsensical texts much appreciated by the cultured public. As a piano virtuoso of working-class origins (origins to which his paralysing shyness attests), Truffaut's protagonist incarnates the idealized figure of the artist as imagined by the New Wave *auteurs*: he is self-made and abandons his concert career in order not to compromise himself within bourgeois milieux, signified in the film by the impresario character. He is a sacrificial hero, and therefore quite unlike the young film-makers of the New Wave, who pragmatically made use of all the openings available to them through their social background or connections in order to produce their films.

The two female characters of *Tirez sur le pianiste* are the conduits through which disaster befalls its male hero. The first of these characters is the pianist's young wife (Nicole Berger), whose own modest origins make her an easy prey for the cynical impresario, as well as preventing her from sharing the artistic emotions of her husband. Her suicide is presented from the viewpoint of Truffaut's protagonist as a tragedy that shatters his life and career. The second is a female fan (Marie Dubois) who, by virtue of the fact that she loves Truffaut's hero, leads him into terrible complications (of which she will be the ultimate victim, though her death is portrayed as the fulfilment of a fatality). The beloved woman, whether or not she is capable of understanding the artist, thus reveals herself in *Tirez sur le pianiste* as the (unwitting) instrument of his defeat. In the best Romantic tradition, the ties of love are cast as an obstacle to the artist's development, and, more generally, as an obstacle to the development of masculine identity. The same angle on the trap that love represents is evident in a host of New Wave films centred on a masculine hero, from Louis Malle's *Ascenseur pour l'échafaud* (1957) to Claude Chabrol's *Les Cousins* (1958), Godard's *A bout de souffle* (1959), and Jacques Rivette's *Paris nous appartient* (1958–1961).

In the limited number of (male-authored) New Wave films that took a female subject as their chief protagonist, the narrative patterns outlined above are not contradicted. The dominant viewpoint still comes across, implicitly or explicitly, as that of a male character who broadly displays the traits of the Romantic hero (cf. Jacques Demy's *Lola* (1961) and *La Baie des Anges* (1963); Truffaut's *Jules et Jim* (1962)). But women's stories were also elaborated within a 'sociological' register that allowed the New Wave *auteur* to describe his female subject from the outside, constructing her not as a consciousness but rather as an instance of a social condition or type (cf. the prostitute in Godard's *Vivre sa vie* (1962); the female employees of Chabrol's *Les Bonnes Femmes* (1960)).[5] That New Wave films admitted such constructions places them in a narrative tradition initiated by Flaubert in *Madame Bovary*.

Claude Chabrol's Flaubertian Inheritance

Claude Chabrol's fourth film, *Les Bonnes Femmes*, offers a prime example of a modernist cinematic vehicle that offsets as polar opposites the male creative subject – as subject-of-the-gaze – and the alienated feminine object. Filming four female sales-assistants in an electrical goods shop in Paris, in order to describe aspects of the working-class 'female condition' in contemporary Paris, Chabrol lays claim to sociological objectivity.[6] But he does not confine himself to mobilizing a 'sociological', detached cinematic look: from the first scene, set in a nocturnal Paris filmed with all the modernist brio of the New Wave, we sense the pleasure he takes in highlighting the vulgarity of the two middle-aged lotharios in their white convertible who 'pull' Bernadette Laffont and Clothilde Joannon and take them to a restaurant and a cabaret, hoping to end the evening in bed. Chabrol's insistence on the grotesqueness of the characters and the ludicrous aspects of the situations he films shapes the whole of *Les Bonnes Femmes*, which follows its women protagonists in their jobs and leisure time over forty-eight hours. A day of interminable work and boredom in the shop, a second night at the music hall, then time at the swimming pool allow Chabrol to sketch out the pathetic limitations of the women's world and aspirations.

But the limits of derision are reached with the phony romantic intrigue of which Joannon, whose face is that of a sad Madonna, is the object. *Les Bonnes Femmes* introduces suspense from the start, through the character of a flamboyant, love-struck biker (played by Mario David) who follows her everywhere without speaking to her until, at the swimming pool, he protects her from two admirers who have become aggressive. A romantic trip to the countryside, an explicit parody of the sentimental narrative mode of the popular *roman-photo*, ends in a sadistic crime. The love-struck romantic proves to be a pervert! He strangles the young woman when she gives herself to him.

If Chabrol reserves his sharpest criticisms for the men to whom his female protagonists inevitably fall victim, he places his spectator in a position of superiority vis-à-vis these young women, who do not seem the least bit aware of the pitfalls of their existence. The fact that they are only permitted to choose between a pitiful Don Juan, a ridiculous *petit bourgeois* and a psychopath testifies to the manipulative dimension of his film. Echoing Flaubert, Chabrol does not adopt in *Les Bonnes Femmes* the tone he employs when his hero is more or less an alter ego, positioned to arouse the empathy of the viewer (cf. *Le Beau Serge* (1959) or *Les Cousins*, Chabrol's first films). When they are female, his characters lose all individuality. The *bonnes femmes* he creates in his ostensible effort to depict social alienation are constructed as Others who are radically lacking in agency and (self-)awareness. Masterful in its structure, as in its narrative tone, *Les Bonnes Femmes* endorses as an objective 'fact' the equation of alienation and the woman subject, working within a cultural tradition very much alive in France since the mid-nineteenth century.

Jacques Rozier's Documentation of Alienation

Adieu Philippine (1960–1962), by Jacques Rozier, uses non-professional actors and offers a narrative of events that is pared down to a minimum. In quasi-documentary vein, it records the months that precede a young conscript's departure for Algeria, showing him at his job (he is a manual worker in television) and on holiday in Corsica with the two girlfriends who share his favours. The film adopts an ironic viewpoint to describe working- or lower-middle-class characters, a viewpoint that has little in common with the idealizing populism of 1930s cinema. The machismo of the male protagonist around whom its narrative is articulated is shown to be ludicrous, as is the coquetry of the two shop-girls who try to seduce him. However, the detached filmic gaze that seems, in Rozier's film, to subject all its players to the same sociological scrutiny, and to position them all as so many social ciphers, is not as objective or even-handed as it might at first appear. The main character, Michel, is presented as unique, while his two conquests, Juliette and Liliane, are cast as interchangeable, not least because they look like one another and are inseparable. Furthermore, Michel has a real job in television, albeit a lowly one, while the girls are shown to be incapable of achieving their professional goals. *Adieu Philippine* dwells smugly upon their absolute incompetence. Even the undying friendship between them, proudly announced at the start of the film, does not survive their rivalry over Michel: a rivalry he exploits in a manner that renders even more ridiculous the two girls' claims to 'personality'.

But the 'ontological' differentiation between masculine and feminine is inscribed in *Adieu Philippine* through reference to the Algerian war. Rozier's film was made between 1960 and 1962, at a time when no one was unaware of the dangers incurred by those called up to participate in a *sale guerre* that dared not speak its name. The spectre of war from the start of *Adieu Philippine* places the sword of Damocles above the head of Rozier's male hero: he must leave to do his national service in three months (that is, at the end of the film). The spectatorial gaze levelled upon Michel is modified immediately by the viewer's awareness of his potential fate.

The theme of the departure for national service recurs as a leitmotif throughout the film, reminding us consistently that a boy runs risks that a girl does not. It affords an additional layer of meaning to the twists and turns of the game of hide and seek Rozier's protagonists embark upon: for the boy, such twists are the last pleasures prior to war, but the girls' indulgence in them simply betrays their 'shop-girl' (*midinette*) nature, as Michel himself reminds them. The Algerian war is not then evoked politically in *Adieu Philippine*, but instead underscores a narrative of sexual difference: a difference that transcends, and is ontologically stronger than, any commonality engendered by shared working-class origins.

Louis Malle's *Vie privée*: A Settling of Scores

The cultural 'distinction' of New Wave cinema is nowhere more apparent than in the relationship between New Wave film-makers and their actors and actresses, especially the most popular amongst them. While an Anna Karina or a Jeanne Moreau function in the films of Jean-Luc Godard or Louis Malle as the director's 'creature', and as a locus, in the cinematic text, of his eroticized projections, Brigitte Bardot the first star in France of the mass-media era, comes across in the context of auteurist film as a 'foreign body'. When Louis Malle agreed to make a film on Bardot with Bardot, at the suggestion of the producer Christine Gouze-Renal,[7] the star, who had established her career in mainstream cinema, had just had her first box-office flop, and her popularity was wavering, due to the hostility provoked by her 'liberated' lifestyle. And *Vie privée* (1962) aimed not to be a homage to Bardot but a denunciation of the alienating character of her popularity, a popularity allied to the forms typically taken by modern mass culture: the tabloid press, fuelled by the paparazzi, and the sort of commercial cinema that took ample advantage of sexual decensorship and the 'public' nature of the private lives of movie stars.

Even though Louis Malle and his screenwriter Jean-Paul Rappeneau claimed to have written their scenario from documents on the 'BB' phenomenon, and from autobiographical material provided by the star herself, a comparison between their scenario and various historical and biographical sources[8] reveals the reconstructive nature of the former. The reconstructive approach that *Vie privée* adopts is underpinned by an opposition between a high culture represented by the *éditeur d'art* played by Marcello Mastroianni, the co-star of the movie, and a passive and alienated mass culture, emblematic of which is the character incarnated by Bardot. The reductive positioning of the female protagonist as object is reinforced by the input of an omnipresent, male narrative voice, who comments on Bardot's actions and moves and lets us know her thoughts, in the manner of the Balzacian omniscient narrator.

When a film-maker spots the photogenic attributes of the well-brought-up girl Bardot plays, her career takes off, but her role is entirely passive: she is a tool in the hands of astute merchandisers, who fabricate her fame. The whole of the first part of *Vie privée*, characterized by a rapid montage of undeveloped scenes that deter the spectator from identifying with the female lead, rehashes clichés about mass culture that construe it as a manufactured product created by the ruling classes as an instrument of social control. Bardot's young woman is simply a commodity, aware neither of her beauty nor of the possibility that she may have any talent (a possibility the film takes care to deny), nor of the manipulations of which she is victim. The only expression of freedom she is allowed in *Vie privée*'s first part is her use of young men as sexual objects, objects that can be discarded like old shirts.[9] Here another stereotype is alluded to: femininity is associated with sexuality as its principal identity, while male characters in the film have a social and pro-fessional identity, if not an artistic gift of the kind possessed by Mastroianni.

The story skims over the Bardot character's rise to fame, changing pace as soon as the scandalous aspects of her career provoke aggressive reactions towards the star. *Vie privée* then shows her as a hunted animal, attempting to rebel against her fate in a purely instinctive and ineffectual manner. We finally see her crack, and her companion parcels her off, hidden under blankets in the back of a car, to her family home in Switzerland. The second part of the film starts with her encounter with Mastroianni, who has been portrayed in its prologue as an unreachable genius with whom, as a young girl, the Bardot figure was secretly in love. Once they meet again when she is an adult star, and a hunted star, the balance alters: the artist is willing now to be attentive to her, but more out of compassion than out of desire or love. At no time does Malle's film suggest that Mastroianni's character is really in love with Bardot's heroine, since art is the centre of his life. She, on the other hand, is in love, but her love brings dependency: she cannot live without the man she desires and attempts suicide as soon as he leaves her to work on his aesthetic project. From the start of their relationship she is shown, moreover, as a concrete obstacle to the artist's achievement, in the time-honoured tradition of the Romantic novel.

The whole of the final part of *Vie privée* is built around an opposition between the autonomy of the male artist and the female, sentimental dependency associated with mass culture. The Mastroianni character stages Kleist's *Das Kätchen von Heilbronn*, an emblem of high or elite culture. Bardot, reduced to the position of an aimless spectator, kills herself by falling from a roof during the first night of the play while attempting to see it without being spotted by the paparazzi who are pursuing her. Her plunge into the void is filmed in slow motion, as if she were flying, to the sound of Verdi's *Requiem*. The film ends on this note of suspended meaning, as if the film-maker could only accord his (anti-)heroine artistic dignity in death.

Louis Malle's film had some box-office success, but less than its producers had hoped for, and its critical reception was mixed. Malle, who had just made *Zazie dans le métro*, adapted from the work of Raymond Queneau, was criticized for being too influenced by mainstream commercial cinema. *Vie privée* has, after all, a linear narrative structure; a big budget; and two major stars. But the film suffers primarily from the (self-) contradictory character of Malle's project. His central female protagonist is portrayed as devoid of interest, autonomy, ambition, intelligence and awareness of her situation. She is depicted, in short, as a cinematographic Madame Bovary, but a Madame Bovary whose construction lacks the austere perfection afforded by Flaubert's writing. On the other hand, Mastroianni, the alter ego of Malle, is valorized in *Vie privée*, but it is not his story that is being told. The 'popular' spectator cannot therefore identify with Bardot's character, or take 'naive' pleasure in identification, while the 'cultured' spectator's more 'sophisticated' impulse toward identification with the cinematic *auteur* is thwarted by the secondary role played by the Mastroianni protagonist.

Le Mépris: Godard's Contradictions

Jean-Luc Godard, who had already made six feature-length films and had come to represent the epitome of 'modern cinema', likewise engaged with Bardot's star persona when he made *Le Mépris* in 1963. Adapted from Alberto Moravia's novel *Il disprezzo* (1954), Godard's film, like Moravia's novel, describes a couple – Camille (Bardot) and Paul (Michel Piccoli) – whose relationship falls apart against the backdrop of the Italian cinematic milieu. Paul has been commissioned to work on a piece for an American movie producer named Jeremy Prokosh (Jack Palance), a new adaptation of the *Odyssey* directed by Fritz Lang (played by himself). The contempt (*mépris*) that Camille feels for Paul, supposedly due to his decision to work for Prokosh, occasions the couple's disintegration, narrated in a scene beautifully and lengthily depicted in their Rome apartment. In Capri, where the whole crew moves to finish Lang's *Odyssey*, Camille starts a liaison with Prokosh. They leave together for Rome and die in a car crash. Paul returns to writing for the theatre, while Lang completes his film.

The artist-figure played by Mastroianni in *Vie privée* is represented in *Le Mépris* by both Paul and Lang who, as Michel Piccoli observed, constitute a kind of 'two-headed monster, Godard's double' ('une sorte de monstre à deux têtes, le double de Godard').[10] Godard himself makes a brief appearance as Lang's assistant in the Capri scenes. Juxtaposed against what is a multifaceted representation of the great male artist, Camille is doubly associated with commercial cinema: she is played by Bardot, and has an affair with the American Prokosh. *Le Mépris* thus reproduces the dichotomy between elite male culture and female mass culture that features in *Vie privée*. However, Godard complicates this topos in several ways.

Not least, he modifies the high cultural script emblematized by the *Odyssey* and the great writers quoted by Lang (Dante, Hölderlin, Brecht) by allying it with 'noble' manifestations of popular culture: *Rancho Notorious*, *Rio Bravo*, the cinema of Griffith, Chaplin and Rossellini. Lang, the maker of the film-within-Godard's-film, and one of Godard's 'twin' doubles, represents the epitome of the cultured male subject and, as Michel Marie puts it, is a flesh-and-blood incarnation of auteurist cinematic politics ('la politique des auteurs en chair et en os')[11], which thus permits Godard to place his own movie within the realm of Art. Lang and Paul, Godard's other alter ego, discuss literature, mythology, cinema. Camille, on the other hand, knows nothing of high culture – the *Odyssey*, she claims, is 'the story of some travelling guy' ('l'histoire du type qui voyage') – nor of the kind of film-making valorized by the *Cahiers du cinéma*. She responds with indifference when Paul offers to go and see *Rio Bravo*. The joke Lang makes about the two BBs (Brigitte Bardot and Bertold Brecht) in the music hall scene, during which popular Italian music is shown as vulgar and inauthentic, underlines for the benefit of the spectator – not without irony – the distance between them, and the cultural modes they exemplify.

In *Le Mépris*, as in *Vie privée*, femininity and consumerism are shown to stifle male creativity. Camille's enthusiasm for her beautiful apartment is the reason why Paul chooses to 'prostitute' his talent to Prokosh. Camille must die in order for Paul to return to his true art, that of the theatre, and Prokosh and Camille must die for the 'real' film to continue. But, unlike the charismatic Fabio in *Vie privée*, Paul is mediocre, and caught between two worlds: he has neither the aura of the great Lang, nor the vitality of the vulgar but powerful Prokosh. Moreover, the ending of *Le Mépris* is not a triumphant affirmation of transcendent (male) creative power, as in *Vie privée*, but rather a comment on the 'death of cinema' and the end of Western civilization (the impossibility of bringing the Ulysses myth back to life). It addresses much more than the fate of the protagonists of the film: the last shot of Lang's movie-within-the-movie shows us a blue but empty sky over which Godard's voice speaks the word 'silence'. Nonetheless, the pessimistic metadis-course that Godard proffers invokes a sexualized notion of creativity, according to which the creative individual can only be male. The cinema for which *Le Mépris* mourns is the cinema of Lang, not of Bardot.

Godard's treatment of Bardot is more complex than that of Malle. *Le Mépris* plays with the gap between the character (Camille) and the star (Bardot), while in *Vie privée* there is a confusion of the two. For example, according to the logic of the narrative of character that *Le Mépris* offers, Camille's decision to join Prokosh (towards whom she is no less contemptuous than she is of Paul) seems inexplicable, but in terms of the logic of the star system that Bardot exemplifies, the Prokosh-Bardot couple makes perfect sense. Camille is an opaque character, devoid of psychological complexity, whereas Bardot brings a visual, oral and semantic depth to Godard's film. As Marie has remarked,[12] Bardot's mythical aura automatically links her to the film's other 'gods'. The dichotomy between the character and the star is particularly in evidence in the portrayal of Bardot's body. Godard, as ever, is both critic and advocate in *Le Mépris* of dominant modes of female represent-ation.[13] He analyses Bardot's iconic dimension, but always returns to her body, her sexuality. Bardot's body becomes the arena wherein elite, high culture (which, in *Le Mépris*, includes auteurist cinema) and mass culture compete for primacy.

Godard was unwilling to show Bardot's naked flesh, but Joe Levine, *Le Mépris*'s producer, demanded that he should add scenes unveiling the star's body. This created one of the *causes célèbres* of French cinema history. Godard's riposte was to add a prologue (located immediately after the film's famous spoken credits) in which Bardot details each part of her body, filmed with stridently coloured filters (blue, red) alternating with natural light. By blatantly transgressing the codes of erotic representation, Godard remained faithful to his aesthetic project: a project of the distanced gaze. And he preserved the loyalty of his cultured audience – an audience that, offered a naked Bardot as a bonus, could recognize and appreciate his creative 'signature' – while alienating the 'popular' spectator (it should come as no surprise that *Le Mépris*, a success in terms of Godard's own career, was one of Bardot's worst flops).

In *Vie privée* and *Le Mépris*, the characters played by Bardot, ciphers both of 'the feminine', are excluded from the world of male creativity. Both films distance and marginalize the popular, as manifested in forms that were most threatening to auteurist cinema as a vehicle of high, elite culture: forms incarnated in the figures of the French female star and the American producer. As Andreas Huyssen has noted, modernism conceals its envy of the popularity of mass culture under the guise of condescension and contempt.[14] It is consequently unsurprising that in *Vie privée* and *Le Mépris*, Bardot dies. Even though, throughout the 1960s, Bardot would incarnate the image of a woman seeking economic, professional and emo-tional independence, an image that was not without significance for the young women of the period, the films discussed in this and the previous section, especially *Vie privée*, imply that the popular female star must inevitably fall victim to the image she (re)presents.

In concluding my analysis, I wish to signal that the cinematic corpus I have chosen to explore has an exemplary status. If the films studied illuminate part-icularly clearly the new representations of sexual and socio-cultural identities that New Wave cinema evolved, and the depiction of the dynamics between such identities that it provided, the same modalities of representation are more or less explicitly in evidence in most of the films issuing from, or associated with, the *Cahiers du cinéma* movement. The so-called 'left bank' film-makers (Alain Resnais, Chris Marker and Agnès Varda, for example) of the 1950s and 1960s were motivated by a different kind of creative commitment, both artistic and political, and their films, at least those of the mid-century era, bear witness to an alternative vision of sexual relationships and of sexual and socio-cultural identities that warrants separate scrutiny. *Hiroshima mon amour* (1959) and *Cléo de 5 à 7* (1962), the sole films from this period to attempt to position a female character as a focal consciousness with whom the subject might identify, not only manifest a common will to examine the imbrication of the political and the private/personal, but were also, significantly, written or directed by women (Marguerite Duras, Agnès Varda). However, the avant-gardist perspectives that these latter films bespeak were far less influential than those mobilized in the central current of late 1950s/early 1960s French cinema, a current that gave rise to the *cinéma d'auteur*. Auteurist cinema has, since the 1960s, remained the emblematic mode of French film-making, evolving from a New Wave cinematic practice whose characteristics I have detailed in the present discussion.

Acknowledgement

The analyses on *Vie privée* and *Le Mépris* offered above are inspired by an article that appeared in *Iris*, 26, Autumn 1998, cowritten with Ginette Vincendeau, whom I thank profusely.

Notes

1. See *Cahiers du cinéma*, 138, December 1962; *Positif*, 46, June 1962. The fortieth anniversary of the emergence of the New Wave has been marked by a proliferation of critical publications on the movement, all of which seek to consolidate its place in the cultural canvas of twentieth-century France as the epitome of 'modern' creativity. These publications include: A. de Baecque (1998), *La Nouvelle Vague: Portrait d'une jeunesse*, Paris; J. Douchet (1998), *Nouvelle Vague*, Paris; a special number of the *Cahiers du cinéma*, entitled *Nouvelle Vague: Une légende en question* (1998: *hors série*); M. Marie (1997), *La Nouvelle Vague: Une école artistique*, Paris. The modernism of the New Wave is a key focus in what follows.
2. See M. Coquillat (1982), *La Poétique du mâle*, Paris, pp. 295–318.
3. See A. Huyssen (1986), *After the Great Divide: Modernism, Mass Culture and Postmodernism*, Bloomington and Indianapolis.
4. See A. Astruc (1948), 'Naissance d'une nouvelle avant-garde, *L'Ecran français*, 144, reprinted in A. Astruc (1992), *Du stylo à la caméra et de la caméra au stylo: Ecrits 1942–1984*, Paris, pp. 324–8.

5. Of interest, in respect of this phenomenon, is L. Mulvey (1989, with C. MacCabe), 'Images of Women, Images of Sexuality: Some Films by J.-L. Godard', in *Visual and Other Pleasures*, Basingstoke and London, pp. 49–62.

6. See C. Chabrol (1976), *Et pourtant je tourne*, Paris.

7. In a gesture typical of *auteur* cinema, Louis Malle radically reworked the project originally proposed to him – that is, an adaptation of Noël Coward's *Private Lives* – by suggesting to its producer, Gouze-Rénal, that he should write with Jean-Paul Rappeneau an original scenario based on BB's life.

8. For auto/biographical data on Bardot, see C. Rihoit (1986), *Brigitte Bardot, un mythe français*, Paris; B. Bardot (1997), *Initiales BB*, Paris.

9. On this subject, we should note that the creators of *Vie privée* plunder and exploit the most turgid of tabloid, scandal-sheet gossip, even though such gossip is contradicted by biographical documentation on BB, who called for a different type of freedom-in-love from that depicted at the start of the film.

10. Michel Piccoli, quoted in P. Vimenet (1991), *Le Mépris*, Paris, p. 104.

11. See M. Marie (1990), *Le Mépris*, Paris, p. 57.

12. See ibid., p. 67.

13. See Mulvey, 'Images of Women'.

14. See Huyssen, *After The Great Divide*, p. 17.

−8−

'Autistic Masculinity' in Jean-Pierre Melville's Crime Thrillers

Ginette Vincendeau

Introduction

Between 1956 and 1971, Jean-Pierre Melville directed seven remarkable crime thrillers: *Bob le flambeur* (1956); *Deux hommes dans Manhattan* (1959); *Le Doulos* (1962); *Le Deuxième Souffle* (1964); *Le Samouraï* (1967); *Le Cercle rouge* (1970); and *Un flic* (Melville's last film, 1971). While clearly genre films in their iconography, Melville's 'thrillers' (I shall call them such for convenience) blur many distinctions: between *auteur* film and popular cinema; between different national intertexts; and within the genre itself, oscillating between gangster film, police film and *noir* thriller. Their representation of masculinity, similarly, fluctuates between the generic and the idiosyncratic, frequently pushing the boundaries of the male gangster/policeman hero beyond established norms. Although Melville's total corpus of thirteen features is highly coherent, for reasons of space and focus I shall leave his other films out of this study.[1] In fact, though I refer to all his thrillers, I shall concentrate on the last three: *Le Samouraï*, *Le Cercle rouge*, and *Un flic*, unified by their use of colour; the performance of the star Alain Delon; and the presence of modernist architecture.

Melville's thrillers display the classic urban iconography of crime, as defined by Colin McArthur.[2] They roam the streets, cafés and night-clubs of Paris, Marseilles and New York. They celebrate the cars, guns and smart attire of the gangster, with his dark suits and ties, his trench coats and hats. Law and lawlessness, loyalty and betrayal, daring heists followed by inevitable failure and death supply their narrative dynamics. Partly because of these generic features, and partly because of Melville's well-known Americanophilia (evident in his choice of pseudonym and the fact that *Deux hommes dans Manhattan* and *L'Aîné des Ferchaux* are set and partly shot in America), these films have traditionally been seen as inspired by American cinema, and, in the most reductive readings, as no more than French imitations of Hollywood movies. Yet Melville's range of intertextual reference is much wider than that. His popularity in France and his cult status outside show that he succeeded in integrating the codes of indigenous crime films (including the specificity of French male stardom) with those of the American gangster film and Western, as well as with codes allied to the figure of the Japanese *samuraï* and to classical tragedy.

To say that Melville's thrillers inhabit a male universe is both self-evident and an understatement. Chronologically, they feature an increasingly bleak, exaggeratedly masculine world that virtually eliminates women (as well as children and the family). The realm of Melville's gangsters is ever more self-enclosed and self-referential, with no perspective on the 'real world', not even at the level of fantasy. This narrative and thematic evolution is paralleled by increasing levels of abstraction and ritualization in the *mise en scène*. However, while this may suggest a difficult avant-garde cinema – on a par, say, with that of Bresson, with whom Melville is sometimes compared – most of Melville's thrillers, and especially *Le Deuxième souffle*, *Le Samouraï* and *Le Cercle rouge*, were extremely popular at the box office. They were not genre movies aimed at a sub-culture of young men (as, arguably, the films of Melville's disciples, Quentin Tarantino and John Woo, are today), but mainstream films – including blockbusters such as *Le Cercle rouge* – destined for a wide audience. This points to the need to relate Melville's textual system and gender ideology to broader social and cultural contexts, as I shall do at the end of this chapter.

Melville and the Critics

The extreme – and by the end almost caricatural – masculine focus of Melville's thrillers has, unsurprisingly, been noted, but has not been explored in any sustained way. This is because, in critical terms, the films have, so to speak, fallen between several stools. In Anglo-American critical discourse, they usually figure as rare examples of French films within studies of the thriller/gangster genre dominated by American cinema.[3] Steve Neale's psychoanalytic exploration of masculinity and Stella Bruzzi's cultural study of clothes in 'Franco-American gangster films' also discuss Melville, especially *Le Samouraï*,[4] but do not focus primarily on his work. These critics do, however, give consideration to questions of gender. The same cannot be said of the more extensive French literature on the director.

French exegeses devoted to Melville raise the issue of gender, only immediately – and defensively – to drop it. In their useful survey of Melville's films, Jacques Zimmer and Chantal de Béchade claim that, if he is generally accused of misogyny, Melville has created two of the most beautiful portraits of women the cinema has offered, in the context of a genre reputed to be exclusively masculine.[5] Here, however, they refer not to women in his thrillers, but to the niece (Nicole Stéphane) in *Le Silence de la mer* and Mathilde (Simone Signoret) in *L'Armée des ombres*. I would add that, powerful as Stéphane's and Signoret's performances certainly are, these critics' assessment is overstated. In her otherwise insightful book on Melville,

Denitza Bantcheva argues that while some have spoken of misogyny and puritanism in respect of his cinema, her own view is that, if he occasionally shows women as humiliated, or leaves off-screen erotic scenes the audience wants to see, no general conclusions may be drawn from this.[6] One of the very few French reviewers of Melville's films to comment on their maleness simply remarked, approvingly, that Melville had done away with 'the usual pretty girls'.[7] These writers' conflation of gender with misogyny or eroticism, and their blindness to masculinity as a gendered mode of sujectivity, testify to the French critical inability to engage with gender as a social construct. Their 'old-fashioned' auteurism also produces a critical impasse, since it refuses to read gender expression in the films through any prism other than that of the potential misogyny of the film-maker, while simultaneously seeking to celebrate him.

My own approach, here, is auteurist too, in that I treat the films as an ensemble whose coherence is supplied by their director. This I regard as an unproblematic procedure, since Melville, from *Bob le flambeur* on, had an exceptionally high level of control over his films, as studio-owner; producer; scriptwriter and director; and, in *Deux hommes dans Manhattan*, as lead actor. I shall not, however, address gender in the films simply in terms of Melville's personal feelings towards women and men. Though these feelings undoubtedly had an impact on his choice of genre, subjects and treatment, of equal importance to the success of his cinema are generic codes; the French star system; source material; and the sociocultural construction of gender in post-war France. The question, in sum, that I shall explore is not 'was Melville a misogynist?' but rather 'why would his male-centred (and misogynist) films be so appealing?' The answer lies, I would argue, in his unique combination of exquisite style with a portrayal of masculinity that is at once cool, intense and tragic.

'Tragically Useless' Women

Let us begin by briefly examining the representation of women before moving on to the men. Nobody will be surprised to learn that in Melville's thrillers, women are marginal. They have no place in the world of gangsters, in terms of narrative agency or screen time, and are thus, in the formulation of a perceptive reviewer, 'tragically useless'.[8] This is reflected in the casting, where no major female star appears. One exception is Catherine Deneuve in *Un flic*, but her narrative role as the mistress of both the main gangster Simon and the *flic* played by Delon is minimal. Deneuve's part in *Un flic* does, however, illustrate two other functions common to Melville's women: that of connective conduits between men, and that of pure representation.

Melville's women serve primarily as links between male subjects. Some are benevolent: Yvonne in *Bob le flambeur*; Manouche in *Le Deuxième Souffle*; Jeanne in *Le Samouraï*; Cathy in *Un flic*. They are the women who feed, clothe, shelter, nurse, run messages and provide alibis for the men. Others are malevolent or just 'bad': Jean's wife in *Bob le flambeur*; Thérèse in *Le Doulos*; the unnamed mistress in *Le Cercle rouge*. They are the women who betray gangsters to the police or (sexually) to each other, and generally get in the way of male bonding. In *Bob le flambeur*, Anne goes from loyalty to betrayal and back; the piano player in *Le Samouraï* is also in turn helper and betrayer, as are the female characters visited by the two male investigators in *Deux hommes dans Manhattan*. In that film, a well-known French politician who was a leader in the Resistance dies in his mistress's flat. The project of the journalist played by Melville, and of his boss, the head of AFP is to erase the 'shameful' death from public view in order to preserve the glorious legend. While this is directly readable as a testament to Melville's well-documented commitment to the ideal of the Resistance, it also symbolically removes the feminine from the grand narrative of male resistance heroism.

But whether facilitators or obstructions, women in Melville's thrillers are equally useless, since none of the helpers (Yvonne, Manouche, Cathy) has any impact on the tragic fate of the male hero. This is visualized in the women's confinement to marginalized feminine spaces: behind a bar; in the bedroom; in bed (Jeanne in *Le Samouraï*, the nameless woman in *Le Cercle rouge*); away from the action. If they happen to be in the streets, they are usually prostitutes. The most prominent prostitute in Melville's thrillers, an (unnamed) informer in *Un flic*, turns out to be a male transvestite. Though extreme, Melville's marginalization of women is hardly unusual for the genre. More interesting is his focus on women as *representation*, especially in his last three thrillers. Here a few words need to be said about the stylistic evolution of Melville's thrillers.

The first two films, *Bob le flambeur* and *Deux hommes dans Manhattan*, use a significant amount of outdoor shooting and embed their male heroes within a more or less realistic universe of cafés and clubs, densely populated by a cast of newspaper-sellers, porters, nurses, actors and journalists. The following two, *Le Doulos* and *Le Deuxième Souffle*, move into the bleaker hinterland of the Paris and Marseilles suburbs. This shift is illustrated by a comparison of the opening of *Bob* (an affectionate tribute to Place Pigalle, with Melville's voice-over and accordeon soundtrack) with that of *Le Doulos*, where Serge Reggiani walks alone, accompanied by Paul Misraki's ominous jazz score, along a grim, dark street under railway lines. In *Le Deuxième Souffle*, Gu spends much screen time on wintry, windswept roads and in solitary suburban rooms. Scenes in *Le Doulos* and *Le Deuxième Souffle* take place in cafés and clubs, but these are no longer the convivial spaces of *Bob*. They are evoked in a melancholy and minimalist fashion, with claustrophobic telephone booths, window panes, staircases, and sets that are empty of warmth and characters. Paradoxically, since Melville has now fully moved on to colour, the last three films inhabit an even sparser and more melancholy universe.

The fewer moments of location shooting depict a dismal suburban street (*Le Samouraï*); soggy, snow-bound fields and woods (*Le Cercle rouge*); and a totally deserted beach on the Vendée coast (*Un flic*). Gone are the companionship and humour of the first two films, gone are the couples of the following two (Maurice and Thérèse in *Le Doulos*; Gu and Manouche in *Le Deuxième Souffle*). Male heroes now live alone (Jef in *Le Samouraï*); with each other (Corey and Vogel in *Le Cercle rouge*); or with their cats (Mattei in *Le Cercle rouge*).

Women in *Le Samouraï*, *Le Cercle rouge* and *Un flic* are kept women, that is, prostitutes, as spelt out to Jeanne by the police inspector in *Le Samouraï*. In *Le Cercle rouge*, the film that features the most minimal feminine presence, Delon places a photograph of his former mistress, now the girlfriend of the rival gangster who sent him to jail, in the latter's safe after he has forcibly taken money from it. Female sexuality and money are exchangeable currencies in the gangsters' economy. But the fact that what he places in the safe is a photograph, whose pose is exactly duplicated by the (nameless) woman herself as she is briefly glimpsed behind a door and in bed, also shows Melville's self-conscious play with female representation. This is expanded in the same film by the brief, though pointed, look at erotic prints on the walls of Delon's flat. Delon enters the flat after a long time in jail, and carefully highlights the prints with a torch. The moment has no narrative purpose. (He could, equally, have used the torch to look for the light-switch.) But the fact that the prints, like the whole flat, are dusty (the telephone is covered with cobwebs), ingeniously signals Delon's dormant sexuality, as well as the redundant nature of women in Melville's system. After showing the prints on the wall, the camera pans to a bedside table where a photo of the former mistress (again in the same pose) stands: Delon picks it up and throws it in the bin. This is the point where he has bonded with Vogel (Gian Maria Volonté), who stands in silence next to him. Not only are women redundant, but in this most extreme film (heterosexual) sexuality is renounced too. In *Le Samouraï*, sex with Jeanne is, literally, an alibi. It is possible to see a suggestion of homosexuality in Melville's films (especially in *Le Doulos* and *Le Cercle rouge*), but it remains just that. More accurately, in Melville's male homosocial world, sexuality is sublimated. In addition to the persona/presence of stars such as Delon and Ventura, which guarantees virility, sexuality, as we shall see later, is displaced into professional action on the one hand, and into the narcissism of clothing on the other.

What the last three films also show is the representation of women as spectacle in a more literal sense. *Le Samouraï*, *Le Cercle rouge* and *Un flic* all feature cabaret scenes constructed around ironically tacky female song-and-dance numbers, staged in the style of Parisian tourist attractions such as the Lido and the Folies-Bergère. *Le Cercle rouge* contains three such moments that occur at Santi's, the cabaret run by the eponymous character played by François Périer. In the first show, the dancers are dressed as prostitutes (short slit skirts, fishnet tights, swinging bags); in the second, they appear as flappers dancing to the Charleston; and in the third, they are 'savages' whose routine is accompanied by a heavy drumbeat. In *Un flic* this phenomenon takes an even more self-conscious form. There is one such scene, a brief one, with women in rhinestone-covered bikinis. But there is also Cathy, played by Deneuve. In Cathy, however, character is simply replaced by star persona. Cathy 'is' Deneuve. Her entrance into the film is telling in this respect. Delon sits down at the piano at 'Simon's', the club that belongs to gangster Simon, Cathy's lover and Delon's friend. Deneuve's entrance in medium shot, out of a grey doorway, resembles a stage entrance. Discreetly made-up, with pink skin tones, glossy lips and blonde scraped-back hair, diamond and coral earrings, she is the glamorous icon popularized by her films and cosmetics adverts. Although he is active (playing the piano) while she just stands there, Deneuve's introduction produces an illusion of equality with Delon through the use of shot/counter-shot. She only reappears three times in the film, however; her total dialogue amounts simply to a few lines.

Women in Melville's last three films perform the function of link/exchange illuminated in previous thrillers. So, for instance, Deneuve's purpose in *Un flic* is sexually to connect crook and policeman. Their situation as kept women and spectacle highlights their consumable status. They are contained, literally, like the photo in the safe, while important business between men goes on around them. At the same time, in the cabaret scenes, Melville foregrounds the mythical status of all his characters: men in conspicuous gangster clothes (or policemen disguised as gangsters, such as Mattei in *Le Cercle rouge*) meet as self-conscious represent-ations of 'gangsters'; while women as spectacle embody feminine myths (the prostitute; the flapper; the savage). Here, representations of masculinity and femin-inity belong equally to the domain of spectacle, and are counterposed in an ever more abstract and self-conscious way. Borrowing Laura Mulvey's argument about Godard,[9] we can say that Melville is both analytical and complicit in his represent-ation of women. He is analytical because he pushes the codes of representation in such exaggerated fashion that they are held up for scrutiny to the audience. But he is also complicit because the cabaret scenes are discrete episodes, 'frozen' in the all-male narratives. Whether as representations that can be contained, locked away or consumed, or as 'helpers' who fail to help, women are fundamentally marginal to the world of Melville's thrillers, indeed useless.

But why may we deem Melville's women 'tragically' useless? We can do so because his thrillers, unlike genre films that celebrate the absence of women with a sense of purpose and adventure (the Western), or with glee (the comedy), offer a sombre portrayal of doomed masculinity. Men do not eliminate women in order to conquer the world or have fun, but rather to perform death-driven rituals. Like the American Western and the Japanese *samuraï* film,[10] the thriller is so evidently male that masculinity in it is both transparent and overwhelming. Sexuality is virtually absent from the screen, but machismo is extensively portrayed. The symbolism of men wielding large guns seems almost too obvious to merit discussion. This is probably why studies of sexuality and gender in crime films have tended to concentrate on *film noir*, where men are more troubled and women more prominent.[11] The thriller meanwhile shares with the Western and the *samuraï* film a vision of an all-male universe of control, ritual, violence and death.

In *West of Everything* (1992), Jane Thompkins sees the Western's androcentric universe as symptomatic of a rejection of the domestic femininity of nineteenth-century religious and literary culture, but also of a reaction to twentieth-century female emancipation.[12] Writers on *film noir* have suggested that its portrayal of masculinity is linked to changes in women's roles brought on by the effects of war. Work on the thriller, on the other hand, has tended to contextualize it in terms of social issues such as capitalism, real crime and censorship. Alternatively, the prominence of death in the thriller has generated cultural readings, and, in particular, comparisons with tragedy, especially since the publication of Robert Warshow's influential 1970 essay 'The Gangster as Tragic Hero'.[13] As Christine Gledhill puts it, 'it is this – the inevitability and mode of the gangster's death – which permits critics' frequent appeal to tragedy as a justification for taking the genre seriously'.[14] Melville himself repeatedly evokes tragedy as the inspiration and underlying structure of his thrillers. Feminist readings of the gangsters' macho posture have tended to view that posture as evidence of weakness; of masked vulnerability; of a 'masculinity in crisis'.[15] Although I am suspicious of the notion of 'masculinity in crisis' as applied to such dominant and popular forms of its representation, I shall look at men in Melville's thrillers in terms of their vulnerability as well as their strengths. And I shall focus my analysis through two prisms: the importance of 'work'; and the celebration of 'autistic' masculinity, set against the context of France in the 1960s.

Men at Work: The Nobility of Professionalism

Purposeful action and movement traditionally characterize virile masculinity.[16] In the Western, this is visualized by horseback pursuit or flights across vast landscapes, and in *samuraï* films by *chambara*, the spectacular sword combats. In Melville's thrillers – which, like most French thrillers, eschew car chases and violent physical fights – action and movement are materialized in the heist, carefully planned, and executed with extreme professionalism (cf. the bank convoy hold-up in *Le Deuxième Souffle*; the break-in at the Place Vendôme jewellers in *Le Cercle rouge*; and the theft of drugs on the train in *Un flic*, which occupy increasingly lengthy periods of screen time). In the light-hearted *Bob le flambeur*, for instance, the robbery of the Deauville casino is minutely thought through if not carried out, because Bob is so busy gambling that he forgets about it. Nevertheless, we are treated to a detailed rehearsal, including a fantasy 'flash forward'.

Through its emphasis on design and skill, the heist is one of the elements that transform the thriller into art, as well as constituting a source of spectatorial pleasure. In Melville's minimalist film-making, where looks and silences are paramount, it becomes a perfect *mise en abyme* of plot and *mise en scène*, as well as of the skills of the director: it is brilliantly conceived, precisely timed, spectacular. The heist contains the potential for violence (its suspense is based on it), but violence is rarely actualized. More important are notions of skill, control and discipline, which also happen to define virile masculinity. In Melville's understated universe, the heist becomes the stage for a display of masculinity in motion.

At this point, it is important to pause briefly to invoke the French star system, and its dominance by male stars. It is no accident that the apogee of Melville's thriller career, with *Le Samouraï* and *Le Cercle rouge*, corresponds to his use of Alain Delon, a star noted for his beauty (and, incidentally, his underworld connections),[17] but also for the controlled virility of his minimalist performance style, inherited from Jean Gabin. Similarly, Lino Ventura (an actor also in the Gabin orbit) imbues the character of Gu in *Le Deuxième Souffle* with the full force of his understated virility: a virility all the stronger because it is given virtually no outlet, as he spends most of his time hidden away. Delon and Ventura were consistently among the top-grossing stars of the period; thus, Melville's conception of masculinity meshed with the dominant (French) style of *performing* masculinity.[18]

The professionalism fetishized by Melville confers nobility on men, a nobility to which women have absolutely no access. The completed heist is presented as a job well done, in the tradition of Jules Dassin (*Du rififi chez les hommes*, 1955) and Jacques Becker (*Le Trou*, 1959), but also of John Huston, whose *Asphalt Jungle* (1950) Melville greatly admired. What these films have in common is their use of the heist or the prison escape to exploit a perverse vision of 'work'. We admire the men for their skills so much that we forget they deploy them in the service of crime. This is because the heist mobilizes the most noble kind of work: that of the superior artisan (cf. Jansen's total concentration, in *Le Cercle rouge*, on the manufacture of the special metal alloy for his alarm-destroying bullets). Heists also require total attention and coordination with other men, and therefore trust. Professional skills are a core element of male bonding. *Le Samouraï* does not feature a heist, but it invests equally in the celebration of accurate professional gestures. This is evident, for instance, in the scenes where Jef and later the policemen patiently and systematically search through a set of keys to find the right one to start a stolen car, or break into Jef's apartment. In the two scenes where Jef visits the mechanic who swaps his number plates, the two men interact in almost total silence. Their trust and the evidence of what needs to be done suffices. Delon's nonchalant yet tight gestures match the mechanic's concentrated work, the scenes punctuated and almost choreographed by François de Roubaix's sparsely evocative music. In *Le Cercle rouge*, Corey and Vogel, from inside the jewellers, open the door at the agreed precise time when Jansen (Yves Montand) is outside, without knowing for sure whether he is there. The success of the operation, and their lives, depend on being able to rely on each other. They look at their watches, at each other, open the door. Jansen is there.

Let me briefly expand here on the role of the Yves Montand character, since he illustrates how, in Melville's films, professional skills are used as a *cure* for ailing masculinity. We are brutally introduced to Jansen in the throes of delirium tremens, rendered expressionistically by animals crawling all over his bed. Reviewers at the time criticized what they saw as a scene out of character with Melville's style (and out of sync with the rest of the film, generally highly praised). Yet, in terms of the character's masculinity, the scene makes perfect sense. Although we are given little information about his past, it emerges that Jansen, an ex-policeman and ace marksman, is in his parlous state because he is *out of work*. A surreal framed picture of a gun on the wall of his dingy room taunts the unshaven, sweaty and uncoordinated figure who pants and shouts as the telephone rings. Corey and Vogel's request that he join them for the heist provides a miraculous cure: he meets Corey at Santi's, smartly dressed; 'cases the joint' at the jewellers; practices his marksmanship; makes the special bullets; and finally, during the burglary, is able to perform the virtuoso shot that disables the alarm system. Aptly enough, he carries his rifle in a violin case and his own skill is emphasized at the key moment: he takes the rifle off the tripod and shoots 'by hand'. This shot, as Bantcheva notes,[19] is ironic, since the lock is inscribed with the initials *JPM* (those of Melville). But the fact that Jansen's crowning achievement is to perform a successful single shot also surely (and rather obviously) attests to his recovered masculinity. Superior professional skills make the man and, here again, this complete, cool and co-ordinated masculine figure accords with the 'normal' persona of the star.

Jansen exemplifies yet another aspect of Melville's use/vision of the heist. Having recovered his masculinity, he gives up his share of the money and later comes to the others' rescue in an act of virtual suicide (in which he dies). In this regard, his fate is no different from that of the other men in *Le Cercle rouge* and, extrapolating further, from that of the male figures of most of Melville's thrillers. A comparison with *Rififi* and *The Asphalt Jungle* illuminates the specificity of these thrillers. In the American film, the bank robbery is accomplished by each member of the group for a stated (and visualized) pupose: the money will help a family; permit an escape; enable the purchase of a dream home. When the men fail, compassion and pathos are triggered in the spectator. In *Rififi*, the hero, Tony, dies as a consequence of the heist. Pathos is evoked through personal ties, articulated via the child who accompanies Tony in his last car ride to death. In *Le Cercle rouge*, as in *Le Samouraï* and *Un flic*, however, the men have absolutely no past and no family connections so emotions are eliminated. (Delon's consignment to the bin of the woman's portrait also makes sense in this respect.) But there is more than that. As Jansen's self-immolatory gesture shows, the ultimate gain, in Melville's films, is of no importance. In Melville, the heist takes place as a proof of professionalism and, per se, bestows nobility on masculinity. At no point does it affect the fatal destiny of the men, predicted in the opening quotation of *Le Cercle rouge*, attributed to Rama Krishna ('When men – unknown to them – are destined to meet one day, anything can happen to them; they can follow divergent paths; on the appointed day they will inescapably be reunited in the Red Circle'). In its emphasis on inevitable failure and fatalism, Melville's cinema echoes the philosophy of the *samuraï* and the *ronin*. In this respect, and notwithstanding the fact that Melville's citation from 'The Book of Bushido' at the beginning of *Le Samouraï* is in fact his own invention, Jef's trajectory in that film is closer to that of the *samuraï*, destined for ritual suicide, than to that of the heroes of American cinema whose fatal end is predicated on censorship and on a Manichean moral code of good and evil.[20]

Melville's representation of masculinity, while it is embedded in the codes of French mainstream cinema (for instance, in his use of stars) and in the generic tropes of the thriller, derived in part from popular American film, also reflects his modernist vision of cinema as art for art's sake, and his existential leanings.[21] Melville's construction of masculinity resides in the following central paradox: the heist celebrates superior skills that underline virility, but it is also evidence of the ultimate futility of (male) life – it is pure *acte gratuit*. In this regard, Melville's treatment of the (gendered paradigm of the) heist signals the bleakness of his vision: a bleakness that can be understood in relation to aspects of French mid-century culture.

'Autistic Masculinity': The Nobility of Death

Melville's avowed desire to elevate his thrillers to the level of 'tragedy' is amply documented.[22] Although there is considerable debate about the terms 'tragedy' and 'melodrama', which I cannot expand on here, there is no doubt that, in the cinema, men dominate the 'tragic' genres of the Western and the thriller, while melodrama is women's province. Gender, then, is enmeshed with the cultural prestige of 'the tragic', and therefore with the tragic aura of Melville's films. But in what sense is Melville's portrayal of masculinity actually 'tragic'? I would argue that it is 'tragic' in two ways: in its concern with death, and in its account of 'autistic' masculinity.

Melville's male protagonists are turned inwards, melancholy and death-driven, yet glamorous and desirable. The 'nobility' of death-driven heroes is powerfully inscribed in the thriller format, no less than in Greek tragedy. André Bazin once called Jean Gabin 'Oedipus in a cloth cap', and one could similarly dub the gangster of the thriller genre 'Oedipus in a trench coat and felt hat'. Critics have dwelt on this phenomenon in their treatments of the American cinematic heritage, especially the glorious period of the 1930s gangster films (*Little Caesar*, *The Public Enemy*) and 1940s *film noir* (*Double Indemnity*, *The Big Heat*). But French cinema, with the emblematic *Pépé le Moko* (1937), as well as its numerous adaptations of French crime literature, also created its own mythology of doomed criminals. Melville, as I have established, crossed these already imbricated traditions with that emblematized in the figure of the Japanese *samouraï*, rendering the crime film-narrative all the richer.

Although Jef, the hero of *Le Samouraï*, is arguably more akin to the *ronin*, or wandering lord-less warrior, he is nonetheless a *samouraï* in that he abides by a (tacit) code of conduct inspired by the Bushido. The West discovered Japanese cinema with Kurosawa's *Rashomon* in 1950. His *Seven Samurai* (1954) also had a major impact. More generally, an interest in Japan permeated French high culture in the 1960s (cf. Alain Resnais's *Hiroshima mon amour* (1959), and Roland Barthes's book on Japan, *The Empire of Signs*, published in 1970). Japanese culture was adulated largely for its exoticism and difference. Melville's recourse to the figure of the *samouraï* does not denote an interest in seventeenth-century Japanese history, but rather an appropriation of a narrative structure and ethical framework whose history conferred credibility and prestige. In this, it reminds us of American remakes of *Yojimbo* (*A Fistful of Dollars*) and *Seven Samurai* (*The Magnificent Seven*). Mitsuhiro Yoshimoto's summary account of an early script for *Seven Samurai* – 'One day of a *samurai*'s life: he gets up in the morning, goes to work at a castle, makes some mistake on the job, and goes home to commit *seppuku*, or ritual suicide'[23] – uncannily evokes *Le Samouraï*. The endings of *Le Samouraï* and of *Le Cercle rouge* can indeed be described as 'ritual suicide', announced in *Le Samouraï* by the garage mechanic, and in *Le Cercle rouge* by the opening quotation.

In order to achieve their death-driven goal, Melville's heroes must be free of any ties. The elimination of women, discussed earlier, means that relationships – with lovers and wives; with family; with children; in short with life – are effectively absent. 'Life' in this context means emotions and passions, femininity and effeminate weakness. It spells vulnerability and, perversely, threatens to distract the hero from his deathly trajectory into the safety of the 'normal world'. For instance, Weber's wife in *Un flic* believes that his trips to perform various robberies are motivated by his search for a job. The concealment of his criminal life preserves his masculine ego while driving him surely to death: he commits suicide when the police knock at the door. His, however, is a slightly ignominious suicide (he is hidden away, in the bathroom), whereas Simon's at the end of *Un flic* is a calm, calculated death, similar to Jef's: he pretends to shoot his friend the policeman (Delon), who then wounds him mortally, only to find that Simon's gun was empty.

The 'positive' side of this construction of masculinity is the culturally prized notion of 'cool' – a display of nonchalance: a disengagement, based on the denial of emotion – which goes towards explaining Melville's exportability and his influence over such figures as Tarantino and Woo. The 'negative' side is a cold and sterile self-absorption: a lack of communication that is close to autism. (Autism, according to dictionary definitions, means an abnormal self-absorption; a limited ability to communicate; a difficulty with language.) Of course, Melville's heroes are not autistic in the strict or clinical sense of the term. They can bond with other men and communicate through shared 'professional' gestures. But these heroes perform their tasks in silence, and live alone or with animals. Their unusual self-absorption includes a high degree of narcissism that chimes with the thriller genre's traditional investment in clothes. However self-consciously, Melville draws excessive attention to the gangsters' narcissistic tendencies. This aspect of his films has already attracted attention from English-speaking scholars.[24] Melville frequently shows his heroes looking at themselves in mirrors (cf. Bob in *Bob le flambeur*; Maurice in *Le Doulos*; Jef in *Le Samouraï*; Jansen in *Le Cercle rouge*): since their personality is all image, it needs constant reaffirmation. As Bruzzi has noted, Jef's downward trajectory is paralleled by the spoiling of his sartorial ensemble (he is shot through his trench coat).[25] Conversely, in *Le Cercle rouge*, we witness Jansen's metamorphosis from abject alcoholic to brilliantly tuned crack shot through his increasing elegance, an elegance that reaches its apogee when he fires the climactic shot that puts the alarm system out of action. Here, Jansen, like Corey and Vogel, completes his attire with an impeccable black silk mask and the Melville trademark white editor's gloves. With elegance in mind, it is time to return to my opening question about the popularity of Melville's representations.

Concluding Remarks

Melville's films may dialogue with the gangster movie of the 1930s (French and American) and with the historic figure of the Japanese *samouraï*, but they also spoke to, and speak about, 1960s France. The last three films inhabit the affluent areas of the Champs-Elysées where the moneyed bourgeoisie meets high-class prostitution, the two worlds intersecting in night clubs and bars. Their gangsters merge with the new *cadres* who rose to prominence in France through the 1950s and 1960s. In *Le Samouraï*, Jef gets rid of his (damaged) trench coat and dons a dark coat and hat to perform his ultimate contract: his own suicide. In *Le Cercle rouge*, Jansen blends perfectly with the rich customers of the jewellers. The opening robbery in *Un flic* is particularly enlightening. Four men raid a seaside bank, men who could equally be gangsters or businessmen. In fact, one of them, Weber, *is* a former bank manager. The sharp suits, dark glasses, neat hair, hats and briefcases connote both gangsterism and the new capitalism reigning over France in the last decade of its post-war economic boom.

The 1960s witnessed the height of France's state-led modernization, manifested by profound political, economic and psychological changes, including the rise of what Roland Barthes envisioned as 'structural man'.[26] As Kristin Ross states, in the new era, 'subjectivity, consciousness, and agency – what passed for *l'homme*, in short, under the now obsolete terms of bourgeois humanism – [were] effaced to the profit of rules, codes, and structures'.[27] One important aspect of this sea-change – the flight from the political, through structuralism – is beyond the scope of this discussion. What I would like to suggest, however, is that, while Melville always professed to make films detached from their immediate context, the intellectual debates of 1960s France invoked above, as well as other cultural manifestations, help us understand how his last thrillers 'spoke' to France in the late 1960s, through an interesting paradox. On the one hand, his self-centred, disconsolate males, obsessed with death and bent on performing *actes gratuits*, are typical of the modernist sensibility, evoking as they do some of the tropes of the French new novel and absurdist theatre. Theirs is not a triumphant rule but a melancholy one, a fact attested to by Melville's numerous images of men seen through rainy window panes. (This is one reason why Delon is the perfect star for the late Melville films.) On the other hand, the supreme professionalism of the gangsters gestures towards the new super-skilled *cadre*-engineer, the lynchpin of the French post-war technocratic establishment. Thus, Melville's configuration of masculinity both celebrates and critiques the shift towards a cool, hard, technocratic new society that mid-century France so markedly underwent. This phenomenon is illustrated by, among other things, Melville's exploitation of modernist architecture.

In *Le Samouraï*, *Le Cercle rouge* and *Un flic*, Melville's pared-down *mise en scène* showcases a cold, linear, modernist world. Colours are washed out and dominated by greys, blues and greens. In *Le Samouraï*, Melville famously aims for 'a black and white film in colour'.[28] It is true that Melville creates a unique fantasy world in which he houses his heroes: an amalgam of French and American locations. At various points, Parisian rooms suddenly open up on to New York vistas (cf. Jef's room in *Le Samouraï*); maps on the walls of police inspectors show the streets of New York (*Un flic*). But location shooting as well as set designs (cf. the cabaret scenes) also show us a brutally real modernist Paris. Like Godard in *Alphaville* (1965) and Tati in *Playtime* (contemporary with *Le Samouraï*), Melville constructs an aesthetically pleasing yet disturbing universe, whose reference points include nightclubs and apartments with white walls, plexiglass bubbles and steel tubes, and the distorted walls of the modern police headquarters in *Un flic*. The ghostly beach at St-Jean de Monts, with its miles of ugly apartment blocks with closed shutters, also depicted in *Un flic*, is a key emblem of the new French leisure society, and, moreover, of the price paid for its realization.

The angular architecture, with its cold colour scheme and images of closure, is likewise a perfect setting for the 'autistic' gangster. As neighbourhoods fragment

Figure 8.1 Masculininty and the fetishism of clothes: Alain Delon (centre) in Jean-Pierre Melville's *Le Samouraï* (1967). Courtesy of Bibliothèque du Film et de l'Image (BIFI), Paris

Figure 8.2 Homosexual love as alibi: Nathalie Delon (left) and Alain Delon (right) in *Le Samouraï*. Courtesy of BIFI, Paris

and central Paris starts its process of *embourgeoisement*, as lifts remove the conviviality of the staircases of old Parisian buildings (lovingly documented in 1930s cinema), so Melville's protagonists must adapt to the new environment, characterized, among other things, by a rise in technologically advanced domesticity. Echoing Jane Thompkins's assessment of the Western, I would suggest that the male(nes)s of Melville's movies may be allied to a flight from an inflated domesticity. The autistic Melville hero responds to a contemporary crisis in 'human' identity (a crisis usefully documented by Ross), and does so in a manifestly gendered fashion. Technology – cars, guns – can be harnessed by men, but is harnessed in order to erase all the more effectively the feminine-oriented technologies that contribute to the 'colonization of everyday life'.[29] It is telling in this context that the few shots of kitchens in the films I have chosen are of kitchens occupied by men who are definitely not cooking: Bob is drinking white wine; Jef dressing his wound; and Jansen making his metal alloy.

The analysis conducted in this chapter does not in any way exhaust the richness and interest of Melville's cinema. But it shows how gender, and especially the construction of masculinity, is intimately linked to all aspects of that cinema: *mise en scène*; performance; decor; themes; and plots. In his brilliant crafting of a unique filmic and cultural hybrid – a self-conscious, nostalgic rewriting of the American and French thrillers of the 1930s and 1940s, enmeshed with a revisiting of the Japanese *samuraï* – Melville succeeds in making the death-driven gangster talk to all of us about universal problems: problems of good and evil, but also problems thrown up by the dehumanization of modern France.

Notes

1. Melville's other films are: his trilogy of war films (*Le Silence de la mer* (1946); *Léon Morin, prêtre* (1961); *L'Armée des ombres* (1969)); his early melodrama *Quand tu liras cette lettre* (1953); his Jean Cocteau collaboration *Les Enfants terribles* (1949); and his adaptation of Georges Simenon's *L'Aîné des Ferchaux* (1962). I am currently working on a book-length study of Melville, to be published by the BFI in 2002.
2. See C. McArthur (1972), *Underworld USA*, London.
3. See ibid.; P. Hardy (1998), *The Companion to Crime*, London.
4. S. Bruzzi (1997), *Undressing Cinema: Clothing and Identity in the Movies*, London and New York; S. Neale (1983), 'Masculinity as Spectacle', *Screen*, 24, pp. 2–16.

5. See J. Zimmer and C. de Béchade (1983), *Jean-Pierre Melville*, Paris, p. 33.

6. See D. Bantcheva (1996), *Jean-Pierre Melville: de l'oeuvre à l'homme*, Troyes, p. 51.

7. See *Les Nouvelles littéraires*, 29 October 1957. No author is indicated.

8. See G. Daussois, *Le Populaire*, 14 November 1967.

9. See L. Mulvey (1989, with C. MacCabe), 'Images of Women, Images of Sexuality: Some Films by J.-L. Godard', in *Visual and Other Pleasures*, Basingstoke and London, pp. 49–62.

10. I am aware that it is reductive to talk of the '*samuraï* film' which, historically, does not exist as a category but as various manifestations of historical films. For a discussion of this issue, see M. Yoshimoto (2000), *Kurosawa*, Durham and London. However, the relation I invoke here is not to *samuraï* films as a genre, but to the *figure* of the *samuraï*, of special interest to Melville.

11. See for example in this context E.A. Kaplan (ed.) (1980), *Women in Film Noir*, London.

12. J. Thompkins (1992), *West of Everything: The Inner Life of Westerns*, New York and Oxford.

13. R. Warshow (1970), 'The Gangster as Tragic Hero', in *The Immediate Experience*, New York, pp. 127–33.

14. C. Gledhill (1986), 'The Gangster/Crime Film', in P. Cook (ed.), *The Cinema Book*, London, pp. 85–91, p. 89.

15. See, for example, P. Kirkham and J. Thumim (1995), 'Me Jane', in P. Kirkham and J. Thumim (eds), *Me Jane: Masculinity, Movies and Women*, London, pp. 11–35, notably pp. 30–1.

16. See ibid., pp. 11–35.

17. I have developed this reading further in my chapter 'One Sings, The Other Doesn't', in G. Vincendeau (2000), *Stars and Stardom in French Cinema*, London and New York, pp. 158–95.

18. The well-known anecdote that, on the set of *Le Cercle rouge*, Melville had to ask the Italian actor Gian Maria Volonté to tone down his 'gesticulations' points to the national specificity of performance styles. With regard to Melville's deployment of male French actors, I shall shortly discuss Montand. I want here to signal briefly, too, that *Le Cercle rouge* makes a startlingly unusual use of the comic star Bourvil, transposed (following his own desire, reportedly) from bumbling 'village idiot' comic to melancholy professional cop.

19. Bantcheva, *Jean-Pierre Melville*, p. 145.

20. See M. Smith (1995), *Engaging Characters: Fiction, Emotion and the Cinema*, Oxford, pp. 216–23, for a discussion of moral code versus moral orientation in *Le Doulos*.

21. See C. McArthur (2000), 'Mise-en-scène degree zero: Jean-Pierre Melville's *Le Samouraï*', in S. Hayward and G. Vincendeau (eds), *French Film: Texts and Contexts*, London and New York, pp. 189–201.

22. See, for example, J.-P. Melville, interview with C.-M. Trémois, *Télérama*, 12 November 1967.

23. Yoshimoto, *Kurosawa*, p. 204.

24. These include Bruzzi; McArthur; and Neale.

25. Bruzzi, *Undressing Cinema*, pp. 80–1.

26. See K. Ross (1995), *Fast Cars, Clean Bodies: Decolonization and the Reordering of French Culture*, Cambridge, Mass. and London, p. 160.

27. Ibid., p. 161.

28. R. Nogueira (1971), *Melville*, London, p. 130.

29. See Ross, *Fast Cars*, p. 77.

9

Gender in the French Fantasy Film 1965–95
Guy Austin

Introduction

As Claude Chabrol has noted, 'there is no real tradition of fantasy cinema in France'.[1] The tradition is, in the main, Anglo-Saxon (Universal horror, Hollywood sci-fi, Hammer horror) rather than Francophone. Hence, it should come as no surprise that a chronological survey of French fantasy cinema since the New Wave would begin and end with Anglophone productions, from Truffaut's *Fahrenheit 451* (1966) and Vadim's *Barbarella* (1967) to Besson's *The Fifth Element* (1997). In this chapter, I shall be using these three films, and some less well-known Franco-phone examples, to map out gender paradigms presented in modern French fantasy cinema. These paradigms range from the readily-identifiable, often-theorized models of the demonized woman, the 'monstrous feminine' and the 'archaic mother', via the Pygmalion myth and its avatars, to the more neglected areas of (constructed/performed) masculinity and, finally, androgyny. Given that 'fantasy cinema is based on archetypes',[2] one might expect it to provide a particularly rigid and unchanging lexicon of gender representations. Certainly, a number of stock gender types were mobilized with repeated success by the numerous British Hammer horror films of the 1960s and early 1970s. And, by virtue of the threadbare nature of the French fantasy film tradition, it is to the Hammer model that I shall turn first.

The Archaic Mother

The stock gender types of Hammer horror and related genres include the 'phallic' female vampire (a figure often imputed with lesbian overtones); the decadently vampiric count; the obsessively puritanical male scientist and/or witchfinder; and the normalized heterosexual couple.[3] The first of these has received by far the most critical attention, notably in Roger Dadoun's seminal essay on fetishism in the horror film, first published in 1970 in *La Nouvelle Revue de psychanalyse*. Concentrating mainly on the Hammer studio, Dadoun spoke of the horror film as mobilizing fears (and desires) related to the 'archaic mother', defined as a 'phallic woman, a woman with a penis, a murderous, all-devouring or castrating mother'.[4] Dadoun's account coincides with the vogue for female vampires that flourished at the start of the 1970s with Hammer's 'sexploitation' trilogy and, in France, Jean Rollin's lesbian vampire series.[5] But the principal importance of Dadoun's thesis lies in its treatment of the gendering of space, according to which the favoured uterine settings of the horror film reveal traces of the archaic mother who 'can be read in a series of enclosures and expulsions, . . . whereby spaces, one inside the other, become progressively smaller and more confining'.[6] Following Dadoun and also Kristeva, Barbara Creed, in her work on the 'monstrous-feminine', has stressed how 'the mythological figure of woman as the source of all life' is rendered pathological and terrifying in many horror and science-fiction films, 'the generative mother seen only as the abyss, the monstrous vagina'.[7] But, illuminating though this paradigm is, the fantasy film does not always demonize the archaic mother and the monstrous-feminine, as I intend to show.

Before leaving Hammer behind, in order to consider French fantasy films of the same period, the rudimentary fantastical trope of doubling requires some attention. At least insofar as it is applied to female figures, doubling can be related to what Bruno Bettelheim identifies as the dual role of the witch in fairy tales: 'The witch . . . in her opposite aspects is a reincarnation of the all-good mother of infancy and the all-bad mother of the oedipal crisis . . . either superhumanly rewarding or inhumanly destructive.'[8] Both of what one might term the 'maternal' tropes of fantasy film (doubling to create good and bad mothers, and the uterine space as the site of terror) are manifest in Hammer's *Twins of Evil* (1971), a film that features twin sisters, one good and one evil. The latter is punished for her ravenous sexuality by becoming a vampire: subsequently one of her victims is attacked in an underground dungeon, another lured into a cave. These tropes reappear in Tim Burton's recent homage to Hammer, *Sleepy Hollow* (1999), with the mother-function split between the good witch (the hero's mother) and the evil witch (the heroine's stepmother). The latter is revealed as the 'archaic mother' when she conjures the decapitated and decapitating Headless Horseman from the womb-like bowels of the Tree of the Dead. And the same tropes can likewise be found in a French science-fiction fable contemporaneous with Hammer horror, François Truffaut's *Fahrenheit 451* (a film actually shot in England, at Pinewood studios and on location in Welwyn Garden City).

Besides its explicit discourse on the respective attributes of television and literature, *Fahrenheit 451* (1966) also engages with French history – Nazism; the Resistance; the importance of remembering in the context of Gaullist myths about the Occupation[9] – and with gender. The protagonist, Montag (Oskar Werner), is asked to choose between the masculine values of the firemen (a kind of fascistic paramilitary group associated with uniformity, discipline and the law) and the more expressive, idealistic values of the underground, the Book People.[10] Put simply,

Montag is challenged to find his 'feminine side', to open up to the emotive and sentimental yet subversive power of literature. The film represents this possibility as utopian, and personifies it in the character of Clarisse (Julie Christie). But the idealized Clarisse is doubled by Christie's other role in the film, as the demonized Linda, Montag's wife. Where Clarisse's appearance is androgynous (tomboy haircut and functional clothes), Linda's is glamorous and feminine, recalling the *femme fatale* of *film noir*. And, like the *femme fatale* – or indeed the lesbian vampire – she is represented, via the insistent mirror compositions, as narcissistic and duplicitous.[11] In short, Linda is the phallic woman, the castrating or archaic mother. This is most apparent in two key sequences that associate her with vampirism and the undead. In the first, Montag finds Linda unconscious on the floor after an overdose: two medics arrive and give her a 'pump out' and a 'blood job', after which she will, they declare, awaken with an 'appetite for all sorts of things'. The next morning, the prediction comes true as Montag, carefully buttoned-up to the neck in his pyjamas, has to fend off his sexually voracious wife. This 'confrontation with the abject (the corpse, bodily wastes, the monstrous feminine)'[12] is later followed by a second confrontation as a book-wielding Montag tells Linda and her friends – all indolent, pill-popping consumers of television – that they are nothing but zombies, who are not living but just killing time in a mindless limbo.

However, our sense that Truffaut is simply rehearsing some split between masculine mind and feminine body is qualified by the nature of the passage read aloud by Montag to his resentful audience. A pathetic lament for a dying wife, the passage at one level expresses Montag's own desire to be rid of Linda (in exchange for Clarisse?). But, by means of the reaction it elicits from its audience, it also represents a return to the good mother; to the traditionally 'feminine' mode of 'the weepie' (in literature or film); to excessive bodily reaction (tears); to nostalgia, loss, an earlier state of things. Hence the troubled responses from Linda, who asks 'Why disturb people with that sort of filth?', and from her friends, one of whom rejects 'novels and tears' while the other breaks down, sobbing 'I'd forgotten all about those feelings'. To a certain extent, then, *Fahrenheit 451* actually celebrates the (monstrous/feminine) body and its 'filth' – when the body and its functions are represented as emotional rather than explicitly sexual. In this regard, the film is comparable to the Hollywood invasion narratives of the 1950s that Mark Jancovich has described as valuing, contrary to the received wisdom about gender in fantasy cinema, 'those qualities which are usually associated with femininity'.[13]

The dichotomy between the 'superhumanly rewarding' good mother and the 'inhumanly destructive' bad mother[14] informs not just characterization but also decor and spatial design throughout Roger Vadim's *Barbarella* (1967). Shot in English, like *Fahrenheit 451*, but based on a French rather than an American source (Jean-Claude Forest's cartoon strip), *Barbarella* stars Jane Fonda as the eponymous superhero, and Anita Pallenberg as the Black Queen, the Grand Tyrant of

Sorgo, City of Night.[15] First seen floating (and stripping) in zero gravity, like a baby in the womb, Barbarella flies a red spaceship that pulses like a heartbeat when preparing for take-off and within which her pilot's chamber is lined with fur. This good maternal craft is to take her on a mission to 'preserve the unity of the stars and our own mother planet', during which Barbarella confronts various forms of masculinity (mostly impotent or destructive) and, ultimately, the archaic mother/phallic woman incarnate, the Black Queen, complete with spiked head-dress and costume, who kills and tortures her victims and whose city lies uneasily on a mass of evil liquid energy called the Matmos. Along the way, Barbarella is 'birthed' down several tubes or out of port-holes – like an earlier version of Besson's super-heroines Nikita and Leeloo[16] – and is attacked not just by the knife-wielding Black Queen but also by a collection of tiny vampire dolls, and by a flock of Hitchockian birds (symbols, in turn, of inappropriately aggressive female and male sexuality). Although the city of Sorgo – like the representations of lesbian vampires in Rollin's films and in Hammer horror[17] – is a phallicized, sadistic realm where sex and violence are always equated, Barbarella's own (hetero)sexuality is ideal-ized: a kind of non-phallic weapon (like her ship), or perhaps more accurately a shield. Her 'good' sexuality is identified again with the mother-ship, in the shots of Barbarella reclining in post-coital poses against warm, golden-brown back-grounds of fur or feathers. Like a male fantasy of the good mother as sex object, Barbarella rejects the Black Queen's lesbian advances, and yet she is finally reconciled with her in order to defeat the overly aggressive masculinity represented by the mad scientist Duran Duran and his phallic positronic ray. The Matmos con-sumes Duran Duran but spares Barbarella and the Black Queen, returning them to safety in a uterine bubble. As in *Fahrenheit 451*, for all the explicit demonizing of the archaic mother throughout the film, it is the abject (in this case, the threatening but nurturing fluid of the Matmos) that ultimately represents a means of escape from fascistic male power.

Claude Chabrol's *Alice ou la dernière fugue* (1977) is stylistically far removed from the camp sexual violence of *Barbarella*. The characterization evades the stock gender types noted above, while the genre is neither horror nor science fiction but pure fantasy, as defined by Todorov: a sustained hesitation between the rational and the supernatural.[18] And yet, even here, the archaic mother can be traced in the claustrophobic enclosures of both narrative and decor. Alice (Sylvia Kristel) is caught between life and death, trapped in a comfortable but sealed limbo that, as the final shot suggests, lasts only as long as it takes her to die as the result of a car crash.[19] Dadoun tells us that in the vampire film, 'a dark, dense, lonely forest . . . is the place for an accident . . . which leaves the hero alone, bereft, as it were lost and enveloped', and that the escape route from this accident is 'the umbilical cord that leads to the castle' of the vampire.[20] Chabrol's film follows this itinerary very closely, with Alice's car accident in the evening rain followed by her stumbling upon the strange, isolated house. Her subsequent escape attempts are futile: all roads and paths return her to the point of departure, the house. The latter is a clear metaphor for the mother's body, in both its nourishing and carceral aspects, so Alice is fed and waited upon but cannot leave. (To this extent, the house represents both the 'good' and the 'bad' mother.) This interpretation holds whether we consider *Alice* to be the story of the protagonist's death or, as Chabrol suggests, the story of her rebirth: 'What happens in the house could represent her period of gestation. Does the film then begin with her death or with her birth?'[21] In Dadoun's paradigm, the horror film's 'series of enclosures' reaches its climax when 'horizontal progression is transformed into vertical descent', usually 'down a twisting staircase' to the crypt or coffin where the 'maternal soil' is found.[22] Alice eventually exits the house through a little wooden door that, we are told, leads down to hell. As Creed affirms, 'the archaic mother is present in all horror films as the blackness of extinction – death . . . a terror of self-disintegration, of losing one's self or one's ego – often represented cinematically by a screen which becomes black'.[23] Hence Alice's final descent into a darkness that fills the screen: 'As we might expect, this horrific emptiness isn't simply negative. It is an emptiness full of fantasmic activity and meaning, a silence full of muffled echoes.'[24] Thus, subterranean noises accompany the image of the abyss where Alice disappears to rejoin (or leave, if one accepts Chabrol's exegesis) the archaic mother.

In *Alice*, as in most of Chabrol's cinema, however, the traditionally maternal space of the house is also rendered a site of patriarchal power by means of surveillance. Like the controlling patriarchs of *Masques* (1986), *Inspecteur Lavardin* (1986) and *Docteur M.* (1990), Alice's male hosts express their power over her by means of voyeurism, observing her undress for a bath by means of a two-way mirror.[25] The fact that Alice's tormentors and captors, seen or unseen, are all male overlays the paradigm of the archaic mother with another recurrent gender motif in fantasy cinema, the Pygmalion myth.

The Pygmalion Complex

'Every major film-maker has a Pygmalion complex: the mad desire to construct a model of the world, and then to give it life.'[26] But the Pygmalion complex, as the original myth and its most famous screen avatars (such as *My Fair Lady*) indicate, is explicitly gendered, turning on the dynamic between male creator and female creature (Pygmalion and Galatea; Professor Higgins and Eliza). In the literature and cinema of fantasy, this myth informs the Frankenstein story and the mad schemes of male scientists and magicians. Lucy Fischer, in her study of Méliès, has memorably detected in the Pygmalion tendency a mode of 'womb envy', whereby the male magician appropriates the female creative powers and erases her from the picture, so that 'woman (as woman) is gone, with only her male-fabricated image remaining'.[27] But, as Mark Jancovich explains, horror's Pygmalion and Frankenstein narratives can be interpreted as being built around a fear of (masculine) science as much as a fear of (female) sexuality:

> Asexuality rather than sexuality is the problem, and this is related to a long history in horror fiction that dates back at least as far as Mary Shelley's *Frankenstein* (1818). Furthermore, asexual reproduction is a problem exactly because of its association with masculinity and science. As in *Frankenstein*, asexual reproduction is associated with the male fantasy of producing life without recourse to women, and it is this fantasy which is defined as monstrous specifically because it is founded on a male fear of female sexuality in particular, and of sexuality in general.[28]

Thus, in *Barbarella*, demonized sexuality is represented not just in female form by the Black Queen and the Matmos, as we have seen, but also by the male scientist Duran Duran, designer of the monstrous organ of torture (a musical instrument that consumes its victims like a huge *vagina dentata*) and the phallic positronic ray, the ultimate form of (masculine) weaponry in the film. His scientific/militaristic discourse and his phallic weapon of mass destruction are rejected by Barbarella with the words 'But that's monstrous!', and he is subsequently defeated by an alliance of the feminine elements in the film: the Matmos, the Black Queen and Barbarella herself.

The perfectibility of a female creature by means of obsessive and monstrous masculine science is a theme common to both the Pygmalion myth (cf. *My Fair Lady*) and the Frankenstein story. This theme informs Hammer's *Frankenstein Created Woman* (Terence Fisher, 1966), a film whose title refers us back to Roger Vadim's *Et Dieu créa la femme* (1956) and also makes us think about the processes behind Vadim's manipulation of Jane Fonda's star image in *Barbarella*. It is equally present in Luc Besson's *Nikita* (1990) – a French action remake of *My Fair Lady* – and *The Fifth Element*, where a male scientist oversees the cloning of a perfect female humanoid from a single alien cell.[29] And it is explored in Jeunet and Caro's futuristic fairy tale, *La Cité des enfants perdus* (1995), where a collection of miserable and malformed creatures – a dwarf woman; a migraine-ridden brain; a sick genius called Krank; and six identical clones with sleeping sickness – testify to the dangers of masculine scientific hubris. The dystopian birth narratives throughout the latter film also include biological 'freaks' such as the circus strongman One and the evil Siamese twins known as the Octopus sisters. Moreover, the numerous children are all orphans, while there is no positive maternal figure to speak of.[30] But nonetheless, in *La Cité des enfants perdus* as in *Barbarella*, the fear of female sexuality crystallized in the abject figures of the Matmos and the Octopus sisters is balanced by a fear of the deranged male scientist, who must be destroyed for closure to be secured.

Masculinities

The mad scientist is not the only role reserved for men in fantasy film. Two other masculine roles predominate in these narratives: the monolithic, proto-fascist male collective and the fetishized, overperformed masculinity of the macho-man. The all-male collective – uniformed, puritanical, violent, a brotherhood with a common cause but no individuation – has largely political connotations. The paramilitary firemen of *Fahrenheit 451*, dressed in black and bent on book-burning, are a direct reference to Nazism, while there are also fascistic echoes in the witchfinders of *Twins of Evil* and the Cyclops of *La Cité des enfants perdus*. In the macho masculinity of the individuated male protagonists – Barbarella's various sexual partners; the double roles played by André Dussollier in *Alice*; and above all, the gentle giant One in *La Cité des enfants perdus* – there are suggestions of role-play, repetition and codification. Particularly in the later films, as I shall shortly demonstrate, these phenomena have connotations of performativity, and even bring to mind the figure of the 'gay clone'.

If male roles are differentiated in the films under scrutiny, it seems to be in order that alternative masculinities might be explored. *Fahrenheit 451* sees Montag leave behind the monolithic masculinity of the firemen and replace their submission to patriarchal authority (symbolized by the magical properties of the firemen's pole) with emotional growth. When the captain's suspicions are aroused, he confronts Montag with the question 'Something wrong between you and the pole?', and insists that 'We've all got to be alike'. *Barbarella* posits the robotic 'leather-men' or Black Guards and the destructively phallic Duran Duran, with his positronic ray, at one extreme, with the hopelessly inept Dildano and the blind angel Pygar at the other. Both Dildano (David Hemmings) and Pygar (John Phillip Law) are presented as objects of desire but to some degree are emasculated: the former, a rebel leader in a leather tunic, is unwilling to have full physical sex (he prefers an orgasm pill) and is associated with broken and useless machinery; the latter, an angel dressed only in a loincloth, is 'cured' by Barbarella of an impotence signified both by his blindness and his temporary inability to fly.[31] The happy medium between violent phallocentrism and impotence is represented by Mark Hand (Ugo Tognazzi), a taciturn primitive who embodies male sexuality: he is hairy and bearded, wears furs, and has sex with Barbarella in a phallic rubber tent. (And, even here, his isolation in the arctic wastes and his name suggest a certain onanistic loneliness.) Full, active and non-destructive masculinity is, in a sense, conferred only by Barbarella herself, in the sex acts by which she rewards Hand, Dildano and Pygar.

But masculinity is also something denoted by appearance, as Richard Dyer has observed: 'Muscles, hairiness, sweat, dirt are conventional signs of masculinity'.[32] Mark Hand is thus coded as the most masculine of Barbarella's lovers not just by his uninhibited performance but also by his costume and his job. (He is dressed in furs and covered in hair; he alone is associated with work.) In other words, his masculinity is performed. A decade after *Barbarella*, the traditional signs of straight masculinity (muscles, workwear, uniform) were appropriated by gay male culture, through the figure of the 'gay clone'. The clone 'fashioned his appearance upon depersonalized, endlessly reproducible images of ideal masculinity', and, in particular, via 'a hypermasculine, highly codified mode of self-presentation which appropriated the roles (cowboys, cops, construction workers) and attributes (moustaches, muscular bodies, laconic speech) of mythic American masculinity'.[33] The gay clone aroused fears, centring on replication without procreation, similar to those aroused by the vampire of horror films or the robotic clone of science fiction.[34] Moreover, because he calls into question the way that masculinity is codified, the figure of the gay clone enables us to open up the question of encoding masculinity in the fantasy films under discussion.

The performative masculinity of the gay clone – a masculinity that turns on dressing-up and role-playing, on 'a kind of self-conscious . . . drag' – distinguishes this 'brand of machismo from its more earnest and tyrannical straight counterpart'.[35] In fantasy film, a theatrical and ludic masculinity (whether interpreted as gay or straight) is often contrasted with monolithic and tyrannical models demonized as monstrous and fascistic. Thus, in Hammer's *Twins of Evil*, the aristocratic and decadent vampire (aided by his butch black manservant) confronts the puritanical brotherhood of witchfinders. In *La Cité des enfants perdus*, One (Ron Perlman), a circus performer whose body is perpetually on display (bare-chested and chained when we first see him at the fair, later bound again but in a night-watchman's uniform, and finally clothed in a seaman's jersey that unravels in the finale to leave him bare-chested once more), battles against the evil Cyclops collective and the six identical clones. Where One's masculine identity is always performed as a display, in a series of different costumes and set-pieces celebrating his appearance and strength, the clones' identity is biological rather than performative: they are scientific clones (created by the Original) rather than role-playing ones. The film also recalls Fassbinder's Genet adaptation *Querelle* (1982) in its setting – a red-lit stone port – and via Gaultier's sailor-chic costumes, that likewise refer back to the gay clones of late 1970s America.[36]

In *Alice*, the 'drag' act is even more self-conscious, since we see one actor, André Dussollier, perform two contrasting masculine roles. He first appears as an urbane passer-by dressed in white, but later figures as a stern macho-man wearing black, complete with baseball cap, aviator shades and moustache. A gay clone, one might say, and certainly at least a theatricalized rendering of a stereotypically male occupation: he plays a garage mechanic, a role that requires as props not only oil can, overalls and cap, but also a gruff voice, comically brusque manner and exaggerated rudeness to Alice (herself now cast in another gender stereotype, as the hapless female motorist). I am not saying, here, that the individuated male characters in the films I am addressing are 'gay'. Rather, the masculinity of these characters is at times distinguished by its performative, costumed nature from the original, background masculinity profiled in the films (that of the clones and the Cyclops, or Alice's captors, seen and unseen), no less than the masculinity of the gay clone is distinguished from the straight original. Their masculinity is a masculinity whose visibly performed, imitative/derivative foundation 'brings into relief the utterly constructed status of the so-called original', just as the performed masculinity of the clone brings into relief the constructed status of straight 'original' masculinity: a masculinity that 'only constitutes itself as the original through a convincing act of repetition'.[37] If, in *Fahrenheit 451*, this pattern appears reversed, with a rather flat male protagonist pitted against a theatrical and cloned male grouping,[38] this is perhaps because Truffaut's film concentrates on the 'original' rather than on the 'copy', showing the firemen learning/repeating the rituals of their masculine activity rather than exploring Montag's own masculinity in any depth.

The notion of gender as performative, associated with the neo-Foucauldian work of Judith Butler, also has implications for the final area of this chapter's investigation, the androgynous. If gender in its 'so-called original' form is, in fact, 'utterly constructed', as twentieth-century theorists affirmed, then what of representations of gender that defy the rigid binary constructions of the masculine and feminine, that circulate between the polarized archetypes of uniformed, fascistic males and zombified, demonized females?

Conclusion: Fantasy and Androgyny

One might expect fantasy film to be a fertile source for the exploration of the androgynous. However, as Constance Penley has observed, science-fiction film in particular has become the site not of androgyny but of difference:

> As men and women are less and less differentiated by a division of labor, . . . science fiction film alone remains capable of supplying the configurations of sexual difference required by the classical cinema. If there is increasingly less practical difference between men and women, then there is more than enough difference between a human and an alien (*The Man Who Fell to Earth, Starman*), a human and a cyborg/replicant (*Android, Blade Runner*) or a human from the present and one from the future (*The Terminator*). In these films the question of sexual difference – a question whose answer is no longer 'self-evident' – is displaced onto the more remarkable difference between the human and the other.[39]

Besson's *The Fifth Element* would fit well into the typology of identities that Penley evokes (human and alien/cyborg). As Susan Hayward notes, the subversive promise of Leeloo, the androgynous alien/cyborg created in the film, is not held. Besson's recurrent Pygmalion complex surfaces once more, so that sexual difference is restored and Leeloo is rendered both Dallas's female lover and 'the (male) scientist's dream cyborg'. Hayward concludes that 'there can, it would appear, be no improper female masculinity for Leeloo'.[40] The film's final image is a freeze-frame of Dallas and Leeloo making love (sexual difference has brought them together and saved the earth). Unlike Dallas in *The Fifth Element*, the would-be hero Dildano in *Barbarella* fails to 'save the day for proper masculine mascu-linity'.[41] But of course the entire narrative of *Barbarella* is a priapic celebration of sexual difference. And, despite the careful elision of sexual implications in the relationship between One and Miette, *La Cité des enfants perdus* finally presents us with the formation of a heterosexual family group, as the dream sequence reconciles an aged, maternal Miette with One (surrogate husband) and Denrée (surrogate son). Since this coincides with the destruction of the male scientist and his monstrous laboratory, the film seems to conclude that 'mothers will be mothers, and they will *always* be women'.[42] So our French examples seem to confirm Penley's assertion that the 'majority of science fiction film works to dissipate the fear of the same and to ensure that there is a difference'.[43]

This 'fear of the same' may also explain the prevalence of the Frankenstein and Pygmalion paradigms in fantasy film and fiction, since it is when the 'division of labour' no longer applies to labour itself, and when the possibility of male birthing is raised, that a horror of sameness ensues. The terror of replication is also present not just in vampire films but in those psychological dramas that investi-gate the vampirizing of one person's personality by another, as in Chabrol's *Les Biches* (1967). The key exception, where sameness is not feared but celebrated, is (ironically, in view of Penley's remarks) offered by the earliest of the French fantasy films I have discussed, namely Truffaut's *Fahrenheit 451*. The film begins with a shot of the firemen's pole and the mobilizing of the group to destroy a cache of books, but such fascistic male collectivity is ultimately replaced by the androgyny of the Book People, whose gender is subsumed beneath their literary identity. They are simply books, and no longer have an 'original' gender identity: hence, both volumes of *Pride and Prejudice* are 'male'; the *Memoirs of Saint-Simon* 'female' (Clarisse); Sartre's *The Jewish Question* and Plato's *Republic* 'female'; *Alice in Wonderland* 'male'; and *Alice through the Looking-Glass* 'female'. Thus, the film ends with a vision of a brave new wilderness where humans are texts and gender has ceased to exist as it did in the codified, polarized society that has been left behind. As the snow falls on this wintry scene, the future is a genderless utopia.[44]

Notes

1. D. Overbey, 'Chabrol: Game of Mirrors', *Sight and Sound*, Spring 1977, pp. 78–81, p. 81. For the purposes of this chapter, I take 'fantasy cinema', as I believe Chabrol does, to include science fiction, horror, pure fantasy and fairy tale, but not the musical, which has been termed a fantasy genre although clearly belongs to a tradition distinct from the other genres mentioned here.

2. 'Le cinéma fantastique . . . travaille à partir de quelques archetypes'. P. Fraisse (1999), 'Entre science et fiction: Un certain cinéma fantastique', *Positif*, 466, pp. 71–4, p. 73.

3. See for example *Twins of Evil* (1971), where all of these archetypes are found. For the male scientist (rather than his alter ego the witchfinder), see *Frankenstein Created Woman* (1966).

4. R. Dadoun (1989), 'Fetishism in the Horror Film', in J. Donald (ed.), *Fantasy and the Cinema*, London, pp. 39–61, p. 50.

5. The films in question are Hammer's *The Vampire Lovers* (1970), *Twins of Evil* (1971) and *Lust for a Vampire* (1971) and Rollin's *La Vampire nue* (1969) and *Requième pour un vampire* (1971). Hammer's 'sexploitation trilogy' is considered in A. Weiss (1992), *Vampires and Violets: Lesbians in the Cinema*, London, pp. 88–96. For an analysis of the way in which Rollin's vampire films seem to escape the closure suggested by the sexploitation genre, see G. Austin (1996), 'Vampirism, Gender Wars and the "Final Girl": French Fantasy Film in the Early Seventies', *French Cultural Studies*, 7, pp. 321–31.

6. Dadoun, 'Fetishism', p. 52.

7. B. Creed (1989), 'Horror and the Monstrous-Feminine: An Imaginary Abjection', in Donald, *Fantasy and the Cinema*, pp. 63–89, p. 79.

8. B. Bettelheim (1991), *The Uses of Enchantment: The Meaning and Importance of Fairy Tales*, London, p. 94.

9. An important precursor to *Fahrenheit 451* is Renoir's *This Land Is Mine* (1942), also shot in English (in Hollywood), and also celebrating the power of Resistance literature in the face of Nazi occupation.

10. See below for more on the representation of masculinity in French fantasy cinema.

11. See, for example, J. Place (1980), 'Women in *Film Noir*', in E. A. Kaplan (ed.), *Women in Film Noir*, London, pp. 35–54, and Weiss, *Vampires and Violets*, p. 94.

12. Creed, 'Horror and the Monstrous-Feminine', p. 72.

13. M. Jancovich (1996), *Rational Fears: American Horror in the 1950s*, Manchester, p. 28. Jancovich contrasts his reading of these films with the theorizing of Peter Biskind and Barbara Creed about gender in the horror film.

14. See note 7, above.
15. The name Sorgo recalls both Sodom and Gomorrah.
16. See in particular the 'birthing' sequences at the restaurant in *Nikita* and at the laboratory in *The Fifth Element*. The latter, with its emphasis on Leeloo's bodily perfection and its gold colour scheme, can be compared to the opening credits of Vadim's film, where Barbarella undresses in a golden chamber while the title song describes her as a 'wonder-woman'.
17. See Weiss, *Vampires and Violets*, pp. 93–4.
18. T. Todorov (1975), *The Fantastic: A Structural Approach to a Literary Genre*, trans. R. Howard, Ithaca and London, p. 25, p. 31.
19. Compare the recent Hollywood thriller *The Sixth Sense*, that also has a frame narrative that ultimately explains the protagonist's position in a kind of undead limbo. Again, this position is expressed spatially by subterranean settings (the cellar) and by the repeated references to falling (the main narrative begins with the legend 'The Next Fall').
20. Dadoun, 'Fetishism', p. 52.
21. Overbey, 'Chabrol', p. 99.
22. Dadoun, 'Fetishism', p. 52. The 'maternal soil' is an allusion to the Dracula story, according to which the vampire could only rest in a coffin full of soil shipped from his homeland.
23. Creed, 'Horror and the Monstrous-Feminine', p. 81. In this regard, it is interesting to note that Chabrol has always declared in interviews that he has 'no ego'. Perhaps he protests too much. *Alice* can certainly be read, contrary to the director's own suggestions, as a film exploring the fear of losing one's ego.
24. Dadoun, 'Fetishism', p. 53.
25. See G. Austin (1999), *Claude Chabrol*, Manchester, pp. 107-23, for a fuller account of patriarchal power in Chabrol's films.
26. 'Il y a dans tout cinéaste majeur un complexe de Pygmalion: le désir fou de construire un modèle du monde, puis de l'animer'. Fraisse, 'Entre science et fiction', p. 74.
27. L. Fischer (1996), *Cinematernity: Film, Motherhood, Genre*, Princeton, p. 39.
28. Jancovich, *Rational Fears*, p. 29.
29. For more on gender in *The Fifth Element* see below, and also S. Hayward (1997), 'Besson's "Mission Elastoplast": *Le Cinquième Elément*', in P. Powrie (ed.), *French Cinema in the 1990s: Continuity and Difference*, Oxford, pp. 246–57.
30. If there is a good mother, she is perhaps to be found in Miette, the young girl seeking a family and saving Denrée by finally defeating Krank as an older, morphed avatar of herself. For a sustained analysis of the representation of the mother in *La Cité des enfants perdus* and other recent French films, see

G. Walsh-Harrington, 'The Function of the Incidental Song in Contemporary French Cinema', unpublished PhD thesis, University of Sheffield, 1999.

31. Dildano's name has an echo of 'dildo', and he represents mediated sexual experience (as in the scene with the orgasm pill, where sexual contact with the partner is minimal). Pygar is at one stage crucified by the Black Queen, and to this extent may be related to sexualized icons of male martyrdom such as Saint Sebastian or Valentino in *Son of the Sheik*.

32. R. Dyer (1990), *Now You See It: Studies on Lesbian and Gay Film*, London, p. 92.

33. R. Meyer (1994), 'Warhol's Clones', *The Yale Journal of Criticism*, 7, pp. 79–109, p. 98. Meyer dates the beginning of the phenomenon as 1978 and sees it as 'a historically specific response to the relentless feminization of the gay male body prior to the 1970s' (cf. p. 100).

34. See ibid., p. 108, on notions of homosexuality as 'replication of the same'.

35. Ibid., p. 100.

36. One's appearance recalls Genet's opening description of the criminal sailor's uniform in *Querelle de Brest*. The influence of Genet's novel on Gaultier's work at the time of *La Cité des enfants perdus* can also be seen in the adverts for his aftershave 'LE MALE', in which twin sailors arm-wrestle each other (an image of gay clones but also perhaps derived from the brothers in *Querelle de Brest*).

37. J. Butler (1990), *Gender Trouble*, cited in Meyer, 'Warhol's Clones', p. 100.

38. The firemen are characterized throughout by doubling: the captain is doubled by the old woman, whom he resembles in appearance and in death; Anton Diffring plays both a fireman and an aged schoolmistress; two cadets have to be separated in class, and so on.

39. C. Penley (1989), 'Time Travel, Prime Scene and the Critical Dystopia', in Donald, *Fantasy and the Cinema*, pp. 197–212, p. 204.

40. Hayward, 'Besson's Mission Elastoplast', p. 254. Hayward concludes that not the alien/cyborg Leeloo but the human Ruby Rhod is the site of transgression in the film (cf. p. 256).

41. Ibid., p. 255.

42. Penley, 'Time Travel', p. 206, italics in original (referring to *Aliens*). Compare the importance of the maternal in ensuring that sexual difference is reestablished at the end of *The Fifth Element*, where Leeloo's first words on waking before the finale are 'Protect life until death'.

43. Ibid., p. 205.

44. Contrast the fantasy portrayals of 'gender wars' that actually followed in the early and mid-1970s in France, as a reaction to the rise of the *Mouvement de Libération des Femmes* (*MLF*) and feminist politics in general. For more on this, see Austin, 'Vampirism, Gender Wars and the "Final Girl"', pp. 321–31.

10

Going Through the Motions: Unconscious Optics and Corporal Resistance in Miéville and Godard's *France/tour/détour/deux/enfants*

Michael Witt

Slow down, decompose (Ralentir, se décomposer)

Introduction

Anne-Marie Miéville and Jean-Luc Godard have employed slow, stop-start, accelerated and reverse motion extensively in their many collaborative ventures and individual projects from the 1970s to the present.[1] In extreme close-up, close-up, mid-shot, or long shot, the defamiliarized gestures of human bodies in motion are superimposed over or drawn into balletic interaction with those of other 'bodies': people walking; cars passing; clouds moving; lights flashing; and so on. Journalistic criticism has identified play with tape and film speed as an index of experimentation and an associated sense of 'difficulty'. But, as Nicole Brenez has suggested recently, the pioneering experimentation of film-makers such as Miéville, Godard, Martin Scorsese and Richard Brooks has encouraged a rediscovery of the medium's full palette of speeds by a range of contemporary film-makers.[2]

A history of Miéville-Godard's manipulation of film and tape speed would need to revisit examples couched in Godard's early work. One recalls, for instance, the staggered camera movement that pans to the rhythms of gunfire in *Vivre sa vie* (1962). Similarly, we might pursue the references to the relationship between human movement and cinematic flow in Godard's early critical writings. In a review of Alexandre Astruc's *Une Vie* (1958), Godard described how unexpected shifts in the pace of human movement – 'that suddenness of gestures that gets the suspense moving every three minutes, that discontinuity latent in the continuity' – had an impact beyond localized questions of narrative or dramatic interest.[3] This early essay foresees an approach to *mise en scène* and a quasi-burlesque conception of performance that informs Godard's *oeuvre*, and I would like to highlight at this stage the self-reflexive relationship between corporal movement and cinematic form that it implies. Gilles Deleuze's suggestive term *acteurs-médiums* captures the flat acting style of the generation of actors who came to cinema with the New Wave, and provides an apt description of the attention paid in Godard's work to the sculptural surface and gestures of the human body at the expense of psychological depth or character development.[4] The self-reflexive charge invested in the body in Godard's art cinema of the 1950s and 1960s is heavily inflected by the phenomenological existentialism of Jean-Paul Sartre and Maurice Merleau-Ponty: as flesh provides a conduit for desire, so all meaning traverses a body. Such reflexivity is increasingly politicized in Godard's collaborative work of the late 1960s and the 1970s, the body coming to serve as a shorthand for the distortions inherent in all processes of representation, and for the materiality of cinema in particular.

The representation of the female body in Miéville-Godard and Godard's work has proved a productive focus for feminist scholarship. Laura Mulvey has discussed the use of the woman's body in Godard as a kind of depository for disparate political, aesthetic and psychosexual meanings that in turn 'inflect the feminine'.[5] At the same time, she charts how that body, inextricably linked to a materialist concern for the demystification of the signifying process in the 1960s and 1970s, comes to represent wider mysteries of cinema and lived experience in Godard's later work.[6] Miéville and Godard have talked little in interviews of their extensive use of altered motion in the second of their collaboratively-made television series, *France/tour/ détour/deux/enfants* (1978). On the one occasion Godard addressed the issue at length, it was to suggest how their discovery of differences in the sequences involving the children, Camille and Arnaud, informed the conception of narrative and character in the fiction film he shot shortly afterwards, *Sauve qui peut (la vie)* (1979):

In *Tour Détour*, I had discovered an intuition, without pursuing it, as I would have needed to discuss it with colleagues and for them to share their experiences with me. We used slow motion and rhythm changes, what I prefer to call decompositions, employing the combined techniques of video and television. I had a little boy and a little girl at my disposal, and we did speed changes, semi-slowed down, semi-accelerated, semi-rhythmic, with loads of different possibilities. As soon as you stop one of twenty-five images (and which isn't enormous, it's five times the number of fingers on your hand, so something you can still conceive of), you realize that a shot you've filmed, depending on how you stop it, suddenly there are thousands of possibilities. All the possible permutations between these twenty-five images represent thousands of possibilities. I concluded that when you change the rhythms, and analyse a woman's movements, even movements as simple as buying a loaf of bread for instance, you realize that there are loads of different worlds inside the woman's movement. Whereas the use of slow motion with the little boy was a lot less interesting. We'd stop the image, and between each image was always the same guiding line. But with the little girl, even when she was doing extremely banal things, you'd go suddenly from profound anguish to joy a split second later. They were real monsters. And I, in my guise as a scientist who knows certain theories, had the impression that they were particles and different worlds, galaxies that were different each time and between which you moved via a series of explosions. Whereas the boy's movement was much more undulatory, with a point of departure, so that the use of slow motion was less interesting plastically.[7]

Taking her cue from Godard's comments, Constance Penley has argued that *Sauve qui peut (la vie)* runs an inevitable course from the breathtaking stop-start celebration of feminine difference proposed at its outset (Nathalie Baye cycling along a country road) to its logical endpoint: the male protagonist dying in the street.[8] Penley approaches the film's bleak portrait of sexual difference through an analysis of the relationship between its use of what she terms 'saccadic stop-motion' and the representation of the blocked traffic between the sexes. By returning to Godard's comments on the videographic somatology of *France/tour/détour/ deux/enfants*, and drawing on a combination of Foucauldian theory and the pre-cinematic science of Etienne-Jules Marey, my aim in this chapter is to foreground the self-reflexive dimension to the representation and decomposition of the body in the series. To begin with, however, I shall introduce three key names: Anne-Marie Miéville, Sonimage and *France/tour/détour/deux/enfants*.

Anne-Marie Miéville

Periodizing the five decades of Godard's work in film, video and television is far from easy. As Michael Temple and James S. Williams have argued in their volume of essays devoted to Godard's later work, the often unexpected turns taken by the ongoing Godardian project demand a constant reassessment of earlier periods in the corpus.[9] Situating the work of Anne-Marie Miéville and Jean-Luc Godard as 'Sonimage', however, is relatively straightforward. The audio-visual experiments conducted by Miéville-Godard in film, video and television in a succession of 'laboratories' from 1973 to 1979 constitute a self-contained and critically under-valued project.[10] Throughout his career, Godard has remained remarkably alert to, and drawn freely on, trends in contemporary thought, blending ideas from disparate thinkers and disciplines – artists; poets; philosophers; and film-makers, but also mathematicians and scientists – into his evolving enterprise. It is perhaps therefore not surprising that the Sonimage project should echo the wider interrogation of totalizing theory characteristic of post-structuralist thought in the 1970s.[11]

Miéville-Godard's aim was clear: to put talk of audio-visual decentralization into practice; work collaboratively; engage with television; and, through ownership of the necessary production equipment, take time to explore the technical and aesthetic potential of video as a compositional medium ('have a little bit of material with which to relearn, and the time to compose with it'[12]). Although their early ambition of producing as many as three low-cost films per year proved unrealistic, the Sonimage experiment was astonishingly productive. Over six years, they made almost nineteen hours of material for television broadcast or cinema release: three films (*Ici et Ailleurs* (1974); *Numéro deux* (1975); *Comment ça va* (1975)), and two monumental television series: *Six fois deux (Sur et sous la communication)* (1976) and *France/tour/détour/deux/enfants* (1978).

Godard has always sought to work with a close-knit group of regular collaborators. But it is the encounter with Anne-Marie Miéville in the early 1970s that marks the beginning of one of modern cinema's great collaborations. In discussions of her and Godard's work, Miéville has frequently been the object of critical injustice. All too often, her input has been ignored or skated over, even when a piece is co-authored or co-directed. It is therefore important to clarify her role in the Miéville-Godard collaboration, and emphasize the extent of her own output. She has forged a strong independent cinematic identity over the past thirty years, producing a body of work whose significance has been acknowledged in a series of retrospectives over the course of the past decade.[13] Independent of her collaboration with Godard, she has worked in a variety of forms: fictional shorts (*Papa comme maman* (1977); *How can I love (a man when I know he don't want me)* (1984); *Le Livre de Marie* (1984); *Faire la fête* (1987)); documentary (*Mars et Vénus* (1991)); and four feature films (*Mon cher sujet* (1988); *Lou n'a pas dit non* (1994); *Nous sommes tous encore ici* (1997); *Après la réconciliation* (2001)). Miéville's cinema comes as close to the crystalline forms of music and poetry as to the conventions of narrative cinema. Compositional precision feeds a loving attention to colour and careful use of direct sound. Running through the films we often find the central figures of the couple and human infant ('creation, creature, and above all creator', as Miéville suggests).[14] In narrative terms, the films return repeatedly to the intertwined themes of language and incommunicability, child-parent relationships and sexual difference. Of particular pertinence to my argument here, as will become apparent, is the pervasive presence of music, song and dance, especially in *Le Livre de Marie*, *Mon cher sujet* and *Lou n'a pas dit non*. The *mise en scène* of the body in *Mon cher sujet* borders on full-scale choreography, especially in the slow-motion fight sequence in the forest. Such is the omnipresence of dance that it erupts periodically through the surface of the films' narratives. Rather than introducing any sense of rupture, therefore, inclusion of a ten-minute filmed sequence of Jean-Claude Gallotta's *Docteur Labeus* in *Lou n'a pas dit non* constitutes the logical extension of a choreographic mode of *mise en scène* running through every film.

Miéville's role within Sonimage was every bit as important as that of Godard. She co-directed, co-authored and co-edited all their joint work of this period with the exception of *Numéro deux*, which she co-wrote. It is tempting to overcompensate for critical neglect of Miéville's contribution by suggesting that hers was perhaps the more significant voice of the two. It would certainly be possible to argue that she was the enterprise's principal creative force, supplying many of the thematic concerns that recur from work to work, and that Godard occupied a more reactive role, channelling her ideas into audio-visual form. In reality, of course, there is little to be gained from pursuing such an argument. The Sonimage work generally, and *France/tour/détour/deux/enfants* in particular, was the fruit of full, equal collaboration. Furthermore, following the Sonimage venture, Miéville has continued to contribute in diverse ways to many of Godard's projects. She co-wrote and co-edited *Sauve qui peut (la vie)*; collaborated on *Scénario du film Passion* (1982); scripted *Prénom Carmen* (1982); co-edited *Je vous salue, Marie* (1983); co-wrote *Détective* (1984); co-produced *Le Dernier Mot* (1989); and worked as art director on *Nouvelle vague* (1990). Above all, a combination of critical sloth and the shadow cast by Godard's star status has served to obscure the fact that Miéville and Godard have co-directed a sizeable body of further collaborative work over the past two decades. Like the Sonimage films and videos, these later collaborations are often essayistic in tone and video-inflected in form. As such, they provide a refreshing counterweight to the precision and intensity of their respective feature filmmaking practices: *Soft and hard* (1985); *Le Rapport Darty* (1989); *L'Enfance de l'art* (1991); *Ecrire contre l'oubli* (aka. *Pour Thomas Wainggai*, 1991); *Deux fois cinquante ans de cinéma français* (1995); and *The Old Place* (2000).

Let me now turn to *France/tour/détour/deux/enfants*. In a sense, the series continues the experimental documentary tradition to which Godard's project has always in part belonged. The documentary aspect of his early work is heavily inflected with the exploration of politics and form manifest in the proto-New Wave documentaries of film-makers such as Chris Marker, Alain Resnais, Jean Rouch and Agnès Varda in the 1950s. Rouch's work looms large over Godard's early art cinema. His influential *cinéma vérité* experiment with Edgar Morin, *Chronique d'un été* (1961), provides an important precursor to the report on the collective national psyche that *France/tour/détour/deux/enfants* proffers.[15] But there are two significant if self-evident differences: *France/tour/détour/deux/enfants* is a series, and it is television. Invoking a musical analogy, Miéville-Godard employ the term *mouvements* (cf. 'programmes') to describe the twelve twenty-six minute episodes that make it up. Each movement is introduced by two or more terms, loose generative metaphors that frame the disparate material that follows: interviews with the children; altered motion sequences; mini documentaries; cryptic 'stories'; and oblique discussions of the nature of television.[16] In his influential 1974 commentary on television as technology and cultural form, Raymond Williams proposed the expression 'planned flow' (or 'programmed flow') to describe the predictable mosaïc of the programming grid.[17] Where Miéville-Godard's previous television series, *Six fois deux (Sur et sous la communication)*, had intervened in the flow through a protracted process of amateurization, *France/tour/détour/deux/enfants* simulates and parodies the conventions of televisual rhetoric. In their respective commentaries, albeit through different means, Miéville-Godard and Williams likewise foreground the question of proportion and mix in television programming. Tongue in cheek, Godard claimed to be playing the scheduling game: 'Yes, I operated like the director of a channel, drawing up a programming grid. And then I began to shoot the follow-up shots . . . It was like a code, certain words of which you'd have, but whose logic had to be retrieved.'[18] Each programme, designed for insertion into the flow on a weekly basis, mimics and lampoons the codes and forms of prime-time television. The usual ingredients are all available – the presenters; talking heads; direct address; reverse angles; bounce lighting; game shows; serials; news bulletins; interviews; and so on – but are redistributed according to obscure rules. As Jean-Paul Fargier observed, Miéville-Godard simply present 'the whole of television simultaneously in each individual programme'.[19]

Commissioned by the second French channel, Antenne 2, and made during 1977–8 in Rolle, the series was immediately shelved for almost two years. Marcel Jullian, head of A2 when *France/tour/détour/deux/enfants* was commissioned, had been replaced by Maurice Ullich by the time it was complete. 'There's no way we're broadcasting *that*', exclaimed Ullich on viewing the first fifteen minutes of the series, 'It's not at all the spirit of the channel'.[20] Eventually broadcast in three blocks of four programmes in Claude-Jean Philippe's *Ciné-Club* on A2 at eleven p.m. on Fridays, the series's serial logic and intended dynamic engagement with the codes, genres and figures of prime-time television were rendered almost wholly redundant. Understandably angry, Godard claimed sabotage, if not censorship: 'They didn't know if it was cinema, television, or what. Whereas it was made to be broadcast just before *Aujourd'hui Madame* . . . The time of broadcast was intentionally chosen to damage my work.'[21] With time, and despite these inauspicious beginnings, the importance of the series has become increasingly apparent, giving rise to something of a critical consensus. Colin MacCabe, for instance, has described the programmes as 'probably the most profound and beautiful material ever produced for television'.[22] An outstanding artistic achievement, the series represents the pinnacle of the Miéville/Godard collaboration in this period. It has also come to constitute an important reference point within the film-makers' respective recent work, notably *Après la réconciliation* (2001) and *Histoire(s) du cinéma* (1988–1998).[23] In the context of Godard's evolution as an artist, its themes and forms pave the way for his third foray into the videographic serial genre, *Histoire(s) du cinéma*. For film and television culture more generally, it remains a unique experiment in televisual composition and major contribution to theoretical reflection on the medium.

Unconscious Optics

Experimentation and reflection in three areas converge in *France/tour/détour/deux/ enfants*: the scientific impetus to the cinematograph; television theory; and historical research. I shall divide the remainder of my discussion into two principal sections: an analysis of the formal tool employed by Miéville-Godard, video, and a Foucauldian reading of their videographic decomposition of the body. Let me begin with a number of observations relating to the altered-motion sequences. First, the brute material revisited, reworked temporally and re-presented is extremely diverse in colour, framing and camera movement. Second, tape speed is manipulated extensively throughout the series (in every movement, and on nineteen separate occasions) but ultimately quite sparingly (the total quantity of such footage amounts to around ten per cent of the total running time). Third, extracts vary greatly in length, from a little under thirty seconds to over three minutes. Fourth, a variety of bodies are surveyed and presented in many different poses and situations: clothed; naked; young; old; big; small; kissing; running; walking; at work; at play; and so on. Fifth, in no fewer than five of the movements, we encounter further altered-motion sequences that are perhaps best considered short test cases. Here the body is examined and decomposed at work (in a café or a supermarket, for instance), or as part of a procession or 'flow' across or beneath the surface of the earth (on escalators; in tunnels; along streets). And sixth, on a general note, the effect of intervention in normal tape speed is such that it has tended to dominate how the series is remembered. Brief perusal of the journalistic commentaries written at the time of the series's initial broadcast in France almost give the impression that all 312 minutes unfold in slow motion. Discussion of altered motion in virtually every account, whether favourable or hostile, is in terms of technical trickery or aesthetic effect. In what follows, my aim is to relate Godard-Miéville's use of video to pre- and early cinema's experimentation with time and altered motion, and so to foreground its properly scientific heritage.

In contrast to many film-makers of his generation, Godard had been eager to use video as early as 1967. When he did eventually begin to explore the medium, his experience would alter his cinema practice forever. He talks of its influence in terms of a profound and lasting democratizing effect. By making the nascent image available to all members of cast and crew, video intrinsically challenges cinema's conventional divisions of labour:

> I still consider myself to be a man who makes films. But I feel that the production apparatus that I've put together myself, with great difficulty, is something closer to a female organism: the way we organize the material, produce a film, or divide our time. There's a kind of democracy, whereas before it was more centrist.[24]

A major attraction of video, for Godard, as for many film-making collectives and community groups who invested in the new technology in the 1970s, was its capacity to by-pass the economic constraints of professional audio-visual production.[25] Etymologically, *video* simply means 'I see'. The combination of 'video' with 'scope' (from the Latin *scopium* and Greek *skopein*: to look at or examine) gives the term 'videoscope'. By placing video alongside other analogous 'scopes' (microscope or telescope), the idea of the 'videoscope' provides a good description of Miéville-Godard's use of the video camera in this period.[26] The blend of slow, fast and stop-start motion in *France/tour/détour/deux/enfants* extends the time-honoured cinematographic tradition of influential precursors such as Dziga Vertov. Indeed the Sonimage studio might be seen as the belated realization of the cinematic research laboratory dreamt of by Vertov. Like Miéville-Godard, Vertov was convinced of cinema's mysterious power to 'make the invisible visible, the unclear clear, the hidden manifest, the disguised overt, the acted non-acted, the untruth truth'.[27] In this context, it is worth recalling that Godard spoke explicitly at the end of the 1970s of having embarked on a conscious journey through the silent period in a quest for a fresh mode of sound film-making.[28] In the process, he and Miéville rediscover the explicitly scientific role for cinema outlined enthusiastically by Walter Benjamin in his 1936 essay, 'The Work of Art in the Age of Mechanical Reproduction'. In a passage that suggests a calling and form for cinema to which the Godardian project has ceaselessly aspired, Benjamin argues that cinema, especially the magic of slow motion, has revolutionized perception through the revelation of hitherto imperceptible processes and movements. He heralds the birth of an 'unconscious optics' comparable in magnitude and import to Freud's account in *Psychopathology of Everyday Life* of the penetration of the unconscious by psychoanalysis:

> The act of reaching for a lighter or a spoon is familiar from routine, yet we hardly know what really goes on between hand and metal, not to mention how this fluctuates with our moods. Here the camera intervenes with the resources of its lowerings and liftings, its interpretations and isolations, its extensions and accelerations, its enlargements and reductions. The camera introduces us to unconscious optics as does psychoanalysis to unconscious impulses.[29]

Perhaps even more influential for Miéville-Godard than the combined weight of Benjamin and Vertov is the pre-cinematic science of Etienne-Jules Marey. As a doctor whose early writings were devoted to the anatomy of the 'human machine', Marey saw the photographic and cinematographic 'camera-scope' as an incomparable scientific aid to the comprehension and demonstration of complex physical, physiological, mathematical and mechanical laws.[30] As early as the 1880s, he was using his photographic rifle to stop and show the intermediate phases of rapid movement. In a letter of 1882, he expressed the 'surprising' revelatory power of serial photography with disarming simplicity: 'I have a photographic rifle which has nothing deadly about it, and which takes the image of a flying bird or running animal in a time of less than a 500th of a second. I don't know if you can imagine this speed but it's something surprising'.[31] If the shot of the hovering seagull in the twelfth movement represents a discreet nod in Marey's direction, the principle of decomposition and recomposition at the heart of his analyses of animal and human movement in the latter half of the nineteenth century is undoubtedly the single most important formal point of reference for the videographic decomposition of body and image in *France/tour/détour/deux/enfants*. In conducting his experiments, Marey not only made an eloquent case for cinema as science, but provided future histories of pre-cinema with much breathtaking imagery. As early as 1878, Eadweard J. Muybridge had begun to analyse animal movement through the use of photography at short intervals in San Francisco. Marey concentrated on the development of 'chronophotography': the decomposition of motion into a series of discrete moments, and the reproduction of the resultant multiple exposures on a single photographic plate. 'Chronophotography', explained Marey in terms that Miéville-Godard might equally have used to describe their practice three-quarters of a century later, 'is the application of instantaneous Photography to the study of movement; it allows the human eye to see the phases that it would not be able to see directly; and it allows one to carry out the reconstitution of the movement that has initially been decomposed.'[32] Video allows Miéville-Godard to rediscover, and literally *animate*, Marey's spatial chronophotographs through an injection of saccadic movement. As Godard observed, video is a kind of intermediate technology between chronophotography and the cinematograph, making possible the unique, jerky, quasi-painterly vibratory visual slippages of *France/tour/détour/deux/enfants* that are neither exactly full-scale decomposition/recomposition (Marey), nor continuous reconstituted movement (Lumière):

> It's the story of Marey, who filmed the decomposition of horses. And when he was told of Lumière's invention, he said: "Completely idiotic. Why film at normal speed what we can see with our eyes? I don't see the interest of a mobile machine" . . . But the machine in between Marey and Lumière is missing, and there comes a time when you need to start again.[33]

As Marey was the first to acknowledge, chronophotography and 'animated photography' were in an embryonic state at the time of his experiments.[34] He was also one of the first to express some disquiet at the excessively trivial uses to which moving images were already being put in the 1890s.[35] But of one thing he was certain: they carried within them extraordinary scientific and pedagogical potential, and would lead to full knowledge of the mechanics of all physical movement. Such advances, he observed, depend on technical simplification and affordability, criteria amply met by video. On numerous occasions in *France/tour/détour/deux/enfants*, we are suddenly conscious that the human body, whether in isolation or viewed as part of a crowd, is being scrutinized in precisely the same way that particle motion is examined by a scientist through a microscope. Miéville-Godard's reinvention of chronophotography through video simply reclaims cinema's scientific heritage in the age of the television. We can rest assured that Marey too would have pounced on the videoscope with unbridled enthusiasm, delighting in the ease at which the tape can be manipulated through simple and quick post-production techniques.

Docile Bodies

Let us now turn to questions of the body, and first to a contextualization of the treatment of the body in *France/tour/détour/deux/enfants* in relation to the partial confluence of feminism and pornography in the years following May 1968. Feminist debate born within the *Mouvement de Libération des Femmes* (*MLF*) served to bring issues of feminine difference, free legal abortion and women's oppression and liberation into the mainstream political arena over the course of the 1970s.[36] The same period witnessed a brief but marked escalation in the pro-duction, distribution and consumption of pornographic films in France, especially between 1973 and 1978. French-only pornographic productions accounted for almost half of all film production in France in 1974 and 1975.[37] The mainstream release of a compilation of American hard-core pornographic shorts, *Anthologie du plaisir* (*History of the blue movie*), in five Parisian cinemas on 23 April 1975 signalled the beginning of a short-lived but influential experiment in censorship relaxation by the Giscard d'Estaing regime. *L'Organe*, a review devoted to porn-ography generally, and to pornographic cinema in particular, first appeared in 1974. The decision not to censor *Anthologie du plaisir*, followed by Paramount's hugely successful nation-wide distribution of the first film in the *Emmanuelle* series, led to an unprecedented escalation in the indigenous production of pornographic films. France's first hard-core pornographic film, Jean-François Davy's *Exhibition* (1975), was quickly made and shown in fifteen theatres in the Paris region, nine owned by the major UGC chain. It was an instant success, followed in July by the release of a further sixteen pornographic films (half of the month's new releases), and in August by an international festival of pornographic films.

This situation provides the backdrop to Miéville-Godard's representation of the body, especially the naked male and female body, and their wider duel with the forms and codes of pornography. On the one hand, the repetition and exploit-ative violence of conventional pornography is roundly dismissed as 'butchery' ('boucherie').[38] On the other, whilst keen to resist easy formulae, Miéville-Godard enthusiastically embrace the possibility of a mature, genuinely 'adult' cinema in which film-makers and their audience are free to grapple with the representation of the body, sexuality and gender in an open and explicit way. 'I tried to include [pornographic images]', said Godard, 'but more gently, and in stories about families, because sex is part of family life.'[39] The deadpan *mise en scène* of the naked pregnant secretary in the fifth movement – described on the sound-track as a sensitive and productive surface condemned within patriarchal society to reproduction, copying and dictation – exemplifies the provocative conjunction of feminist discourse with sexually explicit imagery. Robert Stam has suggested the description 'feminist pornography' for *Numéro deux*'s combination of texts from Germaine Greer's *The Female Eunuch* with recurrent imagery of anal rape, arguing that the film achieves the remarkable feat of politicizing and feminizing an apparently irrecuperable genre.[40] The most enduring impact of the sudden and marked presence of pornography beyond its usual ghetto was perhaps on mainstream film production. Many film-makers were quick to exploit their new-found freedom, integrating depictions of sex and sexuality into their work in a way undreamed of in the preceding decade. Like Miéville-Godard, they tended to view the opportunity of working in hitherto taboo areas as a substantial liberation. But Godard was quick to criticize the way in which such promise was translated into an excuse for the insertion of predictable, trivial, conventionally exploitative pornographic sequences into the most banal of films. With a critical eye on the health of cinema as a vibrant and responsible contemporary art form, he viewed the failure of film-makers to make significant inroads into ground formerly occupied by pornography, or to capitalize on the wealth of fresh material offered so freely and unexpectedly, as a major defeat.

How might Foucauldian theory illuminate *France/tour/détour/deux/enfants*? The series examines the conditioning of the human infant as a docile subject of capitalism through a 24-hour trip to and from school that begins and ends with Camille and Arnaud preparing in turn for bed. A methodological fidelity to the rhythms of the children's day is therefore integral to the structure of the series. With this in mind, let us briefly review the contents of the altered-motion and interview sequences involving the children. This imagery depicts often fleeting and private moments, and records transitional spaces where the children are not on show and television seldom goes to look. Three principal geographical places are represented: home (five sequences); school (four sequences); and various intermediate spaces between the two, notably the street (three sequences). The home and school imagery can be further divided into that which interrogates the children at rest in each of the locations (listening to music or watching television in the home; playing in the playground during a break at school) and that which shows them at work (in class or in detention). Following Foucault and Althusser, school is treated in *France/tour/détour/deux/enfants* not as a place for learning but for enforced incarceration. As suggested in *Leçons de choses*, episode 2a of *Six fois deux (Sur et sous la communication)*, children are really 'political prisoners': detained in school, they are fed instructions and held in reserve for pre-designated future roles. 'Learning and the assignment of social roles', as theorist-polemicist Ivan Illich has put it, 'are melted into schooling.'[41]

In an illuminating article, Constance Penley has discussed Miéville-Godard's relationship to Foucauldian theory in terms of a common concern for 'the institutional organisation of space and time' and 'the power of those spatial and temporal grids' in the normalizing process, relating this to Philippe Ariès's influential account of the shift from the indeterminate education structures of medieval times to the rigorous, highly regimented modern age-based school system.[42] Power is located in the sum of the minutiae of the repetitious and regulatory daily, monthly and annual cycles into which the infant is inserted from birth: going to school; to work; on holiday; and so on. The nascent human animal is caught at the intersection of a series of divisions (between the sexes, labour and leisure, home and work) and repetitions (of the working day and week, of weekends, of holidays). Children are equated by both Foucault and Miéville-Godard with all manner of recording surfaces – 'like paper, a recording surface' ('comme du papier, une surface pour enregistrer'), as formulated in the fifth movement – and decoded as open systems subjected to the effects of myriad socializing norms, which results in the production of an individual 'programmed' to occupy a predetermined social position and function.

Traces of Foucault's *Discipline and Punish: The Birth of the Prison* (1975) might almost be considered as the scenario of the series, informing each of its component segments, as Miéville-Godard scrutinize the body and television through the videoscope.[43] It is certainly as important a source for Miéville-Godard as the celebrated nineteenth-century school primer on which the series is ostensibly based, G. Bruno's *Le Tour de la France par Deux Enfants: Devoir et Patrie*.[44] Indeed, Foucault might be seen as having provided the radical lens through which Bruno's pedagogical primer is read against the grain. Almost as a by-product of his account of the radical metamorphosis of the economy of punishment, and the emergence of the modern prison, Foucault postulates the formation of an all-pervasive 'micro-politics of power' that subjects every body to a monotonous system of regulatory constraints, privations and obligations.[45] Within this perspective, we are all subject to a vast social *mise en scène*, wherein the body is exposed to a finely tuned, quasi-militaristic process of calibration.

Discipline and Punish is coterminous with the work of Sonimage and a major contribution to the intellectual climate of the 1970s. For Foucault, the classical age's discovery of the body as target of power is part of a larger collective intellectual interrogation of the body that developed during the eighteenth century. Borrowing the term 'docility' from the general theory of corporal *dressage* proposed in La Mettrie's *L'Homme-machine*, Foucault charts the emergence of an insidious form of modern slavery located in the body. This is achieved less by appropriation and ownership than the imposition of 'docility-utility' through an accumulation of ostensibly non-ideological constraints, all veiled manifestations of a disciplinary monotony active throughout daily life. A prime example given by Foucault of the regulated relationship between localized gesture and the overall position of the body, and explored visually by Miéville-Godard on numerous occasions in both *Six fois deux (Sur et sous la communication)* and *France/tour/détour/deux/enfants*, is the 'gymnastics' of handwriting. In a key passage, Foucault explains the effects of the disciplines on the docile body:

> The historical moment of the disciplines was the moment when an art of the human body was born, which was directed not only at the growth of its skills, nor at the intensification of its subjection, but at the formation of a relation that in the mechanism itself makes it more obedient as it becomes more useful, and conversely. What was then being formed was a policy of coercions that act upon the body, a calculated manipulation of its elements, its gestures, its behaviour. The human body was entering a machinery of power that explores it, breaks it down and rearranges it. A 'political anatomy', which was also a 'mechanics of power', was being born; it defined how one may have a hold over others' bodies, not only so that they may do what one wishes, but so that they may operate as one wishes, with the techniques, the speed and the efficiency that one determines. Thus discipline produces subjected and practised bodies, 'docile bodies'. Discipline increases the forces of the body (in economic terms of utility) and diminishes these same forces (in political terms of obedience).[46]

For Foucault, therefore, daily life implies subjugation to modes of disciplinary control that are different only in intensity, not substance, from those formalized in the penal system proper. Disciplinary society teaches and imposes a series of specific gestures, thereby conditioning the human body as time-efficient machine. A contagious Taylorization has spread far beyond the factory, infecting all gesture, from the most mundane (washing up) to the most intimate (love-making). We live a punishing routine.

The sequence depicting the technician repairing the video recorder in the fourth movement, or the reference in the sixth to René Clair's *A nous la liberté* (1931) – a film that deals explicitly with the advent of mechanization, mass production and the subjugation of the body to the machine – serve to illustrate Sonimage's general critique of the power of machinery over the human body. Historically, of course, there is a direct relationship between the cinematograph and the calibration of the body. Integral to Marey's scientific exploration of movement was the question of energy efficiency. The principles that informed his experiments were soon adapted by Henry Ford to the elimination of inefficient movement and wasted energy on the factory production line.

Miéville-Godard return to the mechanical impetus of Marey's experiments, giving these a distinctly political spin in the light of Foucauldian theory. Armed with the videoscope and the power of altered motion, they set out to conduct a kind of videoscopic ultrasound of the calibrated body, and so to cast in relief the work of the micro-powers in producing human docility-utility. Foucault draws on

M. de la Salle's prescriptive 1783 blueprint for a meticulous control of routine, elaborated in *Traité sur les obligations des frères des écoles chrétiennes*, to argue that the methods of the timetable used throughout modern institutions (schools, workshops, hospitals) – with their established rhythms, specific operations and regulated cycles of repetition – derive directly from the monastic model.[47] By relating modern disciplinary society directly to the model of the monastic cell, Foucault argues that disciplinary space is essentially cellular. 'Is it surprising', he asks in a question that reverberates across the Sonimage imagery, 'that prisons resemble factories, schools, barracks, hospitals, all of which resemble prisons?.'[48]

Such a model suggests the extent to which Godard was already Foucauldian in his art cinema of the 1960s. 'Cellular theory', as we might call it, provides the logical extension and theoretical confirmation of a form of visual criticism characteristic of much of Godard's earlier work, especially from the mid-1960s onwards where, repeatedly, we encounter tales of solitude narrated through images of back-lit, silhouetted bodies. In *France/tour/détour/deux/enfants*, such characters have mutated into the slothful anonymous hulks or 'monsters' who roam the underground passages of the *métro*. The saturation of the Sonimage imagery in frames and grids provides a visual shorthand for Miéville-Godard's indefatigable pursuit of ossified temporal and spatial relationships. Similarly, earlier films such as *Alphaville* (1965) and *Deux ou trois choses que je sais d'elle* (1966) had long since juxtaposed the soft, vulnerable forms and flesh of the human body against the harsh angles of the city.

To put this another way, is Foucault perhaps as Godardian as Miéville-Godard are Foucauldian? Rather than assuming that Miéville-Godard are simply adopting Foucault, *Discipline and Punish* could be considered an extension of the tales of dehumanized automatons and manufactured desire contained in Godard's science-fiction films of the 1960s (*Le Nouveau Monde* (1962); *Alphaville* (1965); and *Anticipation* (1966)). This proposition is clearly a little far-fetched. But the point is that, in their respective projects, Miéville-Godard, Foucault and indeed Deleuze/ Guattari were all working on parallel tracks in the 1970s. Miéville-Godard's enterprise, however methodologically unconventional, is every bit as serious as that of their contemporaries. In his preface to Deleuze and Guattari's *Anti-Oedipus: Capitalism and Schizophrenia* (1972), Foucault asks how we can begin to ferret out the traces of fascism ingrained in the body. 'By casting in relief the physics of the regulatory micro-powers that subjugate the body to their rhythms through the videoscope', answer Miéville-Godard through their practice. To claim a place for film-makers alongside philosophers, historians and theoreticians will doubtless always be an uphill struggle. But in this period, as Deleuze noted enthusiastically in his oft-quoted commentary on *Six fois deux (Sur et sous la communication)*, Miéville-Godard made a full and original contribution. It just happened to take audio-visual rather than bookish form. Through the videoscope, as Deleuze suggests, they combine a Foucauldian micro-politics of boundaries with systematic videographic revelation (Marey plus Vertov: rendering visible the imperceptible).[49]

Ultimately, Miéville-Godard might best be thought of as bringing Foucault's history up to date, using video as a tool through which to apply the findings of his historical research to Camille and Arnaud's repetitious cycle of home-school-home. They also employ it as a conceptual framework through which to theorize the programming grid of broadcast television. As Penley points out, Foucault's concern for the institutionalized compartmentalization and capitalization of space and time in daily life is eminently applicable to the superficiality and predictability of broadcast television: 'The interrogation of the children's lives in the interviews ceaselessly points to the serialization, the regulated flow and repetition of their domestic, school and leisure schedules.'[50] As Godard has often suggested, if television is essentially a question of scheduling, it is the viewer who ends up 'programmed'. He goes to some length in dialogue with Arnaud in the tenth movement to draw an analogy between the passage of food and television through the body, via an exploration of the expression 'ça fait chier' ('it makes you sick', or, literally, 'it makes you shit'). The Foucauldian timetable is mapped by Miéville-Godard on to Raymond Williams's model of planned flow, and human bodies, dissected for traces of social programming, end up also representing television 'programmes'. This self-reflexive critique operates fluidly through the multiple connotations of terms such as *chaînes* ('channels', but also 'chains') and *programmes*. As Godard suggested, television and the daily routine of the children mirror and figure one another: 'The other logic was that of the day's work. The day of a worker, and so of a schoolchild, since children's work in Western countries is school. We begin at night, but night is just before daybreak, and we proceed to the rhythm of the two children's *programme*, until nightfall.'[51] Here, as often in Godardian discourse, the flow (*défilé*) of people – in this case that of those filing past the camera on political demonstrations, or making their way in waves to and from work – serves as a self-reflexive shorthand for the mechanical *défilement* of televisual or cinematic imagery. The slow-motion sequences represent an active intervention in *both*, and foresee Godard's frequent return to the figure of the *défilé* in his subsequent work (cf. *On s'est tous défilé* (1988)).

Conclusion: Resistance and Recomposition

The centrality and weight of the critical dimension to the Godardian project, where every film and video, immaterial of ostensible subject matter, doubles as an astute commentary on the state of cinema as artistic practice and cultural form, should never be underestimated. *France/tour/détour/deux/enfants*, as Jacques Aumont has suggested, is essentially 'a film about the human body as very paradigm of representation and of expression'.[52] It is the intense self-reflexivity of the exploration of the body in the series that is of enduring significance for our understanding of the development of the Godardian corpus, and of wider changes in cinema over the past fifty years. Godard's commentary on his and Miéville's use of altered motion in *France/tour/détour/deux/enfants*, cited at the start of this chapter, is only partial. He omits any reference to such self-reflexivity, preferring to let the imagery speak for itself. And what we discover as we watch Miéville-Godard manipulating their material in the stop-start sequences is that the body *resists*. Much of the irrepressible vitality and optimism that the series conveys derives from this conviction that the body – human and cinematic – can and does resist. Neo-Foucauldian denunciation of the disciplinary regulation of the body gives way to a systematic search for glimpses of the fissures and disjunctions – sudden and mysterious points of corporal resistance – concealed beneath superficial homogeneity and continuity. As Bérénice Reynaud noted in a perceptive article published in 1986, this idea of the resisting body is central to Godard's art cinema of the 1980s:

> Godard's concern has been to stress that there is an element that resists the geometry of contradictory texts and delineated spaces: the body. The body is this opaque substance that stops light; the body is what emits and receives discourse; the body of a woman is what escapes man's questions about it; the body is that mysterious object, endlessly questioned by philosophers ('One does not know what the body can', wrote Spinoza in the seventeenth century), castigated by some as the ultimate source of sin, overevaluated by others as the ultimate source of pleasure. The body, whose presence is tamed in traditional narrative cinema by the policed training of actors, or reduced to silence by the addition of the voice-over in well-meaning documentaries – the body is what resists becoming a pure signifier. It is thus both the real object of cinema and its more impure elements.[53]

The capacity of the body to evade wholesale machinal conditioning had already been hinted at in the startling flights of the dancing body in *Marcel* (episode 3b of *Six fois deux (Sur et sous la communication)*), where we see Super 8 footage of a young girl ice-skating), and in the vitality and abandon of the young girl's dance that concludes episode 5b (*René(e)s*). These sequences prefigure the project systematized in *France/tour/détour/deux/enfants*, which in turn foresees the centrality of song and dance in Miéville's later work. In particular, *Le Livre de Marie* might be considered an extended fictionalized case study based around the notion of a 'resisting body': an account of how crisis (the emotional turmoil brought about by parental separation) traverses Marie's body, and of how the body fights back (the extraordinary cathartic dance sequence).

There is another form of resistance: that of the breathtaking beauty, vivid colours and dense plasticity of the electronic imagery. Music appears to guide the movements of Miéville-Godard's intervention on the editing table, and often provides a rhythm for the unexpected on-screen choreography of everyday motion. But sometimes its sole function appears to be further to accentuate the aesthetic power discovered at the heart of ordinary imagery. Stripped of sound and extracted from the material in which they are couched, the nineteen altered-motion sequences that punctuate and complicate the smooth flow of *France/tour/détour/deux/enfants* constitute enormously potent self-contained, self-reflexive visual *essais* or *études* on the intertwined themes of human and audio-visual movement. Their roots in social theory, they veer rapidly and irreversibly into the sublime. The revelation of opera in the gestures of the waitresses in the fourth movement, or the celebration of colour in the free-jazz sketch of the children at play in the sixth, both point towards the invention of a unique form of animated painting rather than conventional television. The altered motion sequences carry within them the seeds of cinematic recomposition. Decomposition of the mechanics of an assortment of shapes and ages of human bodies throws up a whole new vocabulary of gesture, movement and corporal interaction. Videographic intervention in television's planned flow leaves a trail of novel video-inflected forms. Together, they provide the basis for a revitalized form of *mise en scène*, performance and cinematic composition that will allow Miéville and Godard to *re*compose differently in images and sounds in the 1980s. If we return to Godard's article on *Une Vie*, it is not hard to see how enthusiasm for the subversive and creative potential of unforeseen movement foreshadows the blend of formal disjunction and corporal liberation in his early work, perhaps nowhere more potently than in his manifesto of cinematic modernity, *A Bout de souffle* (1959). What has changed in the twenty years separating Godard's early criticism and *France/tour/détour/deux/enfants* is the nature of cinema itself. And the cinema of the early 1980s, as it mutated under economic domination and aesthetic infiltration by television, was in sore need of revitalization. Where the Godard of *A Bout de souffle* sought 'discontinuity latent in continuity' as the basis for a belated and rather short-lived glimpse of cinematic modernity, the cinematic and corporal discontinuities revealed by the videographic anatomy of the body in *France/tour/détour/deux/enfants* interrogate the form, nature and existence of film-making in the age of television. By identifying and collating moments of resistance, Miéville-Godard open a gap through which a mature form of cinema can pass. To put this another way, the energy and sheer beauty of the sequences I have been discussing capture forever the oscillation, and ultimate irreversible slippage, from the primacy of the everyday to the new-found metaphysical lyricism of Godard's later work. In the wider context of cinema history, they represent the final transition from cinema's belated adolescence (the Nouvelle Vague) to a post-68, post-television maturity.

Notes

In these notes, all translations are mine unless otherwise stated.

1. A full-length study of the manipulation of film and tape speed in Miéville and Godard's work would include: Miéville-Godard's *France/tour/détour/deux/ enfants* (1978); *Soft and Hard* (1985); *Le Rapport Darty* (1988); and *Deux fois cinquante ans de cinéma français* (1995); Godard's *Scénario vidéo de Sauve qui peut (la vie)* (1979); *Sauve qui peut (la vie)* (1979); *Lettre à Freddy Buache* (1981); *Prénom Carmen* (1982); *Meeting Woody Allen* (1986); *Grandeur et décadence d'un petit commerce de cinéma* (1986); *King Lear* (1987); *On s'est tous défilé* (1988); *Puissance de la parole* (1988); *Closed* (1988); *Les Enfants jouent à la Russie* (1993); *Histoire(s) du cinéma*; and *L'Origine du vingt et unième siècle* (2000); and Miéville's *Mon cher sujet* (1988); and *Après la réconciliation* (2001).
2. N. Brenez (2000), 'Ralenti et accéléré', *Cahiers du cinéma*, Special Issue (November: 'Le Siècle du cinéma'), pp. 94–5.
3. 'cette soudaineté des gestes qui font démarrer le suspense toutes les trois minutes, cette discontinuité latente dans la continuité'. J.-L. Godard (1958), 'Ailleurs', *Cahiers du cinéma*, 89, cited in J.-L. Godard (1985), *Jean-Luc Godard par Jean-Luc Godard*, ed. A. Bergala, Paris, pp. 146–9, p. 149. Henceforth this is referenced as *Godard par Godard I*, and is referenced in preference to the original sites of the essays it brings together.
4. G. Deleuze (1985), *Cinéma 2: L'Image-Temps*, Paris, p. 31.
5. L. Mulvey (1992), 'The Hole and the Zero: The Janus Face of the Feminine in Godard', in R. Bellour and M. L. Bandy (eds), *Jean-Luc Godard: Son + Image, 1974–1991*, New York, pp. 75–88, p. 75. See too Mulvey's essay, co-authored with Colin MacCabe, on 'Images of Woman, Images of Sexuality', in C. MacCabe (1980), *Godard: Images, Sounds, Politics*, London, pp. 79–101.
6. See ibid., p. 81.
7. Godard's claim that the stop-start sequences in *France/tour/détour/deux/enfants* reveal significant differences between the movements of the girl and boy remains to be examined. His comments formed part of a debate coordinated by Jean Douchet at the *Verger* in Avignon in 1980. See *Godard par Godard I*, 'Propos rompus', pp. 458–71, pp. 461–2: 'Dans *Tour Détour*, j'avais découvert une intuition, sans aller plus loin puisqu'il faudrait en parler avec des collègues et qu'ils m'apportent leur expérience. On faisait des ralentis, des changements de rythmes, ce que j'appellerais plutôt des décompositions, en se servant des techniques conjuguées du cinéma et de la télévision. J'avais à ma disposition un petit garçon et une petite fille et on faisait les changements de vitesse, mi-ralenti, mi-accéléré, mi-rythmés avec des tas de possibilités différentes. Dès

qu'on arrête une image dans le mouvement qui en comporte vingt-cinq (ce qui n'est pas énorme, c'est cinq fois les doigts de votre main, c'est quelque chose que vous pouvez encore pensez), on s'aperçoit qu'un plan qu'on a filmé, suivant comme on l'arrête, tout à coup, il y a des milliards de possibilités, toutes les permutations possibles entre ces vingt-cinq images représentent des milliards de possibilités. J'en avais conclu que quand on fait des changements de rythmes, qu'on analyse des mouvements chez une femme, des mouvements aussi simples qu'acheter une baguette de pain par exemple, on s'aperçoit qu'il y a des tas de mondes différents à l'intérieur du mouvement de la femme, alors que les ralentis étaient beaucoup moins intéressants chez le petit garçon, on faisait des arrêts et entre chaque arrêt il y avait toujours la même ligne directrice. Tandis que chez la petite fille, sur des trucs très très banals on passait tout à coup d'une angoisse profonde mais d'un tiers de seconde après c'était la joie, c'étaient vraiment des monstres. Et moi, en tant que scientifique, connaissant certaines théories, j'avais plutôt l'impression que c'étaient des corpuscules et des mondes différents, des galaxies qui chaque fois étaient différentes et qu'on passait de l'un à l'autre avec une série d'explosions, alors que le mouvement du garçon était beaucoup plus ondulatoire avec un départ, ce qui fait que les arrêts étaient moins intéressants plastiquement.'

8. C. Penley (1982), 'Pornography, Eroticism', *Camera Obscura*, 8–9–10, pp. 13–18 (special triple issue devoted to Miéville and Godard's work). Republished in Bellour and Bandy, *Jean-Luc Godard*, pp. 47–9.

9. See M. Temple and J. S. Williams (2000), 'Introduction to the Mysteries of Cinema, 1985–2000', in Temple and Williams (eds), *The Cinema Alone: Essays on the Work of Jean-Luc Godard 1985–2000*, Amsterdam, pp. 9–32, p. 32. This is the best English-language introduction to Godard's later films and videos, and to how we might rethink earlier periods of his work. In the two volumes of Godard's collected texts and interviews, Alain Bergala has proposed a grid through which to organize the phases of Godard's work. These dividing lines remain provisional and open to debate. See *Godard par Godard I*; J.-L. Godard (1998), *Jean-Luc Godard par Jean-Luc Godard II*, 1984–1998, ed. A. Bergala, Paris.

10. The name 'Sonimage' was first used by Godard in late 1972. The Sonimage studio existed in Paris in early 1973 before moving to Grenoble, and finally to Rolle, Switzerland, where Miéville and Godard continue to live and work. The venture ended in 1979, although the company 'Sonimage' continued until 1981, coproducing *Sauve qui peut (la vie)* and *Passion*.

11. One might pursue traces of the work of commentators such as Jean Baudrillard, Gilles Deleuze, Félix Guattari and Jean-François Lyotard into the Sonimage texts.

12. 'avoir un petit peu de matériel pour réapprendre, pour avoir le temps de composer avec lui'. J.-L. Godard (1975), 'Jean-Luc Godard, télévision-cinéma-vidéo-images: paroles . . .', *Téléciné*, 202, pp. 11–13, p. 12.

13. At the Cinémathèque Suisse in January 1992; at the Jeu de Paume (Paris) in July–August 1998; and at the Cinémathèque de Toulouse in January 2001.

14. 'création, créature, et surtout créateur'. Miéville, cited in the press book for *Mon cher sujet*.

15. The dialogue between Rouch and Morin foresees the Miéville/Godard collaboration and its transposition onto their fictional counterparts within the series, Betty and Albert. *Chronique d'un été* is referenced in the second movement through a reworking of the celebrated image of the emergence of Parisians from a *métro* subway into the fresh air that begins the film.

16. 1: OBSCUR/CHIMIE, 2: LUMIÈRE/PHYSIQUE, 3: CONNU/GÉOMÉTRIE/GÉOGRAPHIE, 4: INCONNU/TECHNIQUE, 5: IMPRESSION/DICTÉE, 6: EXPRESSION/FRANÇAIS, 7: VIOLENCE/GRAMMAIRE, 8: DÉSORDRE/CALCUL, 9: POUVOIR/MUSIQUE, 10: ROMAN/ÉCONOMIE, 11: RÉALITÉ/LOGIQUE, and 12: RÊVE/MORALE.

17. See R. Williams (1974), *Television: Technology and Cultural Form*, London.

18. 'Oui, j'ai fonctionné comme un directeur de chaîne, c'est-à-dire en faisant une grille de programmes. Et puis j'ai commencé à faire des suites de plans . . . C'était comme un code, dont on aurait eu certains mots, mais dont il fallait retrouver la logique.' See *Godard par Godard I*, p. 410.

19. 'à la fois toute la télévision en une seule émission'. J.-P. Fargier, 'Le grand méchant loup', *Les Nouvelles Littéraires*, 30 May 1980, p. 36.

20. 'Pas question de diffuser «ça» à l'antenne. Ce n'est pas du tout l'esprit de la chaîne'. Reported in P. Bruneau, 'Un drôle de "tour" avec Godard', *Minute*, 2–8 April 1980.

21. 'Ils ne savait pas si c'était du cinéma, de la télévision, ou quoi. Alors que c'était fait pour passer avant *Aujourd'hui Madame* . . . L'heure de diffusion a été choisie sciemment pour esquinter mon travail.' J.-L. Godard in F. Jouffa, 'Jean-Luc Godard: «La pellicule, c'est complètement chiant!»', *Télé-Ciné-Vidéo*, December 1980, pp. 34–5, pp. 34–5.

22. C. MacCabe (1985), 'Betaville', *American Film*, 10, pp. 61–3, p. 61.

23. The combination of interviews with children and videographic slow motion in the prologue to *Après la réconciliation*, followed by the exchange between the unnamed woman (Miéville) and Robert (Godard) around the creative intensity of a earlier encounter and collaboration, invokes *France/tour/détour/deux/enfants*. Imagery of the children manipulating the microphone or video camera at the beginning of each movement is equated in *Histoire(s) du cinéma* with the power of the cinematograph as a nascent art-form.

24. 'Je me considère toujours comme un garçon qui fait des films, mais je considère que l'appareil de production que j'ai effectivement monté moi-même

avec bien des déboires, c'est plutôt un organisme de type féminin: la manière dont on a organisé le matériel, de produire un film, de repartir le temps; il y a une espèce de démocratie alors qu'avant c'était plus centriste.' *Godard par Godard I*, 'Propos rompus', p. 471.

25. For an account of the use of video by youth and community groups in France in the 1970s, see A. Willener, G. Milliard and A. Ganty (1976), *Videology and Utopia: Explorations in a New Medium*, trans. D. Burfield, London. The authors, based at the University of Lausanne, were themselves responsible for the exploratory practices discussed in the book.

26. Cf. Philippe Dubois's suggestive term *vidéo-scalpel*, in P. Dubois (1990), 'L'Image à la vitesse de la pensée', *Cahiers du cinéma* (November supplement), 437, pp. 76–7, p. 76.

27. Vertov enthuses repeatedly about slow motion. This citation, a definition of 'Kinopravda', is taken from D. Vertov (1984), *Kino-Eye: The Writings of Dziga Vertov*, trans. K. O'Brien, London, p. 15. Reference to the 'laboratory' of which he dreamed can be found on p. 201.

28. See J.-L. Godard (1980), *Introduction à une véritable histoire du cinéma*, Paris, p. 309. I discuss the significance of the silent era in relation to *Histoire(s) du cinéma* in M. Witt (2000), 'Montage, My Beautiful Care, or Histories of the Cinematograph', in Temple and Williams, *The Cinema Alone*, pp. 33–50.

29. W. Benjamin (1973), 'The Work of Art in the Age of Mechanical Reproduction', in *Illuminations*, London, pp. 211–44, pp. 229–30.

30. E.-J. Marey (1873), *La Machine animale: locomotion terrestre et aérienne*, Paris, p. v: 'Very often, and in all epochs, human beings have been compared to machines. But it is now that we can begin to understand the import and accuracy of this comparison' ('Bien souvent et à toutes les époques, on a comparé les êtres vivants aux machines, mais c'est de nos jours que l'on peut comprendre la portée et la justesse de cette comparaison').

31. 'J'ai un fusil photographique qui n'a rien de meurtrier et qui prend l'image d'un oiseau qui vole ou d'un animal qui court en un temps moindre d'un 500ème de seconde. Je ne sais pas si tu te représentes bien cette rapidité mais c'est quelque chose de surprenant'. From a letter to his mother, 3 February 1882. In E.-J. Marey (1994), *Le Mouvement*, Nîmes, p. 319.

32. 'La Chronophotographie, c'est l'application de la Photographie instantanée à l'étude du mouvement; elle permet à l'oeil humain d'en voir les phases qu'il ne pouvait percevoir directement; et elle conduit encore à opérer la reconstitution du mouvement qu'elle a d'abord décomposé'. E.-J. Marey (1899), *La Chronophotographie*, Paris, p. 5. Delivered as a lecture at the Conservatoire des Arts et Métiers on 29 January 1899. Marey lists various ways in which chronophotography could revolutionize science and medicine. His plea for the use of chronophotography and moving images as scientific instruments

through which to study and further our understanding of diseases such as disorders of the nervous system foresees Godard's proposal to the CNRS of cinema and video as tools applicable to the study of cancer. See *Godard par Godard I*, 'Propos rompus', p. 463.

33. 'C'est l'histoire de Marey, qui avait filmé la décomposition des chevaux et quand on lui a parlé de l'invention de Lumière il a dit: complètement imbécile, pourquoi filmer à la vitesse normale de ce qu'on voit avec les yeux, je vois pas quel est l'intérêt d'avoir une machine ambulante . . . Alors la machine manque effectivement entre Lumière et Marey et il y a un moment où tu as besoin de repartir.' Ibid., p. 467.

34. See E.-J. Marey (1886), *Etude sur la locomotion animale par la chrono-photographie*, Paris.

35. Notably through reference to Boleslas Matuszewski's *Photographie Animée*. In the context of Godard's later work, and of *Histoire(s) du cinéma* in part-icular, it is worth noting that Marey cites Matuszewski's prediction that the cinematograph, by capturing and preserving moving images of the present, will alter our relationship to history.

36. For a useful overview of the emergence and consolidation of the feminist movement in post-1968 France, see C. Duchen (1986), *Feminism in France: From May 68 to Mitterrand*, London, pp. 1–25.

37. 45.8 per cent in the first half of 1974, 47.1 per cent in the second half, and 46.8 per cent in the first half of 1975. For a detailed breakdown of statistics, see (1975), 'Porno: les affaires vont bien', *Le Film Français*, 1592, 'Spécial porno', pp. 64–5 (no author is given). A useful overview of production in the period 1975–78 is available in F. Courtade (1982), 'Bilan économique en France sous la Ve République (1975–1985)', in J. Zimmer (ed.), *Cinéma Erotique*, Paris, pp. 108–15.

38. See Godard, in Y. Baby, 'Faire les films possibles là où on est', *Le Monde*, 25 September 1975.

39. 'J'ai essayé de les placer mais plus doucement, et dans des histoires de famille, parce que le cul ça fait partie de la famille.' Godard, *Introduction à une véritable histoire du cinéma*, p. 309.

40. R. Stam (1992), *Reflexivity in Film and Literature: From Don Quixote to Jean-Luc Godard*, New York, p. 62.

41. I. Illich (1971), *Deschooling Society*, London, p. 11.

42. C. Penley (1982), 'Les Enfants de la Patrie', *Camera Obscura*, 8–9–10, pp. 33–58, p. 52. Penley is ultimately unconvinced by Foucault's thesis, dismissing it as 'one of those "global critiques" that brings with it the seductiveness of the sweeping statement and the easy nihilism of its totalness'. See also Part II of P. Ariès (1979), *Centuries of Childhood*, Harmondsworth.

43. See M. Foucault (1979), *Discipline and Punish: The Birth of the Prison*, trans. A. Sheridan, Harmondsworth; M. Foucault (1975), *Surveiller et punir: Naissance de la prison*, Paris.

44. G. Bruno (1878), *Le Tour de la France par Deux Enfants: Devoir et Patrie*, Paris. One could explore in detail the ways in which Miéville-Godard engage with the form and themes of Bruno's book. It is worth noting that Godard professed genuine admiration for the book.

45. See especially the opening to Part III, Chapter One and Part I, Chapter One of Foucault's text.

46. Foucault, *Discipline and Punish*, pp. 137–8. 'Le moment historique des disciplines, c'est le moment où naît un art du corps humain, qui ne vise pas seulement la croissance de ses habilités, ni non plus l'alourdissement de sa sujétion, mais la formation d'un rapport qui dans le même mécanisme le rend d'autant plus obéissant qu'il est plus utile, et inversement. Se forme alors une politique des coercitions qui sont un travail sur le corps, une manipulation calculée de ses éléments, de ses gestes, de ses comportements. Le corps humain entre dans une machinerie de pouvoir qui le fouille, le désarticule et le recompose. Une «anatomie politique», qui est aussi bien une «mécanique du pouvoir», est en train de naître; elle définit comment on peut avoir prise sur le corps des autres, non pas simplement pour qu'ils fassent ce qu'on désire, mais pour qu'ils opèrent ce qu'on veut, avec les techniques, selon la rapidité et l'efficacité qu'on détermine. La discipline fabrique ainsi des corps soumis et exercés, des corps "dociles". La discipline majore les forces du corps (en termes économiques d'utilité) et diminue ces mêmes forces (en termes politiques d'obéissance).' Foucault, *Surveiller et punir*, p. 162.

47. See M. de la Salle (1783), *Traité sur les obligations des frères des écoles chrétiennes*, Rouen.

48. Foucault, *Discipline and Punish*, p. 228. 'Quoi d'étonnant si la prison ressemble aux usines, aux écoles, aux casernes, aux hôpitaux, qui tous ressemblent aux prisons?'. Foucault, *Surveiller et punir*, p. 264.

49. G. Deleuze (1992), 'Three questions about "Six fois deux"', trans. R. Bowlby, in Bellour and Bandy, *Jean-Luc Godard*, pp. 35–41, p. 41. Originally published in 1976, as 'Trois questions sur *Six fois deux*', *Cahiers du cinéma*, 271, pp. 5–12.

50. Penley, 'Les Enfants de la Patrie', p. 34.

51. 'L'autre logique était celle de la journée. La journée d'un travailleur, donc la journée d'un écolier, puisque le travail enfantin dans les pays occidentaux, c'est l'école. On commence la nuit, mais la nuit, c'est juste avant que le jour se lève, et on avance au rythme du *programme* des deux enfants, jusqu'à la tombée du jour'. See *Godard par Godard I*, 'Propos rompus', p. 410.

52. 'Presque, j'exagère à peine, un film sur le corps humain comme paradigme même de la représentation et de l'expression'. J. Aumont (1989), *L'Oeil Interminable: Cinéma et Peinture*, Toulouse, pp. 241–2.

53. B. Reynaud (1986), '"Impure Cinema": Adaption and Quotation at the 1985 New York Film Festival', *Afterimage*, 13, pp. 9–11, p. 11.

–11–

The God, the King, the Fool and ØØ: Anamorphosing the Films of Beineix

Phil Powrie

Introduction

Most of Jean-Jacques Beineix's feature films to date were released in a single decade, the 1980s. He is generally seen as the best example of what came to be known as the *cinéma du look*, which Ginette Vincendeau defined in 1996 as 'youth-oriented films with high production values . . . The *look* of the *cinéma du look* refers to the films' high investment in non-naturalistic, self-conscious aesthetics, notably intense colours and lighting effects. Their spectacular (studio-based) and technically brilliant *mise en scène* is usually put to the service of romantic plots'.[1] Beineix's films were vilified by the critical establishment during the 1980s, to a greater extent than those of Luc Besson, the other major film-maker of the *cinéma du look*. This is in part, no doubt, because Beineix reacted aggressively to his critics. The continuing success of Besson, however, and the popularity of both his and Beineix's films with youth audiences, invite a revision of the critical view still held today in France. In many ways, Beineix is very much a traditional *auteur*, writing his own scripts and controlling production for most of his films. And yet the critics of the *Cahiers du cinéma* considered that the *cinéma du look* undermined the concept of the *auteur*. This chapter proposes a new way of considering Beineix's films, based partly on the auteurist strategy of considering the director's work as a whole, and of isolating a thematics that gives coherence to that work. First, however, I shall give a brief overview of each of his films, placing them in the context of their reception.

Beineix's first feature film, *Diva* (1981), simultaneously invoked high culture, by featuring an opera singer who has never been recorded, and the popular culture of the French police thriller, in the form of a police chief and his thugs involved in trafficking. Between the two is Jules, a young postman, who illicitly records the diva, and is pursued by the thugs when a tape denouncing the police chief ends up in his possession and gets mixed up with his recording of the diva. The film attracted the attention of one of the key theorists of postmodernism, Fredric Jameson, who described it as the first French postmodern film.[2]

The French critical establishment, however, took a dislike to what were considered to be the more superficial aspects of a postmodern style, namely an attachment to objects and to surface effect at the expense of character psychology or moral message. Beineix was singled out as the representative of the *cinéma du look*. The arguments that raged in the pages of the *Cahiers du cinéma* came to a head, as they did for Besson and *Le Grand Bleu* (1988) a few years later, at the Cannes Film Festival, where Beineix showed his second film, *La Lune dans le caniveau* (1983). The film is based on David Goodis's low-life novel, *The Moon in the Gutter* (1953). In it, Gérard Depardieu plays a loner obsessed with discovering the rapist of his sister. The style of the film is consciously operatic, with languorous tracking shots, artificial colour schemes and emphatic music. It was intended to convey the dreamlike atmosphere of the novel, but was seen by critics to be at odds, in its high production values, with its low-life subject. The film was booed when screened, and publicly repudiated by Depardieu.

Beineix's third feature, *37° 2 le matin* (1986), co-produced by his new company Cargo Films, became, as *Diva* had done five years earlier, an even more obviously cult film for youth audiences in France and abroad. This was due in part to the subject, based on a novel by Philippe Djian, a tale of mad love between a world-weary Zorg and a rebellious Betty. The film's success derived, moreover, from its leads, Béatrice Dalle and Jean-Hugues Anglade, who managed to capture the mixture of masculinity in crisis, rebelliousness, innocence and marginalization that characterized the 1980s youth *zeitgeist*.

Beineix's first three feature films had all been adaptations of novels. His last two feature films were based on original treatments in collaboration with Jacques Forgeas. *Roselyne et les lions* (1989) is a vehicle for the actress with whom Beineix was to share his life for several years, Isabelle Pasco. Despite a story-line that, on paper at least, might seem calculated to please the *cinéma du look*'s youth audience – a young couple seek adventure in the world of the big top by training lions – the film did no more than averagely, perhaps because it was too obviously a personal allegory about perfecting one's art. Beineix's last feature film to date, *IP5* (1992), did somewhat better. It is a narrative of initiation as two streetwise youths go on the road in search of romance, only to meet an old man, played by Yves Montand in his last role, apparently doing much the same thing.

Towards the end of the 1980s, the attachment to style manifested by Beineix and the other directors of the *cinéma du look*, Besson and Carax, was redefined as 'neo-baroque'.[3] Less charitable historians and reviewers have categorized Beineix's films as heterogeneous, extended designer clips comprised of advertising images. Susan Hayward describes *37° 2 le matin* as 'a film constructed out of a series of video clips of madness interspersed with "fucking" . . ., a high-tech designer clip-film about nymphomania'.[4]

But we can talk in another way about the *cinéma du look*, by focusing on structures of looking rather than on surface style (how the films look) or surface narrative (how they gather together the styles that generate the look of the films' look). In this discussion, I shall propose a psychoanalytic reading of Beineix's films, focusing on his young male protagonists (YMPs). The rest of the chapter is in three sections. In the first of these, I shall argue that Beineix's YMPs are a lure, a location that allows us to position ourselves. Further, I shall link this phenomenon to Lacan's analysis of Holbein's *The Ambassadors*. In the following section, I shall suggest that Beineix's feature films sketch out a problematic Oedipal trajectory. In the final section, I shall link this trajectory to Beineix's very public railings against the cinematic establishment, railings paralleled by his favourite narrative frame: youth in revolt against the cruel and cynical adult world. The latter parts of my argument can be summed up in the following, inevitably over-simplified statements:

1. Beineix's YMPs, with whom we are called upon to identify, struggle against the Father/establishment whom they need for self-definition.
2. The films' narratives undermine the Father/establishment, leaving an empty space and causing the YMPs to distort.
3. The space is filled by distorted images, at the expense of 'character' or 'message'.

What I find compelling in Beineix's work (as well as in Besson's) is its coherence. Beineix rejects the established cinema inherited from the *Nouvelle Vague* (and is rejected by those critics who adhere to it). That rejection is inscribed not just in the narratives of his films, which are self-destructing, but also in his attraction to images as methods of disruption. Insofar as we may identify part of the time with his YMPs, we are called upon to reject New Wave narrative, and to collapse that identification into a jubilation of the image at the expense of character. That jubilation, in my view, transcends gender-specific identification: the spectator ends up in a no-man's-land constituted by music (which I do not have space to address) and image. This is not to say that Beineix's films (or Besson's) are merely MTV surrogates or advertising clips. Nor does it mean, as so many critics said of both directors' work in the 1980s, that their films are without a message. Without wishing to sound facile, I would suggest that their message is that messages are no longer possible: that pleasure may be possible, but that it is not necessarily enshrined in the concept of message, by which is normally meant a morality. And this, in turn, does not necessarily mean that their films are amoral, escapist fantasies. Rather, in Beineix's case, they are exercises in derision: a derision that affects first and foremost the main focalizers, the YMPs.

In which YMPs/Wimps Morph into Anamorphs

What is striking about Beineix's protagonists is that, although they reject the Law by their marginality, if not their criminality, in a variety of ways, they are fundamentally wimps, albeit artistically-inclined wimps. They are normally over-shadowed by stronger characters who are narratively more pivotal than they are. So, in *Diva*, it is difficult to see who the 'hero' of the film is. Jules does not really set anything in motion; things simply happen to him. Decisions are taken by two older males: the evil police chief, Saporta, and the god-like Gorodish. Jules, the opera-loving postman, acts as a letter-box for the audio-tape that will generate the action. Gérard, in *La Lune dans le caniveau*, is no artist, but is a sensitive docker, who is attracted to the pure, moon-like Loretta, but also to the pull of the gutter: the real gutter where his sister committed suicide after being raped, and the figurative gutter where his girlfriend Bella waits for him. He spends much of the film aspiring to be better, purer and more cultured, but fails and falls in both literal and figurative senses. Zorg, in *37° 2 le matin*, as his extraordinary name suggests, is at the end of everything.[5] He is a failed writer who stops leaks and paints over cracks, but cannot prevent his girlfriend from going mad, from painting herself and from enucleating herself. Played by Jean-Hugues Anglade, one of the new, sensitive breed of mid-1980s actors, Zorg is completely upstaged by Béatrice Dalle's naturalness, to the extent that, taking the sensitivity of the new man to the lengths of a woman's dress, he cross-dresses at the end of the film in order to kill her. Thierry, in *Roselyne et les lions*, is upstaged both in the narrative and in the acting by the whip-wielding Pasco as they create a lion-taming act. Finally, in *IP5*, in his search for his girlfriend, the graffiti artist Tony is paralleled, and again upstaged, by Léon's holy fool, whose apotheosis the film becomes, not least since Yves Montand, who plays Léon, died while the film was being made.

All these male protagonists, ostensibly the identificatory lure of the films, are or become failures. They are all given-to-be-seen, so that we may identify ourselves with them, but they themselves cannot see, in the figurative sense. They are caught in the plot and need a father- or mother-figure to help them see; to help them understand their desires. Jules needs Gorodish; Zorg needs Betty; Gérard needs Bella; Thierry needs the schoolteacher Bracquard; Tony needs Léon. As characters in a film, then, the YMPs exemplify Lacan's formulation of the fading subject. This has been explicated by Robert Lapsley and Michael Westlake, who point out how the subject, for Lacan, is constituted in language. Since language is a system outside us, we are from the outset alienated and divided: 'the subject can only appear if represented in the Other, while simultaneously and consequently all that is repressed as heterogeneous to the identity given through any signifier means that representation is always inadequate to the subject's being'.[6] Beineix's protagonists need the Other, but by the same token they are never where they think they are: they are scattered and deferred, like the drift of signifiers. They are wimps, as I said. To the extent that we identify ourselves at least part of the time with these protagonists, we are also called upon to fade like them; we are wimped, as it were. To put it in a grander, and more obviously Lacanian, way, Beineix's protagonists may be described as 'anamorphic ghosts' (*fantômes anamorphiques*).[7]

An anamorph is the product of anamorphosis, defined as the distortion of an image by the introduction of a differential between the relativities in height and width. The term anamorphosis puts us in mind of morphing, whereby a character assumes a series of faces, indicating either changing identifications or the passage of time. Both these terms – anamorphosis and morphing – more or less encapsulate what I have said so far about Beineix's YMPs. Their position in his films is eccentric, marginal, so that they may appear important, but are less so than other characters. Moreover, because they fade, they end up by distorting. The spectator's view of them will be changed as a result of identifying with other, stronger characters as the youthful protagonists fade, only to return.

Arguably, however, Beineix's YMPs do more than just fade and distort. And Lacan helps us to see how this is so. Lacan is fond of anamorphosis in general and, in particular, of the manner in which it manifests itself in Holbein's *The Ambassadors*. He draws a contrastive parallel between the stable Cartesian subject and the Lacanian subject on the one hand, and geometral or central perspective and inverted anamorphic perspective on the other. Combining this with his analysis of the ostensible theme of *The Ambassadors*, *vanitas*, Lacan is able to say of the anamorphosis, which he likens to fried eggs,[8] that 'it reflects our own nothingness, in the figure of the death's head'.[9] The skull in *The Ambassadors* makes, then, a double comment. As Lacan reminds us, it invokes the well-worn theme of the vanity of worldly affairs. But, in that we can only see the skull by standing in a very specific position, obliquely to it, the skull also makes an oblique reference to the painter himself. ('Hohlbein', according to Hanjo Berressem, means hollow bone (or skull) in German.[10]) The anamorphosis thus comments on the central or geometral perspective without which its dissident and distorted form could not exist, while at the same time annihilating metaphorically the I/eye (the unified subject equivalent to the central perspective) that actualizes the anamorphosis. As Lacan says elsewhere of anamorphs, 'what we seek in the illusion is something in which the illusion as such in some way transcends itself, destroys itself, by demonstrating that it is only there as a signifier'.[11]

What is left in this annihilating perspective? Lacan also relates the anamorphosis in *The Ambassadors* to the phallus (although, typically, he effects a slippage between the phallus as a symbol and the penis as a biological fact): 'How is it that nobody has ever thought of connecting this with the effect of an erection? Imagine a tattoo traced on the sexual organ ad hoc in the state of repose and assuming its, if I may say so, developed form in another state'.[12] He suggests that the distortion represented by the anamorphosis is 'symbolic of the function of lack, of the appearance of the phallic ghost'.[13] Commenting on Lacan's view of Holbein, Berressem suggests that 'visual distortions . . . serve as a (visual) metaphor of psychic distortions; the effects of the interference of the libido within the perceptual apparatus'.[14] Beineix's YMP, and the identifying spectator, can therefore be conceived of as a fading subject, an 'anamorphic ghost', or, to pick up on Lacan's metaphor of the tattooed penis, a bit (quite literally a bit) of a prick, a place for our desire for meaning.

And where are 'we', in this annihilating perspective? Lacan relates anamorphosis to baroque forms, which reminds us of the way in which Beineix's work was redefined as baroque by its attachment to light, colour and movement: 'The Baroque return to the play of forms, to all manner of devices, including anamorphosis, is an effort to restore the true meaning of artistic inquiry: artists use the discovery of the property of lines to make something emerge that is precisely there where one has lost one's bearings or, strictly speaking, nowhere'.[15] Beineix's anamorphs, fading subjects, detumescent penises sunny-side down, are the non-location, the 'nowhere', that undermines the 'there', the 'established view', but cannot completely do so because there is always the Father-figure to restrain the leakage, the stain, introduced by the anamorph. In the narratives of the films, the anamorph revolts by leaving, always precipitously although temporarily, the framework in which we first meet him: Jules takes refuge in a fairy castle; Gérard rejects Vernon Street by getting married in a fairy cathedral; Zorg, who begins in the fairyland beach-houses, takes refuge with Betty in a picture-postcard country cottage; Thierry rejects school and goes on the circus trail; and Tony rejects the city to find his true love in fairy forests.

The anamorphs are thus representatives of the libido that distorts. Unimportant in themselves, they are important in their function. They are our point of identification, the 'nowhere' from which the 'somewhere' is constituted, the letter-box we look through into the signifying system of the film. Lacan uses the term *trompe-l'oeil* to describe the relationship between the painter and the spectator of the painting, although, in the following, we could just as well replace 'painter' by 'film director': 'The relation . . . between the painter and the spectator, is a play, a play of *trompe-l'oeil*'.[16] The anamorphs are lures whose function is to capture our attention, quite literally to bring us to *attend* to the narrative. They are ghostly bodies that force us to take up a position in relation to the film, much as the anamorphosis is what attracts us to place ourselves physically in front of Holbein's *The Ambassadors*. We do not really care much, I suspect, what the painting is about.[17] We simply want to see the anamorphosis out of an almost physical curiosity.[18] What attracts us is the placing of our body so that we can see from that 'nowhere', from that utopian space or place ('utopia' signifies the 'no-place') that anamorphosis establishes. The place where 'we' are is like the blind spot, the point where the optical nerve is fixed, and hence the point that cannot see itself seeing, to recall the formula Lacan uses as the springboard for his discussion of the gaze.[19]

What we see in the films from this nowhere are the aberrant images for which Beineix was censured during the 1980s by the critics of the *Cahiers du cinéma*: wide-angle lens; extreme angles; close-ups on fetishized objects; and so on. These images are truly 'aberrant', in that they wander lazily through the films like floaters (or vitreous opacities, as they are technically called)[20] in the vitreous humour, disturbing the field of vision. If, as I am suggesting, the principal protagonists of Beineix's films are merely fugitive distortions situated in the blind spots, and the images of the world around them are also frequently mobile and distorted, signifying the irruption of desire, then who or what is the (fixed) point of the films?

In which the Films 'Work Through' the Father

In the perspective I have adopted, the (fixed) point of everything is the Father, the Big Fix of the Phallus, the anamorph unmorphed, so that the two fried eggs look less like fried eggs and more like balls. The pun is not entirely spurious, because I mean to suggest that the Fathers in Beineix's films are more rounded characters than the Sons. It is not for nothing that Beineix, according to Denis Parent, is intrigued by power.[21] Beineix's films can be seen as involving a complex Oedipal scenario in which the formless, gormless, anomic anamorph struggles (but fails) to get away from what looms in the perspective, the Father. That Father equates, I would propose, to the establishment against which Beineix spent considerable time railing during the 1980s, because its critics did not take to his perspective, baroque excess. Among other things, the baroque, and by extension Beineix's cinema, includes strategies of fragmentation; vortical turbulence; metamorphosis; and complex structures such as the knot and the labyrinth, whose interest lies in what one writer on the neo-baroque calls 'constructed undecidability'.[22] The pleasure to be gained from such structures is 'primarily the obvious pleasure of getting lost, of wandering, of renouncing that final principle of connection that is the key to the solution of the enigma'.[23] What is the solution to any enigma if not the Father, the Law that, according to Lacan, regulates the Symbolic, the (real) social world and the world of language? In Beineix's films, though, taken as a series, the search for the Father is a *search in reverse*. The anamorph struggles against the stronger Father, who gradually, as one might expect from a film-maker at odds with the critical establishment, is demoted, pulled down from his pedestal. In this section, then, I shall review the films once more, tracing the 'working through' of the Father: his gradual fall from God to King to Fool.

In *Diva*, there are two fathers: the 'bad' father Saporta, the corrupt police chief who has betrayed the Law; and the 'good', God-like, marginal Gorodish, a cross between a magician in supreme control of technology and, as Jameson calls him, a counter-cultural businessman.[24] The film's tortuous double narrative centres on lost and stolen voices. The loss of the voice of the Mother, the enigmatic Diva, forces Jules into an attempt to (re)capture that voice. But he is constantly sucked into the world of the Law (both literally, since the film is partly a police thriller, and figuratively, in the Lacanian sense of the patriarchally-dominated Symbolic), and into that of the Father, the Law's guarantor. The return of the Diva's voice at the end of the film seems to signal narrative and psychical closure, with Jules sinking into his Mother's arms. This misleading, if satisfying, closure is reinforced by Beineix's next two films, *37° 2 le matin* and *La Lune dans le caniveau*, where father- and obvious mother-figures are broadly absent. The Father seems to be manifest merely in shadowy and inconsistent, secondary figures: in antithetical pairs such as the decrepit chalet-owner and the dandy publisher in *37° 2 le matin*, or, in *La Lune dans le caniveau*, the macho foreman and the womanizing drunk of a father. Here, Beineix's narratives focus more on the anamorphs, who try either to recreate their 'family' by an ethos of sibling collectivity (*37° 2 le matin*) or to refuse it (*La Lune dans le caniveau*).

The repressed autocratic Father returns, however, in *Roselyne et les lions*, in a curious and hallucinatory reprise of *Diva*'s characters. The Diva and the young Vietnamese Alba of *Diva* are fused into the ice-cold, leather-wielding dominatrix Roselyne, as Thierry, only slightly less lymphatic than *Diva*'s Jules, clashes with distant relatives of the bad Father Saporta and the good Father Gorodish. First we encounter the bad Father Frazier, the lion-tamer who instructs Thierry and Roselyne, and the Good Father Bracquard, Thierry's schoolteacher, who eventually copies his former pupil by training his domestic cat. Frazier is replaced by big bad Markovitch, the lion-tamer of the provincial and self-referential Cirque Zorglo,[25] and then by Koenig, marked as 'King' by his name, the German owner of the Munich circus that bears his name.

With Beineix's final feature film to date, *IP5*, the Father has become the mystical, Lear-like Fool, held in a contempt that changes to grudging admiration by the two anamorphs of the film, Tony and Jockey. Admiration comes as he initiates these YMPs into an alternative eco-law, where the touching of trees is contrasted with the impatient ejaculations of Tony's graffiti. It is perhaps no coincidence that Beineix has not made a feature film since this apparent acceptance of the 'feminine' Father, whose Law is no longer the bitter rivalry-ridden patriarchal Law of the city, but the feminine Law of the natural Edenic garden.

The indexing of the Father as 'feminine' is, however, ambivalent and troubling. If the Father is accepted, it is at the price of being no longer a patriarchal Father but an excessively visible and visibly fallen Father.[26] The 'feminine' that the Father represents is cast as both positive – by virtue of his connection with an alternative eco-law – and at the same time disturbingly negative, since he remains the location-less emotional Fool. He must therefore, like Lear, roam and die in the wilderness, so as to repair the rupture he represents. The Oedipal trajectory of Beineix's films has it both ways. The lost Good (because 'feminine') Father is found, and the negatively connoted patriarchal Law of the Father is overturned in the process. Conveniently, that same Good Father, who is both Father and Mother, is merely a dying Fool, and the potential Mothers do not take his place. They remain *femmes fatales*, enigmatically unapproachable (the Diva, Loretta, Roselyne) or mad (Betty).

In which the Father Becomes an Idiot and the Anamorph Morphs into the Orphan

What has happened? How could the wimps survive this parental oblation, since – as I pointed out above – Beineix's wimps are dependent on the powerful (paternal) Other? A Lacanian answer would invoke what Lacan says of the subject, who realizes that his father is an idiot: 'the sole function of the father is to be a myth, to be always only the Name-of-the-Father, or in other words nothing more than the dead father'.[27] The wimp has to be only faintly, or 'fadingly', present, so that we may place ourselves in relation to the film's narrative: an anamorphic stain that attracts us into the distraction of the film's narrative. Over the series of five films we attend as witnesses to a gradual deterioration that takes us from Gorodish the God, to Koenig the King, to Léon the Fool, and is located in a fading subject: the sad lost boy. Beineix's protagonists, who oscillate between anomie and revolt, function as our perspective on the degradation of the Father/establishment that Beineix felt was out to get him.

This degradation is enacted through both the narrative and individual images within the *mise en scène*. The anamorphs pull us into a narrative where they constantly fade. They are replaced, one might argue, or at least accompanied, by what many reviewers of Beineix's films saw as an over-emphasis on image at the expense of message or character. But, in the argument I have been developing, these over-emphatic images are, like the anamorphs who lure us into adopting their optic, received as distorted, consciously wrought images of what lurks as unrepresentable: the unconscious. It is no coincidence that Beineix has often said that he was trying to find a language for the unconscious.[28] The degradation of the Fathers and the wilting away of the Sons that occurs on one level of narrative is, which we might call the macro-level, thus paralleled at the micro-level of *mise en scène* and cinematography by moments in the films where excess breaks through, figuring the unconscious.[29]

The representation of characters and the images, I am arguing, distorted and anamorphosed, undermine the film. The fading anamorph undermines a strong sense of agency. The anamorphs are replaced by secondary characters who are stronger, but these secondary characters, over the series of five films, can also be seen to fade away as they are degraded. *The field is left open for images*, themselves anamorphosed, undermining the more realist narrative that many of Beineix's 1980s reviewers, and indeed many of his subsequent critics, felt was lacking, and that they applauded in *Roselyne et les lions*. The *Cahiers du cinéma* reviewer, for example, praised the latter for being 'a pretty documentary on lion-taming',[30] which is to be wilfully blind to Beineix's effort to establish a realist 'ground' that would allow the excess of spectacle to lure the spectator all the more.

Oedipus was, of course, blind, and it is of some interest that the word 'orphan', from the Greek ωρφανος, is linked to the Latin 'orbus', which means 'lacking'. Both words are derived from the Indo-European *orbho*, which, it is presumed, had as one of its primary meanings 'to be blind' (in the sense of lacking sight).[31] I have represented the orphan by the sign ØØ. There is a double O to suggest the phrase Orphan without Origin, the bars representing blindness, in the same way that Lacan's barred S allows the subject 'to distinguish himself from the sign in relation to which, at first, he has been able to constitute himself as subject',[32] and which Lacan likens to a tattoo. The anamorph is a self-made, self-generated Orphan without (and therefore as) Origin. He may fade, but then the Fathers fade even more, and it is the anamorph who survives. He is, literally, an *auteur*, etymologically he who is himself and no Other, the blind and parentless boy-child. He is parentless because he is blind. He refuses to see the inevitability of origin and otherness: he is the blindspot that cannot see itself seeing, and that is therefore the perfect lure for the spectator of Beineix's films. He is the empty hub around which revolve the vortices of images and words in play, something like a fifth of November sparkler describing runic figures in the dark night of the interpretative gesture. ØØ generates himself through the iteration (or, to fall again into etymological habit, the *making Other*) of Images: Images that are *one in the eye* for the adults/cinematic establishment that have rejected him. I am thinking in particular here of the beginning of *IP5*, with its insistence on graffiti: a beginning where Jockey sings of graffiti-painting as a kind of urban terrorism in which one expresses oneself and one's desire. 'I make love with the walls' ('Je fais l'amour avec les murs'), he sings, suggesting that the artist can become incorporated with what imprisons him through the generation of images of desire. He further sings, 'I am nothing more than a signature, a scoring out/failure' ('Je ne suis qu'une signature, une immense rature'). A *rature* is something crossed-out, hence like the bar that crosses out the Ø. This is why it can be translated as 'failure', or, as the film's English sub-titles, themselves a crossing-out of the original, suggest, a 'fail-lure' (the two phonemes are separated in the sub-titles, because Jockey separates them in the French: *ra-ture*).

In *Richard II*, Shakespeare compares anamorphosis (which, until the seventeenth century, was called simply 'perspective') to the blurred vision of sorrow:[33]

> For Sorrow's eye, glazed with blinding tears,
> Divides one thing entire to many objects;

> Like perspectives which, rightly gaz'd upon,
> Show nothing but confusion, – eyed awry,
> Distinguish form.

My argument has been that Beineix's protagonists are merely locations. To finish with a final pun, they are both the *loculus*, which, in Latin, means the small location or coffin, and the *oculus*, or eye. As coffins for the eye, Beineix's protagonists are a series of confusing objects, *trompe-l'oeil* lures that call upon us to *eye them awr(e)y(e)*, so that we can distinguish the ghostly form tattooed upon them. As Lacan says of anamorphosis, it is a 'trap for the gaze', a *piège à regard*.[34] The ghostly form tattooed on the *trompe-l'oeil* protagonists is the dying Father, and the dying (Beineix would have said dead) *cinéma de papa*, that, for Beineix, means the New Wave, the very same cinema that used the term *cinéma de papa* to castigate the cinema of the 1950s.

Notes

1. G. Vincendeau (1996), *The Companion to French Cinema*, London, p. 50.
2. F. Jameson (1992), '*Diva* and French Socialism', in *Signatures of the Visible*, New York and London, pp. 55–62.
3. R. Bassan (1989), 'Trois néobaroques français', *Revue du cinéma*, 449, pp. 44–50.
4. S. Hayward (1993), *French National Cinema*, London and New York, p. 293.
5. 'After the letter Z there is nothing' ('Après la lettre "Z" il n'y a plus rien'), Beineix said in interview. See J. Savigneau, 'Jean-Jacques Beineix: amoureux d'un récit', *Le Monde*, 2 May 1985.
6. R. Lapsley and M. Westlake (1988), *Film Theory: An Introduction*, Manchester, p. 71. The operative passage from Lacan is as follows: 'The signifier, producing itself in the field of the Other, makes manifest the subject of its signification. But it functions as a signifier only to reduce the subject in question to being no more than a signifier, to petrify the subject in the same movement in which it calls the subject to function, to speak, as subject'. J. Lacan (1994), *The Four Fundamental Concepts of Psychoanalysis*, trans. A. Sheridan, Harmondsworth, p. 207. 'Le signifiant se produisant dans le camp de l'Autre fait surgir le sujet de sa signification. Mais il ne fonctionne comme signifiant qu'à réduire le sujet en instance à n'être plus qu'un signifiant, à le pétrifier du même mouvement où il l'appelle à fonctionner, à parler, comme sujet'. J. Lacan (1973), *Le Séminaire. Livre XI. Les quatre concepts fondamentaux de la psychanalyse*, Paris, pp. 188–9.

7. See *Four Fundamental Concepts*, p. 89; *Les quatre concepts*, p. 86.

8. J. Lacan (1992), *The Ethics of Psychoanalysis 1959–1960: The Seminar of Jacques Lacan. Book VII*, trans. D. Porter, London, p. 135; J. Lacan (1986), *Le Séminaire. Livre VII. L'éthique de la psychanalyse*, Paris, p. 161.

9. Lacan, *Four Fundamental Concepts*, p. 92. 'il nous reflète notre propre néant, dans la figure de la tête de mort'. Lacan, *Les quatre concepts*, p. 86.

10. H. Berressem (1996), 'Dali and Lacan: Painting the Imaginary Landscapes', in W. Apollon and R. Feldstein (eds), *Lacan, Politics, Aesthetics*, Albany, pp. 263–93, p. 271. This is, in fact, a questionable interpretation, since although *bein* does mean bone (or leg), there is a difference between *hohl* (long vowel) meaning hollow, and *hol* (short vowel), which does not exist. A more useful point for this chapter is the closeness of 'Holbein' and 'Beineix'. This would suggest that the solution to the enigma posed by the painting (and, as we shall see, to the enigma of the fading Father), is in the 'x', that not only marks a blind spot, but scores out the Name of the Father. I am grateful to Elizabeth Andersen for elucidating the first point, and to Brian MacFarlane for directing me towards the second.

11. Lacan, *Ethics*, p. 136. 'ce que nous cherchons dans l'illusion est quelque chose où l'illusion elle-même se transcende en quelque sorte, se détruit, en montrant qu'elle n'est là qu'en tant que signifiante'. Lacan, *L'éthique*, p. 163.

12. Lacan, *Four Fundamental Concepts*, pp. 87–8. 'comment se fait-il que personne n'ait jamais songé à y évoquer . . . l'effet d'une érection? Imaginez un tatouage tracé sur l'organe ad hoc à l'état de repos, et prenant dans un autre état sa forme, si j'ose dire, développée'. Lacan, *Les quatre concepts*, p. 82.

13. Lacan, *Four Fundamental Concepts*, p. 88. 'symbolique de la fonction du manque – de l'apparition du fantôme phallique'. Lacan, *Les quatre concepts*, p. 82.

14. Berressem, 'Dali and Lacan', p. 270.

15. Lacan, *The Ethics*, p. 136. 'le retour baroque à tous les jeux de la forme, à tous ces procédés, dont l'anamorphose, est un effort pour restaurer le sens véritable de la recherche artistique – les artistes se servent de la découverte des propriétés des lignes, pour faire resurgir quelque chose qui soit justement là où on ne sait plus donner de la tête – à proprement parler, nulle part'. Lacan, *L'éthique*, p. 162.

16. Lacan, *Four Fundamental Concepts*, p. 103. 'le rapport . . . du peintre et de l'amateur, est un jeu, un jeu de trompe-l'oeil'. Lacan, *Les quatre concepts*, p.95.

17. Although, given that we are considering the way the subject is split, it is interesting to note that the painting is in all probability, and unsurprisingly, an oblique reference to a division, that of Henry VIII's divorce from Catherine

of Aragon, which was to lead to the divorce between Henry and Rome. See R. Foster and P. Tudor-Craig (1986), *The Secret Life of Paintings*, Woodbridge, pp. 75–95.

18. This can be ascertained by watching visitors in the National Gallery, London, tricked by the anamorphosis into a physical activity that they are unlikely to resort to in front of other paintings, and that takes little account of the rest of the painting in question, a complex political allegory.

19. Lacan, *Four Fundamental Concepts*, p. 80; *Les quatre concepts*, p. 76.

20. The word 'floater' is used to describe a dead body floating in water, a vagrant, and, in the sense I am referring to here, a vitreous opacity.

21. D. Parent (1989), *Jean-Jacques Beineix: Version originale*, Paris, pp. 112–13.

22. O. Calabrese (1992), *The Neo-Baroque: A Sign of the Times*, Princeton, New Jersey, p. 139.

23. Ibid., p. 140.

24. Jameson, '*Diva*', p. 56.

25. Proving that after Zorg there is a circus rather than nothing.

26. An appropriately neo-Lacanian, but untranslatable, pun would be 'père-chu/perçu' (father-fallen/perceived).

27. Lacan, *The Ethics*, p. 309. 'la seule fonction du père . . . c'est d'être un mythe, toujours et uniquement le Nom-du-Père, c'est-à-dire rien d'autre que le père mort'. Lacan, *L'éthique*, pp. 356–7.

28. 'I wanted to make the subconscious materialize on the screen. I didn't want to be in the service of logic, of reality'. J.-J. Beineix (1983), 'Man in the Moon', *Film Comment*, 19, pp. 16–19, p.17.

29. The position I am adopting here is broadly that adopted by Willemen in relation to Sirk during the 1970s, although I am not claiming the kind of leftist radicalism for Beineix that Willemen arrogated to Sirk. See P. Willemen (1971), 'Distanciation and Douglas Sirk', *Screen*, 12, pp. 63–7; P. Willemen (1972/3), 'Towards an analysis of the Sirkian system', *Screen*, 13, pp. 128–34.

30. 'Un joli documentaire sur le domptage de lions'. I. Katsahnias (1989), 'Roselyne et les lions', *Cahiers du cinéma*, 419–20, p. 78.

31. P. Chantraine (1968), *Dictionnaire etymologique de la langue grecque: Histoire des mots*, Paris, p. 829.

32. Lacan, *Four Fundamental Concepts*, p. 141. 'se distingue du signe par rapport auquel, d'abord, il a pu se constituer comme sujet'. Lacan, *Les quatre concepts*, p. 130.

33. Act II, Scene ii. Quoted by Foster and Tudor-Craig, *The Secret Life*, p. 89.

34. Lacan, *Four Fundamental Concepts*, p. 89; *Les quatre concepts*, p. 83.

–12–

AIDS-Video: Representing the Body in Guibert's *La Pudeur ou l'impudeur*

Alex Hughes

Introduction

In the chapter that follows, I shall focus on a single film – a video-diary of life with AIDS – and on the questions of sexual and bodily self-representation that that film articulates. In order, however, to introduce and situate my analyses, which address the visual work of the contemporary author, journalist and photographer Hervé Guibert, I want to begin by invoking issues of representation and discursification associated with the gay male body.

Reflections on the 'Homosexual Body'

In the first volume of *The History of Sexuality* (1976), Michel Foucault dissects the proliferating discourses around sex that the modern era introduced. Concomitantly, he signals how such discourses enshrined new bodies of knowledge, concerned with particular subjects and bodies, that supported modalities of social control.[1] A central body targeted by the mass of (medical and psychiatric) sexual discourse that emerged in the nineteenth century, and by the disciplinary mechanisms that discourse vehicled, was, Foucault affirms, the 'homosexual body'.[2] Of the perverse male subject to whom this body belonged – a body that, for Foucault, is understood not as an 'unadorned essence' but as discursively and culturally constructed[3] – he famously says the following:

> The nineteenth-century homosexual became a personage, a past, a case history, and a childhood, in addition to being a type of life, a life form, and a morphology, with an indiscreet anatomy and possibly a mysterious physiology. Nothing that went into his total composition was unaffected by his sexuality. It was everywhere present in him: at the root of all his actions because it was their insidious and indefinitely active principle; written immodestly on his face and body because it was a secret that always gave itself away.[4]

Articulated in the remarks cited above, Foucault's vision of the 'homosexual body' as one that came, through deployments of sexual knowledge/power initiated in the late nineteenth century, to be posited (and produced)[5] as excessively significatory – as 'immodest' in what it tells of itself – nourishes Lee Edelman's 1994 essay 'Homographesis'. In the opening sections of this complex exercise in queer theoretical exegesis, Edelman anatomizes the emergence, under the Judaeo-Christian patriarchal symbolic order, of what he terms the 'recurrent tropology of the inscribed gay body'.[6] He invokes a corpus of representational phenomena that, over recent centuries, have sought to privilege the proposition that the gay male body is readably and visibly imprinted with a distinctive homosexual hallmark.[7] He addresses the way in which, even in quite contemporary discursive loci, credence has been accorded to the received idea that the homosexual body is a body on which an array of signifiers attesting to its 'deviant' desiring orientation are publicly recognizable. He establishes the topos of the legible, or 'textual', gay male body as overdetermined, and fundamental to the representational enterprise of Western culture. And he construes that topos, and the definitional barriers or tropes of identification that fuel it, as a product of a defensive anxiety, inspired in the heterosexual cultural imagination by homosexuality's capacity to 'pass', invisibly.[8]

Edelman's claim that modern Western culture needs not only to posit the marker of homosexuality in visual terms[9] but also to envision the gay male body as a body visibly stamped with a plague spot – a body possessed of a potent, if negatively charged, relationship to legibility and signification[10] – feeds his contention that the institutionalization of 'homosexual difference' is central to the project of heterosexist ideology.[11] The imperative to produce gay difference as an object of cognitive and perceptual scrutiny remains, he states, a key element within a contemporary, gay liberationist, affirmative politics 'committed to the social necessity of opening, or even removing, the closet door'.[12] But that imperative is no less a facet of the agenda of a conservative, homophobic sociocultural order that still prevails, and whose labour of social-political regulation turns on processes of identity codification that particularly target homosexuality.

Edelman's intuition that heterosexual culture is subtended by a need to construe homosexuality as visibly marked, and by a need to configure the homosexual body as legibly different from the norm, is echoed in the work of other contemporary commentators who take the gay body as the object of their discussions.[13] Alan Petersen, for instance, informs us that 'by the early twentieth century, the notion that the homosexual male body could be distinguished from the heterosexual male body on the basis of its effeminacy was well established in expert and "popular" writings, and homosexual men began to be routinely derided and persecuted as a result'.[14] Likewise, in a treatment of the representation of AIDS in the UK, Simon Watney suggests the 'homosexual body', as heterosexual culture imag(in)es it, to be a 'garrulous' body that bespeaks its perversity and depravity: a sign-riddled entity disclosed as such in sites that include the photography of nineteenth-century penal anthropology and sexology, and contemporary journalism.[15] It is so constituted, Watney indicates, by the projective fantasies with which it is culturally and symbolically surrounded.[16]

The ideological conceptualization of the 'homosexual body' as a body that reveals the stigmata of its difference/deviance – stigmata writ readably upon it – has, it hardly needs to be said, gained fresh impetus in the era of AIDS. In the specialist and media discourses of contemporary culture (defined by Jan Zita Grover as extra-HIV-community representational loci),[17] AIDS has been presented as offering an 'epidemic of signification':[18] a 'spectacle' of readable, bodily signs.[19] The 'AIDS victim', to cite Watney, has been reductively, dehumanizingly and phobically given as (no more than) an unnaturally over-signed subject, '"withered, wrinkled, and loathsome of visage" – the authentic cadaver of Dorian Gray'.[20] And the 'spectacle' of AIDS has been constituted in an environment in which AIDS has been culturally conceived as an 'intrinsic property of the fantasized "homosexual body"'.[21] Small wonder, then, that the typology of physical, diseased signs that AIDS (like the 'AIDS victim') is habitually reduced to, representationally – a typology whose emblems are extreme emaciation and the lesions of Kaposi's sarcoma – has been collapsed with that existing range of codifying markers already taken as identificatory of the (legible, non-normative) gay male body.[22] As Murray Pratt puts it, the 'symptoms of AIDS [have been] persistently reinscribed as the caricatural signs of sexual difference on which homophobia feeds'.[23] Hence, the phenomenon of AIDS-commentary – a phenomenon in which the 'homosexual body' and the body of the 'AIDS victim' are commonly conflated – has helped to confirm historically entrenched perceptions of the gay male body as a body that indiscreetly discloses the marks of its abnormality: a body with its 'signs affixed', that we must – nay, cannot fail to – read.[24] AIDS-representation, in sum, has served to shore up the culturally-consecrated belief that the 'homosexual body' should be seen as an abject body that speaks its unspeakable difference explicitly: a body on whose textual, 'immodest' surface the heterosexual subject of vision can legitimately train an identificatory, deciphering, ultimately punitive look.[25] So AIDS, as Watney explains, has proved to be of 'inestimable convenience'[26] to that representational project that Edelman views as a fundamental element of heterosexist ideology. It has afforded new momentum to an established cultural enterprise grounded in the will to identify and institutionalize 'homosexual difference', in the service of heterosexual power relations, as a discrete, determinate identity-mode possessed of its own, particularized, readable bodily markers.[27]

Confronted with a matrix of images and narratives that construct the gay male body as a body that is excessively – and deplorably – significatory/legible/textual, what are the self-representational options open to the gay subject who elects to embark on the enterprise of bodily inscription? And, if his subjectivity embraces homosexuality *and* AIDS, how will he engage with that homophobic cultural narrative that envisions AIDS as a multiplicity of readable signs overlaid on, and proper to, the already over-readable body that is the 'homosexual body'?[28] Should he seek to resist the codifications of gay or AIDS identity that are publically available in contemporary culture, by providing alternatives that counter representations produced by the dominant media?[29] Or must he, rather, work deconstructively from within such codifications? And, if homosexuality and the (HIV+) 'homosexual body' are culturally signified as particularly and unnaturally visually marked, how then will he operate in the realm of visual self-representation? And how, in the sphere of the visual, will the gay subject with AIDS deal with that homophobic, normative, reading gaze that unfailingly interprets the symptoms of AIDS as the signifiers of a despised homosexual 'depravity'?

In the remaining sections of this chapter, I shall engage with issues raised by these admittedly rather sweeping questions. I shall do so, finally, in the fourth section, by exploring the manner in which the male body is visually mapped in a French film-text centred on an individual in an advanced stage of AIDS, whose sexuality is grounded in 'homosexual difference'. The film-text in question is Hervé Guibert's *La Pudeur ou l'impudeur*, a video-diary recorded by Guibert between June 1990 and March 1991, edited by Maureen Mazurek, produced by Pascale Breugnot, and shown on French television (TF1) in January 1992, shortly after Guibert's death in December 1991.[30] It is a film-narrative that, as Jean-Pierre Boulé affirms, features Guibert as director, cameraman, scriptwriter and principal *personnage*.[31] Accompanied by a commentary which often simply reprises passages from autofictional texts Guibert wrote in the wake of his HIV-diagnosis, it is no less generically elusive than Guibert's *autofictions*.[32] It can, though, be generically situated, the plurality of its *auteurs* notwithstanding,[33] within the space of filmic autobiography. Moreover, *La Pudeur ou l'impudeur* needs to be culturally contextualized as a work that came into being in a French milieu in which the collective, affirmative gay identity politics and AIDS-communitarian activism associated with the Anglo-Saxon world have not enjoyed a particularly prominent place.[34] To put the latter point slightly differently, *La Pudeur ou l'impudeur* must be aligned with a cultural environment in which, according to commentators, aesthetic responses to AIDS have proved to be more metaphysical (that is, anchored in individualism and notions of personal transcendence) than politicized.[35]

La Pudeur ou l'impudeur (Modesty or Immodesty) was Guibert's first and only film. Since it addresses his situation/status not simply as a subject/body in the grip of AIDS but also as a gay subject, it will constitute, in the closing part of this chapter, a primary focus of my discussion. But before I analyse its contents, I wish to scrutinize briefly another facet of Guibert's visual practice in which, as I shall demonstrate, his representation of the 'homosexual body' merits an examination informed by the analyses of theorists such as Edelman.

Guibert's Bodily Visualizations: I

As Boulé's work on Guibert reveals, in the multifaceted space constituted by his creative productions, the body is omnipresent.[36] That said, it has been claimed that in a particular stratum of his *oeuvre* – his photography – Guibert's treatment of the body is characterized by an unexpected modesty (*pudeur*): a reticence (*retenue*) absent in his literary *écriture(s) du corps*.[37] This reticence is more than manifest in Guibert's photographic self-portraits, some seventeen of which are included in a collection of his photo-images, *Photographies*, published by Gallimard in 1993, after his death. In these *autoportraits*, created between 1976 and 1989, the Guibertian body is never wholly available to the reader's identificatory-documentary gaze. The *pudeur* with which that body is depicted can be attributed to Guibert's dislike of what he saw as his own bodily imperfection, conveyed in his 1983 essay 'Sur une manipulation courante (Mémoire d'un dysmorphophobe)'. (This essay, which serves as the preface to *Photographies*, articulates Guibert's desire to exist, photographically, simply as a 'corps bien indistinct, . . . habité de blancheur lumineuse'). Guibert's *pudeur* can be construed, in short, as a function of a narcissism isolated by Paul Julian Smith as a key stimulus to Guibert's photographic self-construction as an 'immaculate body'.[38] It is my sense, however, that the modesty with which Guibert pursues the activity of photographic, bodily self-representation can be understood as a more complex phenomenon. And I want, now, to elaborate on how Guibert may be taken to photograph his body modestly, and on why I think his habit of so doing can be read in terms of sexual-political resistance. In taking a detour through Guibert's photographic self-portraiture, I am seeking to contextualize more thoroughly the filmic bodily self-representations offered in *La Pudeur ou l'impudeur*.

In *Photographies*, as Raymond Macherel affirms, there are diverse modalities of Guibertian *phautoportrait*.[39] Certain of Guibert's photographic self-portraits simply depict their subject/author's shadow, foregrounding the photographic act and distancing its referent, the Guibertian body, from our scrutinizing *regard*.[40] Others feature Guibert as/in a mirror-image, offering us a purchase not on Guibert's body but on its mere reflection.[41] Others again are produced by techniques of photographic self-portraiture – notably the use of a camera held at arm's length – that ensure that we just cannot see elements of the Guibertian body.[42] Yet others present Guibert's body, or parts of it, as blurred, or covered by veils or bandages. None of these Guibertian self-images portrays his body in such a way as to permit the photographic viewer to construe it as an entity in which we can easily detect signs of its intrinsic 'meaning', or use those signs to interpretative, identificatory ends. All of them work cumulatively and collectively to situate the body they visualize as finally unreadable, or at least as resistant to readability. Moreover, they work to configure the Guibertian body as *sexually* unreadable. Some of the photo-images of *Photographies* – the 1980 photograph of Agathe Gaillard with her breasts challengingly bared; the photograph of a naked T., taken in 1976 – do present us with bodies we can take as stamped with visible, legible sexual signifiers. But Guibert's self-portraits, many of which simply show his upper torso, do not encourage us to decipher or identify the (homo)sexual orientation or desires of the body they represent: a body that, Macherel suggests, they cause to disappear.[43]

Guibert's photographic construction, in the *autoportraits* included in *Photographies*, of his body as unreadable, and as (homo)sexually unsigned, should come as no surprise to readers familiar with *L'Image fantôme*, a collection of essays on photography that Guibert published in 1981. In the penultimate fragment of this text, Guibert tells of how a photo-image depicting an adolescent male body whose homosexual codings are initially quite decipherable deliquesces into blurred illegibility, conveying as he does so his own satisfaction at the loss of (sexual) legibility to which the body of the photograph – a body he seeks to merge with his own – succumbs.[44] What though, finally, are we to make of Guibert's photographic *self*-presentation, in images made in the 1970s–80s, as a body unadorned by sexual signifiers: a body whose homosexual code is undecipherable?

As Pratt's analysis of Guibert's autobiographical and fictional writings proposes,[45] it is possible to understand this phenomenon (Guibert's will to depict himself, in the visual sphere, as (sexually) unreadable; as a body devoid of homosexual markings) as indicative of his collusion with the values of homophobia. Equally, we can take it to reflect the influence of Guibert's cultural environment: an environment that, as Derek Duncan affirms, is not one in which an advanced gay identity politics has evolved.[46] More productively, however, we can view the phenomenon in question as evidence of Guibert's reluctance to implicate himself in, and thereby support, the sexual-discursive structures/system outlined by Foucault and, more particularly, by Edelman. In sum, we can construe Guibert's unwillingness to posit himself photographically as a manifestly sexually signed body as a function of his refusal to inhabit, in the space of visual representation, the place of the over-significatory, excessively visually legible, 'immodest' body that is homophobically allotted to the homosexual male in Western culture and discourse.[47]

Our sense that Guibert sought to effect such a refusal, that he was unwilling visually to give himself as the overly inscribed, 'unnatural' gay body by which heterosexual culture (re)constructs the homosexual, is endorsed by remarks he made about his relationship to homosexuality in an interview with Christophe Donner. In these remarks, Guibert states that homosexuality 'is a word that's never really been relevant to me, strangely, even though it clearly is relevant . . ., it doesn't encapsulate my sense of self, I have the impression of being elsewhere than within those . . .'.[48] In so doing, he signals his reluctance to align himself with those sexual identity-constructions discursively produced, queer theorists affirm, by the policing, disciplinary mechanisms of the heterosexual hegemony.[49] This reluctance can be taken as a testament to the influence on Guibert of Foucault, who was Guibert's intellectual mentor as well as friend.[50] And it can be detected not simply in Guibert's self-representational photography (and writing), but also in his response to the work of a fellow photographer, the American Robert Mapplethorpe. Guibert's assessment of Mapplethorpe's photographic visualization of *le corps homosexuel*, published in 1978, is superficially laudatory ('This homosexual body is tattoed, and harnessed with straps, rivets and metal rings. Its eyes and mouth are sewn shut with zip-fasteners. Its skin is covered with a second skin, of black leather. Its penis, which Mapplethorpe courageously photographs in close-up . . ., is exposed against a backdrop of torn and tattered clothing, offered up as if on a butcher's stall').[51] However, it is permeated by Guibert's unease at the spectacle of the hyper-coded, hyper-readable imagery of the gay male body that Mapplethorpe's S/M iconography proffers, and, I think, by a desire not to reproduce it in his own photographic self-portraiture.

Guibert's Bodily Visualizations: II

At the very end of his life, by the time he came to make *La Pudeur ou l'impudeur*,[52] the possibility of positioning himself, visually and 'modestly', as a non-inscribed, immaculate body was no longer available to Guibert. As he states in *The Compassion Protocol* (1991), the ravages of his advanced and advancing illness, namely its infliction of an emaciation representationally posited as paradigmatic of AIDS, left him no choice but to dwell in the sphere of the readable body: to be a body imbricated in 'textuality and the legibility of signs'[53] ('This shrunken body the masseur pummelled brutally in order to bring back to life . . . was the body I discovered every morning, an Auschwitzian exhibit [*en panoramique auschwitzien*] in the full-length bathroom mirror . . . Not a day passed without my discovering some disturbing new contour, a fresh absence of flesh on the bone structure. The first sign had been a transversal line across the cheeks, exaggerated under certain lights, now the bone seemed to be coming out of the skin'.[54]) Eluding that 'excessive', 'unnatural' corporeal signification that a gamut of representational media have stereotypically and stigmatizingly ascribed to the 'homosexual body', before and during the age of AIDS, was not an option for him.[55] How, though, did this restriction inflect Guibert's visual, bodily self-representational project? How did he engage with the fact that his body with AIDS had become precisely the type of body the homophobic, deciphering subject of vision expects to detect – and despise – in an HIV+ gay man: a body overstamped with readable markings open to reinscription as the ciphers of a devalued homosexual difference? I propose to suggest here that, faced with the reality that AIDS had mutated his body into an over-inscribed entity, writing on it that 'typology of signs' which the homophobic gaze seeks to exploit in order to identify the 'homosexual body' in the 'final moments of its own apparent self-destruction',[56] Guibert sought in *La Pudeur ou l'impudeur* to overinscribe his body, immodestly, in his turn, and to destabilize the viewing and reading habits of his televisual public.

In *La Pudeur ou l'impudeur* (filmed with a camcorder, as my introductory remarks indicated, by Guibert but edited by Maureen Mazurek),[57] Guibert creates a document that, as Ross Chambers explains, deploys the 'chronicle' structure of the home-movie to chart the daily experiences of an advanced AIDS patient.[58] The chronicle Guibert's film-text offers records his life at home; his encounters with the therapeutic professionals in whose hands he finds himself in the terminal phase of his existence; conversations with his Great-Aunts Suzanne and Louise; and a visit to Elba. Some of its sequences feature dialogue, while others, as I signalled above, are punctuated by read passages drawn from Guibert's writings, or from the writings of others. Most involve shots that are fixed, proffering static fields of view into, and out of, which Guibert moves.[59] And the majority of the sequences that compose *La Pudeur ou l'impudeur* confront us with Guibert's weakened, often (semi-)naked body, focusing unwaveringly upon it and obliging us to do the same.[60] How, then, exactly, is that body transcribed in Guibert's film?

In a central sequence of *La Pudeur*, Guibert introduces Rosine, 'la dame de la lettre'. Rosine reads on camera a missive she has previously sent Guibert after a lunch-date at the Coupole. Steeped in sanctimoniousness, her letter communicates her (surprised) 'pleasure' at having been exposed to the sight of Guibert's still handsome body-with-AIDS. ('Seeing you again, looking no less attractive than you did on TV, on "Apostrophes", I was filled with new hope'.[61]) Equally, it informs Guibert that its author will pray for his recovery from AIDS, his release from the mortal fate that awaits him, provided he abandons a homosexual lifestyle contrary to the teachings of the scriptures and castigated, 'du temps du Christ', by the obliteration of Sodom and Gomorrah.

The 'Rosine' episode is centred on the act of reading and on the phenomenon of manifest homophobia. In including it in *La Pudeur ou l'impudeur*, Guibert achieves in my view a number of things. First, he reminds us that the homophobic *regard*, incarnated in Rosine's reading activity and profiled in the words she speaks, is a deciphering, documentary gaze that endlessly trains itself on the body of the homosexual. Second, he contrives to convey how that gaze feasts punitively and sadistically on the AIDS-body in order to find confirming, identificatory evidence of the death-dealing homosexual 'deviance' it deplores. Third, he hints at how that gaze succumbs to frustration when it fails to find in the gay body with AIDS precisely the kind of evidence it seeks. Fourth, he prepares us to receive *La Pudeur*, a narrative of which the 'Rosine' episode forms not just a pivotal but also a particularly unsettling part, as a visual artefact whose bodily articulations work to defy the homophobic reading gaze, and to undermine its cruelly casual consumption of the body of the gay subject with AIDS. How, though, does the Guibertian defiance built into *La Pudeur*'s bodily representations function? And how does it differ from the resistance embedded in the modest bodily configurations of Guibert's *phautoportaits*?

When Guibert stages his body in *La Pudeur ou l'impudeur*, he in fact *overstages* it as that 'hybrid of body and sign' that, Schehr suggests, the 'homosexual body' has been homophobically perceived and posited as, both before and after the advent of AIDS.[62] He does so by repeatedly accentuating its skeletal enfeeblement, in all its amplitude, compelling us to look unremittingly on physical manifestations that the late twentieth-century heterosexual imagination understood not only as the emblems of AIDS but also as the confirmatory cyphers of a homosexual 'dissipation' that is AIDS's root cause. In certain sequences that compose especially the earlier parts of his film-narrative, the totality of Guibert's wasted, hyper-expressive body is powerfully displayed for our scrutiny: curled over the toilet as diarrhoea strikes; extended on a massage table in a muddle of shrivelled nude limbs; caught in a frenetic dance-routine that overexposes its fleshly decomposition. In others, over-significatory bodily segments – a withered arm opening a sachet of medicine or extended for blood-letting; an emaciated pair of naked legs pumping the pedals of an exercise bicycle or rising from a bath – are foregrounded for our inspection. And, in all such sequences, Guibert contrives to 'overfeed' the spectatorial gaze that strives to batten on to the 'textual' stigmata of his seropositive bodily deliquescence, and to reconstruct them as so many clues to his homosexual difference/'guilt'.

The strategy of visual overfeeding that Guibert adopts in *La Pudeur* – his practice of giving us his body, reiteratively, as a hyperexpressive text that contrasts with the 'immaculate' body-text of his *phautoportraits* – should not be understood as accidental, or as just a corollary of his evolving medical condition. Rather, I would say, it should be taken as proof of his effort to thwart, through a process of visual suffusion, the kind of reading *regard* invoked in the 'Rosine' sequence of his film-text. Guibert's strategy, in short, can be construed as indicative of his desire deliberately to effect, in and through his film-narrative, what Murray Pratt terms an 'affront to vision'.[63] The target of Guibert's affront is the scrutinizing look of a heterosexual, homophobic TV viewer who wants to detect all the physical signs stamped on the AIDS-body, and to employ them to censoring and sexually-codifying purpose, but is not prepared to have those signs thrown in his or her face, in a radically immodest, hyperbolic gesture that saps his or her interpretative mastery over them. Guibert's visual challenge, in other words, takes as its object the scopic, identificatory-documentary enterprise of a subject of vision bent on a process of bodily consumption and (d)evaluation. And it works to frustrate that enterprise, or at least to unsettle it, not by eliding the corporeal 'evidence' the homophobe desires to discern in the AIDS-body, but, instead, by providing an *excess* of it that undercuts his or her capacity casually to use it to sadistic interpretative ends.

Guibert's challenge, in sum, turns on a refusal to allow the homophobic deciphering gaze to go about its identificatory, condemnatory reading business with unreflective, heedless ease. His defiance is metaphorized, moreover, within the bounds of his film, in a *mise en abyme* contained in one of its earliest sequences. Here, Guibert confronts us with the spectacle of his upper, emaciated torso, caught in the activity of shadow-boxing. The movements his body makes – movements that seem to penetrate the screen, to assault our voyeuristic viewing stance – emblematize the explicit challenge to prejudicial, thoughtless AIDS/gay body-reading that Guibert's corporeally saturated film-text incorporates.

David Bell and Gill Valentine situate the AIDS activist aesthetic as an 'in your face' representational strategy in which 'the angry body is thrust up against the boundaries of hegemonic subjectivity'.[64] If it eschews the tactics of anger[65] manifest in intra-HIV-community artefacts made in the Anglo-Saxon context, Guibert's video-diary certainly attests, in its 'excessive' depiction of the Guibertian gay+AIDS body as a text overimbued with legibility, to an 'in your face' ethos that proceeds through spectatorial, scopic overkill. And it testifies equally, I believe, to a mode of bodily representation that can be taken to turn on a practice of parodic, defiant mimesis.

In *This Sex Which Is Not One* (1977), Luce Irigaray suggests that the female subject whose identity is devaluatively constru(ct)ed in hegemonic systems of representation can resort to mimetic, hyperbolic parody, in order to 'disturb' the discourses that surround her. Through its 'ludic' deployment of repetition, Irigaray argues, mimetic parody illuminates the ideological, prejudicial basis of the cultural significations to, and through, which the feminine is subjected, opening them up to reconceptualization.[66] In over-flagging filmically his body-with-AIDS as exactly that which the 'hegemonic' heterosexual subject is culturally conditioned to see as the AIDS-body – gaunt, 'loathsome of visage', stamped with signs that symbolize a dehumanized identity delimited by AIDS *and* announce a death invited by sexual 'deviance' – Guibert succeeds, arguably, in performing the deconstructive, parodic rhetorical twist that Irigaray recommends.[67] His *panoramique auschwitzien*[68] mimes and overmimes dominant, dehumanizing representations of the homosexual subject/body-with-AIDS, implicitly highlighting the ideological investments that subtend such representations, and inciting us to perceive them in our turn. In other words, Guibert's AIDS-video may be deemed to play, theatrically, with phobic, reductive visions of the gay body with AIDS, constituted, Watney affirms, 'in a regime of massively overdetermined images, which are sensitive only to the . . . dominant . . . "truth" of AIDS and the projective "knowledge" of its ideally inter-pellated spectator, who already "knows all he needs to know" about homosexuality *and* AIDS'.[69] And its mimetic aspect enables Guibert to call the validity of those dehumanizing visions into question.

That Guibert sought actively to interrogate dominant, homophobic modes of AIDS-representation in mimetic-parodic vein is suggested in several ways in *La Pudeur*. The conscious dimension of Guibert's strategy is highlighted, first, by his re-employment of footage taken from a real home-movie filmed by his father in 1961. The footage he borrows shows us Guibert as a boy, revealing his prepubescent body in all its lively, unblemished purity. It is juxtaposed with Guibert's own filmic articulations of his decomposing, skeletal, adult AIDS-body. Its inclusion permits Guibert manifestly to re-stage – and subvert – a standard media device that censoriously combines 'before-and-after' images of gay men as (i) healthy, erotic, hedonistic (if already overexpressive) gym-bodies, and (ii) moribund PWAs whose bodies are ethereal, lesioned and unnaturally over-signed, and that does so in order to reconstruct the story of AIDS as an anti-gay morality tale.[70]

Guibert's manipulation of the 'before-and-after' trope in no way endorses the stigmatizing message that the 'wages-of-sin' narrative from which it is plundered works to emit. Rather, in a manner that unquestionably situates *La Pudeur* as a resistantly mimetic artefact, Guibert's repetition elaborates its own, alternative, touching rendition of bodily 'innocence lost': a rendition that at once recalls the stereotypical mode of AIDS/gay representation it mimics, and exposes it as riddled with homophobic disdain. Poignantly, and deconstructively, the 'before' images of boyish bodily beauty and the 'after' images of seropositive deterioration that Guibert's mimetic move conjoins are not combined with the lurid, 'tabloid' coarseness typifying accounts that punitively deploy juxtapositional imagery to re-present AIDS as a consequence of, and chastisement for, homosexual degeneracy. Instead, Guibert's 'before' and 'after' sequences are divided/connected by shots of a pair of child's soft toys, positioned in a series of sexualized embraces that invoke not gay 'deviance' but, rather, a (highly personalized, private vision of) homoerotic passion.

Our intuition that Guibert's filmic representation of his gay+AIDS-body was fuelled, at least in part, by mimetic-parodic motives is reinforced by the fact that his 'predictable' (over)visualization of his seropositive body *en panoramique auschwitizien* as the 'authentic cadaver of Dorian Gray' is not actually sustained throughout *La Pudeur*. In a concluding section of his film, introduced by a sequence whose musical accompaniment is a pop-song whose opening line is 'Je suis fatigué/ de faire semblant',[71] Guibert offers us a somewhat different vision of his body. The latter vision is one that refuses simply to mirror/overmime dominant, phobic figurations of the homosexual body-with-AIDS in circulation in contemporary culture.

Guibert's video-diary plays with contrast. It plays off images of the AIDS-body that posit it as less than wholly human, as little more than the emblem of its sickness

– images that chime with standard, stereotypical-devaluative, culturally-sanctioned depictions of the 'AIDS-victim' – against a more restricted set of images, created during Guibert's sojourn in Elba. These last cast Guibert's ailing HIV+ body, nonconformistically, as (nonetheless) that of a *jeune homme en fleur*: a youthful dandy at ease in nature and dressed in the elegant apparel of the *estivant*.[72] Guibert's recourse to contrast encourages us to see that what he is deliberately seeking to do, on one level, in the earlier, far more explicitly 'auschwitzian' parts of *La Pudeur* is less (just) to visualize his own body than to re-present, critically, a dehumanizing mode of AIDS-body depiction that is produced/consecrated in a homophobic cultural climate, and that constitutes the object of his deconstructive endeavours. The representational diversity built into Guibert's corporeally focused film-narrative confirms, in other words, our sense of the mimetic-resistant stratum of his self-inscriptive enterprise. Clearly, Guibert's defiant mimesis was practised at a price. The words of the song he uses to set up the Elba sequence that allows him to effect his contrastive, oppositional rhetorical gesture – 'Je suis fatigué/de faire semblant' – convey the burden his mimetic project imposed upon him.

Mimetic defiance can, of course, miss its mark. It can be misconstrued. That this is the case is indicated by the reception *La Pudeur* elicited in certain quarters. Guibert's film-text was, for instance, deemed by Arnaud Marty-Lavauzelle, president of the French association AIDES, to do no more than reproduce dominant, phobic, prejudicial media-images of AIDS, to fail signally to subvert (*déjouer*) them.[73] But, by the time he created his video-diary, Guibert arguably had little choice but to recur to mimesis in order to produce a film-narrative capable of countering standard, stereotypical representations of the 'AIDS-victim'. And the visual-corporeal narrative that *La Pudeur ou l'impudeur* proffers does, undoubtedly, work to contest such representations, as it likewise works to reorient the manner in which the mainstream public habitually reads, interprets and consumes the homosexual-body-with-AIDS.

Notes

1. For a summary of what Foucault's text says about the modes of power-knowledge the body became subject to, particularly in the nineteenth century, see L. McNay (1992), 'Power, Body and Experience', in *Foucault and Feminism*, Boston, pp. 11–47.
2. M. Foucault (1990), *The History of Sexuality Volume I*, trans. R. Hurley, Harmondsworth, p. 101, p. 104; M. Foucault (1976), *Histoire de la Sexualité I: La Volonté de savoir*, Paris, p. 134, p. 139.

3. As McNay explains (cf. *Foucault and Feminism*, p. 30), the body Foucault addresses in his *History of Sexuality* is a body subject to cultural signification/ production.

4. Foucault, *History of Sexuality*, p. 43. 'L'homosexuel du XIXe siècle est devenu un personnage: un passé, une histoire et une enfance, un caractère, une forme de vie; une morphologie aussi, avec une anatomie indiscrète et peut-être une physiologie mystérieuse. Rien de ce qu'il est au total n'échappe à sa sexualité. Partout en lui, elle est présente: sous-jacente à toutes ses conduites parce qu'elle en est le principe insidieux et indéfiniment actif: inscrite sans pudeur sur son corps et son visage parce qu'elle est un secret qui se trahit toujours.' Foucault, *Volonté de savoir*, p. 59.

5. McNay signals that for Foucault, power-knowledge 'does not simply repress [the body's] unruly forces; rather, it incites, instills and produces effects in the body. There is, therefore, no such thing as the 'natural' or 'pre-social' body; it is impossible to know the body outside of the meaning of its cultural significations'. McNay, *Foucault and Feminism*, p. 38.

6. L. Edelman (1994), 'Homographesis', in *Homographesis: Essays in Gay Literary and Cultural Theory*, New York and London, pp. 3–23, p. 12.

7. Ibid., pp. 5–6, p. 11.

8. Ibid., p. 4, p. 7. Edelman draws here on the work of Eve Kosofsky Sedgwick.

9. Ibid., p. 11.

10. Ibid., p. 6.

11. This contention is central to queer theory which, as Alan Petersen explains, associates all forms of sexual identity-categorization with the regime of dominant heterosexuality and its policing, normative mechanisms. See A. Petersen (1998), *Unmasking the Masculine: 'Men' and 'Identity' in a Sceptical Age*, London, Thousand Oaks and New Delhi, p. 97.

12. Edelman, 'Homographesis', p. 4.

13. We need to recognize that in the arguments of these commentators, the 'homosexual body' is viewed not as an ontological entity but as a finally fictive construct produced by (the anxieties of) the heterosexual order and construed as a stable but 'unnatural' essence.

14. Petersen, *Unmasking the Masculine*, p. 60.

15. S. Watney (1993), 'The Spectacle of AIDS', in H. Abelove, M.A. Barale and D. Halperin (eds), *The Lesbian and Gay Studies Reader*, New York and London, pp. 202–11, pp. 206–7.

16. Ibid., p. 207.

17. J.Z. Grover (1999), 'OI: Opportunistic Identification, Open Identification in PWA Portraiture', in C. Squiers (ed.), *Overexposed: Essays on Contemporary Photography*, New York, pp. 105–22, p. 106. Grover recognizes the problems of dividing AIDS-related communities/representations along binary lines; however, her notion of extra-communitarian AIDS-representation is helpful.

18. I take this phrase from Paula Treichler, who uses it to denote the multiplicity of intersecting narratives surrounding AIDS. See P. Treichler (1996), 'AIDS, Homophobia, and Biomedical Discourse: An Epidemic of Signification', in D. Crimp (ed.), *AIDS: Cultural Analysis, Cultural Activism*, Cambridge, Mass. and London, pp. 31–70.

19. On this phenomenon, see Watney, 'The Spectacle of AIDS', pp. 206–9; Grover, 'OI'; D. Crimp (1992), 'Portraits of People with AIDS', in L. Grossberg, C. Nelson and P. Treichler (eds), *Cultural Studies*, New York and London, pp. 117–33.

20. Watney, 'The Spectacle of AIDS', p. 206.

21. Ibid., p. 208.

22. See ibid., pp. 207–9.

23. M. Pratt (1998), 'A Walk along the side of the Motorway: AIDS and the Spectacular Body of Hervé Guibert', in O. Heathcote, A. Hughes and J.S. Williams (eds), *Gay Signatures: Gay and Lesbian Theory, Fiction and Film in France, 1945–1995*, Oxford and New York, pp. 151–72, p. 151. I shall engage further with this essay, since it has informed my own reading of Guibert's work.

24. In an essay on AIDS-representation entitled 'Body/Antibody', Lawrence Schehr neatly resumes the readability – and textuality – imputed to the AIDS body, linking that readability/textuality to conceptualizations of the gay body as an overly-signed body, a 'hybrid of body and sign'. See L. Schehr (1996), 'Body/Antibody', *Studies in 20th Century Literature*, 20, pp. 405–30, p. 415, p. 419.

25. Watney, 'The Spectacle of AIDS', p. 206.

26. Ibid., p. 207.

27. Edelman, *Homographesis*, p. xiv. His focus, here, is the manner in which Western culture has worked to bring gay men into the realm of representation/ readability for purposes of social discipline and political control.

28. Of interest, here, is Treichler's observation that, under the regime of homophobia, 'whatever else it may be, AIDS is a story, or multiple stories, read to a surprising extent from a text that does not exist: the body of the male homosexual. It is a text people so want – need – to read that they have gone so far as to write it themselves'. Treichler, 'AIDS, Homophobia, and Biomedical Discourse', p. 42.

29. This question, like the others raised in this section of my discussion, is posed in the essays by Crimp, Grover, Pratt and Schehr cited above.

30. On the background to the production/diffusion of Guibert's film, see J.-P. Boulé (1995), 'Hervé Guibert: Autobiographical Film-Writing Pushed to its Limits?', in T. Keefe and E. Smythe (eds), *Autobiography and the Existential Self*, Liverpool, pp. 169–81.

31. J.-P. Boulé (1999), *Hervé Guibert: Voices of The Self*, Liverpool, p. 223.

32. See Boulé, 'Autobiographical Film-Writing Pushed to its Limits?', p. 175. The autofictional texts cited or echoed in Guibert's commentary are *A l'ami qui ne m'a pas sauvé la vie* (1990); *Le Protocole compassionnel* (1991); and *L'Homme au chapeau rouge* (1992). In the latter two, the production, by Guibert's autofictional persona 'Hervé Guibert', of a video-diary we can assimilate with *La Pudeur ou l'impudeur* is addressed. For a summary of what *autofiction* is/does and the autofictional aspect of Guibert's AIDS-writing, see A. Hughes (1999), *Heterographies: Sexual Difference in French Auto-biography*, Oxford and New York, pp. 111–15.

33. See Boulé, *Voices of the Self*, p. 223, p. 228.

34. On gay political history in post-war France, see O. Heathcote, A. Hughes and J.S. Williams, 'Introduction', in Heathcote, Hughes and Williams, *Gay Signatures*, pp. 1–25.

35. See P.J. Smith, 'Blue and the Outer Limits', *Sight and Sound*, October 1993, pp. 18–19, p. 18; D. Duncan (1995), 'Gestes autobiographiques: Le Sida et les formes d'expressions artistiques du moi', *Nottingham French Studies*, 34, pp. 100–11, pp. 100–1.

36. See especially Boulé, *Voices of the Self*.

37. See R. Macherel, 'La Tentation d'image(s): écriture et photographie dans l'oeuvre d'Hervé Guibert', unpublished Masters thesis, ENS de Fontenay-St-Cloud, June 1994, p. 34; Boulé, *Voices of the Self*, p. 225.

38. Smith, 'Blue and the Outer Limits', p. 18.

39. Macherel, 'La Tentation d'image(s)', p. 171. Macherel focuses, as I do here, on those Guibertian photo-images specifically designated as *autoportraits*.

40. Ibid., p. 173.

41. Ibid., p. 173.

42. Ibid., pp. 178–9.

43. Ibid., p. 178. On the bodily effacements operated by Guibert's *phautoportraits*, see also A. Buisine (1995), 'Le Photographique plutôt que la photographie', *Nottingham French Studies*, 34, pp. 32–41, p. 40. In *Le Rose et le noir*, Frédéric Martel describes Guibert's *oeuvre* as imprinted with a 'constante préoccupation homosexuelle'; this is not, however, true of his photographic self-portraiture. F. Martel (1996), *Le Rose et le noir: Les Homosexuels en France depuis 1968*, Paris, p. 320.

44. H. Guibert (1981), 'L'Image cancéreuse', in *L'Image fantôme*, Paris, pp. 165–9. On the political and sexual issues subtending this essay, see Hughes, *Heterographies*, pp. 45–56.

45. M. Pratt (1995), 'De la désidentification à l'incognito: A la recherche d'une autobiographie homosexuelle', *Nottingham French Studies*, 34, pp. 70–81, pp. 71–2.

46. Duncan, 'Gestes autobiographiques', pp. 100–1.

47. For a compelling reading of Guibert's relationship to visuality/visibility, as his AIDS-diary *Cytomégalovirus* (1992) invokes it, see Pratt, 'A Walk along the side of the Motorway'.

48. 'Pour moi c'est un mot qui n'a jamais eu vraiment un rapport avec moi, bizarrement, alors qu'il en a évidemment un . . ., ce n'est pas la façon dont je me sens, j'ai l'impression que je suis ailleurs que dans ces . . .'. H. Guibert, with C. Donner, (1992), 'Pour répondre à quelques questions qui se posent', *La Règle du jeu*, 7, pp. 135–57, p. 157.

49. Critics who address Guibert's refusal (publicly) to 'code' himself as (simply) gay include Pratt, who argues in 'De la désidentification' that Guibert seeks to situate himself outside the sexual definitions/hierarchies of heterosexual ideology, and Duncan. Guibert's sexual self-disidentification, and his aversion to gay identity politics, is also discussed by Martel (cf. *Le Rose et le noir*, p. 320), and in F. Buot (1999), *Hervé Guibert: Le Jeune Homme et la mort*, Paris, pp. 44–5.

50. On the markings, in Guibert's work, of Foucault's influence, see *inter alia* Hughes, *Heterographies*, Chapter Four.

51. 'Ce corps homosexuel est tatoué, et harnaché de sangles, de rivets, d'anneaux. La bouche et les yeux sont cousus par des fermetures à glissière. Toute la peau est doublée d'une seconde peau de cuir noir. Le sexe, que Mapplethorpe ose prendre en gros plan . . ., s'exhibe hors d'un linge troué, déchiré, offert comme sur un étal de boucherie.' H. Guibert, 'L'Influence américaine', *Le Monde*, 28 June 1978.

52. Guibert's move to filmic self-representation coincided, broadly, with his abandonment of photography, notably as practised by others with regard to himself. This phenomenon is discussed, *inter alia*, by Boulé, in 'Autobiographical Film-Writing Pushed to its Limits?', and is anatomized in *Le Protocole compassionnel*. The latter associates Guibert's detachment from photography – from being photographed – with his desire to protect his *corps décharné* from the scrutinizing gaze of the Other. However, as I shall demonstrate, his recourse to video – a medium that he viewed as combining film, photography and writing (cf. Boulé, *Voices of the Self*, p. 228), and that is more immediate than either photography or cinematic film – must be understood as involving an embrace of self-exposure. On Guibert's recourse, as a subject with AIDS, to self-exposure, see Boulé, *Voices of the Self*, pp. 216–17.

53. Edelman, 'Homographesis', p. 7.

54. H. Guibert (1993), *The Compassion Protocol*, trans. J. Kirkup, London, p. 6. 'Ce corps décharné que le masseur malaxait brutalement pour lui redonner de la vie . . ., je le retrouvais chaque matin en panoramique auschwitzien dans

le grand miroir de la salle de bains . . . Il n'y avait pas de jour où je ne découvrais une nouvelle ligne inquiétante, une nouvelle absence de chair sur la charpente, cela avait commencé par une ligne transversale sur les joues, selon certains reflets qui l'accusaient, et maintenant l'os semblait sortir hors de la peau'. H. Guibert (1991), *Le Protocole compassionnel*, Paris, pp. 14–15. This passage, which invokes the (AIDS) body as a readable text, is reprised in the voice-over of *La Pudeur*.

55. See Schehr, 'Body/Antibody', p. 415.

56. Watney, 'The Spectacle of AIDS', p. 207.

57. Boulé, 'Autobiographical Film-Writing Pushed to its Limits?', pp. 172–5.

58. R. Chambers (1997), 'The Suicide Experiment: Hervé Guibert's AIDS Video, *La Pudeur ou l'impudeur*', *L'Esprit Créateur*, XXXVII, pp. 72–82, p. 78.

59. Boulé, 'Autobiographical Film-Writing Pushed to its Limits?', p. 175.

60. Chambers, 'The Suicide Experiment', p. 78.

61. 'En vous revoyant, aussi séduisant que le soir d'"Apostrophes", j'ai repris justement espoir.' Rosine invokes Guibert's appearance on a French literary magazine programme in March 1990.

62. Schehr, 'Body/Antibody', p. 415.

63. See Pratt, 'A Walk along the side of the Motorway', p. 160. Pratt detects in *Cytomégalovirus* the manifestations of a visually combative strategy similar to that deployed, in my view, in *La Pudeur ou l'impudeur*. In 'Gestes autobiographiques', Duncan suggests that if, in *La Pudeur*, Guibert posits his body with AIDS as a text open to spectatorial reading, in a *performance impudique*, this is in order to recuperate control over a body ravaged by illness, and to re-access a sense of the 'coherence' of his *moi* (cf. Duncan, 'Gestes autobiographiques', especially pp. 109–10). I find Duncan's analysis interesting, but am not convinced that it engages properly with the defiance built into Guibert's filmic, bodily, immodest self-representations.

64. D. Bell and G. Valentine (1995), 'The Sexed Self: Strategies of Performance, Sites of Resistance', in S. Pile and N. Thrift (eds), *Mapping the Subject: Geographies of Cultural Transformation*, London and New York, pp. 143–57, p. 155.

65. Ibid., p. 154.

66. L. Irigaray (1985), *This Sex Which Is Not One*, trans. C. Porter, Ithaca, p. 76; L. Irigaray (1977), *Ce Sexe qui n'en est pas un*, Paris, p. 74.

67. On the intense rhetoricity of Guibert's AIDS-video, see R. Chambers (1998), 'Confronting It', in *Facing It: AIDS Diaries and the Death of the Author*, Ann Arbor, pp. 35–60, p. 39. This essay, which reads *La Pudeur* in a very different way from the present analysis, has compelling things to say about the representational and rhetorical politics of Guibert's film. In an earlier section of his study of AIDS diairies (cf. pp. 25–6), Chambers also touches

briefly but interestingly on the issues of gay bodily legibility/identifiability and homophobic reading addressed at length here.

68. This phrase, taken from the segment of *Le Protocole compassionnel* cited above, encapsulates the impact of Guibert's bodily representations.

69. Watney, 'The Spectacle of AIDS', p. 206.

70. Crimp (cf. 'Portraits of People with AIDS', p. 129) and Grover (cf. 'OI', p. 107) address the ideological basis of this dehumanizing, stereotypical representational trope. Given the homophobic nature of much of the AIDS-commentary elaborated in France's mainstream media in the 1980s (cf. Martel, *Le Rose et le noir*, p. 224, p. 240, p. 281, p. 284), it is probable that the trope in question was exploited in it, and came to Guibert's attention. As he confirms to François Jonquet in an interview printed in *Globe* in February 1992, Guibert was an avid consumer of media accounts of AIDS.

71. We can translate this as 'I am tired of pretending', but also as 'I am tired of semblance'.

72. We should note that, inevitably, *La Pudeur*'s Elba shots do also proffer images of Guibert's body as wasted and corrupted. We should also be aware that the 'paradise regained' aspect of Guibert's Elba sequence, and its bodily represent-ations, is not devoid of irony – an irony illuminated by the fact that it is during the Elba segment of his video-dairy that Guibert stages the 'suicide experiment' that is one of its most striking features.

73. For Marty-Lavauzelle's comments on Guibert's film, see *Libération*, 18 and 19 January 1992, p. 22. Guibert's own initial response to a 1988 self-portrait-with-AIDS created by Mapplethorpe, in which Mapplethorpe also, arguably, recurs to a strategy that uses mimetic re-representation to critique dominant, dehumanizing depictions of the PWA, confirms our sense that parodic mimesis is all too likely to be mis-received. As *Le Protocole compassionnel* reveals (cf. pp. 115–16; *The Compassion Protocol*, pp. 98–9), all Guibert could see in Mapplethorpe's self-image, at least on first reading, was a spine-chilling vision of bodily decomposition that, he believed, *Libération* was wrong to have reproduced in the wake of Mapplethorpe's death.

–13–

Gender and Sexuality in New New Wave Cinema
Dina Sherzer

Introduction

New New Wave cinema, it has often been said, is a cinema of the present that engages with issues and preoccupations of contemporary French society. New New Wave directors mark out the psychosocial territory of France, writes Claude-Marie Trémois.[1] Frank Garbaz classifies New New Wave films into testimonies (*films du constat*), emergency alarms (*films signaux d'alarme*) and films of solidarity (*films de la solidarité*), and the categories he establishes point to the New New Wave's involvement with social concerns.[2] And Tonie Marshall, herself a New New Wave director, assesses how New New Wave cinema interacts with the social in the following, pertinent way:

> Committed cinema, in the 1970s, was generally the province of what we called at the time *jeunes bourgeois*, who looked at the world around them and, in doing so consciously, were making an act of commitment. Today, arguably, cinema has penetrated all social strata and geographic environments, drawing its practitioners from a much more comprehensive constituency. People who are making films now come from everywhere, which was not necessarily the case ten years ago. But this brings society back into cinema; it is no longer cinema that seeks society out.[3]

New New Wave directors thematize topics addressed in the French news in the 1980s and after. Eric Rochant explores youth unemployment in *Un monde sans pitié* (1989); Robert Guédiguian depicts the dilemma of working-class individuals who lose their jobs in *Marius et Jeannette* (1997); in *La Vie rêvée des anges* (1998), Erick Zonca examines the plight of young, untrained, single jobless women trying to make ends meet in a difficult world; Cyril Collard invokes the situation of people with AIDS in *Les Nuits fauves* (1993). In addition to social problems, New New Wave directors represent multi-ethnic France. Thus, Mathieu Kassovitz, Thomas Gilou and Jean-Jacques Zilbermann (in, respectively, *Métisse* (1993); *La Vérité si je mens* (1997); and *L'Homme est une femme comme les autres* (1998)) draw attention to French Jewish communities, while Karim Dridi (in *Bye Bye* (1997)), Malik Chibane (in *Hexagone* (1994) and *Douce France* (1995)) and Gilou (in *Raï* (1995)) combat Maghrebi invisibility and underscore the problems that being Maghrebi-French in France entails. Several films offer representations of different social classes or milieux. With the psychological *marivaudage* of *Comment je me suis disputé . . . ma vie sexuelle* (1996), Arnaud Desplechin captures the ways of speaking and living of bourgeois intellectual students. In *Chacun cherche son chat* (1996), Cédric Klapisch proposes a slice of modern life in an old Paris neighbourhood whose diverse population is being displaced little by little by gentrification. In *Pigalle* (1995), Dridi takes spectators into the streets and underworld of Pigalle, with its peep shows and more or less shady characters. In *La Vie de Jésus* (1997), Bruno Dumont illuminates a sleepy, peaceful northern French town, with its working-class inhabitants, as a locus of racial tension, adolescent malaise and gang violence.

History (more precisely, that of the Second World War, the Holocaust and Algeria), a concern of the French news media in the 1990s, is invoked in several New New Wave films, albeit mostly via brief commentaries or remarks made by individual characters. Guédiguian alludes to concentration camps in *Marius et Jeannette*, as does Kassovitz in *Métisse*. Chibane and Dridi, in the films cited above, refer to the Algerian war and issues of immigration. A recurring preocupation in the contemporary French cultural sphere, confronted with the grip of globaliz-ation, is the status of French cinema. In the press, and among film specialists and spectators alike, questions regarding the introspective and intellectual, not to say elitist, tenor of French films and their eschewal of American-style narrative coherence/resolution are regularly raised. Olivier Assayas directly confronts these questions, thematizing them in *Irma Vep* (1996). He constructs his film as a metacinematic work, in which characters discuss French, American and Hong Kong cinema and the power of the image. At the same time, Assayas adopts the New Wave practice of establishing interfilmic relationships, and alludes to Feuillade, Truffaut and others in a witty and naughty fashion, reaffirming and flaunting the intellectual characteristics of his film. Desplechin also indirectly engages with these issues in *Comment je me suis disputé . . . ma vie sexuelle*, by making a film that is provocatively refined and replete with subtle dialogues and psychological intro-spection, thus emphasizing the psychological and intellectual bent of French cinema.

Jean-Pierre Jeancolas has remarked that New New Wave directors represent a personalized realism, their films being both documentaries and the result of their observation and personal experience of contemporary French life.[4] But I shall argue that their films are more than personal renderings of specific issues in present-day French society. They are the work of individuals whose lives have been shaped by feminism, by the gay and lesbian movement, and by post-colonial politics/

thought, that is to say, by major contemporary changes in mentality and behaviour in the domains of gender and sexuality. New perspectives on questions of gender, sexuality and race/ethicity, which have transformed French society, have also entered the films of the New New Wave directors. These directors are not pre-occupied with, or engaged primarily with, these perspectives and questions. But, in an impressionistic way, through treatments of situations, of ways of being and living, they expose spectators to issues of sexual orientation and gender-roles, as well as to the mood and mentality of young people in mid- to late 1990s France.

In what follows, I do not focus on the global meanings of the films I have chosen to discuss, all of which are introduced above. Rather, I concentrate on the constructions of gender and sexuality that they articulate. A notable characteristic of the New New Wave, and one that is significant in terms of its representation of gender, is that New New Wave cinema involves a more or less identical number of male and female directors. This indicates that women directors, in contemporary France, have the same technical capacities, training and artistic sensitivities as their male counterparts, and are able to obtain the same level of financial aid. I could therefore have opted to explore films by men and women *auteurs*, or films made exclusively by women. I have chosen, however, only to consider films by male directors, in order to analyse their particular perspectives on matters of gender and sexuality. My concern is to establish whether the films scrutinized here reflect trends current in modern French society and, if they do not, to see which mirrors they hold up to the social realm.

The New New Wave (*bis*)

Before turning to the main topics of my discussion, gender and sexuality, I wish to offer some general comments about the films I have chosen to examine. Salient features of New New Wave films include the de-dramatization of plot; the lack of a tight progression of events; and the lack of suspense and precision. These features create an atmosphere of availability and openness. Everything can happen; nothing is programmed; nothing is definitely resolved for the protagonists of these films. Their indeterminacy and existential freedom result from a number of aspects of their lives. They are men and women in their thirties, sometimes students, most of the time unemployed. They have no particular political ideology, and no strong professional commitment. They have not yet entered real life. They are single and unattached, sometimes involved temporarily in relationships that could easily break up. Hippo, Halpern and Xavier of *Un monde sans pitié*; Chloe, Djamel and Michel of *Chacun cherche son chat*; Paul, Yvan, Nathan, Patricia, Esther and Sylvia of *Comment je me suis disputé . . . ma vie sexuelle*; and Isa and Marie of *La Vie rêvée des anges*, all fit into this category. Their life is one of mobility, marked by a freedom they are loath to lose. Thus, Michel in *Chacun cherche son chat* breaks up his relationship with his friend. 'I dumped Jean-Yves, he was beginning to get attached to me' ('J'ai plaqué Jean-Yves, il commençait à s'attacher'), he tells Chloe, his room-mate. Paul, in *Comment je me suis disputé . . . ma vie sexuelle*, quoting Kierkegaard, informs Nathan: 'There is nothing more perfumed, inebriating, sparkling than the possible' ('Il n'y a rien de plus parfumé, de plus enivrant, de plus pétillant que le possible').

The family is not a strong presence, reference or influence. In fact, the family is often a single mother to whom the characters do not have any particular attachment (as we see in *La Vie rêvée des anges*) or the provider of food and lodging (cf. *La Vie de Jésus*). In films representing Maghrebi-French life, the family is much more present, but Chibane in *Douce France* and Gilou in *Raï* make a point of showing daughters claiming their independence from the family and moving out on their own. Often the family is replaced by relationships with friends, room-mates or co-workers, and characters are presented as loosely integrated into a neighbourhood or a small town. Marriage is not an option for these protagonists; it is replaced by casual affairs. And religion is not in their mind-set. The films reflect situations and patterns documented in sociologists' analyses of contemporary French society, where family organization is changing: 'unmarriage' rather than marriage is becoming a norm; individualism and autonomy are desired and accepted; and freedom is considered a right.[5]

Gender-Roles

In *La Drôle de guerre des sexes du cinéma français* (1996),[6] Noël Burch and Geneviève Sellier point to many films made between 1930 and 1956 where women are represented as vamps and seductresses; as pathologically sick; as infantile and irresponsible. And the misogyny of New Wave films is amply documented. In contrast, New New Wave films position gender-roles in a strikingly progressive fashion. Men and women are placed on an equal footing; one gender does not dominate the other, and, furthermore, men do not enjoy the masculine privilege of seduction or conquest. Women are given many positive attributes. They are independent from masculine power and do not expect anything from men. They do not seek security in marriage and are not dominated economically. They are active, energetic, assertive and either strong or gaining strength. They are fighters and stand up to men. They have a dynamic control of their bodies, and do not exist as merely physical objects. Several women are associated with movement: they walk, travel, do things. Nathalie in *Un monde sans pitié* goes to teach at MIT; Maggie Cheung in *Irma Vep* comes to make a film in France; Zoe rides with Maggie on her motocycle in the streets of Paris. The old ladies in *Chacun cherche son chat* mobilize Chloe as well as the whole neighbourhood to look for Gris Gris the cat. In *La Vie rêvée des anges*, Isa survives with odd jobs, is resilient and resourceful. Marie rebels, does not let people take advantage of her, and is even powerful in her obsession. In *Ma vie sexuelle*, Esther becomes self-sufficient and begins a career as a translator; Valérie seduces Paul so that he directs her thesis. Jeannette, in *Marius et Jeannette*, and Freddy's mother, in *La Vie de Jésus*, work hard and are strong, courageous single mothers caring for their children. It is Lola in *Métisse* who summons her two lovers Félix and Jamal and enjoins them to live with her, forcing them to get along and be the fathers of the child she is expecting. Maghrebi-French young women are active and take initiatives on their own, such as preventing the arranged marriage of Moussa by taking the bride-to-be to the airport in *Douce France*. Even the traditional mothers are enlightened: Moussa's mother drives a car, Mouloud's aunt helps her daughters to learn English in *Bye Bye*. The cinematography also contributes to this positive representation of women characters, since the New New Wave directors' camera is not voyeuristic or harsh, and does not aggressively display the female body.

In watching these films, spectators are not observing women playing mythic roles, but women of today with their questions, their problems, their hopes, their strengths and their weaknesses. There is certainly an osmosis between the characters in the films and the ways women lead their lives in the real world. Equally, the construction of male characters is strongly anti-patriarchal, and traditional features of masculinity are definitely played down. Most male figures are weak, vulnerable, disaffected and disenchanted with life. In *Un Monde sans pitié*, Hypo lacks direction and purpose. The male protagonists in *Comment je me suis disputé . . . ma vie sexuelle* feel and live with doubt, whereas in the women we detect the beginnings of a possible solution. It is Paul's thesis director who has Alzheimer's disease, not his wife. In *Marius et Jeannette*, Marius is a recovering alcoholic and cannot tolerate sorrow or stress; Dédé is constantly made fun of for the stupidity and gullibility that made him join the *Front National*; and the *instituteur* is led by the nose by his lively girlfriend who survived a concentration camp. The ageing director in *Irma Vep* is another example of a man assailed by doubts, who has to be sent to a psychiatric hospital. Maghrebi-French films chronicle a sick masculinity. Fathers are authoritarian and backward, with ideas unadapted to the life of young people in France. They are victims of immigration, emasculated by their marginal condition. All the directors display sympathy for their masculine characters, for their existential problems and the difficulties that they face, at times showing that men are less resilient, more fragile, than women. Men's lives are revealed as difficult and painful.

On the one hand, the films discussed here reflect current trends in French society observed by sociologists: namely, the waning influence of institutions such as marriage and religion, accompanied by the growing independence and autonomy of women, and the redefinition and transformation of masculinity.[7] But, on the other, these New New Wave films also challenge sexist, conservative, macho attitudes concerning men's and women's roles in society. They unquestionably dismantle (notions of) conventional male and female gender-positionality, offering more complex, attentive visions of gendered subjectivity.

Sexuality

Whereas French mainstream cinema previously offered representations of desire that were mainly heterosexual and addressed desire between French-French men and women, New New Wave films offer a *mise en scène* of sexual diversity. Spectators are exposed to a panorama of sexual orientations and arrangements. These include heterosexual, interreligious and interracial couplings, and various forms of homosexuality, involving bisexual and transvestite characters. Contemporary French cinema no longer works as the medium of a restricted sexual code, but is instead open to difference(s). In all the films I have mentioned hitherto – *Marius et Jeannette*; *La Vie de Jésus*; *La Vie rêvée des anges*; *Comment je me suis disputé . . . ma vie sexuelle*; *Un Monde sans pitié*; and *Chacun cherche son chat* – casual heterosexual relationships between two French individuals are presented as normal for adults who are unmarried. There is the unsaid assumption that it is natural and desirable for adult subjects to have sexual relationships outside marriage. Men and women tolerate and enjoy sexual freedom and have several sexual partners, sometimes simultaneously. In *La Vie de Jésus*, Freddy and Marie make love in Freddy's bedroom in his mother's house, and the mother accepts this as normal. Jasmina in *Bye Bye* and Sahlia in *Raï* are portrayed as no less free than the French-French women of their age.

The sexual emancipation depicted in New New Wave cinema is not a novelty but an accepted type of behaviour to which spectators have, in fact, been exposed for several decades, since the New Wave first portrayed liberated women in the 1960s.[8] What is different, however, is that women protagonists of New New Wave films are not punished by men for their sexually free behaviour, and there are no ambiguities concerning sexual freedom, as there were, for instance, in *Et Dieu créa la femme*, with regard to Bardot.[9] Furthermore, women's sexuality is not coded as having a dangerous power leading men to destruction. But sexual freedom is not necessarily posited as synonymous with a happy relationship: in essence, the contrary is true. All the relationships shown in the films I am addressing are fraught with difficulties and problems. Dumont focuses on the violence that dogs the intercourse between Freddy and Marie, and makes it an important reason for Marie's decision to break up their liaison. The *marivaudage* of Desplechin's characters, their indecision, their instability and their doubt, leaves them frustrated and unsatisfied. Zonca documents the fascination and infatuation of Marie for Chris and highlights Chris's exploitative behaviour. Klapisch underscores the selfishness of the drummer who has his tryst with Chloe and then dumps her. And the young men of *Un monde sans pitié*, Hippo, Xavier and Halpern, all have difficult relationships, starting an affair with women, abandoning them, then going back to them or being deserted by them. All the characters play a game of cat and mouse. The directors describe an unstable heterosexual economy, where notions of faithfulness and continuity are absent.

New New Wave directors map a multi-ethnic France, whose populace includes Jews, Blacks of African and Caribbean origin, and Maghrebi-French subjects. In their films, they inscribe interreligious, interracial heterosexual relationships that raise issues of ethnicity, race, religion and xenophobia. Some films offer positive images of successful mixed relationships. In the very popular comedy *La Vérité si je mens*, some of Gilou's protagonists engage in discussions about ethnic differences between Sephardic and Ashkenazi Jews. But such differences are transcended in the film when the prominent Ashkenazi business man comes back from Israel with a blond Scandinavian model and when, after many ups and downs, the goy and the devoutly religious Sephardic girl finally marry. Love, sexual attraction and money triumph over religious and ethnic differences. In *Métisse*, with a solid dose of wit and mocking irony, Kassovitz mingles two potentially uneasy combinations: the *ménage à trois* and the interracial union. Lola, a model of wisdom, patience and beauty, summons her two lovers, one black and one Jewish, to come and live with her in order to help with her baby who is about to be born. Lola loves the two men, and wants the relationship to work. The men even manage to overcome some divergence and differences and we see the three of them peacefully sleeping together, Lola in the middle of her two lovers, each of whom has a hand on her stomach. Despite the xenophobic overtones very much present in the whole film – overtones that Kassovitz underscores in his role-reversals and deconstructions of stereotypes of sexuality and race – the final message of this ambiguously unrealistic comedy is positive.[10] In the realistic register, Guédiguian expresses the same affirmative message in *Marius et Jeannette*. The film is set in L'Estaque, a neighbourhood of Marseilles, in the region that is the fief of the violently anti-Arab National Front. But spectators hear Jeannette describe to Marius with regret and nostalgia the love-making abilities of her deceased Algerian husband. She praises his expertise and sexual *savoir faire*. Furthermore, from this man, who was killed in a work-related accident, she had a child, loves him dearly, and raises him with his sister born from a French-French father. Guédiguian, in sum, underscores the possibility of interracial love even in an environment plagued by racism targeted against the Maghrebi population.

In these three narratives, Gilou, Kassovitz and Guédiguian offer representations where ethnic and religious differences are overcome. They give a message of hope and convey a desire for acceptance of the Other. But other New New Wave films present a much grimmer view of interracial relations. In this latter group of films, the society and individuals around the interracial couple are shown to exert a negative influence that manifests itself in the form of verbal and even physical violence. In *Bye Bye*, Dridi sets his interracial couple in the same environment that Guédiguian chooses in *Marius et Jeanette*: a working-class sector of Marseilles. The relationship between Jacki and Jasmina is marred by the attraction that brings Ismael and Jasmina together, and by the racism of Jacki's brother, Ludo, who reveals with hate Jasmina's infidelity and provokes the break-up. Continuing their racist binge, Ludo and his friends disturb the wedding party of a black man and a white woman, hurling insults at them. The Maghrebi-French Ismael and the French Ludo do not tolerate Jasmina's relationship with Jacki, and Ludo and his friends do not tolerate the marriage between the French woman and the African man. In *Hexagone*, Chibane also brings out the racism of Annick, the young French girl protagonist. On hearing that Annick lives in Paris because, in the suburbs, there are too many Blacks and *beurs* (second-generation Maghrebi-French), Nacera feels compelled to deny his Algerian origin. Annick does not rebuff Nacera because she thinks his name is Xavier and his parents are Italian. In *La Vie de Jésus*, Dumont stages the most strident, painful case of violence provoked by an interracial relationship. He opposes a good-looking, innocent and daring Maghrebi-French boy, Kader – who is irresistibly attracted to Marie – to the mentally sick Freddy, who is unsure of himself and is tormented by sexual jealousy, racism and irrational impulses. Freddy unleashes his gang of French boys on the Maghrebi-French youth, but he is the one who savagely beats his rival and leaves him like an animal on the side of the road. We cannot envisage a more powerful representation of irrational violence, provoked by the fear of interracial sexual concourse.

Whether they are comedies or not, the films analysed above address the complexities and difficulties of interracial relationships. Such relationships are represented as possible. Desire and attraction exist between individuals of different ethnicities, the films affirm, but society does not tolerate such unions because stereotypes, prejudice, racism and xenophobia prevail. We should note that in their *mise en scène*, these films avoid showing sexual scenes between characters of different ethnic backgrounds, as if to do so would be too disturbing. Spectators do not see lovemaking episodes between Jacki and Jasmina; Dridi simply lets us imagine their physical pleasure, suggested in the moans coming from their room. Similarly, Dumont's camera captures in a hyperrealist fashion the sexual anatomy and the violent movements of the intercourse between Freddy and Marie, but refrains from depicting Kader and Marie. And Kassovitz shows Jamal and Lola frolicking together in bed, but we never see Felix and Lola naked together.

Comparing these representations with what sociologists report in a 1998 collection of essays entitled *Liberté, égalité, mixité . . . congugales: Une sociologie du couple mixte* is informative.[11] The essays of the collection address interracial, interreligious and homosexual couples, precisely the kinds of 'mixed couples' encountered in the films I discuss here. That they do so signals that the phenomenon of ethnic, religious and sexual mixing constitutes a trait of contemporary French society, and a focus of interest for sociologists. The conclusions the sociologists reach are strikingly similar to the messages conveyed by the New New Wave film-makers: messages that tell us that foreignness and difference are reacted to with suspicion and rejection. French subjects do not readily accept interracial couples; they are more likely to tolerate a homosexual couple than an interracial union. The fact that homosexuality is frequently thematized in New New Wave films intended for wide audiences with different sexual orientations is significant. In their presentation of homosexual relationships, New New Wave directors create different moods and tones. The first French film of the 1990s on homosexuality that comes to mind – not least because of its enormous success, the death of its director and the consequences of his death – is Collard's *Les Nuits fauves*. Many critics have commented on this film, its impact and its reception.[12] What is important for the scope of this discussion is the fact, noted by several critics, that the film figures different forms of gayness and of male desire for male bodies, and that its main character Jean is bisexual, leading an overtly gay life while having a female lover. In his film, in short, Collard confronts heterosexual audiences with protagonists who have multiple identities and who cannot be conventionally or reassuringly labelled.

In a less excessive, urgent and violent vein, in *L'Homme est une femme comme les autres*, Jean-Jacques Zilbermann approaches the same subject matter with a different slant. His main character Simon is overtly gay; his Jewish mother and uncle accept this fact, but coerce him into getting married. Gradually he is forced to assume a bisexual persona. Despite his physical inhibition, he manages to have intercourse with his wife and enjoys married life for a while, but returns subsequently to his gay identity; his heterosexual relationship founders.[13] However, he will become a father and his family will have a descendant, as his uncle wished. In this bittersweet comedy, Zilbermann makes male desire and male/male attraction the central theme of the film, visually concretizing it through the camera work. Simon and other young men are on display in all the shots, undressed, dressing or undressing themselves in various circumstances, in a manner that enables the camera to focus on the young male bodies.[14] Here, the gaze would appear to be primarily targeted at a male homosexual spectator, but is also designed to please a female and heterosexual audience.

Two other directors, Assayas in *Irma Vep* and Klapisch in *Chacun cherche son chat*, stage situations involving homosexual and lesbian protagonists, but the sexual orientation of these protagonists is not the main theme of the films in which they feature. It constitutes one among a number of aspects of their identities. These homosexual and lesbian characters are not involved in unhappy and difficult situations, and are represented as friendly and positive individuals. In *Chacun cherche son chat*, Klapisch plays out the euphemism alluded to in his title. *La chatte*, in French, is a euphemism for female sexual parts, so by extension, in the film, if the old ladies are looking for Gris Gris, the young people are looking for sexual partners. Constructing a symmetrical arrangement of scenes that mirror each other, Klapisch shows Chloe being propositioned by the female bartender and refusing lesbian intercourse, then Michel being propositioned by Chloe and refusing heterosexual intercourse. Pursuing this symmetrical arrangement and mirroring of scenes, Klapisch has Chloe in bed with the drummer, then Michel making love with his new lover. And the film ends with another symmetry, since Michel is happy with his new lover, and Chloe is happy to have met Bel Canto. With these couplings, Klapisch conveys the message that physical attraction can be homosexual or heterosexual, and that individuals cannot and do not want to be what they are not. The most remarkable lesson of his film turns on the tolerance that young people display with regard to the sexual orientation of others. Chloe and Michel can be room-mates and friends; Chloe is not upset by the presence of Michel's new lover. She can see and hear through the curtain the intercourse between the two men without being shocked or disturbed. And Klapisch is willing to show graphically, if in a somewhat veiled fashion, images of the two men making love. This is a daring move, for while heterosexual audiences are used to seeing heterosexual lovemaking scenes, mainstream films have not generally depicted, realistically, episodes of homosexual sex.

In *Irma Vep*, it is around the Hong Kong actress Maggie Cheung, dressed in the black cat costume of Feuillade's Irma Vep, that questions of cinema are debated. But Assayas inserts a side-story in which Maggie Cheung, a beautiful exotic fetish-object in black latex, becomes the focus of desire for men but also for several women. Only the female attraction of which Maggie is the target is developed by Assayas. However, he does not show any kissing or intercourse between women. Rather, he focuses on female desire for female bodies. He sets up conversations between women about Maggie. Thus Zoe, the costume girl and the intertextual counterpart of Arlette in Truffaut's *Le Dernier Métro* (1980), explains to her friend Mireille what she feels for Maggie: 'she is good-looking, I like her a lot, you feel like touching her, playing with her' ('Elle est jolie, elle me plaît bien, on a envie de toucher, de jouer avec'). 'Go ahead, take advantage, it's time to do it' ('Vas-y, profites-en, c'est le moment'), says Mireille. Maggie's double is also attracted to Maggie and wants to know if Zoe slept with Maggie. Mireille, fascinated too by Maggie's beauty, interrogates her about her sexual preferences, asking her abruptly in English: 'Do you like girls, do you sleep with girls?'. Assayas displays lesbian desire and sexual attraction with simplicity. His characters talk overtly about their feelings, do not hide their lesbian orientation, and are confortable with their sexuality.

Selected for a prize at the Venice festival in 1994, *Pigalle*, by Karim Dridi, takes place in the Paris underworld of prostitution and drug dealing, homosexuals and transvestites. Tension, violence and murder shatter the lives of the main protagonists. But, in this raw and hard world, Dridi focuses on the deep sorrow that Polo, the young bisexual, feels after Divine, the transvestite he loved, has been savagely murdered because of a bad drug deal. In addition, he creates a very moving character in Fernande, the older transvestite singer, ready to give everything to Polo out of love. The film ends with Fernande visiting Polo in jail. For this occasion, she dresses and 'performs' as a man in order to be accepted in the regular world of heterosexuals.[15] It is obvious that Dridi is committed to giving a positive picture of the transvestite characters. He portrays them as human beings with feelings, tenderness and generosity, and not as transgressive or abject characters.

With the exception of *Les Nuits fauves*, these films offer a soft and non-threatening vision of homosexuals, lesbians and transvestites. The characters are represented in sensitive ways, as subjects whose sexuality and personality are not marked as deviant, dangerous or monstrous. Furthermore, gay characters are not represented in negative terms intended to valorize and promote normative heterosexuality. Such representations capture the evolution of mentalities in France, where sociologists have registered an increased visibility and normalization of homosexuality and a concomitant tolerance of it. Against a backdrop of social and cultural factors that have facilitated and encouraged hedonism, free sexuality and the pursuit of personal gratification in France (and in the Western world in general), New New Wave directors put into circulation images of heterosexuals, homosexuals, transvestites, *ménages à trois* and mixed couples, and do so without misogyny or homophobia. The 'normal', their films suggest, is but one existential possibility. If, moreover, the 'normal' is constituted by a stable relationship between two heterosexual individuals, it does not hold sway any longer. It has been displaced by casual and frequently changing relationships. Sexuality then, as New New Wave directors represent it, is but one component of identity, and a component that can take many forms.

Cinema of the Present

As Tonie Marshall's remarks imply, society has certainly entered New New Wave cinema. Its realism not only reflects tendencies that exist in French society today, but is also shaped by them. 'With reality, politics enters films', writes Jeancolas.[16] New New Wave films are not overtly political, but their representations of gender and sexuality challenge sexist, racist and heteronormative forces in French culture. They do so by imagining a France not hostile to women's freedom or to racial mixing, and tolerant of sexual differences. But are New New Wave directors pointing to the disarray of today's society? In response to this question, we can say that they are registering changes of mentality and social mutation, portraying models of being, of subjectivity, consonant with a freer, more fluid and precarious way of life in which men and women are more individualist, more lonely perhaps, but not necessarily pessimistic. Old ways of living are outmoded in France, and new ways are emerging, notes sociologist Pierre Ronsanvallon.[17] New New Wave directors have caught the pulse of a country where it is now imperative to think about subjectivity – gendered and sexual subjectivity included – in terms of individualism, and multiple and complex identities.

Notes

1. 'Les cinéastes balisent ce territoire psychosocial'. C.-M. Trémois (1997), *Les Enfants de la liberté*, Paris, p. 48. The label New New Wave – a label that has, on occasion, been deemed to be excessively homogenizing but provides a useful umbrella term to categorize (aspects of) contemporary French cinema – was used in 1995 in *L'Express* (cf. *L'Express*, 18 May 1995), in a piece devoted to the 1995 Cannes festival. General studies include R. Prédal (1996), 'Trente ans après ou le cinéma des années 90: 1991–1995', in *50 ans de cinéma français (1945–1995)*, Paris, pp. 650–704; P. Powrie (1999), 'Heritage, History, and 'New Realism', in P. Powrie (ed.), *French Cinema in the 1990s*, Oxford, pp. 1–21.
2. F. Garbaz (1997), 'Le Renouveau social du cinéma français', *Positif*, 442, pp. 74–5.
3. 'Le cinéma engagé des années 70 était la plupart du temps une pratique de ce qu'on appelait à l'époque de jeunes bourgeois, qui avaient un regard sur le monde et qui, dans ce déplacement intentionnel, faisait acte d'engagement. Peut-être qu'aujourd'hui le cinéma a pénétré plus profondément dans tous les milieux sociaux et tous les espaces géographiques pour constituer ses troupes. Les gens qui font du cinéma maintenant viennent de partout, ce qui n'était pas forcément le cas il y a dix ans. Mais cela ramène la société dans le cinéma, ce n'est plus le cinéma qui va chercher la société'. T. Marshall (1997), 'Les Intermittents de la politique', *Positif*, 436, pp. 44–7, p. 47.
4. Jeancolas uses the expression 'un réel de proximité', which I translate as a personalized realism. J.-P. Jeancolas (1997), 'Une bobine d'avance: du cinéma et de la politique en février 1997', *Positif*, 434, pp. 56–8, p. 57.
5. For analyses of various aspects of French contemporary society see O. Galland and Y. Lemel (eds) (1998), *La Nouvelle Société française: 30 années de mutation*, Paris.

6. N. Burch and G. Sellier (1996), *La Drôle de guerre des sexes du cinéma français: 1930–1956,* Paris.

7. See Galland and Lemel.

8. Other New New Wave films that treat of women's sexual freedom include *Personne ne m'aime* (1994), by Marion Vernoux, and *Vénus beauté (Institut)* (1998), by Tonie Marshall.

9. Burch and Sellier suggest that this turns on a patriarchal *rappel à l'ordre* that paved the way for the misogyny of the New Wave, emergent in the aftermath of the freedom displayed by/in films during the Occupation and the Liberation. See *La Drôle de guerre,* p. 277.

10. See D. Sherzer (1999), 'Comedy and Interracial Relationships: *Romuald et Juliette* (Serreau, 1987) and *Métisse* (Kassovitz, 1993)', in Powrie, *French Cinema in the 1990s,* pp. 148–59.

11. See C. Philippe, G. Varro and G. Neyrand (eds) (1998), *Liberté, égalité, mixité . . . congugales: Une sociologie du couple mixte,* Paris.

12. See for instance B. Rollet and J.S. Williams (1998), 'Visions of Excess: Filming/Writing the Gay Self in Collard's *Savage Nights*', in O. Heathcote, A. Hughes and J.S. Williams (eds), *Gay Signatures: Gay and Lesbian Theory, Fiction and Film in France, 1945–1995,* Oxford and New York, pp. 193–208; C. Tarr (1999), 'Gender and Sexuality in *Les Nuits fauves*', in Powrie, *French Cinema in the 1990s,* pp. 117–26. See also B. Rollet (1999), 'Unruly Woman? Josiane Balasko, French Comedy, and *Gazon maudit*', in ibid., pp. 127–36.

13. This film brings to mind Ettore Scola's *Una Giornata particolare* (1977), where Marcello Mastroianni, the gay man who has just lost his job, and Sophia Loren, the prolific mother serving Fascist Italy, spend the day together and have a memorable sexual encounter.

14. In *Presque rien* (1999), Sébastien Lifshitz recounts the love affair that develops between two young men. Again, in this latter film, the camera emphasizes the beauty of the male bodies, the tenderness, desire and attraction the two boys feel for each other. Anne Fontaine, in *Nettoyage à sec* (1998), also displays the beauty of a young man's naked body, that of Loïc, a character who lives his bisexuality as perfectly normal and natural.

15. Dridi's film offers, here, a concrete instance of (or metaphor for?) the performed nature of gender and sexuality, as discussed by Judith Butler in *Gender Trouble: Feminism and the Subversion of Identity,* New York and London, 1990.

16. 'Avec le réel c'est la politique qui entre dans le film'. Jeancolas, 'Une bobine d'avance', p. 58.

17. See an interview with Pierre Ronsanvallon entitled 'La France en révolution', *Le Nouvel Observateur,* 8–14 October 1998. His ideas are developed in P. Ronsanvallon (ed.) (1998), *France: Les Révolutions invisibles,* Paris.

14

Running Out of Place: Gender, Space and Crisis in Ferreira Barbosa's *Les Gens normaux n'ont rien d'exceptionnel* and Lvovsky's *Oublie-moi*

Julia Dobson

Introduction

The title of this chapter evokes notions of movement, crisis, lack and displacement: notions that play a fundamental role in any consideration of the representation of gender and, more specifically perhaps, of the female subject in film. In the chapter, a detailed discussion is offered of two French films of the 1990s that manifest striking parallels in their portrayals of women in crisis in the city. Through my discussion, I seek to engage with the topics of cinema, space, gender and the city, and with the different configurations these elements admit: configurations that belong to a vast canvas, the lineaments of which this study can only point towards.

The myths and topologies of urban France are ceaselessly represented and redefined through the cultural medium of cinema. Yet, if our relationships to the urban environment shift constantly, the city persists as a primary and recurrent site of fascination, intrigue and alienation. Contemporary critical discourse signals a dominant concern with the construction, representation and interpretation of space and place. Over a decade ago, Edward Soja suggested that 'space and geography may be displacing the primacy of time and history as the distinctively significant interpretative dimension of the contemporary period'.[1] The tendency he refers to has been amplified over the intervening years, across many disciplines and discourses.

The fundamental role of space and place in contributing to constructions of subjectivity, identity, an individual's sense of his or her 'place in the world', cannot be underestimated. Feminist geographers have long called for the demystification of masculinist discourses of place and space, recognizing that 'space itself – and landscape and place likewise – far from being firm foundations for disciplinary expertise and power, are insecure, precarious and fluctuating'.[2] Equally, contemporary philosophers, architects and historians have revealed the political significance of representations of the gendered body in space, asserting the importance of:

exploring the ways in which the body is psychically, socially, sexually, and discursively or representationally produced, and the ways, in turn, bodies reinscribe and project themselves onto their sociocultural environment so that this environment both produces and reflects the form and interests of the body.[3]

Within recent critical discourse on film, considerable attention has been paid to the role of urban environments in narratives and representations of gender construction. Such discourse has focused almost exclusively on the identification of a 'masculinity in crisis', represented in films from classic *film noir* and gangster movies to present-day mainstream Hollywood products.[4] This critical phenomenon should, one senses, have opened up space for new and different narrative tropes of women in the urban fabric. It should have allowed for identifications of the female subject that construe her as other than the *femme fatale* whose inevitable punishment for transgressions of conventional femininity removes her agency and capacity for direct engagement with the city, while simultaneously ensuring her fetishized inscription in the landscape as a trace of dangerous sexuality.[5] There has, however, been remarkably little exploration of the construction of femininity and the representation of the female subject in urban settings. The question addressed by Elizabeth Mahoney to film studies – 'To what extent, and in what ways, can we trace connections between the spatial and sexual politics of a text?'[6] – has, to date, received only partial answers.

Since the dawn of the city, Western culture has endowed the urban landscape with the metaphors and narrative functions of a dangerous and exotic femininity, yet it continues to consign women to the margins of its cultural, economic and social mappings. From the intricate spatial networks of class and gender in Flaubert's novels to the surrealist urban muse fantasies of Breton's *Nadja*, from the complex mappings of sexuality and space in Vigo's *'Atalante* to Godard's problematic employment of female sexuality as a locus for his critique of the alienating effects of mass-consumerism, the representation of Paris has served as a prime example of this displacement.

A desire to address questions such as Mahoney's to French cinema of the 1990s subtends this spectator's frustration at the lack of new filmic representations, or narrative configurations, of women in the city: a frustration that targets, specifically, French film's continuing, marked indifference to the female *flâneur*, a figure whose absence has been extensively explored in the context of other narrative genres/ disciplines.[7] French cinema of the last thirty years of the twentieth century has paid much more heed to the female protagonist in the urban realm, and this can be read as a belated, but nonetheless welcome, challenge to the conventionally ascribed gender of public and private spaces. However, while it is clear that the female protagonists of recent French films are no longer defined solely in relation to the feminized, interior spaces of domesticity, privacy and romance, representations of an independently and assertively mobile female subject remain rare indeed.[8]

The vast majority of these female characters fail to attain the status of the female *flâneur*: a role they could only achieve by resisting their sexual objectification through a subversion of the directionality of the erotic gaze.[9] If the presence of the female subject in the city has been reasserted, the archetypal narrative tropes within which that presence is contained remain all too familiar. The negotiation between female subjectivity and the city space is resolved predominantly in ways that avoid disruptions of both gender norms and the city. Resolutions involve, for example, a displacement to the hinterlands of the city that permits the foregrounding of different (and equally problematic) mappings of otherness (cf. Yolande Zauberman's *Clubbed to Death* (1997)), or the elision of the discovery of a new identity/sexuality with an escape to, or at least a weekend away in, the country (cf. Sylvie Verheyde's *Un frère* (1997)). The most common and recurrent reconciliation of female subject and city continues to be effected through the legitimization of the female subject's place in the city as part of a couple, and the consequent validation of a romance sub-plot. Thus, as Chloe apparently reconquers the city streets in the gloriously vital and exhilarating final sequence of Cédric Klapisch's *Chacun cherche son chat* (1996), her new-found mobility, agency and direction are inextricably linked to her freshly discovered future as part of a couple, and to her recuperation into the romance narrative. The long tracking shot of the final sequence does not foreground an innovative response to the female subject's previously problematic relationship with the spaces of the city, but rather celebrates a final conventional narrative progression that ultimately suggests the fixity of Chloe's identity and the transcendence of place.[10]

There is insufficient space here to embark upon a detailed discussion of the more general, and still-emerging, relationships of gender and space that might be taken to characterize French cinema of the 1990s, or indeed the films of the so-called New New Wave.[11] I want to turn instead to a close examination of what, I suggest, is a more radical exploration of the relation between the female subject and the city space in two films of striking similarity released in 1994: Laurence Ferreira Barbosa's *Les Gens normaux n'ont rien d'exceptionnel*[12] and *Oublie-moi* by Noémie Lvovsky[13]. The films are directed by women, and could be successfully accommodated in Teresa de Lauretis's description of the characteristics of women's cinema:[14]

> From the inscription of subjective space and duration inside the frame to the construction of other discursive social practices . . . women's cinema has undertaken a redefinition of both private and public space that may well answer the call for 'a new language of desire'.[15]

De Lauretis offers these observations in the context of a discussion of what are manifestly counter-cinemas – those of Chantal Akerman and Lizzie Borden. Yet to claim a specific and generalized relationship between women (directors) and the spatial is to risk playing into the hands of the essentialist discourses that define conventions of gendered space. The two films under scrutiny here present central female protagonists who, apparently disturbed by the recent breakdown of a sexual relationship, undertake a desperate search for an identity and a place in the city. Their quests involve chaotic movement and the disruption of coherent mappings and narratives of the city. The established and fertile relationship between film studies and psychoanalysis has included a positing of the city, in film and psychoanalytic theory alike, as the primary site and reflection of identities in flux and in crisis. As Lapsley suggests:

> The Lacanian subject . . . experiences the city as inseparable from subjective dereliction and destitution. . . . the city is at once the metaphor and site of this process: metaphor of an order experienced as a disordering; site of the space which, constituted by signifiers, promises but forever denies self-realization.[16]

The employment of the cityscape as the scene of identity formation and disruption is clearly important to the films addressed below. But I wish to focus rather upon the implied role the city plays in the crises of their protagonists, and on these women's responses to the tropes of displacement and exclusion that dominate their experience of urban space. Both films situate the female subject's quest for identity in public spaces rather than in the conventionally feminized domestic interiors of melodrama: the historically dominant, generic site of female crisis. Both foreground the role of the urban spatial environment in the emotional and mental disturbances of their central protagonists, and present spatial metaphors of identity. In what follows, I shall focus not only on the gendered nature of the spaces occupied by the two films' female characters, but also on the films' concomitant disruption of the cinematographic space: a disruption that has implications for narrative coherence, spectatorial unity and identification.

Urban Fabric: *Les Gens normaux*

Les Gens normaux and *Oublie-moi* situate their narratives of crisis firmly in the urban fabric of Paris. Their thematic coincidences and their use of the same actress, Valeria Bruni-Tedeschi, in their lead parts is intriguing in the contexts both of the key role played by a select group of actors in the representation of the New New Wave,[17] and of the construction of Bruni-Tedeschi's star persona, a phenomenon that dominated many reviews of the films. Their central characters – Martine in *Les Gens normaux* and Nathalie in *Oublie-moi* – make constant demands on others to describe and define them, to narrate or reflect their selves, as they struggle to assert their presence and agency in the face of explicit rejections by their ex-partners, and more abstract rejections from the established, gendered spaces of the city. In the discussion offered here, I shall examine the two films in turn, before moving to a comparison of the different spatial and narrative trajectories in which the protagonists they present are engaged.

The very first sequence of *Les Gens normaux* announces the implication of the urban environment in Martine's crisis. The use of direct sound is at its most striking here, as the noise of city traffic resonates over the opening credits and continues to form a sharp contrast to Martine's silence. Martine is seen running across the frame, yet the camera does not track her, remaining in long shot and revealing her spectacular failure to negotiate the rules and signs of road crossings. Her direct interventions in the conventions and regulations of urban space can be read as an emphatic challenge to dominant definitions of space,[18] but her obvious lack of control and direction undermines a radical reading of her relationship to space at this point in the film. Her erratic and unexplained flight stops, only for her to be framed in close-up against the metal grid of a metro bridge that denotes imprisonment and exclusion. As Martine cries out in despair, the sequence ends with a visual reference to the archetypal image of modern alienation, Münch's 'The Scream'. After aggressing customers, colleagues and her ex-partner, whom she encounters and taunts in the arena of a miserable *espace vert*, Martine's chaotic run continues until she stops, exhausted and apparently lost, in front of a shop-window and head-butts the image of her own face she sees reflected in it. This attempt at an explicit obliteration of self halts her movement and leads to her occupation of an entirely different space as, confused by her amnesia and continued agitation, Martine agrees to spend the night in a psychiatric hospital and then leaves. The next sequence sees her unexplained admission to the clinic in which half of the film is set.

Ferreira Barbosa's comments clearly acknowledge her will to foreground the role of the urban in Martine's breakdown. She affirms that 'Paris is rather the setting of all adventures; it's not a direct route to the asylum but you are crushed by a reality which is oppressive'.[19] A lack of place in the city is shown to be at the heart of Martine's crisis. Indeed, when informed that she must leave the clinic to make room for people who are in greater need of its resources, her protests are articulated in spatial terms: 'And what about me? Do you think that there is a small place for me in the world?' ('Et moi? Vous croyez qu'il existe une petite place pour moi dans le monde?').

Martine's trajectory constitutes a retreat from the city to the conventionally marginalized spaces of the psychiatric hospital in which she resides on a voluntary basis. These institutional spaces provide a blurring of boundaries between the public and the private, as they are removed from the public realm yet offer little privacy and recognition of individuality. Martine's recuperation takes place in a pastoral, communal setting that is clearly contrasted with the cityscapes and traffic noise of the opening sequences. Indeed, Martine's sorties from the clinic (a visit to her sister; the pursuit of a fellow patient's imaginary relationship) are undertaken after dark, in a chauffeur-driven car that allows her access to others without initiating any contact with the urban fabric. The dominant long shots of this section of the film emphasize the expanse and verdure of the clinic's grounds, in which Martine is able to indulge her most naïve and altruistic fantasies as she undertakes increasingly desperate attempts to form a social group, to engineer the personal relationships of others, to 'reorganize the world'.[20] The clinic is presented as a communal space – there are no scenes of individual characters alone in their rooms – and this is underlined by the framing of Martine with other residents and the greater depth of shot employed in the clinic sequences.[21] Her existence in the city had been characterized by her incessant demands that male others should define her,[22] yet in the clinic she is shown to be concerned only for others, and to desire immersion in a group-identity.

Martine's ill-advised attempts to resolve others' problems, primarily through romantic interpretations and a refusal to accept solitude as a mode of being,[23] are represented through her relationship to space. Her desire to find a space is seen as concomitant with her desire for shared spaces: a desire that is symbolized through her persistent efforts to organize the other patients into spatially defined activities, including a game of tennis and her farewell picnic. The latter activity descends into farce. The repeated use of the long shot reveals her positing of a communal space (a bright pink picnic rug) as deluded and oppressive: she tries to restrict the movements of the other residents who are in dogged pursuit of their own personal and spatial configurations. Martine finally succeeds in engineering a group photo-graph, yet this is revealed as an artificial exercise reliant upon notions of fixity and framing that are evidently undermined by the dominant cinematic language of the film itself, with its insistence on an unpredictable mobility and inconsistent point of view.

No consideration of the different spaces represented within a film can be complete without an acknowledgement of the film's constructions of cinema-tographic space, and of the implications of such constructions for characterization, narrative coherence, and spectatorial situation:

> The visual language of the cinema, although confined within the rectangular space of the film frame, strains toward sequentiality in its depiction of narrative. It flourishes on juxtapositions and metonymies, on the reflection of drama in *mise-en-scène* carried forward in editing or camera movement and gradually unfolding the proximities of people and things into a connotative chain of associated meanings. The cinema's articulation of its own space carries with it a momentum that is subsumed into the linear pattern of narrative and overflows onto the narrative's dramatic figurations. And these linear patterns of narrative space, transmuted into characters in the drama on the screen, are inevitably themselves informed by the ideologies and aesthetics of gendered place.[24]

The camera movement and position in *Les Gens normaux* reflects Martine's changing state of mind and her accompanying relationship to space. The opening sequences of the film that present her chaotic and increasingly desperate flight through the city are filmed with a hand-held camera that cuts from extreme close-ups to long shots and does not adopt Martine's point of view, but remains independently mobile.[25] However, as Martine's confusion subsides, and as she herself becomes capable of the creation of spatially and temporally cohesive narratives, the camera position and spectator identification become more legible, and conventional progressive linear movement is asserted within the screen space. The scenes in the clinic are filmed with a predominantly static camera and appear as a series of tableaux. As Martine enters a period of apparent stability, the intro-duction of tracking shots that accompany her movement from left to right across the screen assert the conventional filmic visualization of linear narrative progress and coherence. The camera reflects her more stable identity and the disjointed, panicky movements of the early sequences are lost. The female subject becomes more legible and the spectator is encouraged, through the increasing use of close-up and point-of-view shots in the final sequences of the film, to identify with Martine.

The film's final sequence can be interpreted as Martine's reconciliation with the spaces of the city, yet some ambiguity remains. Martine leaves the clinic in a taxi, her new-found stability articulated by her confident return of the spectatorial gaze, yet the taxi serves as a continuation of the recuperative cocoon that separates her from the space of the city. She returns to her apartment, throws open a window and leans out, her body forming a potential bridge between the private domestic space and the public/urban domain. She opens the door to a recent acquaintance, and now potential romantic partner, but quickly slams it in his face and dissolves into laughter. While her apparent recovery is indicated by her continuing confident occupation of centre screen, the introduction of her domestic space at such a late point in the film is striking. It encourages us to read *Les Gens normaux*'s closure as turning on a conventional recuperation of the female subject into the traditional, domestic spaces of femininity and impending romance. Martine is comfortable engaging with the city from the spatial enclosure of her apartment, yet her alienation from the urban fabric remains unrepresented and unresolved.

Non-places: *Oublie-moi*

Noémie Lvovsky's *Oublie-moi* contains similar narrative elements, and the two films' opening sequences display noticeable points of overlap. However, the relationship between the female subject in crisis and the gendered nature of urban space is depicted differently and, I would argue, more radically in *Oublie-moi*. Lvovsky employs explicit spatial terms to indicate her characters' concerns, as she conceptualizes her film as the story of people who cannot get their lives together, or find a place.[26] Its central protagonist, Nathalie, is constantly on the move, in a ceaseless displacement of self and an obsessive mapping of her desires. She is seen to reject her current partner, Antoine, in order to besiege an ex-lover, in search of an explanation of the breakdown of their relationship. The tone of the film is claustrophobic, as Nathalie embarks upon a series of crazed journeys through the city, hurtling herself against the routes, maps and plans of both spatial and narrative coherency.

Nathalie does not occupy the conventional spaces of the female subject. She is not seen in her own domestic interior – indeed, she has apparently forfeited her apartment, through non-payment of rent – and the rejection or ejection that meets her repeated and insistent attempts to enter the domestic spaces of other people is striking. However, I do not propose to read *Oublie-moi* in such a way as to define Nathalie's crisis as a consequence of her alienation from the conventional realms of the feminine, but will suggest, rather, that hers is a struggle to assert a gendered identity in specific, impersonal spaces of urban life. Nathalie's crisis is acted out in the public spaces of the city from which she can find no retreat. Like Martine in *Les Gens normaux*, Nathalie seeks desperately to gain acknowledgement of her presence and identity from others, yet her quest for recognition leads her not to the illusion of a shared social space, but to a defiant occupation of the transient spaces of the city.

The spaces that come to characterize the trajectory of the central protagonist of *Oublie-moi* are spaces of transition and threshold: the corridors and platforms of the *métro*; bus shelters; public telephone kiosks; entrances; hallways; and landings. The *métro* figures largely here not as the allegory of a predominantly masculine quest narrative, as it does in several French films of the 1980s and early 1990s,[27] but as a marker of Nathalie's lack of direction, her failed journeys and abandoned trips. The choice of such settings is strikingly consistent throughout the film, encouraging a focus on the nature of what anthropologist Marc Augé has defined as the 'non-places' (*non-lieux*) that increasingly characterize contemporary social existence.[28]

Anthropological studies of place are founded upon a set of conditions and principles wholly different from studies of gendered space, or indeed cinemato-graphic space, yet share abiding concerns with the latter studies: 'Identity and relationships are at the heart of all the spatial systems that constitute the classical objects of study of anthropology'.[29] The 'non-place' is a space that has no identificatory, relational or historic functions and that privileges 'solitary individu-ality, the transitory and the provisional'.[30] Non-places do not therefore work as part of a social spatial structure, but represent instead 'the opposite of utopia: they do exist and they shelter no kind of organic society'.[31] Such sites do not, though, constitute the opposite of a sense of social place: rather, their coexistence with places provides 'palimpsests where the confused play of identity and relation is constantly reinscribed'.[32] It is this inscription that lies at the heart of Nathalie's exhausting battle, and, while some critics have (predictably) discussed Lvovsky's central character in terms of lack, it is her determination to assert her presence in these spaces that is most noticeable. If, as Augé claims, the 'non-place' is characterized by its lack of historical, social and personal investments and referents, then this type of space, one that is apparently uncolonized by conventions of gendered space, may provide the most suitable and accommodating sites in which to assert the presence of the female subject. Augé discusses the 'non-place' in terms of individual experience, but stops short of attending to individual subjective differences (of race, class and gender). That he does so could lead one to conclude that the occupancy of *non-lieux* might be problematically homogeneous. That notwithstanding, his concept of the *non-lieu* remains a valuable and provocative addition to a reconfiguration of the gendered spaces of the city, enabling us better to understand how the female subject in *Oublie-moi* stages an inscription of her presence and identity in uncharted sites of the kind Augé invokes.

Oublie-moi also attests to a consistent disruption of cinematographic space, as rapid editing, the dominant use of hand-held camera, and a lack of conventional camera position or movement combine to undermine the spectator's sense of distance or perspective. When accompanied by the obsessive repetition of dialogue – a repetition that functions as a Godardian device to foreground notions of performance and to alienate the spectator – and by a complete lack of any indication of a conventional temporal landscape,[33] the formal aspects of the film create a more radical disruption of narrative coherence and spectatorial unity than that mobilized in *Les Gens normaux*.[34] In other words, the spaces represented in the film and the cinematographic space are in no way subsumed by a linear narrative.

It is once again through a dissection of the final sequence of the film under discussion that I wish to develop these points. Having initiated and rejected a series of relationships, Nathalie's chaotic negotiation of the city spaces comes to an abrupt and unsignalled halt as she stops suddenly and enters a public telephone kiosk, the very space in which we first see her at the start of the film. She then makes a call to Antoine, the partner whom she abandoned at the beginning of the story. However, the potentially cyclical resolution of the narrative is disturbed as the call is answered by an ambiguous respondent, who claims to be Antoine's new lodger but who may indeed be Antoine disguising his identity. Nathalie flirts, describes herself flatly in negative terms that are neither playful nor confessional ('I am a real pain, a poison, an ordeal'[35]), and waits for him to come down and meet her. The last shot of the film is a close-up of a luminous Nathalie smiling as someone approaches in the distance. In interviews, Lvovsky has insisted that Nathalie is rejoining Antoine and is recovering from her obsessive state,[36] yet the spectator's unease at such a sudden, apparent change of behaviour is considerable.

Our uncertainty is reinforced by Nathalie's non-contestatory definition of self: a definition that seems more performative than revelatory, and evinces a continuation of her defiant unwillingness to be recuperated in/by the gendered spaces and narratives with which the female subject in the city is habitually associated.

Open Endings

The representations of the female subject in crisis offered in *Les Gens normaux* and *Oublie-moi* culminate in open endings that hint at a possible repositioning of the films' main protagonists vis-à-vis the gendered spaces of the urban realm. Both Martine and Nathalie remain atypically stationary, and to some extent passive, as they consider their situation in relation to the prospect of a resolution of the crises that have befallen them: a resolution that operates through the re-establishment of a romance narrative and through a (potential) renewed occupancy of domestic space. As Martine sits on her bed laughing, she returns the camera's gaze. But her agency and control are undermined by the striking incongruity of the domestic interior and the sense of enclosure that reigns therein, for all her emphatic opening of the window. Nathalie stands on the threshold of the telephone kiosk and waits for Antoine (or the new tenant) to come and seek her out. Yet the forceful contrast between this scene and her perpetual movement in the main body of the film suggests that any resolution that might occur may be illusory, or temporary.

Martine and Nathalie can find no space for themselves in the city. An urban landscape is employed to reflect the boundaries, barriers and limits that these characters both defy and deny, in processes that result in a ceaseless displacement of their selves and of the city itself. Their different trajectories of spatial identification – in relation both to the space of the city and to the cinematographic space on screen – reflect different responses to gendered mappings of space. A search for identity leads Martine to reject the alienating public spaces of the city in favour of a retreat into the artificial pastoral and communal space of the clinic, whose potential for new configurations of gendered space remains unexplored. Having failed to integrate herself there into any coherent social spaces, Martine returns to the conventionally feminized domestic interiors in which, it is implied, her crisis of identity and space will be resolved by the emergence of a romantic closure. The central protagonist of *Oublie-moi* finds refuge neither in the domestic nor in the social spaces of the city. In occupying the *non-lieux* of the urban fabric, as sites where she chooses to assert her presence and identity, she seems to effect a breakdown of conventions of gendered space: a breakdown that might permit her to escape 'recuperation'. But that breakdown, we must recognize, may or may not prove transitory.

Notes

1. E. Soja (1987), 'The Postmodernisation of Geography: A Review', *Annals of the Association of American Geographers*, 72, pp. 289–94, p. 289.
2. G. Rose (1993), *Feminism and Geography: The Limits of Geographical Knowledge*, Oxford, p. 160.
3. E. Grosz (1992), 'Bodies-Cities', in B. Colomina (ed.), *Sexuality and Space*, New York, pp. 241–53, p. 242.
4. See for example Joel Schumacher's *Falling Down* (1992). For a more oppositional reading of this text, see E. Mahoney (1997), 'The People in Parentheses: Space under Pressure in the Post-Modern City', in D.B. Clarke (ed.), *The Cinematic City*, London and New York, pp. 168–85.
5. In fact, the discourses of a masculinity in crisis arguably constitute narrative and critical strategies that ultimately ensure the continued marginalization of others.
6. See Mahoney, 'The People in Parentheses', p. 168.
7. See, for example, G. Pollock (1988), *Vision and Difference*, London and New York, pp. 68–74, and J. Wolff (1989), 'The Invisible Flâneuse: Women and the Literature of Modernity', in Andrew Benjamin (ed.), *The Problems of Modernity*, New York and London, pp. 141–56.
8. There are welcome exceptions, the most striking of which is Chantal Akerman's *Nuit et jour* (1991).
9. I would question the equation of an increased number of female subjects in the city with a reconfiguration of their function and status in both narrative and urban space. On this subject, see E. Wilson (1999), *French Cinema Since 1950: Personal Histories*, London, p. 125.
10. In this particular instance, the romance will also entail a removal of the female protagonist from the city to the suburbs.
11. It is interesting to note, however, that many films of the late 1990s witnessed a switch of attention from the sites of Paris to the provincial cities of central and Northern France. See, for example, Eric Zonca's *La Vie rêvée des anges* (1998).
12. Laurence Ferreira Barbosa made several successful short films in the early 1980s: *Paris ficelle* (1982); *Adèle Frelon est-elle là?* (1983); *Sur les talus* (1987); and a documentary on Ingmar Bergman, before receiving the *prix Georges Sadoul* and the *prix Cyril Collard* for *Les Gens normaux n'ont rien d'exceptionnel*. Her next film *J'ai horreur de l'amour* (1997) was also a critical success.
13. Noémie Lvovsky received critical acclaim for her two short films: *Dis-moi oui, dis-moi non* (1990) and *Embrasse-moi* (1991). 1999 saw the release of *La Vie ne me fait pas peur*, an extended version of her film for the acclaimed

Arté series 'Tous les garçons et les filles de leurs âges'. She collaborated with Arnaud Desplechin on *La Sentinelle* (1992) and co-wrote Yolande Zauberman's *Clubbed to death* (1997).

14. Clearly the definition of a women's cinema remains complex and intersects with gendered conventions of theme, genre, audience and auteur.

15. T. de Lauretis (1988), 'Aesthetic and Feminist Theory: Rethinking Women's Cinema', in D. Pribran (ed.), *Female Spectators: Looking at Film and Television*, London, pp. 174–95, p. 193.

16. R. Lapsley (1997), 'Mainly in Cities and at Night', in Clarke, *The Cinematic City*, pp. 186–208, p. 186.

17. For a reflection of this status, see C.-M. Trémois (1997), *Les Enfants de la liberté*, Paris, pp. 221–41.

18. As described in the work and situationalist projects of Michel de Certeau. See M. de Certeau (1990), *L'Invention du quotidien. 1. Arts de faire*, Paris.

19. 'Paris c'est plutôt le lieu de toutes les aventures, c'est pas la route directe vers l'asile mais on est ecrasé par une réalité qui est oppressante.' Laurence Ferreira Barbosa (1996), 'J'ai horreur de l'amour', *Cinélibre*, 39, pp. 16–17, p. 16.

20. See ibid., p. 17.

21. The other residents of the clinic are presented as stereotypes of neurosis reminiscent of the categories represented in *One Flew over the Cuckoo's Nest*: the paranoid who complains about the running of the institution; the builder of matchstick monuments (here hilariously the Eiffel tower); the male adolescent who uses absorption in music as a barrier to communication with others.

22. She asks a male colleague whether he finds her pretty, her father how he finds her, and her ex-partner if they loved each other.

23. She entreats Florence to go back to François: 'Separation is irrational. Stay together . . . make a good life . . . well, normally' ('La séparation n'est pas raisonnable. Restez ensemble . . . faites une belle vie . . . fin . . . normalement').

24. L. Mulvey (1992), 'Pandora: Topographies of the Mask and Curiosity', in Colomina, *Sexuality and Space*, pp. 52–71, p. 56.

25. For example, the camerawork encourages the spectator to assume that we are accompanying Martine as we enter her place of work, yet we find her already at her desk.

26. See Thierry Jousse and Frédéric Strauss (1995), 'Entretien avec Noémie Lvovsky', *Cahiers du cinéma*, 448, pp. 20–3, p. 21.

27. See for example Jean-Jacques Beineix's *Diva* (1981); Luc Besson's *Subway* (1985); and Leos Carax's *Les Amants du Pont neuf* (1991).

28. M. Augé (1992), *Non-lieux: Introduction à une anthropologie de la surmodernité*, Paris. The translations that follow are my own.

29. 'L'identité et la relation sont au coeur de tous les dispositifs spatiaux étudiés classiquement par l'anthropologie.' Ibid., p. 76.
30. 'un monde promis à l'individualité solitaire, au passage, au provisoire'. Ibid., p. 101.
31. 'Le non-lieu est le contraire de l'utopie: il existe et il n'abrite aucune société organique.' Ibid., p. 140.
32. 'les palimpsestes où se réinscrit sans cesse le jeu brouillé de l'identité et de la relation'. Ibid., p. 101.
33. There is no room here to discuss the detailed implications of such (Deleuzian) models of time-image, yet a consideration of their relation to the subversion of gendered space in film is much needed.
34. The temporal movement of *Les Gens normaux* is clearly demarcated as Martine asks what day it is and plans to leave the clinic on a Friday. In the closing scenes, we learn that the narrative has spanned just ten days.
35. 'Je suis une vraie plaie, un poison, un calvaire.'
36. See, for example, F. Audé (1995), 'Entretien avec Noémie Lvovsky: Une belle personne', *Positif*, February, pp. 39–42, p. 40.

15

Identification and Female Friendship in Contemporary French Film
Emma Wilson

Introduction

In *The Bell Jar*, Sylvia Plath writes:

> I looked at Joan. In spite of the creepy feeling, and in spite of my old, ingrained dislike, Joan fascinated me. . . . Her thoughts were not my thoughts, nor her feelings my feelings, but we were close enough so that her thoughts and feelings seemed a wry, black image of my own.

> Sometimes I wondered if I had made Joan up. Other times I wondered if she would continue to pop in at every crisis of my life to remind me of what I had been, and what I had been through, and carry on her own separate but similar crisis under my nose.

> 'I don't see what women see in other women', I'd told Dr Nolan in my interview that noon. 'What does a woman see in a woman that she can't see in a man?'

> Dr Nolan paused. Then she said, 'Tenderness.'
> That shut me up.[1]

These same issues of fascination and distaste, crisis and tenderness, are brought into focus in the French female friendship films that will be my subject here. The female friendship movie is developing a history: Karen Hollinger, author of *In the Company of Women* (1998), locates the development of the genre first in the 1970s, but links it with 1930s and 1940s women's films.[2] Hollinger's study stops in the early 1990s: its latest film, not insignificantly, is Rose Troche's 1994 *Go Fish*. My interest is in what happens to the female friendship movie through the 1990s, in the light precisely of the new queer cinema of which Troche's film is a part.

Until very recently, screen images of lesbians have hovered between hysteria and homicide, offering few points of identification for the female viewer, lesbian or otherwise.[3] Arguably, in the wake of such incendiary and melodramatic imaging, the female friendship movie offered a space for homoerotic fantasy. Films such as

Fred Zinneman's *Julia* (1977), in their idealization of romantic friendship and women's loyalty one to another, seem to court such a response. Addressing the issue of lesbian viewers' recuperative readings, in *The Celluloid Closet* (1995), one woman speaks of her pleasure watching *Rebecca* (1940), for example, and of her love of the scene where Mrs Danvers fingers the flimsy clothes, the furs in Rebecca's closet. As lesbianism finally starts to enter mainstream cinema in the 1990s, the need for such fantasy viewings is obviated. The female friendship movie can itself in turn evolve, no longer merging desire and identification, but arguably offering new charged analyses of the very fascination Plath has made her focus in my opening quotation. Fascination, critical proximity, identity in production: these typify the dynamics of friendship as it is dissected in late 1990s film.

Hollinger's study has six affirmative chapters – on sentimental, erotic, political and other female friendship films – and one distressed chapter, a seventh, 'Backlash: The Anti-Female Friendship Film', where she re-views films such as *Single White Female* (1992), *Poison Ivy* (1992) and others. My films come from the hinterland between her chapters, where friendship is contingent, fantasized, non-reciprocal, yet still in its tenderness and formative power scores the female subject deep within.

Theory

In *The Practice of Love* (1994), Teresa de Lauretis stresses the importance of distinguishing female friendship movies and lesbian cinema. She outlines what she sees as the risks of conflating identification (female friendship) and desire (lesbian sexuality). Crucially, she refuses the 'sweeping of lesbian sexuality and desire under the rug of sisterhood, female friendship and the . . . mother-daughter bond'.[4] De Lauretis works here to criticize the position taken up by Jackie Stacey in her important 1987 article 'Desperately Seeking Difference'.[5] Stacey looks at such films as *All about Eve* (1950) and *Desperately Seeking Susan* (1985). She argues that while these are not lesbian films, they offer women spectators particular pleasures connected with 'women's active desire and the sexual aims of women in the audience in relationship to the female protagonist on screen'.[6] For De Lauretis, this is problematic since, as she puts it plainly, 'in these representations, desire between women is not sexual'.[7]

Stacey's position, and interest in the merger of identification and desire in representations and viewing relations, is closer to the queer theoretical engagement with psychoanalysis developed by Judith Butler, Diana Fuss and others. As Butler contends: 'Some psychoanalytic theories tend to construe identification and desire as two mutually exclusive relations to love objects that have been lost through prohibition and/or separation. Any intense emotional attachment thus divides into either wanting to have someone or wanting to be that someone, but never both at once.'[8] Butler continues, in terms germane to Stacey's argument: 'It is important to consider that identification and desire can coexist, and that their formulation in terms of mutually exclusive oppositions serves a heterosexual matrix'.[9] I concur absolutely with Butler's analysis, as developed through her work in *Gender Trouble*, in its emphasis on the coexistence of identification and desire in the formation of identity. May it still not be useful, nevertheless, to distinguish lesbian desire and female friendship as differently invested affective relations in both personal experience and cinematic representation? It seems that, in espousing and affirming such divisions between lesbianism and female friendship, De Lauretis's aim is to keep lesbianism sexy, to find its fantasy structures in cinema (as she does in her analysis of the construction of a lesbian primal scene in Sheila McLaughlin's 1987 film *She Must Be Seeing Things*). Conversely, here, my aim is to explore the alternate implication of De Lauretis's division between female friendship and lesbian desire. What happens as we divorce homoeroticism from female friendship? If ignoring the erotic, can female friendship films still pose a challenge to heterosexism and patriarchal configurations of desire?

The French Female Friendship Movie

The French female friendship movie has a far less rich history than its US counterpart. A pertinent question indeed is whether the notion of a female friendship movie, developed in the US, as progeny of the woman's film and as counterpart to the buddy movie, is of relevance in a European context. Hollinger's study is devoid of reference to European film. I would say, however, that such exclusive divisions seem untimely in the light of the extraordinary presence and influence of US films in Europe, if not vice versa. Evidence of the influence of the US female friendship movie in European film-making can be found, for example, in the playful homage to George Cukor's *Rich and Famous* (1981) at the end of Pedro Almodóvar's *The Flower of My Secret* (1995). An inverse influence can be traced too, indeed, in the tributes to Jacques Rivette's *Céline et Julie vont en bateau* (1974) found in *Single White Female* or *Before Sunrise* (1995). Certainly cross-influences exist. Yet it is perhaps important to consider, too, certain specific differences between the female friendship movie in the US and its European counterparts. Arguably, European art-house film-makers have been more concerned to interrogate the psychoanalytic bases behind female friendship. Such influence is felt in the explorations of merger and imperfect individuation developed in Margaretta von Trotta's *The German Sisters* (1981) or its seminal influence, Bergman's *Persona* (1966). Consciously or not, this is the European inheritance that, cross-bred with the specific US genre, develops in new, committed French female friendship movies. Such film-making eschews psychoanalytic or aesthetic abstraction, yet largely avoids sentiment or idealization too, in order to pay serious attention to the complexities of female friendship and the (feminist) identity issues it raises.

This is a hybrid genre in French film-making, then. Films of the *Nouvelle Vague*, those of Chabrol or Truffaut for example, predominantly show male friendship. Exceptions come in Eric Rohmer's early and increasing emphasis on female friendship. Where films such as *Quatre aventures de Reinette et Mirabelle* (1986) tend to exploit the visual pleasures of representations of two *jeunes filles en fleurs*, more recent films such as *Conte d'automne* (1998) look in more complex terms at issues of identity and identification, both within and across generations of women. There have been relatively few female-directed studies of female friendship in French cinema, however. Agnès Varda's *L'Une chante l'autre pas* (1976) stands out here, of course. Interestingly, it may be seen as one implicit point of reference for the films to which I shall turn my attention below in its focus on women's creativity, exploring as it does the friendship between a photographer and a singer. Varda's film charts the development and transformation of the women's friendship in the context of the women's movement in France during the 1960s and 1970s. It is as much a film about a generation as it is a film about two individual women. Its interest lies largely in the possibility of reconciling sexual relationships with men with emotional relationships with women (a conflict similarly explored in a 1978 US film, Claudia Weill's *Girl Friends*). The following decade likewise produced one really outstanding exploration of female friendship in French film-making: Diane Kurys's autobiographical *Coup de foudre* (1983). Again the film aligns female creativity and female friendship, exploring the (platonic) friendship that develops between Madeleine, a sculptor, and her friend Léna. It has been read, in accordance with my initial comments on female friendship movies, as one of the few French films to offer homoerotic representations that are recuperable for a lesbian spectator.

In the 1990s, with Josiane Balasko's ground-breaking comedy, *Gazon maudit* (1995), lesbianism entered mainstream French cinema. In addition to this direct representation, lesbian sexuality has increasingly become less an issue, more an accepted subject within a broader spectrum of French representations of sex, sexuality and emotional relations. In Olivier Assayas's 1996 *Irma Vep*, lesbian desire for Maggie Cheung is just one of the facets to the film's exploration of impossible investments in relations to the Other. In Cédric Klapisch's *Chacun cherche son chat* (1996), Chloe is shown to be an impossible object of desire for a waitress in the bar where she drinks, just as her gay room-mate Michel is an impossible object of desire for Chloe herself. Where these examples, despite their sexual diversity, may still suggest further interest in lesbianism as impossible passion, Catherine Corsini's *La Nouvelle Eve* (1999) is all the more relaxed in placing a lesbian couple as the example of monogamous relations against which the main protagonist's own (hetero)sexual wanderings are set in relief.

While lesbianism is now part of the sexual landscape of current French cinema (as it is in independent US film), the female friendship movie is increasingly divorced from its role as vehicle for the representation of women's positive (homo-erotic) attention to each other. Female friendship is not seen merely as a refuge from the misunderstandings and conflict of heterosexual relations. This new inter-rogation does not downplay the intensity of female friendship, but reveals further the challenge that friendship can pose to female autonomy and individuation as much as the tenderness that can be evinced. In the 1990s, more first films were directed by women in France, and this too is perhaps one of the reasons why more complex representations of female friendship have gained currency in French film-making. Films by young women directors such as Pascale Ferran's *L'Age des possibles* (1995) and Noémie Lvovsky's *La vie ne me fait pas peur* (1999), neither of which received a cinema release in the UK, explored the impact and imprint of women on each other's lives. But perhaps most influential within this generation and genre have been two films by Martine Dugowson that have taken as their subject the desire to be and not to have the other woman. These will be my point of focus in the next part of this chapter, before I turn finally to an analysis of *La Vie rêvée des anges* (1998), perhaps the most revelatory friendship film in late 1990s French film-making.

Portraits Chinois/Mina Tannenbaum

In Dugowson's 1995 film *Portraits Chinois*, a crucial emotional scene takes place between the two central female protagonists near the culmination of the drama. Ada (Helena Bonham-Carter) has been a successful dress designer, living with her writer partner, Paul. In the course of the film she has lost her partner and her place in the fashion house. In both positions she is usurped by Lise (Romane Bohringer), her younger alter ego. In a set piece scene, Ada, together with various other characters whose interwoven lives make up the subject of the film, attends Lise's signature *défilé*. Leaving the party afterwards, Ada slips behind the scenes in the fashion house, entering a room that has previously been her workshop and the setting for the construction of her identity.

Alone in this hidden space, Ada fingers material that is stretched out on the table. We are offered a close-up of her hand in contact with the fabric: a tactile image (obliquely reminiscent of Mrs Danvers in *Rebecca*) and one that frames her creative profession, her sensory nostalgia and her sensuality. While Ada remembers a former self, her former life and her work with Sandre, the male dress designer who founded the fashion house and with whom she has been in partner-ship, tears come to her eyes. Into this memory space, this space of identity formation and loss (aptly a costume design workshop), comes Lise. The exchange between Ada and Lise is central to the film. Dugowson presents it as a shot/reverse shot sequence. Lise faces Ada, and the camera, as she confides 'You inspired the collec-tion' ('J'ai pensé à toi en dessinant la collection'). She admits 'You were my guide'

('C'était toi le fil conducteur'). At this moment, as the two women stand face to face, almost mirror-images of one another, Lise reaches out her hand to touch Ada's cheek, to touch the ego ideal Ada has been for her. At this moment, in the failed gesture of contact and tenderness, the film almost crosses the line of identi-fication and desire, as Lise's gaze lingers longer on Ada and the scene is pregnant with Lise's emotion towards Ada. Yet her words, and Ada's resistance, confirm the real set of relations that are at stake here. Lise continues 'I wanted to know you', 'I wanted to impress you', 'Be as pretty as you' ('moi, je voulais te connaître', 'je voulais t'impressionner', 'être aussi belle que toi'). Lise's desire is confirmed as a desire to be Ada, whether or not she also wants to have her. She invites her to return to work for the fashion house. Lise reminds Ada that she, Lise, and Sandre are alike, that she and Ada could work together. Ada rejects this offer, walking out of this space of memory and mirroring identification.

The scene seems to work as one of expiation for Ada, allowing her to cut ties with the past and permitting her to perceive the idolization and envy that have motivated Lise. While the film is largely negative in its representation of female/female relations – this act of usurpation is hardly friendship – it is significant in privileging an identificatory relation over a desiring relation. Far less important and intense than Lise's brief affair with Paul, whom she leaves, is her identification with Ada, the woman whose role she wishes to play. Despite its lack of reciprocity, and its conflict, the same-sex relation holds sway over heterosexual desire in the film, allowing the viewer to question the relative import of each. This same relativ-ization, this privileging of women's attention, positive or negative, to each other, is found equally in Dugowson's earlier, more frequently discussed film, *Mina Tannenbaum* (1993).

Mina Tannenbaum is partly a nostalgia film: its tone is uneven, mingling humour and elegy. It is set in Paris in the 1970s and 1980s, implicitly paying homage to the period of the development of the women's movement and its ideals (and films) of sisterhood and female friendship. Critics discussing the film allude to Varda and Kurys.[10] They speak also of the influence of the Hollywood melodrama or 'weepie'.[11] Beyond this, in some moments of sheer intensity, the film addresses the impossibility and regret of a friendship whose roots lie in identification. The friend-ship *Mina Tannenbaum* traces, from split screen birth scene through childhood, adolescence and young womanhood, is that between Mina (Romane Bohringer) and Ethel (Elsa Zylberstein). The film is narrated in retrospect, after Mina's suicide. In this sense, it is a film dominated by a mourning aesthetic: by an attempt to deny the loss which is located at its inception. This disavowal, as Mina's image is re-animated in the memory sequences that make up the film's narrative, does not preclude a painful critique of the conflict of power that pulls the friendship apart.

We first gain a sense of the intensity of this friendship in one of the scenes intercut with the titles. Ethel walks towards the camera, in busy discussion with work colleagues. She seems oblivious to the fact that she is being filmed. But suddenly she stops in response to an unheard question. Her forward trajectory is interrupted as she appears jolted, halted, numbed for a moment. Facing directly to the camera she says 'Mina Tannenbaum? We met when I was seven . . . What could I tell you? It'd take too long . . .' ('Mina Tannenbaum? J'avais sept ans quand je l'ai connue . . . Qu'est-ce que je pourrais vous dire? Ça serait trop long . . .'). Ethel's words seem to suggest that the subject necessarily exceeds any narrative form. We have a sense at the start that the film can only encompass a very small part of its subject: the intensity and importance of the friendship is confirmed. The silences between Ethel's words equally signal that much will be left out.

The film is at its finest, in my view, in creating childhood images of the two protagonists. Importantly, both girls are established as individuals before their friendship develops. Delicately the film seems to offer a few images that show the loneliness that subtends the friendship. We see a tiny Mina taken to the optician and later teased because of her glasses. We see Ethel at a bar mitzvah, her face expectant, in close-up, as she swings her legs and watches other little girls being invited to dance. These memory images, that have the quality of home-movie sequences, reveal the film's attention to detail, not merely period detail (which is nevertheless lovingly respected) but the detail of childhood emotions, wishes and friendships.

The friendship begins after dance class. Ethel, the gentler and plumper of the two, is fascinated by a painting Mina has in her bag. It is Mina's copy of Gainsborough's portrait of his daughters: two little girls sitting close together. Mina and Ethel sit on a bench talking about who will keep the picture. Mina tells Ethel that she has changed the image and made one sister whisper in the other's ear. The scene seems to hold a set of meanings. Dugowson as film-maker points to the tradition of images of sisterhood and sentimental friendship that her film will copy and subvert, offering new images of complicity between women. Mina's creativity, her role as artist, and Ethel's fascination with this role, crucial to much of the film, are signalled even in a childhood scene. More insidiously, a trail of images of copying is initiated. Mina's skill and expertise as a copyist are confirmed here, looking forward all too fatefully to the late collapse of her career as painter and her need to supplement her income with money gained from copying the great masters. The theme of copying is also linked to a further thematics of crisis in the film: the crisis in identity that is wrought by Ethel's repeated over-identification with Mina. The importance of the Gainsborough copy is signalled too by its return at the very end of the film. The camera approaches the image as we hear the phantom voices of the young Mina and Ethel. Ethel is whispering a secret to Mina, just as Gainsborough's daughters, in Mina's copy, whisper to one another. The identification between art and life is confirmed as the image of the painting now catalyses an aural memory.

As in *Portraits Chinois*, Dugowson is fascinated by the ways in which women may take each other as models as they construct and perform their identities. Such a subject has its own self-reflexive resonance in cinema, where work has been done on the questions of identification and identity construction that inform affective spectatorial relations. In *Mina Tannenbaum*, narrative cinema is used as a means to reveal the tensions and abuses of such narcissistic identifications. It is predominantly in the second half of the film that these issues come to the fore, as the viewer begins to question the ascendancy of Mina in the friendship between the two girls. The presentation of the friendship is notably selective. Interestingly, the film entirely elides the period at which we may assume the friendship is at its most intense and exclusive. In a fluid 360-degree shot, the film moves from the image of the little girls on the bench to an image of their teenage counterparts. The film's intense interest is, from this point on, in the betrayals and deformations of friendship. These are wrought by identification and ambition.

As Mina's career as an artist goes from strength to strength, Ethel is seen to attempt subtly to usurp her position. The first real conflict we see takes place at Mina's *vernissage*. Ethel compliments Mina on the paintings and on what she has achieved: 'They all love you here' ('Tout le monde est amoureux de toi, ici'). She continues: 'You've got talent, brains, beauty . . . Will you talk to me when you're famous? . . .' ('Si! Tu as le talent, l'intelligence et la beauté . . . Tu me parleras encore quand tu es célèbre? . . .'). The lines belie Ethel's insecurity. Yet she will profit by Mina, as she says: 'Being your friend opens doors for me . . .' ('Tu sais quoi? C'est une carte de visite pour moi de dire que je suis ta meilleure amie . . .'). Ethel's words, as she is drunk, work to lay bare the foundations of their friendship. The film details the ways in which she makes use of her identification with Mina. She pretends to be Mina Tannenbaum, the painter, as she organizes an interview with a reclusive artist. Mina, horrified by this appropriation of her identity, affirms bitterly that the differences between herself and Ethel are far more striking than the similarities. In this scene, the two women sit in a café, both facing the camera. As they argue, they turn to face one another, their images inescapably mirroring one another. Despite this visual and emotive bond, the friendship seems entirely ruptured: Ethel affirms 'our friendship's beginning to weigh on me' ('cette amitié finit par me peser'). She leaves the café. As the camera follows her it pans upwards, with some irony, to a *Belle Epoque* image of two nymphs. Signalled here seems to be the distance between friendship experienced and the ideal of the female-female couple. Yet we find too the inescapability of the bond that binds the two women, despite their best efforts, through the course of the film. As Mina herself exits the café, she neglects to watch as she crosses the road and is knocked down by a van. This accident seems a rehearsal for the suicide that closes the film. The last parts of the film indeed seem to depend on a series of repetitions of the friendship's rediscovery and renewed rupture.

Ethel's quest to usurp Mina continues as she comes close to marrying the art dealer, Dana, whom Mina too has desired. Mina questions Ethel bitterly as to why she has always wanted what she had. An irony of the film comes, however, as close to the end Ethel informs Mina 'You're no model for me anymore. Understand?' ('Tu n'es plus un modèle pour moi, tu sais?'). What we find is that Ethel survives this identification, as she survives her asphyxiating relation to her mother, while Mina is its victim. As Mina loses Ethel, her life falls apart and we are left to surmise that outside the affirming gaze of the Other, Mina's identity has no value. The film subtly realigns our impressions of the power relations, of the losses and gains in the drama of identity that is its subject.

La Vie rêvée des anges

Erick Zonca's 1998 film *La Vie rêvée des anges* is unusual in the current trend of French female friendship movies, since it is the work of a male director. But it bears the mark of a female cinematographer, Agnès Godard. Further, the film is inextricably linked to the image – the very faces – of its two lead players, Elodie Bouchez (Isa) and Natacha Régnier (Marie). In this way it is comparable to *Mina Tannenbaum*, equally associated with the couple formed by its iconic lead actresses, Bohringer and Zylberstein. Bouchez and Régnier shared the best actress award for their work in *La Vie rêvée des anges* at Cannes in 1998. Critics comment on the way the film is animated by the extraordinary rapport, the tactile emotion, established between the two actresses. Emphasis on the complementarity between Bouchez and Régnier – one dark, one fair, one child-like, one sardonic – has dominated discussions of the film, and its marketing.

This focus on the couple in fact ignores one of the greatest achievements of the film that is, following *Mina Tannenbaum*, to interrogate and undermine the dyadic structure of female friendship. In all the more complex terms, the film shows the ways in which identifications are never brought to full closure, are vehicles for one another, haunted by other needs and other losses. It is this knowledge about friendship, identity and identification that the film seems to bring. *La Vie rêvée des anges* is a film dependent on phantom doubling, on echoes and displacements. It opens following Isa as she walks down a country road with a large back pack. Her missed encounter with a friend leads her to spend the night alone in the van where they have sold crêpes in the past. We follow her to Lille, the main location of the film. One of the first signature images of Isa comes as she sits in a café carefully cutting out pictures from old magazines, pasting them on to card to sell in the street. The film typically pays patient, tender attention to such minor acts. The cinematography is deliberately underplayed: hand-held camerawork is used to follow the protagonists as they move around, to establish the space between them, yet there are significant moments of stillness where the unmoving camera merely observes the characters unobtrusively. Zonca's decision to shoot in 16 mm, the consequent grainy effect, the muted natural colours of the film add to this apparent lack of artifice, this intimate unstaged encounter.

The patterns of the film, its repetitions, belie this, however. As we watch Isa cutting out the images she will sell as Christmas cards we find ourselves watching the first of a series of scenes that illustrate her creativity, comparable to that of Mina or Ada in Dugowson's more bourgeois contexts. Isa attempts to make a montage out of reality; to recycle and reincarnate the images and objects of her very sparse material existence. This is witnessed in her laying out the hand-made Tarot cards, an understated symbol of her mobile destiny. One of these cards will be a gift in her friendship with Marie: an artist has given the cards to Isa who in turn asks Marie to choose a card, recirculating friendship and exchange.

Friendship in the film follows this pattern of displacement and exchange. Isa inserts herself into Marie's life, countering her resistance, and indifference, with open responses and sheer faith. The friendship is haphazard and hesitant. A series of scenes in the first third of the movie show the friendship at its warmest, most reciprocal. Isa prepares breakfast for Marie and the camera frames her entering Marie's bedroom, which is shadowy, a still warm dream-like space. As they sit up in bed, the camera holds both women within the frame in long takes, then moves to intercut close-ups of their faces as we find a first reference to the elusive dream-life, the dreamed life, of the film's title. Marie tells Isa 'tu rêves beaucoup' ('you dream a lot' – words that reflect back precisely on Marie's own destiny within the film).

Even in this scene, the closest between Marie and Isa, we gain a phantom impression of the second female friendship of the film: a friendship all the more tenuous, and illusory, than the first. The telephone rings and Marie leaves it unanswered (foreshadowing her own repeat calls to Chriss later in the movie). She tells Isa it will be for the other women, the mother and daughter, whose house they are living in. Mother and daughter have been in a car crash; the daughter is now in hospital in a coma. The film takes place in the limbo time of the daughter's unconsciousness, of her living death and fragile survival. Marie is indifferent to the fate or identity of these other women. Isa, on the other hand, becomes fascinated by the daughter Sandrine. The film cuts from the scene of Isa and Marie in bed, to shots of Isa alone in Sandrine's room, looking at a montage of photos on Sandrine's wall. She looks in fascination at an image of Sandrine herself. In the careful detail of the film's set, we see a poster from the Louvre on Sandrine's wall, a Botticelli fresco of two girls arm in arm (reminiscent of the Gainsborough image copied in *Mina Tannenbaum*).

Isa's friendship with Marie is displaced in the film by her growing fascination with Sandrine. As Marie embarks on her suicidal affair with Chriss, Isa begins to develop a relation to the girl imagined and remembered in the spaces of the apartment. She reads Sandrine's journal, the camera again painstaking as it follows the childish handwriting as Isa reads. She visits Sandrine in hospital, watching her unconscious form with avid attention and care, learning to become a channel of sensory and mnemonic triggers to help Sandrine return to consciousness. Isa reads the words of Sandrine's journal to her. Then she takes up the writing of the journal, addressing her in the second person, creating a compensatory witness to Sandrine's existence, filling the gaps in the journal, pasting together the dissembled parts of Sandrine's life-writing.

This relation to the Other is utterly non-reciprocal. Isa has not known Sandrine before the accident. Her friendship with her is the product of Isa's living in the literal spaces of Sandrine's past life. In the pathos of Isa's dreamed, fantasized relation to the absent Other, the film seems to evoke a Freudian understanding of identification as a mechanism to avoid or manage loss. Diana Fuss explores this phenomenon in *Identification Papers* (1995), where she shows how identification invokes phantoms, arguing that 'all identification begins in an experience of traumatic loss and in the subject's tentative attempts to manage that loss'.[12]

As Sandrine remains poised between life and death, Isa can deny her loss for a time, incorporating her alterity, blurring the boundaries between herself and the girl with whom she identifies. The fragile status of this identification as friendship is foregrounded brutally, as we see Sandrine's all but inanimate form in the hospital bed. We begin to see how this illusory relation to Sandrine shadows Isa's friendship with Marie. Sandrine appears an uncanny double of Marie. The first words Isa reads in Sandrine's journal – 'on the edge of the abyss I feel this crazy urge to jump' ('je suis au bord d'un gouffre avec la folle envie de m'y jeter') – are themselves realized in Marie's suicide. Sandrine's unmoving shape is doubled and echoed in Marie's abject form as Isa looks down to see her on the ground below. The film moves between the two non-reciprocal friendship relations, letting each show up the absences of the other. Close to the end of the film, we see the final rupture between Marie and Isa, their faces mirroring each other in contortion and anger. The film cuts to a scene in the hospital where, with sheer pathos, Isa now holds Sandrine's hand. The new image of tenderness is pasted over the inverse mirror-image of the former friendship. Yet we are painfully aware of Isa's impossible investment in each friendship as fantasy.

In making female friendship its subject, *La Vie rêvée des anges*, like *Mina Tannenbaum*, reveals how identification depends on loss and illusion. (A reviewer in *Interview* writes that 'you are left wondering if there is anything worse that can happen between adults than the process of becoming strangers'.)[13] Yet, over and above this, what I find most startling is the film's investment in the continued possibility of movement into the future. Isa, angel of the film's title, resembles the images of innocence and faith found in the heroine of Fellini's *La Strada* (1954), or even in Bess in *Breaking the Waves* (1996). Where each of these figures is sacrificed, Isa survives, in another act of displacement. The film's last scene shows her taking her place in a new set of relations. As the film plays out, we see the camera pause rhythmically as it comes face to face with each of the women in the factory. For Zonca, in interview, these other portraits of women make Isa's story universal. For the reviewer in *Sight and Sound*, 'as the camera pauses at each female assembly-line worker, it suggests the potential for new friendships (and similar women's stories)'.[14] For me, these virtual existences seem to form the film's own dream-life beyond its ending. (*Mina Tannenbaum* would seem to find a more conventional view into the future as Ethel names her small daughter Mina, in a possible tribute to lost friendship.)

La Vie rêvée des anges dissects female friendship, and its dependence on an impossible dream of unity, symbiosis, reciprocity. (Here, the film's symbolic location in the house of the absent mother and daughter seems evident.) It shows the conflict, jealousy and breakdown of female friendship, refusing the lyrical idealization common in the genre, critiqued by Hollinger for offering a false illusion to female viewers. Yet, in articulating doubts over female friendship and identification, the film, I would argue, still bears its own feminist message.

Conclusion

In her 1998 essay 'The Postmodern in Feminism', Barbara Johnson looks at what can be gained from conflicts in feminism. She argues: 'But conflicts amongst feminists require women to pay attention to each other, to take each other's reality seriously, to face each other. This requirement that women face each other may not have anything erotic or sexual about it, but it may have everything to do with the eradication of the misogyny that remains within feminists, and with the attempt to escape the logic of heterosexuality'.[15] Contemporary French female friendship film, by placing women face to face as friendship shades into antagonism and betrayal, by making the viewer face the sometimes illusory nature of women's wishes for each other and themselves, itself escapes the logic of heterosexuality, by making differences between women its compelling and insistent subject. Here, then, the female friendship film offers a challenge to heterosexism. This can be witnessed in both *Mina Tannenbaum* and *La Vie rêvée des anges*. The latter film is perhaps all the more heartening in feminist terms, where a reckoning with conflict and difference does not undermine the film's confidence in the very tenderness of which Plath speaks. (The *Interview* review of *La Vie rêvée des anges* is titled 'Tenderness in the Strangest Places'.) Tenderness, for me, is part of the feminist politics of *La Vie rêvée des anges* and part of the possible future, the new virtual existence, of the contemporary female friendship film. Such tenderness not only marks Isa's attention to others, but saturates the very aesthetic of the film: its pace, its patience, its understatement. The film makes its own moving montage of women's relations with each other, pasting image against image, reminding us of cinema's capacity to reflect, and reflect on, the image-production and incorporation on which identity depends.

Notes

1. S. Plath (1963), *The Bell Jar*, London, pp. 209–10.
2. K. Hollinger (1998), *In the Company of Women: Contemporary Female Friendship Films*, Minneapolis.
3. A. Weiss (1992), *Vampires and Violets: Lesbians in the Cinema*, London, pp. 51–83.
4. T. de Lauretis (1994), *The Practice of Love: Lesbian Sexuality and Perverse Desire*, Bloomington and Indianapolis, p. 116.
5. J. Stacey (1987), 'Desperately Seeking Difference', *Screen*, 28, pp. 48–61.
6. Ibid., p. 49.
7. de Lauretis, *The Practice of Love*, p. 120
8. J. Butler (1991), 'Imitation and Gender Insubordination', in D. Fuss (ed), *Inside/Out: Lesbian Theories, Gay Theories*, New York and London, pp. 13–31, p. 26.
9. Ibid., p. 26.
10. D. Toscan du Plantier, 'Romane et Elsa', *Figaro Magazine*, 12 March 1994.
11. G. Austin (1996), *Contemporary French Cinema: An Introduction*, Manchester, p. 96.
12. D. Fuss (1995), *Identification Papers*, New York and London, p. 38.
13. D. Fuller, 'Tenderness in the Strangest Places', *Interview*, April 1999, p. 76.
14. G. Smith, '*La Vie rêvée des anges*', *Sight and Sound*, November 1998, p. 64.
15. B. Johnson (1998), *The Feminist Difference: Literature, Psychoanalysis, Race, and Gender*, Cambridge, Mass. and London, p. 194.

Filmography

Allégret, M., *Zouzou* (1934)
Assayas, O., *Irma Vep* (1996)
Beineix, J.-J., *Diva* (1981)
   La Lune dans le caniveau (1983)
   37°2 le matin (1986)
   Roselyne et les lions (1989)
   IP5 (1992)
Bernard, R., *Faubourg Montmartre* (1931)
Besson, L., *The Fifth Element* (*Le Cinquième Elément*) (1997)
Buñuel, L. and Dalí, S., *Un chien andalou* (1929)
Carné, M., *Hôtel du Nord* (1938)
   Le Jour se lève (1939)
   Les Visiteurs du soir (1942)
   Les Enfants du paradis (1945)
Chabrol, C., *Les Bonnes Femmes* (1960)
   Alice ou la dernière fugue (1977)
Chibane, M., *Hexagone* (1994)
   Douce France (1995)
Clair, R., *Entr'acte* (1924)
Clouzot, H.-G., *Les Diaboliques* (1955)
Cocteau, J., *Le Sang d'un poète* (1932)
   La Belle et la bête (1946)
   L'Aigle à deux têtes (1947)
   Les Parents terribles (1948)
   Orphée (1950)
   La Villa Santo-Sospir (1951)
   Le Testament d'Orphée (1960)
Collard, C., *Les Nuits fauves* (1993)
Desplechin, A., *Comment je me suis disputé . . . ma vie sexuelle*
Dridi, K., *Pigalle* (1995)
   Bye Bye (1997)
Duchamp, M., *Anémic cinéma* (1926)
Dugowson, M., *Mina Tannenbaum* (1993)
   Portraits Chinois (1995)

Dulac, G., *La Coquille et le clergyman* (1928)

Dumont, B., *La Vie de Jésus* (1997)

Ferreira Barbosa, L., *Les gens normaux n'ont rien d'exceptionnel* (1994)

Genina, A., *Paris-Béguin* (1931)

Gilou, T., *Raï* (1995)
  La Vérité si je mens (1997)

Godard, J.-L., *Le Mépris* (1963)

Godard, J.-L. and Miéville, A.-M., *France/tour/détour/deux/enfants* (1978) (video)

Guédiguian, R., *Marius et Jeaneette* (1997)

Guibert, H., *La Pudeur ou l'impudeur* (video, first shown on French TV on 20 January 1992)

Jeunet, M. and Caro, J.-P., *La Cité des enfants perdus* (1995)

Kassovitz, M., *Métisse* (1993)

Klapisch, C., *Chacun cherche son chat* (1996)

Leterrier, F., *Les Mauvais Coups* (1961)

L'Herbier, M., *Le Bonheur* (1935)

Lvovsky, N., *Oublie-moi* (1994)
  La vie ne me fait pas peur (1999)

Malle, L., *Vie privée* (1962)
  Ascenseur pour l'échafaud (1957)

Man Ray, *Retour à la raison* (1923)
  Emak Bakia (1926)
  Etoile de mer (1928)

Melville, J.-P., *Bob le flambeur* (1956)
  Deux hommes dans Manhattan (1959)
  Le Doulos (1962)
  Le Deuxième Souffle (1964)
  Le Samouraï (1967)
  Le Cercle rouge (1970)
  Un flic (1971)

Rochant, E., *Un monde sans pitié* (1989)

Rozier, J., *Adieu Philippine* (1960–1962)

Truffaut, F., *Tirez sur le pianiste* (1960)
  Fahrenheit 451 (1966)

Vadim, R., *Barbarella* (1967)

Zilbermann, J.-J., *L'Homme est une femme comme les autres* (1998)

Zonca, E., *La Vie rêvée des anges* (1998)

Selected Bibliography

Selected Secondary and Critical Reading on Directors, Actors and Films

Arletty

Arletty, in collaboration with Souvais, M. (1987), *'Je suis comme je suis . . .'*, Paris: Carrère.

Audé, F. (1992), 'Arletty', *Positif*, 382, pp. 66–71.

Demonpion, D. (1996), *Arletty*, Paris: Flammarion.

Forbes, J. (1997), *Les Enfants du paradis*, London: BFI.

Perrin, M. (1952), *Arletty*, Paris: Calmann-Lévy.

Souvais, M. (1999), *Arletty, de Frédéric Lemaître aux Enfants du paradis*, Paris: Dualpha.

Turk, E.B. (1989), *Child of Paradise*, Cambridge, Mass. and London: Harvard University Press.

Bardot

Bardot, B. (1997), *Initiales BB*, Paris: Grasset.

Rihoit, C. (1986), *Brigitte Bardot, un mythe français*, Paris: Orban.

Beineix

Bassan, R. (1989), 'Trois néobaroques français', *Revue du cinéma*, 449, pp. 44–50.

Beineix, J.-J. (1983), 'Man in the Moon', *Film Comment*, 19, pp. 16–19.

Jameson, F. (1992), '*Diva* and French Socialism', in *Signatures of the Visible*, New York and London: Routledge, pp. 55–62.

Katsahnias, I. (1989), 'Roselyne et les lions', *Cahiers du cinéma*, 419–20.

Parent, D. (1989), *Jean-Jacques Beineix: Version originale*, Paris: Barrault.

Savigneau, J., 'Jean-Jacques Beineix: amoureux d'un récit', *Le Monde*, 2 May 1985.

Besson

Hayward, S. (1997), 'Besson's "Mission Elastoplast": *Le Cinquième Elément*', in P. Powrie (ed.), *French Cinema in the 1990s: Continuity and Difference*, Oxford: OUP, pp. 246–57.

Buñuel

Drummond, P. (1977), 'Textual Space in *Un chien andalou*', *Screen*, 18, pp. 55–118.
Evans, P. W. (1995), *The Films of Luis Buñuel: Subjectivity and Desire*, Oxford: Clarendon Press.

Chabrol

Austin, G. (1999), *Claude Chabrol*, Manchester: MUP.
Chabrol, C. (1976), *Et pourtant je tourne*, Paris: Robert Laffont.
Overbey, D., 'Chabrol: Game of Mirrors', *Sight and Sound*, Spring 1977, pp. 78–81.

Cocteau

Albersmeier, F.-J. (1997), 'Tensions intermédiales et symbolique multimédiale dans *Le Sang d'un poète* de Jean Cocteau', *Oeuvres et Critiques*, 22, pp. 162–9.
Chaperon, D. (1990), *Jean Cocteau: La Chute des angles*, Lille: Presses Universitaires de Lille.
—— (1994) 'Jean Cocteau, un enfer tapissé de plumes', *Revue des Sciences Humaines*, 233, pp. 7–10.
Cocteau, J. (1943), *Le Mythe du Gréco*, Paris: Au Divan.
—— (1956), *Discours d'Oxford*, Paris: Gallimard.
—— (1972), *Cocteau on the Film: Conversations with Jean Cocteau recorded by André Fraigneau*, trans. L. Traill, New York: Dover Publications.
—— (1979), 'Inédit féodal', *Cahiers Jean Cocteau*, 8, pp. 142–4.
—— (1981), 'Notes autour d'une anamorphose: un phénomène de réflexion', *Cahiers Jean Cocteau*, 9, pp. 245–7.
—— (1985), *Two Screen Plays: The Blood of a Poet/The Testament of Orpheus*, trans. C. Martin-Sperry, London and New York: Marion Boyars.
—— (1988), *Du cinématographe*, Paris: Pierre Belfond.
—— (1995), *Jean Cocteau: Romans, Poésies, Oeuvres diverses*, Paris: Livre de poche.

Dittrich, D. (1997), 'Les Chiffres du poète – Les "Trucs" du cinématographe', *Oeuvres et Critiques*, 22, pp. 170–84.

Domarchi, J. and Laugier, J.-L. (1960), 'Entretien avec Jean Cocteau', *Cahiers du cinéma*, 19, pp. 1–20.

Fargier, J.-P. (1992), 'La Marche arrière', *Vertigo*, 9, pp. 101–3.

Foucart, C. (1997), 'Cocteau et l'écriture du corps', *Oeuvres et Critiques*, 22, pp. 185–96.

Freeman, E. (ed.) (1992), *Jean Cocteau, Orphée: The Play and the Film*, London: Bristol Classical Press.

Gercke, D. (1993), 'Ruin, Style and Fetish: The Corpus of Jean Cocteau', *Nottingham French Studies*, 32, pp. 10–18.

Greene, N. (1988), 'Deadly Statues: Eros in the Films of Jean Cocteau', *The French Review*, 61, pp. 890–8.

Milorad (1979), 'Esquisse d'une théorie de la sexualité', *Cahiers Jean Cocteau*, 8, pp. 132–41.

—— (1981), '*Le Sang d'un poète*: Film à la première personne du singulier', *Cahiers Jean Cocteau*, 9, pp. 269–334.

Mourier, M. (1997), 'Quelques aspects de la poétique cinématographique de Cocteau', *Oeuvres et Critiques*, 22, pp. 152–61.

Pillaudin, R. (1960), *Jean Cocteau tourne son dernier film*, Paris: La Table Ronde.

Rolot, C. and Ramirez, F. (1992), 'Le Rôle des trucages dans la "Poésie de Cinéma" de Jean Cocteau ou "les tours d'Orphée"', *Quaderni del Novecento Francese*, 15, pp. 163–75.

Williams, J.S. (forthcoming), *Jean Cocteau*, Manchester: MUP.

Collard

Durham, C.A. (1999), 'Codes of Contagion: Cyril Collard's *Les Nuits Fauves*, *French Forum*, 24, pp. 233–50.

Marshall, B. (2000), 'The national-popular and comparative gay identities: Cyril Collard's *Les Nuits fauves*', in D. Alderson and L. Anderson (eds), *Territories of Desire in Queer Culture*, Manchester: MUP, pp. 84–95.

Rollet, B. and Williams, J.S. (1998), 'Visions of Excess: Filming/Writing the Gay Self in Collard's *Savage Nights*', in O. Heathcote, A. Hughes and J.S. Williams (eds), *Gay Signatures: Gay and Lesbian Theory, Fiction and Film in France, 1945–1995*, Oxford and New York: Berg, pp. 193–208.

Tarr, C. (1999), 'Gender and Sexuality in *Les Nuits fauves*', in P. Powrie (ed.), *French Cinema in the 1990s*, Oxford: OUP, pp. 117–26.

Duchamp

de Duve, T. (ed.) (1991), *The Definitively Unfinished Marcel Duchamp*, Cambridge, Mass. and London: MIT Press.

Judovitz, D. (1996), 'Anemic Vision in Duchamp', in R.E. Kuenzli (ed.), *Dada and Surrealist Film*, Cambridge, Mass. and London: Harvard University Press, pp. 46–57.

Lebel, J.-J. (1959), *Sur Marcel Duchamp*, Paris: Editions Trianon.

Martin, K. (1975), 'Marcel Duchamp's *Anémic cinéma*', *Studio International*, 189, pp. 53–60.

Mussman, T. (1966), 'Anemic Cinema', *Art and Artists*, 1, pp. 48–51.

Dugowson

Toscan du Plantier, D., 'Romane et Elsa', *Figaro Magazine*, 12 March 1994.

Ferreira Barbosa

Ferreira Barbosa, L. (1996), 'J'ai horreur de l'amour', *Cinélibre*, 39, pp. 16–17.

Godard

Aumont, J. (1990), 'The Fall of the Gods: Jean-Luc Godard's *Le Mépris*', in S. Hayward and G. Vincendeau (eds), *French Film: Texts and Contexts*, London and New York: Routledge, pp. 217–29.

Baby, Y., 'Faire les films possibles là où on est' (interview with Godard), *Le Monde*, 25 September 1975.

Bellour, R. and Bandy, M.L. (eds) (1992), *Jean-Luc Godard: Son + Image, 1974–1991*, New York: The Museum of Modern Art.

Brenez, N. (2000), 'Ralenti et accéléré', *Cahiers du cinéma*, Special Issue ('*Le Siècle du cinéma*'), pp. 94–5.

Bruneau, P., 'Un drôle de "tour" avec Godard', *Minute*, 2–8 April 1980.

Godard, J.-L. (1980), *Introduction à une véritable histoire du cinéma*, Paris, Albatros.

—— '«France Tour Détour Deux Enfants»: Déclaration à l'intention des héritiers', *Caméra Stylo*, September 1983, pp. 64–5.

—— (1985), *Jean-Luc Godard par Jean-Luc Godard*, ed. by A. Bergala, Paris: Cahiers du Cinéma/Editions de l'Etoile.

—— (1998), *Jean-Luc Godard par Jean-Luc Godard*, Vol. 2, 1984–1998, ed. by Alain Bergala, Paris: Cahiers du Cinéma.

Jouffa, F., 'Jean-Luc Godard: «La pellicule, c'est complètement chiant!»' (interview with Godard), *Télé-Ciné-Vidéo*, December 1980, pp. 34–5.

Loshitzky, J. (1995), *The Radical Faces of Godard and Bertolucci*, Detroit: Wayne State University Press.

MacCabe, C. (1980), *Godard: Images, Sounds, Politics*, London: BFI/Macmillan.

—— (1985), 'Betaville', *American Film*, 10, pp. 61–3.

Marie, M. (1990), *Le Mépris*, Paris: Nathan.

Mulvey, L. (1989, with C. MacCabe), 'Images of Women, Images of Sexuality: Some Films by J.-L. Godard', in *Visual and Other Pleasures*, Basingstoke and London: Macmillan, pp. 49–62.

Penley, C. (1982), 'Pornography, Eroticism', *Camera Obscura*, 8–9–10, pp. 13–18.

—— (1982). 'Les Enfants de la Patrie', *Camera Obscura*, 8–9–10, pp. 33–58.

Reynaud, B. (1986), "Impure Cinema': Adaption and Quotation at the 1985 New York Film Festival', *Afterimage*, 13, pp. 9–11.

Silverman, K. and Farocki, H. (1998), *Speaking about Godard*, New York: New York University Press.

Stam, R. (1992), *Reflexivity in Film and Literature: From Don Quixote to Jean-Luc Godard*, New York: Columbia University Press.

Temple, M. and Williams, J.S. (eds) (2000), *The Cinema Alone: Essays on the Work of Jean-Luc Godard 1985–2000*, Amsterdam: Amsterdam University Press.

Vimenet, P. (1991), *Le Mépris*, Paris: Hatier.

Guibert

Boulé, J.-P. (1995), 'Hervé Guibert: Autobiographical Film-Writing Pushed to its Limits?', in T. Keefe and E. Smythe (eds), *Autobiography and the Existential Self*, Liverpool: Liverpool University Press, pp. 169–81.

—— (ed.) (1995), 'Hervé Guibert Special Issue', *Nottingham French Studies*, 34.

—— (1999), *Hervé Guibert: Voices of The Self*, Liverpool: Liverpool University Press.

Buot, F. (1999), *Hervé Guibert: Le Jeune Homme et la mort*, Paris: Grasset.

Chambers, R. (1997), 'The Suicide Experiment: Hervé Guibert's AIDS Video, *La Pudeur ou l'impudeur*', *L'Esprit Créateur*, XXXVII, pp. 72–82.

—— (1998), 'Confronting It', in *Facing It: AIDS Diaries and the Death of the Author*, Ann Arbor: University of Michigan Press, pp. 35–60.

Hughes, A. (1999), *Heterographies: Sexual Difference in French Autobiography*, Oxford and New York: Berg.

Pratt, M. (1998), 'A Walk along the side of the Motorway: AIDS and the Spectacular Body of Hervé Guibert', in O. Heathcote, A. Hughes and J.S. Williams (eds),

*Gay Signatures: Gay and Lesbian Theory, Fiction and Film in France, 1945–
1995*, Oxford and New York: Berg, pp. 151–72.

Schehr, L. (1996), 'Body/Antibody', *Studies in 20th Century Literature*, 20,
pp. 405–30.

Smith, P.J., 'Blue and the Outer Limits', *Sight and Sound*, October 1993, pp.
18–19.

Lvovsky

Audé, F., 'Entretien avec Noémie Lvovsky: Une belle personne', *Positif*, February
1995, pp. 39–42.

Bouquet, S. (1995), 'Attache-moi', *Cahiers du cinéma*, 448, pp. 24–5.

Jousse, T. and Strauss, F. (1995), 'Entretien avec Noémie Lvovsky', *Cahiers du
cinéma*, 448, pp. 20–3.

Man Ray

Bouhours, J.-M. and de Haas, P. (eds) (1997), *Man Ray directeur du mauvais
movies*, Paris: Editions du Centre Pompidou.

Hedges, I. (1996), 'Constellated Visions: Robert Desnos's and Man Ray's *Etoile
de mer*', in R.E. Kuenzli (ed.), *Dada and Surrealist Film*, Cambridge, Mass.
and London: Harvard University Press, pp. 99–109.

Man Ray (1963), *Self-Portrait*, Boston: Little Brown.

Melville

Bantcheva, D. (1996), *Jean-Pierre Melville: de l'oeuvre à l'homme*, Troyes:
Librairie Bleue.

Bruzzi, S. (1997), *Undressing Cinema: Clothing and Identity in the Movies*, London
and New York: Routledge.

McArthur, C. (2000), 'Mise-en-scène degree zero: Jean-Pierre Melville's *Le
Samouraï*', in S. Hayward and G. Vincendeau (eds), *French Film: Texts and
Contexts*, London and New York: Routledge, pp. 189–201.

Neale, S. (1983), 'Masculinity as Spectacle', *Screen*, 24, pp. 2–16.

Nogueira, R. (1971), *Melville*, London: Secker and Warburg.

Smith, M. (1995), *Engaging Characters: Fiction, Emotion and the Cinema*, Oxford:
Clarendon Press.

Zimmer, J. and Béchade, C. de (1983), *Jean-Pierre Melville*, Paris: Edilig.

Miéville

Anon., 'Entretien avec Anne-Marie Miéville', press book for *Mon cher sujet* (Lasa Films, 1988).

Signoret

Durant, P. (1988), *Simone Signoret: Une vie*, Lausanne: Editions Favre.
Hayward, S. (1995), 'Simone Signoret 1921–1985: The Star as Sign – the Sign as Scar', in D. Knight and J. Still (eds), *Women and Representation*, Nottingham University of Nottingham Press (WIF occasional papers): pp. 57–74.
Josselin, J.-P. (1995), *Simone: Deux ou trois choses que je sais d'elle*, Paris: Grasset.

Zonca

Fuller, D., 'Tenderness in the Strangest Places', *Interview*, April 1999, p. 76.
Smith, G., '*La Vie rêvée des anges*', *Sight and Sound*, November 1998, p. 64.

General and Further Reading

Abel, R. (1984), *French Cinema: The First Wave 1915–1929*, Princeton: Princeton University Press.
—— (1994), *The Cine Goes to Town: French Cinema 1896–1914*, Berkeley and London: University of California Press.
Abelove, H., Barale, M.A. and Halperin, D. (eds) (1993), *The Lesbian and Gay Studies Reader*, New York and London: Routledge.
Adamowicz, E. (1998), *Surrealist Collage in Text and Image: Dissecting the Exquisite Corpse*, Cambridge: CUP.
Andrew, D. (1995), *Mists of Regret: Culture and Sensibility in Classic French Film*, Princeton: Princeton University Press.
Ariès, P. (1979), *Centuries of Childhood*, Harmondsworth: Peregrine Books.
Astruc, A. (1992), *Du stylo à la caméra et de la caméra au stylo: Ecrits 1942–1984*, Paris: L'Archipel.
Audé, F. (1981), *Ciné-modèles, cinéma d'elles: Situation des femmes dans le cinéma français 1956–1979*, Lausanne: Editions L'Age d'homme.
Augé, M. (1992), *Non-lieux: Introduction à une anthropologie de la surmodernité*, Paris: Seuil.
Aumont, J. (1989), *L'Oeil Interminable: Cinéma et Peinture*, Paris: Séguier.
—— (ed.) (2000), *La différence dés séxes, est-elle visible? Les hommes et les femmes du cinéma*, Paris: Cinémathèque française.

Austin, G. (1996), *Contemporary French Cinema: An Introduction*, Manchester: MUP.

—— (1996), 'Vampirism, Gender Wars and the "Final Girl": French Fantasy Film in the Early Seventies', *French Cultural Studies*, 7, pp. 321–31.

Austin, J.L., *How to Do Things with Words*, Oxford and New York: OUP, 1975.

Baecque, A. de (1998), *La Nouvelle Vague: Portrait d'une jeunesse*, Paris: Flammarion.

Baecque, A. de and Jousse, T. (1996), *Le Retour du cinéma*, Paris: Hachette.

Baudry, J.-L. (1974), 'The Ideological Effects of the Basic Cinematic Apparatus', *Film Quarterly*, 27, pp. 39–47.

Beauvoir, S. de (1949), *Le Deuxième Sexe*, Paris: Gallimard.

—— (1972), *The Second Sex*, trans. H. Parshley, Harmondsworth: Penguin.

Bell, D. and Valentine, G. (1995), 'The Sexed Self: Strategies of Performance, Sites of Resistance', in S. Pile and N. Thrift (eds), *Mapping the Subject: Geographies of Cultural Transformation*, London and New York: Routledge, pp. 143–57.

Bellmer, H. (1957), *Petite Anatomie de l'inconscient physique ou l'anatomie de l'image*, Paris: Eric Losfeld.

Benjamin, W. (1973), *Illuminations*, London: Fontana.

Berressem, H. (1996), 'Dali and Lacan: Painting the Imaginary Landscapes', in W. Apollon and R. Feldstein (eds), *Lacan, Politics, Aesthetics*, Albany: State University of New York Press, pp. 263–93.

Best, V. and Collier, P. (eds) (1999), *Powerful Bodies: Performance in French Cultural Studies*, Bern: Peter Lang.

Betsky, A. (1997), *Queer Space: Architecture and Same-Sex Desire*, New York: Morrow.

Bordo, S. (1993), *Unbearable Weight: Feminism, Western Culture, and the Body*, Berkeley and London: University of California Press.

Breton, A. (1951), 'Comme dans un bois', *L'Age du cinéma*, 4–5, pp. 26–30.

Burch, N. and Sellier, G. (1996), *La Drôle de guerre des sexes du cinéma français: 1930–1956*, Paris: Nathan.

Butler, J. (1990), *Gender Trouble: Feminism and the Subversion of Identity*, New York and London: Routledge.

—— (1993), *Bodies That Matter: On the Discursive Limits of 'Sex'*, New York and London: Routledge.

Cairns, L. (1998), '*Gazon Maudit*: French National and Sexual Identities', *French Cultural Studies*, 9, pp. 225–37.

Calabrese, O. (1992), *The Neo-Baroque: A Sign of the Times*, Princeton: Princeton University Press.

Calvet, L.-J. (1981), *Chanson et société*, Paris: Payot.

Caws, M.A., Kuenzli, R.E. and Raaberg, G. (eds) (1991), *Surrealism and Women*, Cambridge, Mass. and London: MIT Press.

Chauveau, P. and Sallée, A. (1985), *Music-hall et café-concert*, Paris: Bordas.

Clarke, D. B. (ed.) (1997), *The Cinematic City*, London and New York: Routledge.

Cohan, S. and Hark, I. (eds) (1993), *Screening the Male: Exploring Masculinities in Hollywood Cinema*, London and New York: Routledge.

Colomina, B. (ed.) (1992), *Sexuality and Space*, New York: Princeton Architectural Press.

Cook, P. (ed.) (1986), *The Cinema Book*, London: BFI.

Coquillat, M. (1982), *La Poétique du mâle*, Paris: Gallimard.

Corbin, A. (1990), *Women for Hire: Prostitution and Sexuality in France after 1850*, trans. A. Sheridan, Cambridge, Mass. and London: Harvard University Press.

Cowie, E. (1984), 'Fantasia', *m/f*, 9, pp. 76–105.

Creed, B. (1993), *The Monstrous-Feminine: Film, Feminism and Psychoanalysis*, London and New York: Routledge.

Crimp, D. (1992), 'Portraits of People with AIDS', in L. Grossberg, C. Nelson and P. Treichler (eds), *Cultural Studies*, New York and London: Routledge, pp. 117–33.

—— (ed.) (1996), *AIDS: Cultural Analysis, Cultural Activism*, Cambridge, Mass. and London: MIT Press.

Deleuze, G. (1967), *Présentation de Sacher-Masoch*, Paris: Minuit.

—— (1985), *Cinéma 2: L'Image-Temps*, Paris: Minuit.

—— (1991), *Masochism*, trans. J. McNeill, New York: Zone Books.

Doane, M.A., (1987), *The Desire to Desire: The Woman's Film of the 1940s*, Bloomington and Indianapolis: Indiana University Press.

—— (1991), *Femmes Fatales: Feminism, Film Theory, Psychoanalysis*, London and New York: Routledge.

Doane, M.A., Mellencamp, P. and Williams, L. (eds) (1984), *Re-Vision: Essays in Feminist Film Criticism*, Los Angeles: University Publications of America.

Donald, J. (ed.) (1989), *Fantasy and the Cinema*, London: BFI.

Douchet, J. (1998), *Nouvelle Vague*, Paris: Cinémathèque française/Hazan.

Dubois, P. (1990), 'L'Image à la vitesse de la pensée', *Cahiers du cinéma* (November supplement), 437, pp. 76–7.

Duchen, C. (1986), *Feminism in France: From May 68 to Mitterrand*, London: Routledge and Kegan Paul.

—— (1994), *Women's Rights and Women's Lives in France, 1944–1968*, London and New York: Routledge.

Dyer, R. (ed.) (1977), *Gender and Film*, London: BFI.

—— (1979), *Stars*, London: BFI.

—— (1986), *Heavenly Bodies: Film Stars and Society*, New York: St. Martin's Press.

—— (1990), *Now You See It: Studies on Lesbian and Gay Film*, London: Routledge.

Dyer, R. and Vincendeau, G. (eds) (1992), *Popular European Cinema*, London and New York: Routledge.

Edelman, L. (1994), *Homographesis: Essays in Gay Literary and Cultural Theory*, New York and London: Routledge.

Evans, R. (ed.) (1998), *Simone de Beauvoir's The Second Sex*, Manchester: MUP.

Ezra, E. (2000), *Georges Méliès: The Birth of the Auteur*, Manchester: MUP.

Fallaize, E. (ed.) (1998), *Simone de Beauvoir: A Critical Reader*, London and New York: Routledge.

Fischer, L. (1979), 'The Lady Vanishes: Women, Magic, and the Movies', *Film Quarterly*, 33, pp. 30–40.

—— (1996), *Cinematernity: Film, Motherhood, Genre*, Princeton: Princeton University Press.

Flitterman-Lewis, S. (1990), *To Desire Differently: Feminism and the French Cinema*, Urbana and Chicago: University of Illinois Press.

Forbes, J. (1992), *The Cinema in France After The New Wave*, London: Macmillan.

Fotiade, R. (1995), 'The Untamed Eye: Surrealism and Film Theory', *Screen*, 36, pp. 394–407.

Foucault, M. (1975), *Surveiller et punir: Naissance de la prison*, Paris: Gallimard.

—— (1976), *Histoire de la Sexualité I: La Volonté de savoir*, Paris: Gallimard.

—— (1979), *Discipline and Punish: The Birth of the Prison*, trans. A. Sheridan, Harmondsworth: Peregrine.

—— (1990), *The History of Sexuality Volume I*, trans. R. Hurley, Harmondsworth: Penguin.

Fraisse, P. (1999), 'Entre science et fiction: Un certain cinéma fantastique', *Positif*, 466, pp. 71–4.

Fuss, D. (ed.) (1991), *Inside/Out: Lesbian Theories, Gay Theories*, New York and London: Routledge.

—— (1995), *Identification Papers*, New York and London: Routledge.

Galland, O. and Lemel, Y. (eds) (1998), *La Nouvelle Société française: 30 années de mutation*, Paris: Armand Colin.

Gallop, J. (1988), *Thinking Through The Body*, New York: Columbia University Press.

Garbaz, F. (1997), 'Le Renouveau social du cinéma français', *Positif*, 442, pp. 74–5.

Gatens, M. (1996), *Imaginary Bodies: Ethics, Power and Corporeality*, London and New York: Routledge.

Gever, M., Greyson. J and Parmar, P. (eds) (1993), *Queer Looks: Perspectives on Gay and Lesbian Film and Video*, London and New York: Routledge.

Grant, C. (2001) 'Secret Agents: Feminist Theories of Film Authorship', *Feminist Theory*, 2, pp. 113–30.

Grosz, E. (1994), *Volatile Bodies: Toward a Corporeal Feminism*, Bloomington and Indianapolis: Indiana University Press.

—— (1995), *Space, Time, and Perversion*, New York and London: Routledge.

Grover, J.Z. (1999), 'OI: Opportunistic Identification, Open Identification in PWA Portraiture', in C. Squiers (ed.), *Overexposed: Essays on Contemporary Photography*, New York: New Press, pp. 105–22.

Hanson, E. (ed.) (1999), *Out Takes: Essays on Queer Theory and Film*, Durham and London: Duke University Press.

Hardy, P. (1998), *The Companion to Crime*, London: Cassell.

Hayward, S. (1993), *French National Cinema*, London and New York: Routledge.

Hayward, S. and Vincendeau, G. (eds) (1990), *French Film: Texts and Contexts*, London and New York: Routledge. 2nd edn 2000.

Heath, S. (1979), *Questions of Cinema*, London: Macmillan.

Heathcote, O., Hughes, A. and Williams, J.S. (eds) (1998), *Gay Signatures: Gay and Lesbian Theory, Fiction and Film in France, 1945–1995*, Oxford and New York: Berg.

Hill, J. and Gibson, P.C. (eds) (1998), *Oxford Guide to Film Studies*, Oxford: OUP.

Hollinger, K. (1998), *In the Company of Women: Contemporary Female Friendship Films*, Minneapolis: University of Minnesota Press.

Hughes, A. and Witz, A. (1997), 'Feminism and the Matter of Bodies: From de Beauvoir to Butler', *Body and Society*, 3, pp. 47–60.

Huyssen, A. (1986), *After the Great Divide: Modernism, Mass Culture and Postmodernism*, Bloomington and Indianapolis: Indiana University Press.

Illich, I. (1971), *Deschooling Society*, London: Calder and Boyars.

Irigaray, L. (1977), *Ce Sexe qui n'en est pas un*, Paris: Minuit.

—— (1985), *This Sex Which Is Not One*, trans. C. Porter, Ithaca: Cornell University Press.

Jackson, S. and Scott, S. (eds) (1996), *Feminism and Sexuality: A Reader*, Edinburgh: Edinburgh University Press.

Jancovich, M. (1996), *Rational Fears: American Horror in the 1950s*, Manchester: MUP.

Jeancolas, J.-P. (1997), 'Une bobine d'avance: du cinéma et de la politique en février 1997', *Positif*, 434, pp. 56–8.

Johnson, B. (1998), *The Feminist Difference: Literature, Psychoanalysis, Race, and Gender*, Cambridge, Mass. and London: Harvard University Press.

Kaplan, E.A. (ed.) (1980), *Women in Film Noir*, London: BFI.

—— (1983), *Women and Film: Both Sides of the Camera*, London and New York: Routledge.

—— (ed.) (1990), *Psychoanalysis and the Cinema*, London and New York: Routledge.

Kirkham, P. and Thumim, J. (eds) (1995), *Me Jane: Masculinity, Movies and Women*, London: Lawrence & Wishart.

Klein, J.-C. (1991), *La Chanson à l'affiche: Histoire de la chanson française du café-concert à nos jours*, Paris: Du May.

Krauss, R. and Livingston, J. (eds) (1986), *L'Amour Fou: Photography and Surrealism*, London: Arts Council.

Kristeva, J. (1983), *Histoires d'amour*, Paris: Denoël.

—— (1987), *Tales of Love*, New York: Columbia University Press.

Kuenzli, R.E. (ed.) (1996), *Dada and Surrealist Film*, Cambridge, Mass. and London: MIT Press.

Lacan, J. (1953), 'Some Reflections on the Ego', *International Journal of Psychoanalysis*, 24, pp. 11–17.

—— (1973), *Le Séminaire. Livre XI. Les quatre concepts fondamentaux de la psychanalyse*, Paris: Seuil.

—— (1986), *Le Séminaire. Livre VII. L'éthique de la psychanalyse*, Paris: Seuil.

—— (1992), *The Ethics of Psychoanalysis 1959–1960: The Seminar of Jacques Lacan. Book VII*, trans. D. Porter, London: Tavistock/Routledge.

—— (1994), *The Four Fundamental Concepts of Psychoanalysis*, trans. A. Sheridan, Harmondsworth: Penguin.

Lagny, M., Ropars, M.-C. and Sorlin, P. (1986), *Générique des années 30*, Paris: Presses Universitaires de Vincennes.

Laplanche, J. (1970), *Vie et mort en psychanalyse*, Paris: Flammarion.

—— (1976), *Life and Death in Psychoanalysis*, trans. J. Mehlman, Baltimore: Johns Hopkins University Press.

Lapsley, R. and Westlake, M. (1988), *Film Theory: An Introduction*, Manchester: MUP.

Lauretis, T. de (1984), *Alice Doesn't: Feminism, Semiotics, Cinema*, Bloomington and Indianapolis: Indiana University Press.

—— (1988), 'Aesthetic and Feminist Theory: Rethinking Women's Cinema', in D. Pribran (ed.), *Female Spectators: Looking at Film and Television*, London: Verso, pp. 174–95.

—— (1994), *The Practice of Love: Lesbian Sexuality and Perverse Desire*, Bloomington and Indianapolis: Indiana University Press.

Lauretis, T. de and Heath, S. (eds) (1980), *The Cinematic Apparatus*, New York: St Martin's Press.

Marey, E.-J. (1873), *La Machine animale: locomotion terrestre et aérienne*, Paris: Germer Baillière.

—— (1886), *Etude sur la locomotion animale par la chrono-photographie*, Paris: Association Française pour l'avancement des Sciences.

—— (1899), *La Chronophotographie*, Paris: Gauthier-Villars.

—— (1994 [1894]), *Le Mouvement*, Nîmes: Jacqueline Chambon.

Marie, M. (1997), *La Nouvelle Vague: Une école artistique*, Paris: Nathan.

Martel, F. (1996), *Le Rose et le noir: Les Homosexuels en France depuis 1968*, Paris: Seuil.

Mayne, J. (1990), *Women at the Keyhole: Feminism and Women's Cinema*, Bloomington and Indianapolis: Indiana University Press.

—— (1993), *Cinema and Spectatorship*, London: Routledge.

Mazdon, L. (ed.) (2001), *France on Film: Reflections on Popular French Cinema*, London: Wallflower.

McArthur, C. (1972), *Underworld USA*, London: Secker and Warburg.

McNay, L. (1992), *Foucault and Feminism*, Boston: Northeastern University Press.

Metz, C. (1974), *Language and Cinema*, trans. D. Jean, The Hague: Mouton.

—— (1982), *The Imaginary Signifier: Psychoanalysis and Cinema*, trans. B. Brewster, C. Britton, A. Guzzetti and A. Williams, Bloomington and Indianapolis: Indiana University Press.

Meyer, R. (1994), 'Warhol's Clones', *The Yale Journal of Criticism*, 7, pp. 79–109.

Mirzoeff, N. (ed.) (1998), *The Visual Culture Reader*, New York and London: Routledge.

Modleski, T. (1988), *The Women Who Knew Too Much: Hitchcock and Feminist Theory*, New York: Methuen.

Moi, T. (1994), *Simone de Beauvoir: The Making of an Intellectual Woman*, Oxford and Cambridge, Mass.: Blackwell.

Morin, E. (1972), *Les Stars*, Paris: Seuil.

Mulvey, L. (1975), 'Visual Pleasure and Narrative Cinema', *Screen*, 16, pp. 6–18.

—— (1989), *Visual and Other Pleasures*, Basingstoke and London: Macmillan (also 1989, Bloomington and Indianapolis: Indiana University Press).

Naumann, F. (1994), *New York Dada 1915–23*, New York: Harry N. Abrams.

O'Shaughnessy, M. (2000), *Jean Renoir*, Manchester: MUP.

Ory, P. (1985), *L'Anarchisme de droite*, Paris: Grasset.

Passek, J.-L., (ed.) (1987), *Dictionnaire du cinéma français*, Paris: Larousse.

Penley, C. (ed.) (1988), *Feminism and Film Theory*, London: BFI.

—— (1989), *The Future of an Illusion: Film, Feminism, and Psychoanalysis*, Minneapolis: Minnesota University Press.

Petersen. A. (1998), *Unmasking the Masculine: 'Men' and 'Identity' in a Sceptical Age*, London, Thousand Oaks and New Delhi: Sage.

Philippe, C., Varro, G. and Neyrand, G. (eds) (1998), *Liberté, égalité, mixité . . . congugales: Une sociologie du couple mixte*, Paris: Anthropos.

Pollock, G. (1988), *Vision and Difference*, London and New York: Routledge.

Powrie, P. (1997), *French Cinema in the 1980s: Nostalgia and the Crisis of Masculinity*, Oxford: Clarendon Press.

—— (ed.) (1999), *French Cinema in the 1990s: Continuity and Difference*, Oxford: OUP.

Prédal, R. (1996), *50 ans de cinéma français (1945–1995)*, Paris: Nathan.

Rearick, C. (1985), *Pleasures of the Belle Epoque: Entertainment and Festivity in Turn-of-the-Century France*, New Haven and London: Yale University Press.

—— (1997), *The French in Love and War: Popular Culture in the Era of the World Wars*, New Haven and London: Yale University Press.

Roberts, M.L. (1994), *Civilization Without Sexes: Reconstructing Gender in Postwar France 1917–1927*, Chicago and London: University of Chicago Press.

Rodowick, D.N. (1991), *The Difficulty of Difference: Psychoanalysis, Sexual Difference, and Film Theory*, London and New York: Routledge.

Ronsanvallon, P. (ed.) (1998), *France: Les Révolutions invisibles*, Paris: Calmann-Lévy.

Rose, G. (1993), *Feminism and Geography: The Limits of Geographical Knowledge*, Oxford: Polity Press.

Ross, K. (1995), *Fast Cars, Clean Bodies: Decolonization and the Reordering of French Culture*, Cambridge, Mass. and London: MIT Press.

Russo, V. (1987), *The Celluloid Closet: Homosexuality in the Movies*, New York: Harper and Rowe.

Schefer, J.L. (1995), *The Enigmatic Body: Essays on the Arts*, trans. P. Smith, Cambridge: CUP.

Sedgwick, E.K. (1990), *Epistemology of the Closet*, Berkeley and Los Angeles: University of California Press.

—— (1993), *Tendencies*, Durham and London: Duke University Press.

Shaviro, S. (1993), *The Cinematic Body*, Minneapolis: University of Minnesota Press.

Shelton, A. (ed.) (1995), *Fetishism: Visualising Power and Desire*, London: South Bank Centre.

Showalter, E. (ed.) (1989), *Speaking of Gender*, New York and London: Routledge.

Siclier, J. (1957), *La Femme dans le cinéma français*, Paris: Cerf.

Silverman, K. (1988) *The Acoustic Mirror*, Bloomington and Indianapolis: Indiana University Press.

—— (1992), *Male Subjectivity at the Margins*, London and New York: Routledge.

—— (1996), *The Threshold of the Visible World*, London and New York: Routledge.

Soja, E. (1987), 'The Postmodernisation of Geography: a Review', *Annals of the Association of American Geographers*, 72, pp. 289–94.

Stacey, J. (1987), 'Desperately Seeking Difference', *Screen*, 28, pp. 48–61.

—— (1994), *Stargazing: Hollywood Cinema and Female Spectatorship*, London and New York: Routledge.

Stich, S. (1991), *Anxious Visions: Surrealist Art*, New York: Abbeville Press.

Studlar, G. (1988), *In The Realm of Pleasure: Von Sternberg, Dietrich, and the Masochistic Aesthetic*, Urbana: University of Illinois Press.

Suleiman, S.R. (ed.) (1986), *The Female Body in Western Culture: Contemporary Perspectives*, Cambridge, Mass. and London: Harvard University Press.

—— (1990), *Subversive Intent: Gender, Politics and the Avant-garde*, Cambridge, Mass. and London: Harvard University Press.

Tarr, C. (1998), '*L'Eternel retour*: Reflection of the Occupation's Crisis in French Masculinity?', *Sub-stance*, 87, pp. 55–72.

Thompkins, J. (1992), *West of Everything: The Inner Life of Westerns*, New York and Oxford: OUP.

Todorov, T. (1975), *The Fantastic: A Structural Approach to a Literary Genre*, trans. R. Howard, Ithaca: Cornell University Press.

Trémois, C.-M. (1997), *Les Enfants de la liberté*, Paris: Seuil.

Vertov, D. (1984), *Kino-Eye: The Writings of Dziga Vertov*, trans. K. O'Brien, London: Pluto.

Vincendeau, G. (1987), 'Women's Cinema: Film Theory and Feminism in France', *Screen*, 28, pp. 4–18.

—— (1988), '"Daddy's Girls" (Oedipal Narratives in 1930s French Films)', *Iris*, 8, pp. 70–81.

—— (1989), 'Melodramatic Realism: On some French Women's Films in the 1930s', *Screen*, 30, pp. 51–65.

—— (1992), 'From the Bal Populaire to the Casino: Class and Leisure in French Films of the 1930s', *Nottingham French Studies*, 31, pp. 52–70.

—— (ed.) (1996), *The Companion to French Cinema*, London: Cassell and BFI.

—— (2000), *Stars and Stardom in French Cinema*, London and New York: Continuum.

Warshow, R. (1970), *The Immediate Experience*, New York: Atheneum Books.

Weiss, A. (1992), *Vampires and Violets: Lesbians in the Cinema*, London: Cape.

Willener, A., Milliard, G. and Ganty, A. (1976), *Videology and Utopia: Explorations in a New Medium*, trans. D. Burfield, London: Routledge & Kegan Paul.

Williams, J.S. (ed.) (2000), *Revisioning Duras: Film, Race, Sex*, Liverpool: Liverpool University Press.

Williams, L. (1981), *Figures of Desire: A Theory and Analysis of Surrealist Film*, Urbana: University of Illinois Press.

—— (1981), 'Film Body: An Implantation of Perversions', *Ciné-Tracts*, 12, pp. 19–35.

—— (1991) 'Film Bodies: Gender, Genre, and Excess', *Film Quarterly*, 44, pp. 2–13.

—— (ed.) (1994), *Viewing Positions: Ways of Seeing Film*, New Brunswick: Rutgers University Press.

Williams, R. (1974), *Television: Technology and Cultural Form*, London: Fontana.

Wilson, E. (1999), *French Cinema Since 1950: Personal Histories*, London: Duckworth.

Yoshimoto, M. (2000), *Kurosawa*, Durham and London: Duke University Press.

Zimmer, J. (ed.) (1982), *Cinéma Erotique*, Paris: Edilig.

Index

A bout de souffle 128, 187
Adèle Frelon est-elle là? 251n12
Ades, Dawn 33n48
Adieu Philippine 130–1
Adorno, Theodor 29
Against the Wind 111
Age des possibles, L' 259
Aigle à deux têtes, L' 36, 79, 82
Aîné des Ferchaux, L' 139
Akerman, Chantal 243
Alice ou la dernière fugue 160–1, 163, 164–5
All about Eve 256
Allégret, Yves 114
Alphaville 151, 184
Amants, Les 108
Amants du Pont-Neuf, Les 8, 252n27
Anderson, Bibi 116
André, Marcel 78
Andrew, Dudley 57
Android 165
Anémic cinéma 20, 21, 28
Anglade, Jean-Hugues 196
Annabella 35, 67–8, 71
Année dernière à Marienbad, L' 127
A nous la liberté 183
Anthologie du plaisir (History of the blue movie) 180
Anticipation 184
Après la réconciliation 176
Arletty 10, 36, 63–76 *passim*, 108–9, 122n8
Armée des ombres, L' 140
Artaud, Antonin 20, 30n4
Ascenseur pour l'échafaud 108, 128
Asphalt Jungle 146–7
Assayas, Olivier 7, 228, 235
Astruc, Alexandre 127
Atalante, L' 242
Audé, Françoise 6
Audiard, Jacques 7
Augé, Marc 248–9

Aumont, Jean-Pierre 67–8
Aurenche, Jean 67
Austin, J.L. 64
Aznavour, Charles 128

Baie des Anges, La 128
Baker, Josephine 36–7, 44–51, 58, 60n22
Balasko, Josiane 8, 258
Balin, Mireille 35
Ballet mécanique 20, 21, 28
Bantcheva, Denitza 140–1, 147
Barassat, Philippe 7
Barbarella 12, 157, 159–60, 162, 163–4, 166
Bardot, Brigitte 109, 113, 120, 122n19, 131–5, 137n9, 232
Barencey, Odette 38, 40–4, 47, 57, 58
Barendt, Rachel 53
Barrault, Jean-Louis 71–4
Barthes, Roland 149, 151
Bataille, Georges, 24
Batcheff, Pierre 27
Baume, Georges 109
Baur, Harry 35
Baye, Nathalie 173
Bazin, André 148
Beau Travail 9
Beauvoir, Simone de 1–4, 15n11, 66
Beauvois, Xavier 7
Béchade, Chantal de 140
Before Sunrise 257
Beineix, Jean-Jacques 12–13, 195–207 *passim*
Bell, David 218
Belle Equipe, La 35, 69
Belle et la bête, La 77–9 *passim*, 81, 82, 88, 95
Benjamin, Walter 23, 178
Bergala, Alain 189n9
Berger, Nicole 128
Bergman, Ingmar 115–6
Bernard, Armand 35
Bernhardt, Sarah 80

Bernstein, Henry 55
Berressem, Hanjo 199–200
Berry, Jules 35, 68–9, 70–1
Bersani, Leo 85
—— and Ulysse Dutoit 105n51
Besson, Luc 9, 12, 195–6, 197, 160
Best, Victoria 64
Betsky, Aaron 92–3
Bettelheim, Bruno 158
Biches, Les 166
Big Heat, The 149
Blade Runner *165*
Blier, Bernard 68
Bob le flambeur 139, 141, 142, 145, 150
Bohringer, Romane 259, 260, 263
Boléro 122n8
Bonham-Carter, Helena 259
Bonheur, Le 36, 38, 44, 55–58
Bonnes Femmes, Les 129–30
Borden, Lizzie 243
Botticelli, Sandro 264
Bouchez, Elodie 263
Boulé, Jean-Pierre 212, 213, 224n52
Bourvil 154
Boyer, Charles 44, 55–7
Brasseur, Pierre 71–4
Bray, Yvonne de 82
Breaking the Waves 265
Brecht, Bertold 134
Breillat, Catherine 7
Brenez, Nicole 171
Bresson, Robert 115
Breton, André 20, 23–5, 29, 242
Breugnot, Pascale 212
Brooks, Richard 171
Bruni-Tedeschi, Valeria 244
Bruzzi, Stella 140, 150
Brynner, Yul 96
Buffet, Eugénie 45
Buisine, Alain, 223n43
Buñuel, Luis 10, 20
Burch, Noël and Geneviève Sellier, 8, 230
Butler, Judith 2–4, 15n11, 64–5, 67, 256–7
Bye Bye 228, 231, 232, 234

Cairns, Lucille 8, 18n47
Caravaggio (Michelangelo Merisi) 105n51
Carax, Leos 8, 196

Carné, Marcel 65, 67, 70–1, 72
Carol, Martine 108–9, 113
Casarès, Maria 72
Casque d'Or 113, 139, 140
Castagno, Andrea del 83
Cawelti, John, 22
Caws, Mary Ann 32n33, 32n34
Céline et Julie vont en bateau 257
Celluloid Closet, The 256
Cercle rouge, Le 11, 140, 142–4, 145–51
    passim
Chabrol, Claude 11, 129–30, 160–1, 168n23,
    258
Chacun cherche son chat 229–30 *passim*,
    235–6, 243, 258,
Chambers, Ross 216, 225–6n67
Chancel, Jacques 107
Chant d'amour, Un 7, 24, 28
Chaperon, Danielle 77
Chaplin, Charles 134
Charef, Mehdi 7
Chéreau, Patrice 7
Cheung, Maggie 230, 258
Chibane, Malik 7, 228, 230
Chien andalou, Un 20, 21, 22, 23, 26–28
    passim
Christie, Julie 159
Chronique d'un été 175
Cité des enfants perdus 162–4 *passim*, 166,
    168–9n30, 169n36
Cixous, Hélène, 4
Clair, René 10, 19
Clavius, Laurence 61n26
Cléo de 5 à 7 136
Clift, Montgomery 63
Clouzot, Henri-Georges 118
Clouzot, Vera 118–9
Clubbed to Death 243, 251–2n13
Cocteau, Jean 7, 8, 10–11, 77–106 *passim*
Coeur de Lilas 51
Colette 36
Collard, Cyril 7, 227, 235
Collier, Peter 64
Coquillat, Michelle 126
Coquille et le clergyman, La 20, 21, 23, 26
Comment ça va 174
Comment je me suis disputé . . . ma vie sexuelle
    228–231 *passim*

Condamné à mort s'est échappé, Un 114
Conte d'automne 258
Coup de foudre 258
Cousins, Les 128
Coward, Noël 137n7
Cowie, Elizabeth 5
Creed, Barbara 5, 158, 161
Crime de Monsieur Lange, Le 51
Cronenberg, David 85
Cuny, Alain 70–1

Dadoun, Roger 157–8, 161
Daïnah la Métisse 61
Dali, Salvador 10, 20
Dalle, Béatrice 196
Damia 36, 38, 40
Darrieux, Danielle 35
Déa, Marie 70–1
Dédée d'Anvers 112
Delannoy, Jean 8
Deleuze, Gilles 72–3, 77, 99n4, 171, 184–5
— and Félix Guattari 184
Delluc, Louis 18n51
Delon, Alain 139, 141–4, 146, 149, 151
Delorme, Danielle 120
De Mayerling à Sarajevo 36
Demonpion, Denis 64
Démons de l'aube, Les 109, 111
Demy, Jacques 7
Deneuve, Catherine 141, 144
Denis, Claire 9
Depardieu, Gérard 196
Dermit, Edouard 78, 86, 92, 105–6n57
Dernier Métro, Le 236
Dernier Mot, Le 175
Desnos, Robert 20
Desperately Seeking Susan 256
Desplechin, Arnaud 7, 228, 232
Détective 175
Deux hommes dans Manhattan 139, 141, 142
Deuxième Souffle, Le 139, 140, 141–4, 145–6
Deux ou trois choses que je sais d'elle 184
Diaboliques, Les 10, 108, 111, 113, 114, 118–21
Dietrich, Marlene 66, 71
Dis-moi oui, dis-moi non 251n13
Diva 195, 198, 202, 252n27
Divine 38

Doane, Mary Ann, 4, 57
Docteur M. 161
Doisneau, Robert 105–6n57
Donner, Christophe 214
Double Indemnity 149
Douce France 228, 230, 231
Doulos, Le 139, 142–3, 150
Dridi, Karim 7, 228, 234, 236–7
Dubois, Marie 128
Duchamp, Marcel 10, 19, 25, 28, 30n3
Duchesse de Langeais, La 36
Dufrenne, Oscar 59–60n18
Dugowson, Martine 14, 259–63
Dulac, Germaine 10, 20, 30n4
Dumont, Bruno 7, 228, 234
Duncan, Derek 214, 225n63
Duras, Marguerite 7, 136
Du rififi chez les hommes 146–7
Durozoi, Gérard. 25
Dussollier, André 163, 164
Dutoit, Ulysse and Leo Bersani 105n51
Duvernois, Henri 38
Dyer, Richard 63, 99n8, 163

Eck, Marcel 78
Ecrire contre l'oubli (Pour Thomas Wainggai) 175
Edelman, Lee, 6, 95–6, 210, 214
Eggeling, Viking 28
El Greco 82
Elsaesser, Thomas, 28
Emak Bakia 2–4 *passim*, 27, 31n24
Embrasse-moi 251n13
Enfance de l'art, L' 175
Enfants du paradis, Les 10, 36, 64, 66, 71–4
Entr'acte 19, 23–5 *passim*
Ernst, Max, 28
Escamotage d'une dame, L' 22
Et Dieu créa la femme 122n19, 232, 162
Eternel retour, L' 8, 82
Etoile de mer 20, 23
Exhibition 180

Fahrenheit 451 12, 157–9, 160, 163, 165, 166
Faire la fête 174
Falling Down 251n4
Fantômas 30
Fargier, Jean-Paul 80, 176

Fassbinder, Rainer Werner 85, 164
Faubourg Montmartre 36, 38–44, 45, 51, 54, 57, 58, 59n12
Femme du boulanger, La 35
Ferreira Barbosa, Laurence 7, 13, 243, 244–7, 251n12
Feuillade, Louis 228, 236
Feuillère, Edwige 36
Fifth Element, The (Le Cinquième Elément) 9 12, 157, 158, 165–6, 168n16
Fischer, Lucy, 30n17, 161–2
Flaubert, Gustave 126, 129, 130, 133
Flic, Un 11, 139, 141–4 *passim*, 145, 147, 149–51 *passim*
Flitterman-Lewis, Sandy, 6
Florelle, Odette 36–7, 39–40, 43, 60n22
Flower of My Secret, The 257
Fonda, Jane 159
Fontaine, Anne 239n14
Forbes, Jill 6, 72, 75n14
Forgeas, Jacques 196
Foucart, Claude 82, 101n21
Foucault, Michel 182–5 *passim*, 209–10, 215
Francesca, Piero della 83
France/tour/détour/deux/enfants 12, 172–87 *passim*
Frankenstein Created Woman 162, 167n3
Freaks 83
Fréhel 36, 38, 40, 45
Frère, Un 243
Freud, Sigmund 178
Freytag-Loringhoven, Baroness Elsa von 19, 29–30n1
Fuss, Diana 256, 265

Gabin, Jean 35, 44, 45–55, 58, 61n27, 61n31, 63, 68–70, 146
Gaillard, Agathe 214
Gallotta, Jean-Claude 174
Garat, Henri 35
Garbaz, Frank 227
Garbo, Greta 70–1
Garçonne, La 65
Gaulle, Charles de 64
Gaultier, Jean-Paul 164, 169n36
Gauthier, Xavière, 22, 24
Gazon Maudit 258
Genet, Jean 7, 164

Gens normaux n'ont rien d'exceptionnel, Les 13, 243, 244–7, 250, 253n34
Gercke, Daniel 77–9, 99n2
German Sisters, The 257
Gesmar 54
Gibier de potence 65
Gilou, Thomas 227, 230, 233
Giornata particolare, Una 239n14
Girl Friends 258
Gledhill, Christine 145
Godard, Agnès 263
Godard, Jean-Luc 11, 80, 133–5, 144, 151, 171–87 *passim*
—— and Anne-Marie Miéville 7, 12, 171–87 *passim*, 189n10
Go Fish 255
Goodis, David 127, 196
Gouze-Renal, Christine 131
Grand Bleu, Le 196
Grande Illusion, La 35
Greene, Naomi 77–8, 98n1
Greer, Germaine 181
Grémillon, Jean 61n26
Griffith, D.W. 134
Grover, Jan Zita 211
Guédiguian, Robert 7, 9, 227, 228, 233
Gueule d'amour 35
Guibert, Hervé 13, 209–26 *passim*
Guilbert, Yvette 45

Hannoteau, Guillaume 64
Hanson, Ellis 6
Hayes, Graham 8
Hayward, Susan 6, 63, 95, 104n48, 165–6, 196
Heath, Stephen, 4
Hemmings, David 163
Hepburn, Katharine 63, 66
Herrand, Marcel 70–4
Hexagone 228, 234
Hiroshima mon amour 136, 149
Histoire(s) du cinéma 80, 176
Hitchcock, Alfred 95–6
Holbein, Hans (The Younger) 94, 197, 199–200, 206n10
Hollinger, Karen 255, 257, 266
Holmlund, Christine, 6
Homme est une femme comme les autres, L' 227, 235

Hôtel du Nord 10, 35, 36, 64, 65, 67–8, 69, 71
How can I love (a man when I know he don't want me) 174
Huis clos 65
Huyssen, Andreas 126–7, 135

Ici et ailleurs 174
Inspecteur Lavardin 161
IP5 196, 198, 202, 204
Irigaray, Luce 218
Irma Vep 228, 230, 231, 235, 236, 258

J'ai horreur de l'amour 251n12
James, Henry 97, 105–6n57
Jameson, Fredric 195
Jancovich, Mark 159, 162
Jaque-Catelain 56
Jarman, Derek 105n51
Jeancolas, Jean-Pierre 9, 228, 237
Jeanson, Henri 67
Je vous salue, Marie 175
Joannon, Clothilde 129
Johnson, Barbara 266
Jour se lève, Le 10, 35, 36, 64, 66, 67, 68–70, 71
Jouvet, Louis 67–8
Judovitz, Dalia, 28
Jules et Jim 108, 128
Julia 256
Jullian, Marcel 176

Kahn, Cédric 7
Kassowitz, Mathieu 7, 227, 228, 233, 234
Klapisch, Cédric 7, 228, 232–3, 235–6, 243
Krauss, Rosalind, 24–5
Kristel, Sylvia 160
Kristeva, Julia 5, 72–3, 158
Kuenzli, Rudolf 31n28
Kurosawa, Akira 149
Kurys, Diane 7, 258, 260

Lacan, Jacques, 27, 197, 198–201, 203–5, 205n6
Lafont, Bernadette 129
La Mettrie, Julien Offray de 182
Lang, Fritz 133–4
Laplanche, Jean 85, 102n32
Lapointe, Bobby 128

Lapsley, Robert 198
Larquey, Pierre 45
Laurent, Jacqueline 35, 68–9, 71
Lauretis, Teresa de, 4, 256–7
Law, John Phillip 163
Lebel, Jean-Jacques 33n51
Lebon, Yvette 47
Leclerc, Ginette 35, 65
Ledoux, Fernard 70–1
Lee, Spike 9
Léger, Fernand 10,19–21
Leterrier, François 114–5, 123n20
Levine, Joe 135
Lifshitz, Sébastien 239n14
Little Caesar 149
Livre de Marie, Le 174, 186
Lola 128
Loren, Sophia 239n13
Lou n'a pas dit non 174
Lumière, Auguste and Louis Lumière 21
Lune dans le caniveau, La 196, 198, 202
Lvovsky, Noémie 7,13, 243, 247–250, 251–2n13

Macadam 109
McArthur, Colin 139
MacCabe, Colin 176
Macherel, Raymond 213–4
Magritte, René 31n18
Mahoney, Elizabeth 242
Malle, Louis 11, 108, 131–3, 137n7
Man Ray 10, 19–21, 25, 28–9, 30n8, 31n24
Man Who Fell to Earth, The 165
Mapplethorpe, Robert 215, 226n73
Marais, Jean 8, 79, 84, 95, 105–6n57
Marey, Etienne-Jules 12, 173, 178–80, 182, 185, 191–2n32
Marie, Michel 134, 135
Marius et Jeannette 227, 228, 231, 233, 234
Marker, Chris 135, 175
Marnac, Jane 36–7, 51–5, 58
Marseillaise, La 8
Mars et Vénus 174
Marshall, Tonie 7, 227, 237
Martel, Frédéric 223n43, 224n49
Marty-Lavauzelle, Arnaud 220
Masques 161
Mastroianni, Marcello 131–3, 239n13

Matuszewski, Boleslas 192n35
Mauvais Coups, Les 10, 108, 114–8, 120–1
Max, Jean 53
Mazdon, Lucy 18n48
Mazurek, Maureen 212
Méliès, Georges 21–2, 161
Melville, Jean-Pierre 11–12, 139–55 *passim*
Mépris, Le 133–5
Mercer, Kobena, 6
Merleau-Ponty, Maurice 172
Merry, Ila 46
Métisse 227, 228, 231, 233
Metz, Christian 4–5
Meurisse, Paul 118
Miéville, Anne-Marie 171, 173–6
—— and Jean-Luc Godard 7, 12, 171–87
    passim, 189n10
Miller, D.A., 6, 105n52
Milorad 78, 90, 99n7, 103n43
Mina Tannenbaum 14, 260–3, 265, 266
Misraki, Paul 142
Mistinguett 36–7, 40, 45, 53, 54
Mon cher sujet 174
Monde sans pitié, Un 227, 229, 230, 231, 233
Montand, Yves 147, 198
Montparnasse, Kiki de, 23–4, 28
Moravia, Alberto 133
Moreau, Jeanne 108
Morgan, Michèle 120
Morin, Edgar 63, 175
Morlay, Gaby 38, 55–7, 59n12
Mort en ce jardin, La 113
Mourier, Maurice 106n58
Mulvey, Laura 5–6, 144, 172
Musidora 30n10
Muybridge, Eadweard J. 179
My Fair Lady 161, 162
Mystères de New York, Les 30

Neale, Steve 140
Nettoyage à sec 239n14
Nikita 162, 168n16
Noro, Line 38
Nous sommes tous encore ici 174
Nouveau Monde, Le 184
Nouvelle Eve, La 258
Nouvelle vague 175
Nuit et jour 251n8

Nuits fauves, Les 7, 8, 227, 235, 237
Numéro deux 174, 181

One Flew over the Cuckoo's Nest 252n21
On s'est tous défilé 185
Ophüls, Max, 38
Orphée 77–84 *passim*, 88, 89, 94, 95, 97, 99n8
O'Shaughnessy, Martin 8
Oublie-moi 13, 243, 247–250
Ozon, François 7

Palance, Jack 133
Papa comme maman 174
Parent, Denis 201
Parents terribles, Les 78, 82
Paris-Béguin 36, 38, 44, 51–5, 56, 57, 58
Paris ficelle 151n12
Paris nous appartient 128
Pasco, Isabelle 196
Pasolini, Pier Paolo 98n1
Penley, Constance 165, 166, 173, 182, 185
Pépé le Moko 36, 61n27, 61n31
Périer, François 143
Perlman, Ron 164
Perrin, Michel 64–5
Persona 257
Personne ne m'aime 239n8
Peterson, Alan 4, 221n11
Petit Soldat, Le 127
Philippe, Claude-Jean 176
Picabia, Francis 28, 30n12
Piccoli, Michel 133
Pigalle 228, 236–7
Pisanello (Antonio) 83
Plath, Sylvia 255, 256, 266
Plato 166
Poison Ivy 256
Playtime 151
Pointe courte, La 125
Portraits Chinois 14, 259–60, 262
Powrie, Phil 6, 9, 18n53
Pratt, Murray 211, 214, 217, 224n49, 225n63
Préjean, Albert 35
Prénom Carmen 175
Presle, Micheline 120
Presque rien 239n14
Prévert, Jacques 70
Princesse Tam-Tam 45, 50

Printemps, Yvonne 55, 60n22
Prowse, Derek 119
Public Enemy, The 149
Pudeur ou l'impudeur, La 13, 212–20 *passim*

Quatre aventures de Reinette et Mirabelle 258
Queen Christina 71
Queneau, Raymond 133
Querelle 164

Radiguet, Raymond 99n7
Raï 228, 230, 232
Raimu, 35
Ramirez, Francis and Christian Rolot
    99–100n9
Rancho Notorious 134
Rappeneau, Jean-Paul 131,137n7
Rapport Darty, Le 175
Rashomon 149
Raynaud, Bérénice 186
Rear Window 95–6
Rebecca 256
Reggiani, Serge 142
Régnier, Natacha 263
Renoir, Jean 8
Requième pour un vampire 167n5
Resnais, Alain 135, 175
Retour à la raison 19–20, 25, 29
Rich and Famous 257
Richter, Hans 10
Rio Bravo 134
Rivero, Enrique 90
Rivière, Joan 72
Robbe-Grillet, Alain 127
Rochant, Eric 7
Rodowick, D.N. 4, 6
Rolot, Christian and Francis Ramirez
    99–100n9
Romance, Viviane 35, 65–6, 69
Roselyne et les lions 196, 198, 202, 204
Rosenvallon, Pierre 238
Ross, Kristin 151, 153
Rossellini, Roberto 134
Roubaix, François de 146
Rouch, Jean 175
Rousseau, Jean-Jacques 126
Roux, François 7
Rozier, Jacques 11,130–1

Sacher-Masoch, Leopold von 73, 77, 85
Salle, M. (Jean-Baptiste) de la 184
Samouraï, Le 10, 139, 140, 142, 143, 146–51
    passim
Sang d'un poète, Le 7, 77, 78, 83, 84, 89, 91–7
    passim, 99n7, 101–2n24
Sartre, Jean-Paul 166, 172
Sauve qui peut (la vie) 172–3, 175
Schefer, Jean Louis 83
Schehr, Lawrence 222
Scorsese, Martin 171
Sedgwick, Eve Kosofsky, 4, 72, 97, 105–6n57
Sellier, Geneviève and Noël Burch 8, 230
Sentinelle, La 251–2n13
Serreau, Coline 7
Seven Samurai (The Magnificent Seven) 149
Shakespeare, William 204–5
Shaviro, Steven 6, 85
She Must Be Seeing Things 257
Siclier, Jacques 65
Signoret, Simone 11, 63, 107–123 passim,
Silence de la mer, Le 140
Silverman, Kaja, 5
Simon, Michel 56, 66
Single White Female 256, 258
Sirk, Douglas 207n29
Six fois deux (Sur et sous la communication)
    174, 175, 181, 183, 184, 186
Sixth Sense, The 168n19
Sleepy Hollow 158
Smith, Paul Julian 213
Soft and Hard 175
Soja, Edward 241
Son of the Sheik 169n31
Sorcières 111
Spaak, Charles 61n26
Stacey, Jackie 67, 256
Stam, Robert 181
Starman 165
Stéphane, Nicole 140
Stewart, Alexandra 115
Stich, Sidra, 26
Strada, La 265
Studlar, Gaylyn, 66, 73
Subway 252n27
Suleiman, Susan Rubin, 24
Sur les talus 251n12
Sylvia Scarlett 66

Tarantino, Quentin 140, 150
Tarr, Carrie 8
Tati, Jacques 151
Téchiné, André 7
Temple, Michael and James S. Williams 173
Terminator, The 165
Testament d'Orphée, Le 77–98 *passim*, 99–100n9, 105n51
Tête d'un homme, La 36
Thérésa 37
Thérèse Raquin 113
This Land is Mine 167n9
Thompkins, Jane 145, 153
Thompson, David 66
Tirez sur le pianiste 127–8
Tognazzi, Ugo 163
Treichler, Paula 222n18, 222n28
Trémois, Claude-Marie 227
37°2 le matin (Betty Blue) 196, 198, 202
Trou, Le 146
Truffaut, François 11,12, 127–8, 258, 228, 236
Turk, Edward Baron 70, 71, 73
Twins of Evil 158, 164, 167n3
Tzara, Tristan, 25

Uccello, Paolo, 83, 101–2n24
Ullich, Maurice 176
Ullmann, Liv 116
Une chante l'autre pas, L' 258

Vaché, Jacques 20
Vadim, Roger 12
Vailland, Roger 115, 123n22
Valentine, Gill 218
Vampire Lovers, The 167n5
Vampire nue, La 167n5
Vanel, Charles 35, 38, 61n26
Varda, Agnès 7, 125, 135–6, 175, 258, 260
Varna, Henri 59–60n18, 60n20
Vecchiali, Paul 7
Ventura, Lino 146
Vénus beauté (Institut) 239n8
Vérité si je mens, La 227, 233

Vernoux, Marion 7
Vertov, Dziga 178, 185
Vie, Une 171, 187
Vie de Jésus, La 228–34 *passim*
Vie ne me fait pas peur, La 251–2n13, 259
Vie privée 131–3, 134, 135, 137n9
Vie rêvée des anges, La 14, 227, 229–31 *passim*, 259, 263–6, 251n11
Villa Santo-Sospir, La 92–5
Vincendeau, Ginette 6, 18n51, 58n3, 63, 195
Visiteurs du soir, Les 10, 36, 64, 70–71
Vivre sa vie 129, 171
Voile bleu, Le 59n12
Volonté, Gian Maria 143, 154
Vormittagsspuk 20, 25–6, 29

Warhol, Andy 85
Warshow, Robert 145
Watney, Simon 210–1, 218–9
Weisweiller, Mme Alec 92, 94–5
Werner, Oskar 158
Westlake, Michael 198
Wheeler, Rose, 23
White, Patricia, 6
Whitman, Walt 104n48
Willemen, Paul 207n29
Williams, James S. and Michael Temple 173
Williams, Linda 22
Williams, Raymond 175–6, 185
Wilson, Emma 8
Winnicott, D.W. 26
Wittig, Monique, 4
Woo, John 140, 150

Yojimbo (A Fistful of Dollars) 149
Yoshimoto, Mitsuhiro 149

Zazie dans le métro 133
Zilbermann, Jean-Jacques 227, 235
Zimmer, Jacques 140
Zonca, Erick 14, 263–6, 227, 230
Zouzou 36, 38, 44–51, 52, 57, 58
Zylberstein, Elsa 260, 263